SUPREME COURT DECISIONS

AND

WOMEN'S RIGHTS

SUPREME COURT DECISIONS
AND
WOMEN'S RIGHTS

Milestones to Equality

EDITED BY CLARE CUSHMAN

FOREWORD BY ASSOCIATE JUSTICE
RUTH BADER GINSBURG

SPONSORED BY
THE SUPREME COURT HISTORICAL SOCIETY

CQ PRESS

A DIVISION OF CONGRESSIONAL QUARTERLY INC.
WASHINGTON, D.C.

CQ Press
A Division of Congressional Quarterly Inc.
1414 22nd Street, N.W.
Washington, D.C. 20037
(202) 822-1475 ; (800) 638-1710
www.cqpress.com

Printed and bound in the United States of America

04 03 02 01 00   5 4 3 2 1

⊗ The paper used in this publication meets the minimum requirements of the American National Standard
for Information Sciences—Permanence of Paper for
Printed Library Materials, ANSI Z39.48-1992.

LIBRARY OF CONGRESS CATALOGING-IN-PUBLICATION DATA

In process

CONTENTS

CONTENTS

CONTRIBUTORS

FOREWORD

Etched above the entrance to the majestic building that houses the Supreme Court of the United States are the words: "Equal Justice Under Law." Those four words express a fundamental, still evolving American ideal. In eleven enlightening chapters, this fine work of the Supreme Court Historical Society tells of the gradual realization of the equal justice ideal for the nation's once disenfranchised majority—its women.

Readers of the Constitution of the United States will search in vain for the word "equal" or "equality" in the seven articles composing our fundamental instrument of government as framed in 1787, or in the ten amendments, ratified in 1791, composing the Bill of Rights. Why should that be so in view of the 1776 Declaration of Independence, which declared in ringing tones the "self-evident" truth "that all men are created equal"?

The existence of slavery in all but five of the thirteen states of the United States when our nation was new is part of the answer, but the reason is more encompassing. John Adams, who became second president of the United States, wrote a revealing letter to a friend in 1776, the very year the Declaration of Independence was proclaimed. Adams explained to his friend why he thought voting qualifications should not be lowered in his home state of Massachusetts:

[I]t is dangerous to open so fruitful a source of controversy and altercation as would be opened by attempting to alter the qualifications of voters; there will be no end of it. New claims will arise; women will demand a vote; lads from twelve to twenty-one will think their rights are not enough attended to; and every man who has not a farthing, will demand an equal voice with any other, in all acts of state. It tends to confound and destroy all distinctions, and prostrate all ranks to one common level.[1]

Concerning women, one must place in the context of the early nineteenth century, the words of Thomas Jefferson, principal author of the Declaration of Independence, later third president of the United States. Jefferson said in 1816:

Were our State a pure democracy . . . there would yet be excluded from deliberations . . . women, who, to prevent depravation of morals and ambiguity of issues, should not mix promiscuously in the public meetings of men."[2]

Not until 1868, after the Civil War ended slavery, did the Constitution provide, as it has ever since, that no state "shall . . . deny to any person . . . the equal protection of the laws." And women did not become a part of the U.S. political community until 1920 when, by constitutional amendment, they at last gained the right to vote.

Thurgood Marshall, leader of the struggle in the courts for an end to odious racial classifications, said prior to his 1991 retirement as a Supreme Court justice, that he did not celebrate what the Constitution was in the beginning. (As originally framed, the Constitution protected the slave trade until 1808 [art. I, sec. 9] and it required the return of persons who had escaped from human bondage, a provision in force until the Civil War [art. IV, sec. 2].) Instead, Thurgood Marshall celebrated how our fundamental instrument of government had evolved over the span of two centuries. The "true miracle," he said, is the Constitution's "life nurtured through two turbulent centuries."[3]

I share that view, but I appreciate, too, that the equal dignity of individuals is part of the constitutional legacy, shaped and bequeathed to us by the framers, in a most vital sense. The founding fathers rebelled against the patriarchal power of kings and the idea that political authority may legitimately rest on birth status. Their culture held them back from fully perceiving or acting upon ideals of human equality in rights, obligations, and opportunities, and of individual freedom to aspire and achieve. But they stated a commitment in the Declaration of Independence to equality and in the Declaration and Bill of Rights to individual liberty. Those commitments had growth potential. They received further expression in the nineteenth century, after the Civil War ended slavery, through the addition of the Equal Protection Clause to the Constitution, and again in the twentieth century, when women were made voting citizens. As historian Richard Morris wrote, a prime portion of the history of the U.S. Constitution, and a cause for celebration, is the story of the extension (through amendment, judicial interpretation, and practice) of constitutional rights and protections to once ignored or excluded peo-

ple: to humans who were once held in bondage, to men without property, to the original inhabitants of the land that became the United States, and to women.[4]

With that background in mind, one can put in proper perspective the story told in this book of when, why, and how women came to count in constitutional adjudication and as participants, in full partnership with men, in diverse aspects of the nation's economic and social life. A great American, Susan B. Anthony, made a prediction a century ago, bold for her time, but now, as the following chapters show, within hailing distance. She forecast a time when "[t]he woman . . . will be the peer of man. In education, in art, in science, in literature; in the home, the church, the state; everywhere she will be acknowledged equal, though not identical with him."[5]

It is my hope and expectation that readers of this book will experience the realization of Susan B. Anthony's ultimate vision: "man and woman working together to make the world the better for their having lived."[6]

RUTH BADER GINSBURG
Associate Justice
Supreme Court of the United States

Notes

1. Letter from John Adams to James Sullivan (May 26, 1776), in 9 *The Works of John Adams* 378 (Charles F. Adams ed., 1854).

2. Letter from Thomas Jefferson to Samuel Kercheval (Sept. 5, 1816), in 10 *The Writings of Thomas Jefferson* 46 n. 1 (Paul L. Ford ed., 1899).

3. Thurgood Marshall, *Reflections on the Bicentennial of the United States Constitution*, 101 Harv. L. Rev. 1, 5 (1987).

4. See Richard B. Morris, *The Forging of the Union, 1781–1789*, at 193 (1987).

5. Lynn Sherr, *Failure Is Impossible: Susan B. Anthony in Her Own Words* 305 (1995).

6. *Ibid.*

INTRODUCTION

In 1923 Justice George Sutherland wrote:

In view of the great—not to say revolutionary—changes which have taken place since [1908], in the contractual, political and civil status of women, culminating in the Nineteenth Amendment, it is not unreasonable to say that the [differences between the sexes] have now come almost, if not quite, to the vanishing point.

Although the Nineteenth Amendment had granted women the right to vote in 1920, Justice Sutherland was unreasonably optimistic about the demise of laws that treat men and women unequally. It would take a vigorous women's movement in the late 1960s to lead legislatures and the courts to reconsider such laws and find them discriminatory.

The Supreme Court has searched for an appropriate standard for gauging whether sex-based laws deny women equal protection of the laws. This book tells the story of the Supreme Court's role in reviewing laws based on gender distinctions and explains how and why it went from upholding such laws, to allowing them to stand if they had a "rational basis," to presuming—absent "an exceedingly persuasive justification"—that they were discriminatory.

The justices have made rulings affecting women—and men—in a broad range of areas: employment, jury duty, abortion, maternity leave, military service, and single-sex schooling, to name a few. Their decisions are described in these pages in a way that we hope makes them meaningful to the general reader.

Throughout the chapters are also woven profiles of the plaintiffs, to give complex legal principles a human dimension and to examine the specific inequality in question. In addition, the reader will find that there are essays—marked by a quill and paper icon—discussing the legislative advances that have prompted the Supreme Court's changing interpretation of gender law. Finally, the last chapter in the book describes the milestones marking women's affiliation with the Supreme Court as an institution: as spouses, clerks, advocates, employees, and justices.

In *United States v. Virginia* (1996), the Court ruled that all-male Virginia Military Institute could not keep its doors closed to women. In her majority opinion, Justice Ruth Bader Ginsburg took the opportunity to recount how far the Court had come in helping women achieve equality since it struck down a sex-based law for the first time in 1971:

[T]he Court has repeatedly recognized that neither federal nor state government acts compatibly with the equal protection principle when a law or official policy denies to women, simply because they are women, full citizenship stature—equal opportunity to aspire, achieve, participate in and contribute to society based on their individual talents and capacities.

While women are now largely treated as equals, Justice Sutherland's "vanishing point" is still beyond the horizon and indeed may never be achieved. Nor should it, perhaps, as legisla-tures and the courts continue to accommodate the differing biological and cultural roles of men and women in areas such as military service and pregnancy. But for the most part the legal barri-ers to women's full equality have fallen. This is in no small measure due to the decisions by Justice Sutherland's successors on the Supreme Court.

LEON SILVERMAN
President
The Supreme Court Historical Society

ACKNOWLEDGMENTS

The Supreme Court Historical Society is indebted to the many individuals who assisted in the preparation of this book. First and foremost, we gratefully acknowledge the work of all the writers who contributed essays and profiles. We wish to thank the editorial advisors, Jeffrey Rosen, Susan Deller Ross, and Wendy Webster Williams, who lent their expertise and provided considerable guidance in editing the manuscript. The Society is also extremely grateful to Justice Ruth Bader Ginsburg and her law clerk, Deirdre von Dornum, for carefully reviewing the manuscript and for making a variety of suggestions for improvement.

Savina Lambert deserves special praise for her dedicated efforts to find and secure the more than 120 illustrations that appear in these pages. The Society is also indebted to Gail Galloway, Franz Jansen, and the staff of the Curator's Office at the Supreme Court of the United States, who provided access to the Court's extensive illustrations collection.

Librarians Barbara Bridges, Jill Duffy, Patricia R. Evans, and Richard Evans are to be commended for their tireless efforts at checking all the facts and citations in this reference work. The Society also wishes to thank Supreme Court librarian Shelley Dowling and her staff for facilitating research in the Court's library.

The Society is enormously grateful to all the plaintiffs, plaintiffs' families, counsel, and other individuals who consented to be interviewed or who provided us with personal photographs: Martha Field Aschuler, Patricia Dwinnell Butler, Connie and Monty Camp, Sharron Frontiero Cohen, Wilbur O. Colom, Curtis Craig, Allen Derr, Helen B. Feeney, Joseph Frontiero, Jane De Hart, Ann Hopkins, William F. Horsley, Maureen E. Mahoney, Lorelyn Penero Miller, Donald Ross Patterson, (Dianne) Kim Rawlinson, Nancy Stanley and Chuck Reichel, Sally Reed, Harriet S. Shapiro, Barbara D. Underwood, Penny Weaver and the Southern Poverty Law Center, Carolyn Whitener, and Jason and Stephen Wiesenfeld. We are also indebted to Professor Robert Darcy of Oklahoma State University for assistance in contacting individuals associated with *Craig v. Boren* and for providing us with an advance copy of the article about that case he coauthored with Jenny Sanbrano of the University of Tulsa.

The editor further wishes to thank Beth Hanlon for providing skillful editing advice, Carolyn Lerner for contributing her expertise on sexual harassment law, and Jamin B. Raskin for sharing his glossary. The editor is also grateful to those people who gave invaluable support to this project in a variety of different ways: Paulette B. Cushman, Izette and Neil Folger, Mary Stewart Irion, Maricel V. Mariano, Meg de Toledo, and, especially, Amédée S. Prouvost. In addition Connie Corson, librarian at the Spence School, deserves credit for pointing out the need for this reference work.

The Society's Publications Committee, chaired by E. Barrett Prettyman Jr., approved this project and shepherded it to completion. Tommy Port Beaudreau of Fried, Frank, Harris, Shriver & Jacobson generously gave his time to draft and finalize the copublishing agreement between the Society and CQ Press.

The Supreme Court Historical Society gratefully acknowledges its members for their ongoing financial support in its endeavors to educate the public about the Court's history. Similarly, all the firms, individuals, corporations, and foundations who have contributed to the Society deserve our appreciation as well.

Finally, the Society wishes to thank Patricia Gallagher, Adrian Forman, Talia Greenberg, and their colleagues at CQ Press for their dedication to this project.

SUPREME COURT DECISIONS
AND
WOMEN'S RIGHTS

1

ROMANTIC PATERNALISM

Most nineteenth-century legal decisions involving women's issues were based on an attitude that historians now call "romantic paternalism." This was not a legal doctrine but a belief, based on the "romantic" notion that women are the weaker or gentler sex, that the law should provide them increased protections. Women were expected to perform specific functions, such as domestic chores and raising children, and were sheltered from the harshness of life outside the home. The downside to this protective attitude was that women were also considered unfit to participate in civic life, branded as inferior to men, denied economic rights, and subjected to their husbands' rule in the family.

Women thus held many fewer rights in eighteenth- and nineteenth-century society than men. The law did not allow them to vote, hold office, or serve on juries. They were excluded from most educational institutions and professions. When they married, they became legally subordinate to their husbands under the principle of "coverture," a term defined in 1765 by British jurist William Blackstone.

By Marriage, the husband and wife are one person in law: that is, the very being or legal existence of the woman is suspended during the marriage, or at least is incorporated and consolidated into that of the husband; under whose wing, protection and cover, she performs every thing; . . . and her condition during her marriage is called her coverture.

Under coverture rules, a woman could not make contracts; write wills; sue or be sued in court; or own property such as money, clothing, and household goods—these belonged solely to the "head of the household," the husband. This meant that if the wife worked for pay for someone else, her husband owned the wages that she earned. If the wife came from a wealthy family, she could have restricted rights to own real property such as land and a house that her father might give her, but since her husband had the sole right to manage or sell such property, and to keep the profits, her right was of little use unless her father made special, optional, legal arrangements to give her management rights as well.

A married man also had the legal right to have sexual relations with his wife. This could be accomplished forcibly, if necessary, because the legal definition of rape specifically excluded husbands and wives. A husband also had control of their children, so if they divorced he was awarded custody automatically.

As a result of increasing pressure from a grow-ing women's rights movement in the mid–nine-teenth century, a number of states passed laws, known as "married women's property acts," to ad-dress the problems of coverture. These laws led to incremental increases in the rights of married women to control their own property, but signifi-cant limitations on married women's ability to conduct business remained. And these gains were economic rather than political in nature: protect-ing wives' property against the claims of their husbands' creditors rather than responding to the notion of equal rights.

In the midst of this limited progress in women's civil status, and passage of the Four-teenth Amendment in 1868 guaranteeing all citi-zens equal rights, the Supreme Court issued a de-cision that reflected the old order. In *Bradwell v. Illinois* (1873) it upheld the right of the state of Illinois to deny a woman the right to practice law. Far less surprising, given that the Fourteenth Amendment did not guarantee women's political rights, was the Court's decision in *Minor v. Hap-persett* (1875), which dealt a blow to the growing political strength of women by holding that they had no constitutional right to vote. Likewise, in an 1880 decision the Court indirectly allowed states to deny women another political right: to serve on a jury.

Romantic paternalism persisted far into the twentieth century. Although passage of the Nine-teenth Amendment in 1920 gave women voting rights, it took many more decades before men and women began to be more equally protected by the law. It was not until the 1970s that the modern view of gender discrimination took hold in Supreme Court decisions. Now the Court views with great skepticism laws that treat men and women differently. It strongly presumes that such laws are discriminatory, especially if they rely on old-fashioned stereotypes about the traditional roles of men and women in society, or if they "cre-ate or perpetuate the legal, social, and economic inferiority of women." But the Court does allow sex-based laws if they are "used to compensate women for particular economic disabilities [they have] suffered," to "promot[e] equal employment opportunity," or "to advance full development of the talents and capacities of our Nation's people."

EARLY EXCLUSION

Barred from Being Lawyers

Bradwell v. Illinois, 16 Wall. 130 (1873)

Before the 1870s the opportunities for women to work as paid employees were limited, not only because of cultural traditions, but also legal barri-ers. In terms of employment, property rights, or contracts, the law failed to offer significant pro-tections or equality for women. In fact, laws often did the opposite; they provided the legal means for men to treat women as second-class citizens. This barricade was especially evident in the op-portunities, or lack thereof, for women to learn and practice law, with statutes in many states that specifically limited to men the right to become a member of the state bar association.

The Thirteenth, Fourteenth, and Fifteenth Amendments to the Constitution (known as the Civil War Amendments) were enacted between 1865 and 1870 to guarantee the rights of African American slaves freed at the close of the Civil War. Congress did not intend the amendments to provide similar rights for women. Nevertheless, a group of women's rights advocates began to assert the idea that the provisions in these amendments should also apply to women and other victims of discrimination. Their efforts yielded some limited progress.

In 1869, for instance, the St. Louis Law School became the first American law school to admit women. The following year, the first American woman to receive a law degree graduated from an accredited institution, the Union College of Law in Chicago. Yet women continued to face legal barriers that prevented them from becoming full, practicing members of the profession. In Iowa, for instance, a state law limited admission to the bar "to any white male person." It took a very expansive reading of that law by the Iowa Supreme Court in 1869 for Iowa to become the first state to admit a woman to the practice of law in the United States. It was not until several years later that the legislature changed the law and the admission requirement of "white male" was removed.

These slow gains were countered by a number of backward steps, the most significant of which was the Supreme Court's 1873 decision in *Bradwell v. Illinois.* That ruling upheld a lower court decision that allowed the state of Illinois to deny a woman membership in the state bar solely because of her sex.

Myra Colby Bradwell was an early advocate of women's rights. As the founder and chief editor of the *Chicago Legal News,* one of the most important legal publications outside the East Coast, she was also an esteemed member of the legal community. Bradwell had studied law with her husband, James B. Bradwell, a respected attorney and judge. With her sharp legal mind, she easily passed the Illinois Bar Exam and, as required, applied to the Illinois Supreme Court in 1869 for admission to the state bar.

Bradwell included with her application the required letter from an inferior court showing that she was a "person" of good character, along with proof that she had passed the bar exam. The Illinois Supreme Court nonetheless refused her request and denied her admission. The clerk's written denial of her application informed her that the court was "compelled" to turn down her license request "by reason of the disability imposed by your marriage condition." In other words, as a married woman Bradwell would not have the power to uphold the implied contracts that were standard between attorney and client. Under existing laws, married women could not legally contract on their own behalf without their husband's consent.

In response, Bradwell filed an additional brief, insisting that "it is neither a crime nor a disqualification to be a married woman." More substantively, she argued that married women often acted as legal agents for their husbands, entering into contracts on their spouse's behalf. How was that different from the role of an attorney, who acts as an agent for clients? Moreover, since passage of Illinois's Married Women's Property Act of 1861, a married woman was now permitted to contract with respect to any property she might hold separately from her husband.

As a practical matter, the court's decision made little sense since Bradwell, in her capacity as an editor and publisher, had already been doing what the state court said she was unable to—make and uphold contracts. Ironically, she even had a contract with the legislature to publish the opinions of the Illinois Supreme Court in her *Chicago Legal News.* Bradwell had noted in her arguments that a woman like herself who carried out business contracts without the express consent of her husband was considered a "femme sole" (single woman) under common law. In fact, she had become a femme sole trader through a private legislative act—an option available to all married women.

Bradwell concluded that if a married female attorney were to "fail to perform her duty, or to [fail to] comply with all her contracts as an attorney," then the court could simply "strike her name from the roll." She predicted that the court's decision would "strike a blow at the rights of every married woman in the great State of Illinois who is dependent on her labor for support."

But these arguments did not sway the court. When Bradwell subsequently appealed the denial, the Illinois Supreme Court, in a full opinion, reiterated and expanded upon the reasoning for its earlier refusal. It admitted that the real barrier was not Bradwell's married status but her sex.

[T]hat God designed the sexes to occupy different spheres of action, and that it belonged to men to make, apply, and execute the laws, was regarded as an almost axiomatic truth. In view of these facts, we are certainly warranted in saying that when the legislature gave to this court the power of granting licenses to practice law, it was with not the slightest expectation that this privilege would be extended to women.

In preparing her appeal to the U.S. Supreme Court, Bradwell and her lawyer, Matthew Carpenter, a senator from Wisconsin who was also a women's rights supporter and an experienced advocate, had an unusual opportunity. No Supreme Court decisions interpreting the Fourteenth Amendment yet existed, so Bradwell's arguments could be formed on a clean slate. The difficulty was to choose which of the three clauses of the amendment—the Equal Protection Clause, the Due Process Clause, or the Privileges and Immunities Clause—to use to mount the challenge (see text of amendment, p. 37).

There is some debate as to whether Bradwell assisted Carpenter in preparing the brief. Its preface contains a lengthy assurance that giving women the right to be lawyers would not imply that they could also gain the right to vote. According to her biographer, Jane M. Friedman, Bradwell directed Carpenter to make that argument to allay the fears of the conservative justices (who would in fact soon rule that suffrage was not a privilege of citizenship). Other sources suggest, however, that she was not consulted in the brief's preparation. That Bradwell, an ardent suffragist, would consent to compromise one cause to promote another is not improbable; the consti-

tutional argument for suffrage was weak and the one for contracts strong. In any case, Susan B. Anthony, the leader of the women's suffrage movement, wrote Bradwell a letter scolding her for the brief.

In the end Carpenter, with or without Bradwell's input, premised the claim on the Privileges and Immunities Clause, asserting that admission to the bar, or the pursuit of "other ordinary avocations," was one of the national privileges and immunities that could not be abridged by a state's laws. He suggested that the Privileges and Immunities Clause should be interpreted broadly: "[I]f this provision does protect the colored citizen, then it protects every citizen, black or white, male or female. . . . Intelligence, integrity and honor are the only qualifications that can be prescribed as conditions precedent to an entry upon any honorable pursuit or profitable avocation."

It was an unprecedented assertion, anticipating future equal protection arguments. "Of a bar composed of men and women of equal integrity and learning," the brief declared, "women might be more or less frequently retained as the taste or judgment of clients might dictate. But the broad shield of the Constitution is over all, and protects each in the measure of success which his or her individual merits may secure."

The Right to Practice a Trade

Slaughter-House Cases, 16 Wall. 36 (1873)

With these arguments before the Court, Bradwell's challenge had all the makings of a landmark case. But law does not proceed in a vacuum, and the case fell victim to a number of outside factors that minimized its impact, not the least of which was timing. *Bradwell* was argued the month before *Slaughter-House Cases*, a set of three consolidated suits by Louisiana butchers who were responding to a state law—enacted for

Justice Joseph P. Bradley wrote a concurring opinion in *Bradwell v. Illinois* (1873) maintaining that state legislatures should retain the power to keep women out of certain occupations because women belonged at home in the "domestic sphere."

health reasons—mandating that their slaughter-house businesses be located in one spot in New Orleans. The butchers complained that the state had created a monopoly, and that the manner in which the site was selected was unfair and violated not only state laws but also their rights under the Fourteenth Amendment, specifically the Privileges and Immunities Clause. Included in that protection, argued their attorneys, was the fundamental right to freely pursue a profession without government interference.

Writing for a 5–4 majority, Justice Samuel F. Miller disagreed, concluding that the federal protection of privileges and immunities involved only those rights "which own their existence to the Federal government, its National character, its Constitution or its laws." This did not include the right of a person to choose a certain type of employment or occupation, which, the Court said, was within the state's regulatory power.

The Court issued its opinion in *Slaughter-House* a day before *Bradwell*, and thus it became the first decision by the Court interpreting the Fourteenth Amendment as it related to the rights of individual citizens to conduct their trade. It was also the ruling that would be forever remembered as the one that seriously weakened the Privileges and Immunities Clause. *Bradwell* would become just an opportunity for the Court to amplify that reasoning.

It took little discussion for the Court in *Bradwell* to explain why the "just delivered" opinion in the *Slaughter-House* case

renders elaborate argument in the present case unnecessary; for, unless we are wholly and radically mistaken in the principles on which those cases are decided, the right to control and regulate the granting of license to practice law in the courts of a State is one of those powers which are not transferred for its protection to the Federal Government, and its exercise is in no manner governed or controlled by citizenship of the United States in the party seeking such license.

If the Court had stopped there, *Bradwell* would probably have been relegated to a historical footnote. Instead, because of a notorious concurring opinion by Justice Joseph P. Bradley, joined by Justices Stephen J. Field and Noah H. Swayne, *Bradwell* has a more lasting place in American legal history. That opinion took on far broader issues than the Privileges and Immunities Clause by addressing the claim for equal rights for women. Bradley defined in the most paternalistic terms a woman's role in society as one that should be subservient to men, relegated to the home.

Man is, or should be, woman's protector and defender. The natural and proper timidity and delicacy which belongs to the female sex evidently unfits it for many of the occupations of civil life. The constitution of the family organization, which is founded in the divine ordinance, as well as in the nature of things, indicates the domestic sphere as that which properly belongs to the domain and functions of womanhood.

Bradley explained that, under the common law, the husband was regarded as the wife's "head and representative in the social state," and that laws flowing from and depending upon this "cardinal principle still exist in full force in most States." While he acknowledged that many women are unmarried and therefore unaffected by any of these "duties, complications and incapacities," Bradley concluded that these exceptions were irrelevant.

The paramount destiny and mission of woman are to fulfill the noble and benign offices of wife and mother. This is the law of the Creator. And the rules of civil society must be adapted to the general constitution of things, and can not be based upon exceptional cases.

Although Bradley's paternalistic opinion was clearly a product of its time, he tempered it by supporting the advancement of women in some fields. "The humane movements of modern society, which have for their object the multiplication of avenues for woman's advancement, and of occupations adapted to her condition and sex, have my heartiest concurrence," the justice wrote. But, he explained, this does not mean they have the right to be admitted into every office and position, including those that require special qualifications and demanding responsibilities. State legislatures, he maintained, must retain the power to decide where women belong.

A few footnotes on the *Bradwell* case are in order. First, it is worth noting that while the butchers in *Slaughter-House Cases* were denied their constitutional right to pursue a profession by a narrow 5–4 vote, Bradwell lost her appeal by an 8–1 margin, a result that reflects at least in part the views of Bradley's concurrence. (The one dissenting vote came from Chief Justice Salmon P. Chase, who was not only a strong antislavery voice as a senator and member of Abraham Lincoln's

Cabinet, but also a distant cousin of Myra Bradwell. He died a few weeks after the *Bradwell* decision, and was too ill to write an explanation of his dissenting vote.)

Also worth noting are the seemingly inconsistent alignments of both Carpenter and Justice Bradley in the two cases. Carpenter defended Bradwell's right to become a lawyer, but argued against the butchers' position in *Slaughter-House* because he believed the Louisiana law to be a valid health regulation. Conversely, Bradley argued in dissent in *Slaughter-House* for the butchers' constitutional right to adopt and pursue a lawful employment, but was in the majority in *Bradwell* asserting that she did not have that freedom.

Denied: The Right to Vote

Minor v. Happersett, 21 Wall. 162 (1875)

Two years after its decisions in *Slaughter-House Cases* and *Bradwell*, the Supreme Court applied similar reasoning and analysis of the Fourteenth Amendment to the issue of women's right to vote. As the *Bradwell* brief had anticipated, the justices were not willing to consider the right to vote a privilege of national citizenship. Under its weak interpretation of the Fourteenth Amendment—which the Court interpreted as conferring civil, not political rights—the Court allowed the states to deny women suffrage.

Virginia L. Minor and her husband, Francis Minor, were both committed and energetic suffragists. The first woman to speak out for women's voting rights in her state, she was the founder of the Missouri Woman's Suffrage Association, and a passionate and effective public speaker. He was a Princeton and University of Virginia–educated lawyer who stayed out of the spotlight to draft resolutions, legal briefs, and letters to newspapers. Together, the couple began to

raise the notion that the Fourteenth Amendment was intended to provide an expanded view of women's voting rights.

One way they sought to achieve this interpretation was by creating a test case to raise their theory in court. In 1872 Virginia made an unsuccessful effort to register to vote in St. Louis, which led her and her husband to file a suit (as a married woman she could not sue independently) against the registrar, Reese Happersett. After initially losing they appealed to the Missouri Supreme Court, and finally to the Supreme Court of the United States.

Francis, presenting their case himself, argued that the right to vote was a national privilege and immunity protected by the Fourteenth Amendment. States had certain regulatory functions to determine who is qualified to vote, the Minors asserted, but under the Constitution, states could not deny, solely on the basis of gender, what was a core right of national citizenship.

While this argument seemed initially like it might be more viable than the assertion put forth in *Bradwell*, the Court, in an opinion by Chief Justice Morrison R. Waite, did not agree. Not only did the justices endorse the holding in *Bradwell*, their decision in *Minor v. Happersett* (1875) further limited the protections of the Privileges and Immunities Clause. The unanimous decision also further curtailed the rights of women while extending the Court's paternalistic treatment of them.

Waite's opinion started by addressing whether women were even citizens of the United States. While finding that indeed they were, the chief justice suggested that the Fourteenth Amendment played no role in that conclusion.

[S]ex has never been made one of the elements of citizenship in the United States. In this respect men have never had an advantage over women. The same laws

As the great fire swept through Chicago on the evening of October 8, 1871, Myra Bradwell gathered a few valuables and gave them to her husband to bury in their front lawn to save them from destruction. She then fled to Lake Michigan, where, along with her family and other Chicago citizens, she stood in the lake for the duration of the night. The fire raged for three days, destroying virtually the entire city. Adding to the panic of that first evening was the discovery that her thirteen-year-old daughter, Bessie, was missing. Bessie was found, alive and well, the following afternoon. The reason for her disappearance: she had rushed to her mother's office to save the lengthy subscription list to her mother's publication, the *Chicago Legal News*, before the premises were consumed by flames.

Nothing was of greater value to Bradwell than those lists. With the city still smoldering and most law offices and law libraries burned to the ground, copies of the *News*, especially back issues, became more useful than ever to its subscribers. And Bradwell ensured that her publication became indispensable to a new clientele—landowners—when she persuaded the Illinois legislature to choose the *News* as the official medium for the publication of all court records, including notices of land title, that had been burned by the fire and then re-created. Displaying her keen business sense, Bradwell capitalized on the disaster by promising potential advertisers that "in no place in the world will there be such a demand for law books as in Chicago during the next few months."

Even before the great fire, the *Chicago Legal News* had flourished. Founded by Bradwell in 1868, the weekly had quickly become the most important legal publication in the Midwest. A year after its founding, the Illinois legislature passed a bill providing that any statute, ordinance, notice, or court

Myra Bradwell, editor of the influential legal trade journal *Chicago Legal News*, appealed her case to the Supreme Court after Illinois refused to grant her a license to practice law because of her sex.

opinion published therein would be admissible as evidence in court. And the *News* was able to publish the latest legislation by the Illinois legislature very quickly, capitalizing on the time lag of several months it took the state to publish its own laws. As a result, no lawyer could practice in the Chicago area without having first read the *News*. Within a decade of its launching, the *News* had become the most widely circulated legal newspaper in the country.

Bradwell was responsible for all aspects of the journal's content, which included general news of interest to lawyers and business leaders, and for the financial operations of the business. But her contribution was even greater, for once she had secured her reputation as a solid legal journalist, she began to editorialize about the need for social reform, wisely using wit and jokes that went further toward persuading her readers than any political tract.

In addition to her newspaper, Bradwell ran a printing and binding company that produced her newspaper, as well as bound volumes of legislation that had appeared in its pages. Praised for its accuracy and efficiency, the company received requests from out-of-state courts to publish in a month what was taking their states years to produce. It also offered subscribers seventy-five different printed legal forms, all compiled by Bradwell, who had studied law for several years under the tutelage of her husband, James B. Bradwell, a county judge. Her business success made Bradwell one of the most prosperous businesswomen of the post–Civil War era, and enabled her to buy a large mansion on the shores of Lake Michigan. But she sought more than success as a publisher: Bradwell wanted to be licensed to practice law. To that end, in 1869 she applied to the Illinois state bar, having passed a qualifying exam with high honors that certified her for admission. She was not the first woman to do so; a young teacher named Arabella B. Mansfield had passed the bar exam in Iowa just six weeks before. But unlike Mansfield, who did receive her license, Bradwell was turned down for being a "married woman."

Under the centuries-old principle of "coverture," a woman was not a separate legal entity from her husband and could not legally enter into contracts without the consent of her husband as a cosigner. Bradwell had been allowed to run her business without supervision by her husband only after receiving special permission from the state. But being licensed as a lawyer was another matter entirely.

When Bradwell contested the Illinois court's decision, it eventually conceded that she had been denied admission because of her sex, not her marital status. In 1873 the Supreme Court of the United States upheld the lower court's decision in *Bradwell v. Illinois* on the ground that the right to practice a profession was not guaranteed by the Fourteenth Amendment.

In the meantime, Bradwell and two of her young protégés, Ada Kepley and Alta Hulett, had been busy drafting and lobbying for an Illinois statute providing that "no person shall be precluded or debarred from any occupation, profession or employment (except military), on account of sex." After its passage, the Illinois Supreme Court had no choice but grudgingly to admit women. Never one to rest on her laurels, Bradwell also drafted legislation, which her husband then introduced, making women eligible to hold elective office in the Illinois public school system—quite a feat considering women were not actually allowed to vote in the elections (that right would not come until 1892, again at Bradwell's urging). Two years later, the Bradwells pushed legislation through the Illinois House of Representatives making all women, married and single, eligible to be notaries. In her editorials, Bradwell faithfully trumpeted gains made by women in business, politics, and law in every state. She commented wittily on Belva Lockwood's efforts to become a member of the Supreme Court bar (see p. 207), asking male skeptics of women's abilities not to " 'man-dam-us' before we have had a hearing" (a mandamus is a type of court order).

Bradwell was an ardent suffragist, but she allied herself with the moderate wing of the movement. Unlike the more radical Susan B. Anthony, she believed that the vote would more readily be gained by "sensible and devoted mothers, wives and daughters" asking their fathers, husbands, and brothers to "give women the right to vote" than by militant unmarried women. Bradwell served as an officer of the moderate American Woman Suffrage Association and unsuccessfully sought a women's suffrage amendment to the Illinois constitution. She was, however, victorious at lobbying for married women's property laws, which finally granted women some control over their property and earnings.

(continued)

(continued)

Bradwell's penchant for social reform was fostered at an early age. Born Myra Colby in Manchester, Vermont, her family was staunchly abolitionist. The story of Elijah Lovejoy, a newspaper publisher and friend of the family who had been killed in 1837 by a pro-slavery mob, made a deep and lasting impression on the young girl. When Myra was twelve, the family moved to Elgin, Illinois, where she finished high school. She attended the Ladies Seminary in Kenosha, Wisconsin, and then returned to Elgin to teach school.

In 1852 Myra married James B. Bradwell, the son of poor English immigrants, who had just finished college and was preparing to be a lawyer. They both secured jobs at a private school in Memphis, Tennessee, where James's duties as headmaster did not prevent him from continuing his study of law. Upon their return to Chicago in 1855, he was admitted to the bar and started a legal practice. James was elected county judge of Cook County in 1861 and often used his influence in the community to support legislation furthering reforms advocated by his wife.

Myra was determined to read law with her husband so that they could "work side by side and think side by side." Her studies were interrupted by the births of her four children (only two of whom survived early childhood). In addition to Bessie, the Bradwells had a son, Thomas, who, like his sister, eventually became a lawyer. Bessie Bradwell Helmer would succeed her mother as publisher of the *Chicago Legal News* in 1894; Thomas would join his father in the management of his mother's printing company.

In addition to advancing women's rights, Bradwell was passionate about reforming the legal system. She advocated the adoption of uniform rules of legal practice throughout the state and urged lawyers in large cities to specialize in specific areas of the law. She inveighed against disreputable lawyers, particularly those who bribed jurors (a rampant practice at the time), stole clients' money, drank heavily, or obtained quick divorces for their clients. She successfully waged war on the corrupt practice of jury-packing. She insisted on good manners in the courtroom, punctuality in judges, and keeping side conversations to a minimum. She urged the legislature to raise judicial salaries and to improve courtroom facilities and conditions. She considered it unconstitutional for a judge to run for higher political office without first resigning his judicial office, and she supported the adoption of laws requiring compulsory retirement for judges at the age of sixty-five.

Very little that affected her community escaped Bradwell's critical assessment and bold commentary. Yet she routinely published others' articles that severely criticized her own positions. She often prevailed when she wrote editorials challenging court decisions, many of which were reversed or revised through appeal or legislation.

Although denied admission to the state bar, Bradwell was an early supporter of the formation of the Chicago and Illinois Bar Associations. She became an honorary member of both, and served four consecutive terms as an honorary officer. Despite having pushed through legislation in 1872 providing that all persons, regardless of sex, were guaranteed freedom to pursue an occupation, she never reapplied to the bar. In 1890, however, the Illinois Supreme Court decided to act on its own accord. An order was entered granting Bradwell's original application for admission to the bar, and she became the first person in Illinois granted a license to practice law on the court's own motion. Two years later, on March 28, 1892, Bradwell was admitted to the bar of the Supreme Court of the United States on the motion of Attorney General W. H. H. Miller.

Bradwell died of cancer in 1894, leaving behind a legacy of achievement in the business and legal world that still stands as a model of industry, civic responsibility, and professional success. Her words and deeds, not to mention her personal model, caused many to reconsider and amend social customs and legal restrictions that were no longer defensible.

In 1872 Virginia L. Minor, claiming women's suffrage as a right and not a favor, unsuccessfully tried to register to vote in St. Louis. Her husband, Francis Minor, argued her case all the way to the Supreme Court, which held that suffrage was not a privilege of citizenship and that states could therefore deny women the right to vote.

alone have the power to regulate this kind of activity. "The Amendment did not add to the privileges and immunities of a citizen," said the Court, "[i]t simply furnishes an additional guaranty for the protection of such as he already had." "The power of the State in this particular," wrote Waite, "is certainly supreme until Congress acts." From this point it was an easy matter for the Court to take the next step—a state-by-state review of the status of women's voting rights. It found that each state determined for itself who should have that electoral power, and that no state allowed all of its citizens to vote.

[I]f the courts can consider any question settled, this is one. For nearly ninety years the people have acted upon the idea that the constitution, when it conferred citizenship, did not necessarily confer the right of suffrage. If uniform practice long continued can settle the construction of so important an instrument as the Constitution of the United States confessedly is, most certainly it has been done here.

precisely apply to both. The [F]ourteenth [A]mendment did not affect the citizenship of women any more than it did of men. In this particular, therefore, the rights of Mrs. Minor do not depend upon the amendment. She has always been a citizen from her birth, and entitled to all the privileges and immunities of citizenship.

Having set up this straw woman argument about citizenship and then torn it down, the Court next turned to the more problematic second question: whether all citizens are necessarily voters, or, more specifically, whether suffrage is one of the national privileges and immunities of citizens. The Court's conclusion was an emphatic "no," based on its understanding that the states

Finally, the decision reaffirmed the idea that if the Privileges and Immunities Clause had been intended to create a woman's right to vote, there would have been no need to adopt the Fifteenth Amendment, which prevented the right to vote from "being denied on account of race." "Nothing is more evident," wrote Waite, "than that the greater must include the less, and if all were already protected, why go through with the form of amending the Constitution to protect a part?"

The Court's decision in *Minor v. Happersett* placed a significant roadblock in the way of the women's suffrage movement. The result meant that women had fewer rights than the recently freed slaves, whose right to vote was specifically protected by the Fifteenth Amendment. It would take nearly another half century, and passage of the Nineteenth Amendment, to change this situation and bring to a close more than a century's effort to achieve national women's suffrage. Several commentators have suggested that the *Minor* decision and its impact on women was similar to the impact on African Americans of the 1856 *Dred Scott v. Sandford* decision, which held that African Americans were not citizens. In both cases it took a constitutional amendment to overturn a decision that relegated the affected party to second-class citizenship.

Susan B. Anthony on Trial

Before the Supreme Court rejected their arguments, the Minors' interpretation of the Privileges and Immunities Clause had a great impact on the National Woman Suffrage Association (NWSA), and its leaders Susan B. Anthony and Elizabeth Cady Stanton. Convinced that, as citizens, women already possessed the right to vote, women suffrists in several states began casting ballots or setting up alternative polling booths to cast mock votes. In the best-known instance Anthony and fifteen associates persuaded the registrar in Rochester, N.Y., to permit them to vote—an act that got suffrists and election supervisors arrested and thrown in jail. Anthony was keen to remain imprisoned to gain publicity, but her lawyer, Henry R. Selden, posted bail out of a "sense of gallantry."

Anthony's case went to trial in June 1873 before U.S. Supreme Court justice Ward Hunt, who was fulfilling his duty to sit as judge on a circuit court in New York. He refused to instruct the jury that proof of the defendant's belief in good faith that she had a constitutional right to vote would render her not guilty. Anthony, Hunt observed, "had knowingly voted, not having a right to vote." He concluded that "her belief did not affect the question."

Pronouncing Anthony guilty, Hunt sentenced her to pay a fine of $100 and the costs of prosecution. She refused, pleading that she was already $10,000 in debt for publishing her radical newspaper, the *Revolution*. The government did not enforce the fine, and it is likely that Selden eventually paid it. The prosecutor dropped the criminal charges against the women "voters," but the election inspectors were judged guilty and sent to jail. Hundreds of Rochester supporters came to visit them, and the suffrists brought them their dinner daily. At Anthony's urging, Selden eventually obtained a pardon for the inspectors from President Ulysses S. Grant. Nine years later, the circuit court reversed its decision, admitting that it had "erred in charging the jury to find the defendant guilty."

Perhaps the most interesting aspect of the case was Anthony's reply to Justice Hunt's routine inquiry as to whether "the prisoner [had] anything to say why sentence [should] not be pronounced?" Indeed Anthony had quite a bit to say, which she did despite the judge's frequent requests to sit down and be silent. "Robbed of the fundamental privilege of citizenship," she raged, "I am degraded from the status of a citizen to that of a subject; and not only myself individually, but all of my sex, are, by your honor's verdict, doomed to political subjection." Anthony further objected that she was neither defended, prosecuted, nor judged by peers because "jury, judge, counsel, must all be of the superior class [male]." She explained that she had been defended by a man because women were not admitted to the bar, prosecuted by male judges chosen by male politicians because women could not vote, and judged by an all-male jury because women were not permitted to serve on juries.

Two years after sentencing Anthony, Justice Hunt voted with the unanimous Supreme Court in *Minor v. Happersett*, which denied women the right to vote. With the defeat in *Minor*, the NWSA tactically reverted back to the pursuit of legislative victory. In 1878, at its Tenth Convention, the NWSA's leaders drafted a constitutional

A delegation of female suffragists came before the Senate Judiciary Committee to argue that the Fourteenth and Fifteenth Amendments to the Constitution provided for women's voting rights. Many suffragists, including Susan B. Anthony (below), also tried to cast ballots in state elections to exercise a broad interpretation of those amendments.

amendment that prohibited disenfranchisement on the basis of sex. That language would not become law until 1920, when the Nineteenth Amendment was finally ratified.

 The Nineteenth Amendment

The Constitution left it up to the individual states to decide who was qualified to vote in federal elections. So women's groups initially focused their efforts on persuading state legislatures to authorize women's suffrage. But passage of the Fourteenth and Fifteenth Amendments guaranteeing voting rights for African Americans created an opportunity to bring the debate to the national level. Women's rights advocates began to push for a broader reading of those amendments

that would extend that right to women as well. Their efforts proved unsuccessful.

Taking a new tack, at its Tenth Woman's Rights Convention in 1878 the National Woman's Suffrage Association introduced a constitutional amendment (known as the Susan B. Anthony Amendment) enfranchising women. It was not until twelve years later that the Senate finally considered the amendment, only to reject it by a large margin.

Meanwhile, women's voting rights groups were experiencing some success at the state level. Wyoming enfranchised women in 1890 when it became a state, although women had been allowed to elect territorial officials as early as 1869. Colorado followed in 1893, and in 1896 both Utah and Idaho granted suffrage to women.

But elsewhere progress was slow and opposition remained strong. It was not until the Progressive era that other states followed: Washington in 1910; California in 1911; Arizona, Kansas, and Oregon in 1912; Montana and Nevada in 1914; and New York in 1917.

Opposition to women's suffrage was fierce and vociferous. Antisuffrage groups claimed that women, by nature, were incapable of making political decisions and would not know how to choose a candidate or cast a ballot. They also cautioned that the relationship between the sexes would suffer, because women would act more like men. Some went so far as to suggest that giving women the vote would lead to the end of marriage, the breakup of the family—even to communism. Women's rights groups countered that women's suffrage would purify the political landscape because women would vote out all of the corrupt forces.

The militant wing of the suffrage movement, the National Woman's Party (NWP), took the lead on the eve of World War I to agitate for a constitutional amendment granting women the right to vote. President Woodrow Wilson was

Although women's rights groups had little success in passing a national suffrage amendment, they did meet with victory in state legislatures. Wyoming, which had allowed women to elect territorial officials as early as 1869, was the first state to enfranchise women. Above are women voters in Cheyenne, two years before Wyoming gained statehood in 1890.

adamantly opposed to a federal solution, maintaining the decision belonged to the states. Rallied behind suffragist Alice Paul, members of the NWP demonstrated noisily outside the White House. Their protest drew much public scrutiny, and ultimately they were arrested. Members of the armed forces, who found such demonstrations unpatriotic during wartime, were especially harsh. The demonstrators countered that their disenfranchised status was particularly objectionable when the country was at war for the very purpose of "making the world safer for democracy."

In jail, the protesters found the overcrowding, inhumane treatment, and unsanitary conditions unbearable. They staged a hunger strike to protest, prompting the authorities to force feeding. Their plight gave rise to enormous public sympathy and helped focus national attention on their cause.

On January 9, 1918, Wilson finally announced that he would support the proposed suffrage amendment. The next day it was introduced in the House by Jeannette Rankin of Montana, the first woman elected to Congress. The House approved it by a vote of 274–136—only one vote more than the necessary two-thirds majority. But in a 62–34 vote, the Senate failed the next day to assemble the necessary majority. Wilson tried to squeeze the amendment through after the Republicans won the November election, but the lame-duck Democratic Senate mustered only a 55–29 vote. In a surprising turnabout, however, the amendment was quickly approved at a special session of the new Republican Congress: House 304–89 on May 21, 1919, Senate 56–25 on June 4. But in order to win the support of southern male voters, progressive northern women distanced themselves from African Americans seeking to establish political rights in the south.

When Tennessee became the thirty-sixth state to pass the amendment on August 18, 1920, the

Legal counsel to the National Woman's Party, Burnita Shelton Matthews was photographed on the steps of her party's building in 1923, three years after ratification of the Nineteenth Amendment. When the building was later condemned, Matthews won the largest condemnation award the United States had ever paid. The government put the land to good use: it became the site of the current Supreme Court building. Matthews was appointed to the United States District Court for the District of Columbia in 1949, becoming the first female to gain a life-tenured trial court judgeship in the nation. In part to make up for her colleagues' refusal to hire women clerks, Judge Matthews engaged only women as her clerks.

three-fourths majority necessary for ratification was achieved. On August 26 the final proclamation was signed, and these words added to the Constitution: "The right of citizens of the United States to vote shall not be denied or abridged by the United States or by any State on account of sex."

The passage of the Nineteenth Amendment effectively nullified all state laws that did not already grant women full suffrage. State courts interpreted the amendment to require that voting qualifications be the same for both sexes. For example, a Kentucky law that required that only women, but not men, be literate in order to vote was struck down by the state court, and an Ohio woman was told she must provide her exact age, like a man, if she wished to register.

The Supreme Court did, however, decide to permit unequal qualifications in *Breedlove v. Suttles* (1937) when the voting requirement was more burdensome for men, not women. At issue was a Georgia law that required all citizens—except children, the elderly, women not registered to vote, and the blind—to pay a poll tax of one dollar. The rationale for exempting women: "[T]he laws of Georgia declare the husband to be the head of the family and the wife to be subject to him. To subject her to the levy would be to add to his burden." In *Breedlove*, a man who was denied the right to vote because he had not paid the tax charged that the law unfairly discriminated against men under the Equal Protection Clause of the Fourteenth Amendment, as well as under the Nineteenth Amendment. The Court upheld the law on the ground that neither of those amendments regulated the enforcement of taxes, and that the poll taxes did not interfere with the right of either sex to vote.

In other states, however, poll taxes were used to discourage women, and especially African Americans, from voting. The issue was finally put to rest when poll taxes were effectively abolished with adoption of the Twenty-fourth Amendment in 1964.

PROTECTING WOMEN'S HEALTH AND MORALS

The Nature of Women's Work

Wages were less of an issue for most American women at the turn of the nineteenth century than they are now because they worked on family farms and were essentially self employed. Women who did earn wages generally opted for work that was home based or part time, allowing them to be near their children. Women comprised one fifth of the paid labor force in 1905, and sixty percent of those working women were either employed as domestics in private households or as home-based workers taking in laundering, sewing, or lodgers. Young, single women, most of whom were waiting to get married, constituted two thirds of women wage earners, while married women (mostly poor immigrants and African Americans) just under one fifth.

By 1930 married women had entered the workforce in greater numbers, and represented fully one third of women wage earners. By then working-class women were expected to labor for longer periods during their lives and to continue working after having children. The shortage of men during World War II drew even more married women into the labor force. By the end of the 1940s the number of working married women with husbands also in the workforce equaled the number of working single, divorced, and widowed women combined.

But the prevailing attitudes about women, the family, and work did not change as rapidly as the composition of the workforce. The interests of various groups often overshadowed the struggle to improve women's working conditions and access to better jobs. For example, a man's dominance in the family was threatened by his wife's paycheck. Middle-class reformers were intent on keeping women workers home as much as possible to preserve the family unit and to protect children. And employers were eager to prevent women from joining increasingly powerful unions.

The Ten-Hour Working Day

Muller v. Oregon, 208 U.S. 412 (1908)

On September 15, 1905, Emma Gotcher, a laundress from Portland, Oregon, charged her employer, Curt Muller, with violating the state law that limited a woman's workday to ten hours. An active member of the Shirt, Waist, and Laundry-workers Union, she had been forced to work long hours on Labor Day, a new legal holiday on which employers were supposed to give workers the day off. Backed by the Laundry-Owners' Association, Muller changed his guilty plea to a complaint that the ten-hour, women-only law violated the Due Process Clause of the Fourteenth Amendment. The protective law had been passed two years earlier in the state senate at the instigation of the Oregon Federation of Labor. The Oregon Supreme Court upheld the law restricting women's hours in a brief, unanimous opinion. Muller appealed.

At this point the National Consumers' League (NCL) joined the fray. Founded in 1899 to advocate patronizing only employers who treated working women well, the NCL pushed women-only protective labor legislation. Its head, Florence Kelley, asked fellow activist Josephine Goldmark to persuade her brother-in-law, the prominent Progressive attorney (and later Supreme Court justice) Louis D. Brandeis, to take the case.

Brandeis devised an extraordinary brief consisting of only 2 pages of legal argument but 111 pages of fact regarding working conditions for women. This revolutionary brief (which would spawn similar "Brandeis briefs") marshaled statistics, doctor's reports, and copies of protective laws in seven other countries to prove that overwork was particularly harmful to women. This legal technique was inspired by Kelley's masses of statistics in her legal briefs arguing for an eight-hour day in Chicago sweatshops.

Dangers to women's reproductive capacity were of particular concern. One expert cautioned against the pressure of the sewing machine on the abdomen. Another warned that an overtired mother's milk could induce "spasmodic diarrhea" in babies and lead to death. The evidence presented may not all have been accurate, but the Supreme Court was persuaded. Justice David J. Brewer's unanimous opinion swiftly distinguished the case from *Lochner v. New York* (1905), an important precedent that had overturned a New York law setting a ten-hour day for *all* bakery workers. In order for the Court to distinguish this case from *Lochner*, it needed to emphasize the difference between the sexes in the same manner that Justice Bradley had in *Bradwell*. The resulting opinion put woman into "a class by herself" because "she is not an equal competitor with her brother."

The two sexes differ in structure of body, in the functions to be performed by each, in the amount of physical strength, in the capacity for long-continued labor, particularly when done standing, the influence of vigorous health upon the future well-being of the race, the self-reliance which enables one to assert full rights, and in the capacity to maintain the struggle for subsistence. This difference justifies a difference in legislation. . . .

Justice Brewer further argued that restrictions on women's hours were necessary not to endanger their reproductive and maternal functions.

That woman's physical structure and the performance of maternal functions place her at a disadvantage in the struggle for subsistence is obvious. This is especially true when the burdens of motherhood are upon her. Even when they are not, by abundant testimony of the medical fraternity continuance for a long time on her feet at

When his overworked laundresses accused him of violating Oregon's ten-hour working day law, laundry owner Curt Muller (arms folded, in the doorway) challenged the law as discriminatory because it covered only women. In 1908 a unanimous Supreme Court upheld the law on the ground that women's health was vital "to the future well-being of the race."

work, repeating this from day to day, tends to injurious effects upon the body, and as healthy mothers are essential to vigorous offspring, the physical well-being of woman becomes an object of public interest and care in order to preserve the strength and vigor of the race.

Although the good of society was clearly the Supreme Court's main concern, the opinion did note that protective legislation would "compensate" for "some of the burdens which rest upon [women]." Was this progress? Women were not free, as men were, to work as many hours as they chose and to earn the money that brings. But they were protected from being forced to work long, punishing days. Women's groups were seriously divided over this issue. The NCL declared victory, but the National Woman's Party, a feminist group, opposed special protection and called

for maximum working hour legislation covering all workers. It pointed out that some women workers—for example, printers and streetcar conductors—were fired from jobs that had formerly been reserved for men because they could not work long hours. Those occupations paid more than the jobs into which women were segregated, like cleaning homes. If hours laws covered all workers, employers would not have the option of firing one sex; the other would be subject to the same restrictions.

There were other damaging consequences to women. Because they were "protected" by maximum working hour laws, women were not eligible to join unions, which meant they did not benefit from the bargains struck by unions with employers in terms of working conditions and compensation. The protective laws also limited women's ability to compete for jobs. And they reversed women's inroads into traditionally male jobs and helped ensure their continuous segregation into low-paid women's work.

In the next few years after *Muller,* the Supreme Court consistently upheld laws limiting women's hours. In *Hawley v. Walker* (1914), *Miller v. Wilson* (1915), and *Bosley v. McLaughlin* (1915) the Court resisted challenges to female hour limits in several states. *Radice v. New York* (1924) concerned a law that made an exception for entertainers and ladies' room attendants, but forbade waitresses from working the night shift. Yet, in *State v. Bunting* (1917), the Court also upheld as constitutional a maximum hours law from Oregon covering both women *and* men. Interestingly, the brief prepared for the NCL by Harvard Law School professor Felix Frankfurter (who took over when Brandeis was appointed to the Supreme Court) emphasized the importance of evening opportunities for workers' self-betterment, such as night school and visiting libraries, which had not been stressed in *Muller* because women were expected to take care of their families after work.

Although social reformers could have used this 1917 victory to campaign for hours laws for *all* workers, unions opposed the move, fearing it would undermine support for unions. The women-only hour limits remained the law in most states until they were struck down in the 1960s.

Minimum Wage Laws

Adkins v. Children's Hospital of D.C., 261 U.S. 525 (1923)

West Coast Hotel Co. v. Parrish, 300 U.S. 379 (1937)

As thirty-nine states passed laws limiting women's working hours, the National Consumers' League and other progressive groups next devoted themselves to establishing minimum wage laws for women. Massachusetts adopted such a law in 1912 and eight states followed suit the next year. Nonindustrial states resisted, however, and by the time the Supreme Court ruled on their constitutionality in 1923 only seventeen states had adopted minimum wage laws for women.

In practice, these laws did not always benefit the women they were trying to protect. Willie Lyons was a twenty-one-year-old elevator operator employed by the Congress Hall Hotel in Washington, D.C., for $35 a month and two meals a day. She liked her job and her employers were satisfied with her performance. However, in 1918 the District of Columbia enacted a minimum wage law that required women to earn a high enough wage—in Lyons's case $71.50 a month—to ensure that they were not "receiving wages inadequate to supply them with the necessary cost of living, maintain them in health and protect their morals." The result: Lyons was fired and a man hired to replace her at the market rate of $35 because he was not "protected" by the law. Furious, she joined female employees at the local children's hospital to contest the law.

The Supreme Court struck down the District of Columbia's law in *Adkins v. Children's Hospital* (1923) as a violation of the liberty of contract guaranteed by the Due Process Clause of the Fifth Amendment. In his majority opinion, Justice George Sutherland noted approvingly the political strides women had made since *Muller* and argued that women should not be subjected to greater restrictions on their liberty of contract than men.

In view of the great—not to say revolutionary—changes which have taken place since that utterance, in the contractual, political, and civil status of women, culminating in the Nineteenth Amendment, it is not unreasonable to say that these differences have now come almost, if not quite, to the vanishing point.

Willie Lyons was fired from her job at the Congress Hall Hotel (building with the large awning) in Washington, D.C., because it could not afford to pay her the salary that the city's minimum wage law required women elevator operators be paid. A man was hired to replace Lyons at the market rate of less than half that salary, prompting her to join with local children's hospital workers to challenge the city's minimum wage law for women.

He held that the physiological differences between men and women justified the one-sided maximum working hour legislation but not the minimum wage laws.

As to morality, Sutherland argued that it was not possible to determine a living wage at which a woman's morals were guaranteed protection. The correlation between wage level and morality depended on the situation: the woman's sense of frugality, whether she lived alone or with her family, or whether she had outside income. And was it fair to assume that all poor women were less trustworthy or less honest? Sutherland also expressed concern about the social burden placed on employers in making them responsible for a female employee's virtue by keeping her out of poverty. That welfare function belonged to society at large, he admonished. Finally, Sutherland cautioned against the financial burden placed on small employers who could not afford to pay the higher wage. He concluded that the free market was the best way to determine wages.

Fifteen years later, the Court overturned *Adkins*, as well as another decision, *Morehead v. New York ex. Rel. Tipaldo,* made just five months earlier, in which the Court had struck down a New York minimum wage law for women only. Its decision to uphold Washington state's women-only wage law in *West Coast Hotel Co. v. Parrish* (1937) reflected a striking change of heart for the Court. Previously, the justices had declared unconstitutional Franklin D. Roosevelt's aggressive initiatives for helping the country out of the economic devastation of the Great Depression. Starting with the minimum wage law for women in *Parrish,* they finally began upholding controls on prices, wages, and rents.

Chief Justice Charles Evans Hughes's majority opinion in *Parrish* declared that the state legislature was "entitled to consider the situation of women in employment, the fact that they are in the class receiving the least pay, that their bargaining power is relatively weak, and that they are ready victims of those who would take advantage of their necessitous circumstances." Justice Sutherland, remaining true to his opinion in *Adkins,* dissented. He argued that women were being discriminated against arbitrarily because their right to make wage contracts freely would be restricted. Women should not, he wrote, "be denied, in effect, the right to compete with men for work paying lower wages which men may be willing to accept." Sutherland firmly believed that women were no less adept than men at negotiating wages with their employers. "The ability to make a fair bargain, as everyone knows, does not depend upon sex," he wrote.

Ending Protective Legislation for Women

Two years after *Parrish* was handed down, the Fair Labor Standards Act of 1938 established a national minimum wage for workers of both sexes and required that overtime be paid when they worked longer than an eight-hour day. Labor Secretary Frances Perkins, formerly of the National Consumers' League, was chief architect of the bill. Yet its successful passage was not achieved by agitation for equal rights on the part of women's groups, but rather by organized labor's realization that wage-and-hours legislation for men might be a way of combating unemployment. The new law helped women working in manufacturing, but—following in the footsteps of the women-only laws—did not cover domestic service or agriculture, the leading female occupations in terms of numbers.

Protective legislation that limited women's hours, restricted night work, forbade women from lifting heavy materials, and barred them from jobs in mining and bartending remained on the books in many states for decades. Blue-collar women successfully challenged these laws as discriminatory, not protective, after passage of Title VII of the Civil Rights Act of 1964 (see p. 119), which prohibited employment discrimination because of sex. But some women's rights groups and unions wanted to retain the protective legislation, and they initially opposed the Equal Rights Amendment (ERA) in the early 1970s because its passage would render such laws unconstitutional. The dissenters eventually rallied behind the ERA when most protective legislation for women was invalidated by the courts under Title VII.

No Place for a Lady: Women Bartenders

Goesaert v. Cleary, 335 U.S. 464 (1948)

The notion of "romantic paternalism" was especially evident in laws prohibiting women from buying or selling liquor. This attitude grew out of the temperance movement that emerged in the last quarter of the nineteenth century, which pressured state legislatures into prohibiting women from bars—either as customers or as workers.

Working with Jane Addams, the prominent Chicago reformer, Florence Kelley crusaded successfully for Illinois's first factory inspection law to monitor safety and working conditions. As a result of her victory, the governor appointed Kelley Chief Inspector of Factories in 1893. But failure to secure passage of an eight-hour law for women workers left her frustrated. In 1899 Kelley was invited to head the National Consumers' League (NCL), a New York–based group advocating improved working conditions for women through the use of consumer power (patronizing and publicizing benevolent employers). She prevailed on fellow NCL reformer Josephine Goldmark to persuade the great Progressive attorney Louis D. Brandeis (who was later named to the Supreme Court) to become the NCL's lawyer in *Muller v. Oregon*, the Supreme Court case that would uphold the constitutionality of a maximum working hour law for women. Kelley had finally found the way to win her crusade.

Drinking establishments were portrayed as dens of sin and vice, unfit for women, where men used coarse language and engaged in manly camaraderie. The Women's Christian Temperance Union, which spearheaded the campaign, became the largest women's group of the era. It was particularly persuasive at denouncing bars as places where men squandered their money, drank too much, and then left to return home and inflict abuse on their families.

In that climate, it was not surprising that the Supreme Court in *Cronin v. Adams* (1904) upheld a Denver ordinance prohibiting the sale of alcohol to women and forbidding them from working in bars or liquor stores. But less predictable was the outcome of a Michigan case, *Goesaert v. Cleary,* that took place four decades later—after the demise of Prohibition and the eclipse of the temperance movement.

After Prohibition ended in 1933, all-male bartender unions in San Francisco, New York, and Ohio sought new laws to exclude women from practicing the lucrative, and now legal, profession. "Liquor alone causes enough trouble, why add women?" became the slogan of the International Bartenders Association. The state of Michigan consequently drafted a statute prohibiting women from bartending, as did many other states. Under pressure from proprietors of family-run bars, however, the language of the Michigan law was modified to forbid a woman from becoming a licensed bartender unless she was "the wife or daughter of the male owner."

A group of women bartenders and bar owners from Dearborn, Michigan, formed a class action suit to dispute the statute. Margaret and Valentine Goesaert, a mother who owned and tended a bar and her daughter who helped her bartend, teamed up with Caroline MacMahon, a bar owner, and Gertrude Nadrski, a bartender. Their attorney, Anne R. Davidow, also represented another woman bar owner and twenty-two female

During his two terms as senator from Utah, George Sutherland (pictured here with his wife, Rosamond) was an early champion of the right of women to vote. "Any argument which I may use to justify my own right to vote," he reasoned, "justifies as it seems to me, the right of my wife, sister, mother, and daughter to exercise the same right." A brilliant orator with an impressive knowledge of the Constitution, Sutherland made an artful case for suffrage in a 1915 speech.

[To] deprive [women] of the right to participate in the government is to make an arbitrary division of the citizenship of the country upon the sole ground that one class is made up of men, and should therefore rule, and the other class is made up of women, who should, therefore, be ruled. To say, and to prove if it were capable of proof, that such a division will not materially affect the government is not enough.

Appointed to the Supreme Court in 1922, Sutherland became one of the Four Horsemen—a quartet of conservative justices who systematically opposed the legislative reforms of the New Deal era. These justices believed that the government's initiatives infringed on the rights of individuals to make their own contracts as guaranteed by the Due Process Clause. Some have seen inconsistency in Sutherland's pro–women's rights stand in Congress and his anti–protectionist-laws-for-women opinions on the Court. But his belief in liberty of contract and women's rights can also be seen as quite consistent. That explains why, in *Adkins v.*

Children's Hospital, he sided with Willie Lyons, an elevator operator who had been fired because her employer could not afford to pay her under a minimum wage law designed to guarantee her a decent wage, rather than with the government whose law left employers free to hire cheaper male workers. Sutherland felt that women were perfectly capable of negotiating their own contracts and competing against men for jobs. It was their liberty to compete freely that needed protecting.

bartenders who claimed that their livelihood was threatened.

Davidow had graduated from Detroit Law School in 1920, one of five women in a class of thirty-four. In order to ensure her right to practice law under her own name, she had delayed marriage—and taking her husband's name—until after being admitted to the bar.

Several of the plaintiffs were waitresses who had switched to bartending for the better pay.

Many supported children (one had seven), and four supported husbands who were ill and could not work. As a group, the plaintiffs each averaged eight years of bartending experience. The women who owned bars complained that male bartenders cost more, and that—unlike barmaids—they drank on the job. These owners had invested their whole life savings in their bars and the law threatened to put them out of business.

The three-judge federal court that heard the case upheld the legislation. One of the three judges vigorously dissented, however, going so far as to argue that women bartenders were better than men at protecting public health, safety, and morals.

On appeal to the Supreme Court in 1948, the Michigan law was upheld in a 6–3 decision by Justice Frankfurter. He made a lighthearted refer-ence to the presence of barmaids in literature ("We meet the alewife, sprightly and ribald, in Shakespeare") to make the point that bartending was a historic calling for women. Despite this tradition, Frankfurter wrote, "Michigan could, beyond question, forbid all women from working behind a bar" because "liquor traffic is one of the oldest and most untrammeled of legislative powers." He held that it was permissible for the state to treat the sexes differently when it came to regulating vice.

The fact that women may now have achieved the virtues that men have long claimed as their prerogatives and now indulge in vices that men have long practiced, does not preclude the States from drawing a sharp line between the sexes, certainly, in such matters as the regulation of the liquor traffic.

But what about the question of Michigan's allowing one group of women (wives and daughters of owners) to bartend while discriminating against the rest? Frankfurter did not consider this to be discrimination because there was a moral rationale for the double standard. "Ownership of a bar by a barmaid's husband or father," he wrote, "minimizes hazards that may confront a barmaid without such protecting oversight." The Michigan legislators, he held, had drawn a line that had "a basis in reason."

Justice Wiley Rutledge, joined by William O. Douglas and Frank Murphy, dissented on the ground that the statute violated the Equal Protection Clause. The Michigan law, Rutledge argued, discriminated between male and female bar owners.

A male owner, although he himself is always absent from the bar, may employ his wife and daughter as barmaids. A female owner may neither work as a barmaid herself nor employ her daughter in that position, even if a man is always present in the establishment to keep order.

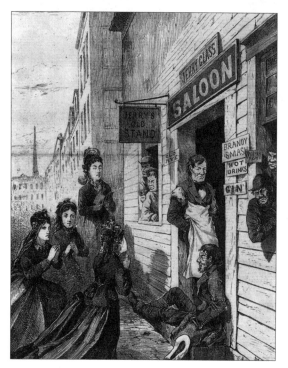

The women's temperance movement in the late nineteenth century successfully portrayed saloons as places of vice and sin and demanded state laws prohibiting women from buying liquor or working in bars.

When Prohibition was repealed in 1933 and saloonkeeping became legal again, all-male bartender unions sought to keep women out of their lucrative profession. In 1948 the Supreme Court upheld a Michigan law forbidding women from working in bars unless they were the wife or daughter of the owner, who presumably would protect their virtue.

Because of this discrepancy, Rutledge reasoned, the majority opinion "[b]elies the assumption that the statute was motivated by a legislative solicitude for the moral and physical well-being of women." In other words, women were more harmed than protected by the statute.

Given Frankfurter's earlier support of protective legislation for women and his work for the National Consumers' League, his conviction that he was protecting women's morals was genuine. Yet his urging the Court not to "give ear to the suggestion that the real impulse behind this legislation was an unchivalrous desire of male bartenders to try to monopolize the calling" now seems naive. In fact, campaigns by male bartenders to exclude their female cohorts from bartending continued into the 1970s. But so long as the Court could conceive of a good reason for the Michigan law, Frankfurter believed it could ignore the discriminatory motive behind it.

The immediate effect of the Supreme Court's decision was minimal because the Michigan Liquor Commission simply had been ignoring the statute. A year after *Goesaert* the law was amended, probably at the behest of widow bar owners, to permit women owners and their daughters to bartend. It was repealed after six years, but similar laws persisted in other states.

At the national convention of the bartenders union in 1949, it was reported that seventeen states had laws forbidding the employment of women bartenders, and that in the wake of the Supreme Court's decision in *Goesaert*, unions were working in eight other states to get such laws passed.

But after the 1964 Civil Rights Act became law, women bartenders won federal court victories declaring that these laws discriminated against women and were invalid under Title VII. And in 1971, a unanimous California Supreme Court invalidated a statute barring women from tending bar because it violated the federal Equal Protection Clause as well as a clause in the 1879 California Constitution: "No person shall on account of sex be disqualified from entering upon or pursuing any lawful business, vocation or profession." In *Sail'er Inn v. Kirby* the California court declared that *Goesaert* was antiquated, signaling that the reign of romantic paternalism was coming to a close. "The pedestal upon which women have been placed," wrote the California court, "has . . . , upon closer inspection, been revealed as a cage." Finally, in 1976, the Supreme Court officially repudiated *Goesaert*.

2

JURY DUTY

WOMEN AS "THE CENTER OF HOME AND FAMILY LIFE"

The same paternalistic attitude toward women characterized by the *Bradwell, Minor, Muller,* and *Goesaert* decisions was apparent in a series of cases involving another fundamental right of citizenship denied to women: jury membership. Like voting, jury service is a ritual that allows citizens to participate in the democratic process. But it is also an obligation: citizens who do not respond to a jury summons face sanctions ranging from fines to contempt of court. Because jury service takes citizens away from their daily responsibilities, it had been considered too burdensome for women, who were "protected" from having to perform it. The stated rationale was that women had a more essential duty to perform than jury service: taking care of their home and family. Lurking behind this justification was the romantic paternalist belief that women needed to be sheltered from the crudeness of criminal trials and that women did not make competent jurors. As a result, women were prohibited, discouraged, or excused from serving on juries until the 1970s.

Strauder v. West Virginia, 100 U.S. 303 (1880)

The first of the Supreme Court's decisions pertaining to discrimination in jury service, *Strauder v. West Virginia* (1880), concerned the appeal by an African American man of his murder conviction for killing his wife. The man challenged the verdict of a West Virginia court because the state's laws prevented blacks from serving on juries by limiting jury service to "all white male persons." The Court found the statute "practically a brand upon [African Americans], affixed by the law, an assertion of their inferiority," and therefore unconstitutional under the Fourteenth Amendment's Equal Protection Clause.

Because jury service, like voting, is a political right, the Supreme Court did not see a constitutional basis for extending that right to women before Congress granted women voting rights. In what is known as dicta, a judicial opinion suggesting how some issue might be decided in the future, but which is not legally binding, the Court made clear that the rights of citizenship that the Fourteenth Amendment guaranteed for African American men concerning jury membership did not pertain to women of any color. "The very idea of a jury is a body of men composed of the peers

The Little Closed Spaces Where Men Are Men

NO WOMEN ALLOWED

By CARL ROSE

Women were prohibited or discouraged from serving as jurors until the 1970s because it was thought that the burden of jury service would interfere with their ability to care for their home and family. Many also believed that women did not make competent jurors and that they should be protected from the crudeness of criminal trials.

or equal of the person whose rights it is selected or summoned to determine," the Court asserted in *Strauder*.

The Court similarly acknowledged that a state has the right to make certain limitations and "discriminations" in terms of qualifications for jury service in state courts. Thus the state "may confine the selection to males, to freeholders [property owners], to citizens, to persons within certain ages, or to persons having educational qualifications." The purpose of the Fourteenth Amendment, said the Court, was not to disallow the state from privileging these categories, but solely to prevent "discrimination because of race or color." Though not legally binding on future courts, the dicta about the constitutionality of excluding women from jury service under the Fourteenth

Amendment would nonetheless have long-term consequences.

Hoyt v. Florida, 368 U.S. 57 (1961)

More than eighty years later, in *Hoyt v. Florida* (1961), the Supreme Court would not only maintain the underlying premise of the dicta in *Strauder*, but also convert it to legal precedent. In *Hoyt*, a Tampa, Florida, woman named Gwendolyn Hoyt had been convicted of the second degree murder of her husband, Clarence Hoyt. Although she had suffered mental and physical abuse in her marriage, and showed neurotic, if not psychotic, behavior, a six-man jury deliberated for just twenty-five minutes before finding her guilty. The male judge sentenced the thirty-three-year-old Hoyt to thirty years hard labor. In appealing her conviction she challenged the constitutionality of Florida's statutory system of jury selection, which discouraged most women from service by requiring them to register for jury duty with the clerk of the circuit court. In contrast, males were registered automatically, even if they were entitled to apply for an exemption because of age, body infirmity, or occupation. Most women did not register, so women were effectively excluded from jury service in Florida.

The Supreme Court began its analysis by stating that it would not reexamine what it called "the continuing validity" of the language in *Strauder* supporting the right to confine jury duty to males. "This constitutional proposition has gone unquestioned for more than eighty years in the decisions of the Court," wrote Justice John Marshall Harlan in a unanimous decision. "Even were it to be assumed that this question is still open to debate," he added, "the present case tenders narrower issues."

The most crucial of those "narrower issues" was that the statute did not exclude women from jury service but merely spared them the obligation in recognition of their place at "the center of home and family life." Exemption was therefore a matter of privilege. Harlan concluded that such a system did not deny due process or equal protection of the laws because the differences within the statute "were based on some reasonable classification," relating to women's home-based role in society, and therefore were constitutional. He left the choice of whether to participate up to each individual woman based on her own constraints.

Despite the enlightened emancipation of women from the restrictions and protections of bygone years, and their entry into many parts of community life formerly considered to be reserved to men, woman is still regarded as the center of home and family life. We cannot say that it is constitutionally impermissible for a State, acting in pursuit of the general welfare, to conclude that a woman should be relieved from the civic duty of jury service unless she herself determines that such service is consistent with her own special responsibilities.

Harlan's opinion further explained that while the state could have limited this exemption only to women who actually have "family responsibilities," it was not "irrational" for it to apply the broader exemption, whether for public policy reasons or administrative convenience. In other words, women could be equal, but society did not require them to be. They were exempted from having to fulfill the same duties as men to allow them to carry out their "special" responsibilities as homemakers and mothers.

The Court carefully distinguished the issue of gender discrimination in jury selection from that of racial discrimination in jury selection, which it had struck down in previous cases. "This case in no way resembles those involving race or color," wrote Harlan, "in which the circumstances shown were found by this Court to compel a conclusion of purposeful discriminatory exclusions from jury service." This distinction apparently persuaded even several of the more liberally inclined justices

on the Court. A brief concurring opinion by Chief Justice Earl Warren and Justices Hugo L. Black and William O. Douglas concluded that "from the record" it cannot be said "that Florida is not making a good faith effort to have women perform jury duty without discrimination on the ground of sex." This result seemed to fly in the face of the Court's finding that a proportion of less than .01 percent of the 46,000 registered women voters who were eligible for jury service had made the jury list.

"A Fair Cross Section of the Community"

Taylor v. Louisiana, 419 U.S. 522 (1975)

Ballard v. United States, 329 U.S. 187 (1946)

Twelve years after *Hoyt* the Women's Rights Project of the American Civil Liberties Union, led by Ruth Bader Ginsburg, assisted in preparing an appeal to the Supreme Court from a state court decision upholding a Tennessee law that allowed women to opt out of jury service. The appellant was a young woman, Edna Stubblefield, who had been convicted of murdering a rival for her boyfriend's affections. Although the justices declined to hear *Stubblefield v. Tennessee*, the arguments presented on behalf of Stubblefield were restated in subsequent Women's Rights Project briefs. Women's easy exemption from jury service, Ginsburg wrote, is "ultimately harmful to them," because it reinforces the notion that they are not "persons with full civic responsibilities as well as rights" and that their "assistance in the administration of justice is not really needed by the community."

Ginsburg made the same point in briefing another 1973 case, *Healy v. Edwards*, which challenged a jury selection system in Louisiana that was similar to the one Florida used at the time of *Hoyt* but had since abandoned. Louisiana law provided that a woman could not be selected for jury

Gwendolyn Rogers Hoyt claimed that she had a special need for a jury that included women. It was unfair, she argued, for an all-male jury to pass judgment on a woman's "state of mind," especially when the state of Florida required proof of a "depraved mind regardless of human life" for a second degree murder charge. What was so special about her story that she believed female jurors might have judged it differently from male jurors?

By all accounts Gwendolyn and Clarence Hoyt had a turbulent and violent marriage. High school sweethearts, they married in 1942 when Gwendolyn Rogers was seventeen. After Clarence returned from an overseas assignment with the air force, his wife caught him with another woman in their apartment and divorced him. They remarried a few years later, but during the time they were divorced Gwendolyn was convicted of stabbing her ex-husband and his girlfriend. She was put on probation and ordered to pay a $500 fine. Gwendolyn blamed her unstable behavior on her epilepsy, which had first developed when she was twenty years old and her husband was posted overseas. According to the defense, the epilepsy had damaged her brain in a way that made it difficult for her to control her emotions.

She was also a victim of her husband's neglect and degradation. In 1956, after they had remarried

In 1957 mentally unstable Gwendolyn Hoyt (right) struck and killed her husband, Clarence Hoyt (left), with their son's broken baseball bat. She was charged with second degree murder and sentenced to thirty years hard labor. On appeal, her lawyers argued unsuccessfully that if women had been represented on the all-male jury that tried her case she would have been convicted of a lesser crime.

and a year before his murder, Clarence, an air force captain, was transferred from a base near their home in Tampa to Homestead Air Force Base south of Miami, away from his wife and eight-year-old son. Initially, he spent his weekends and leave driving nearly 250 miles to be with his family. Within a year, however, he began visiting less often, and showed signs of having an adulterous affair. Distraught, Gwendolyn twice drove to the Homestead base to beg her husband to move his family down to be with him. Although he promised to arrange to do so, Clarence continued his elusive conduct. On one of his rare visits home, according to Gwendolyn's later testimony, he "became extremely angry" and "beat her unmercifully."

When Clarence stopped returning his wife's calls, she lured him home by falsely leaving word that their son was dying. Once he was home, Gwendolyn made a desperate attempt to reconcile with her husband, including trying to seduce him. He spurned all her overtures, refusing any discussion. Enraged and humiliated, she struck him several times on the head with their son's broken baseball bat. He died the next day from his injuries. After her arrest, she was admitted to a psychiatric ward at Tampa General Hospital, where she stayed for almost two weeks.

Hoyt was convicted of second degree murder by a six-man jury that deliberated for just twenty-five minutes before finding her guilty. The male judge sentenced her to thirty years hard labor. (She was paroled after three and a half years of imprisonment because she posed no further threat to the community.)

In her appeal, Hoyt claimed that women jurors would have been more compassionate and understanding of her plight and more receptive to her claim of "temporary insanity." She firmly believed that a female jury would have convicted her of the lesser offense of manslaughter. Her lawyer cited articles written by sociologists demonstrating that women and men behave differently as jurors, because women are more empathetic to the social and emotional aspects of a case and tend to side with defendants. The lawyer representing Florida in the appeal countered with this argument: "Impartiality is a *state of mind.* Its existence or absence does not depend on whether the juror is male, female, black, white or what have you."

In his majority opinion Justice John Marshall Harlan dismissed the notion that a jury for this type of crime should necessarily include women.

These premises misconceive the scope of the right to an impartially selected jury assured by the Fourteenth Amendment. That right does not entitle one accused of crime to a jury tailored to the circumstances of the particular case, whether relating to the sex or other condition of the defendant, or to the nature of the charges to be tried. It requires only that the jury be indiscriminately drawn from among those eligible in the community for jury service, untrammeled by any arbitrary and systematic exclusions.

He concluded that the result of Hoyt's appeal "must therefore depend on whether such an exclusion of women from jury service has been shown," and found, of course, that it had not.

service unless she had filed a written declaration of her desire to serve. This process became known as the "opt-in" system.

Among the plaintiffs in *Healy* was a woman who had purchased a defective beauty product that caused her hair to break off at the roots. She claimed that women jurors would be more understanding of the embarrassment caused by her hair loss and would be more likely to award her higher damages. *Healy* was a class action suit that included three discrete groups: women litigants who said they were disadvantaged because Louisiana's system deprived them of a jury of their peers, potential women jurors who objected to the pre-registration requirement, and men who complained that they were called to jury service too often because women were not required to serve. The plaintiffs challenged the broad exemption on equal protection grounds of all women from jury service and sought an injunction against continued enforcement of the exemption.

Ginsburg persuaded a three-judge federal court to hold that *Hoyt* had been rendered obsolete by later decisions. "When today's vibrant principle is obviously in conflict with yesterday's sterile precedent," the court reasoned, "trial courts need not follow the outgrown dogma. Hence we consider that *Hoyt* is no longer binding." The absence of women from jury panels, the court concluded, "is significant not because all women react alike, but because they contribute a distinctive medley of views influenced by differences in biology, cultural impact and life experience, indispensable if the jury is to comprise a cross-section of the community."

Healy was argued before the Supreme Court together with a criminal case, *Taylor v. Louisiana,* which the Court used to override *Hoyt.* Ironically, Taylor involved a man convicted of a crime of violence against a woman. Armed with a butcher knife, Billy J. Taylor had abducted her and forced her to drive her car to a deserted area where he raped and robbed her. In the backseat of the car were her daughter and baby grandson.

Taylor was convicted of aggravated kidnapping. Grasping at every straw, he sought to have his indictment voided on the ground, among others, that women "were systematically excluded" from the jury selection process. Taylor contended that the absence of women from the pool of potential jurors deprived him of his federal constitutional right to "a fair trial by jury of a representative segment of the community." He pointed out that although 53 percent of the eligible population was female, no more than 10 percent of the people in the so-called "jury wheel," those with a possibility of being picked for service, were women. Indeed, in his case, *no* women were in the pool of 175 prospective jurors.

The Court noted that over time it had "unambiguously declared" that, to satisfy the Sixth Amendment jury trial guarantee, jury pools must reflect "a fair cross section of the community." In an earlier decision, *Ballard v. United States,* the Court had stated that a representative segment of the community would not exclude women.

In that 1946 precedent, the Court had reversed a federal court conviction challenged on the ground that women had been specifically excluded from the jury selection process. (It is important to distinguish *Hoyt* and *Taylor,* in which the Court was concerned with the right and power of *states* to regulate jury membership, from *Ballard,* in which the Court exercised its supervisory power over lower federal courts to hold that women's exclusion from jury service in *federal* cases was impermissible.) The 5–4 decision by the Court in *Ballard* reaffirmed the importance of having a jury pool truly representative of a democratic society. In doing so it addressed what it called the "indefinable" differences between men and women.

The thought is that the factors which tend to influence the action of women are the same as those which influence the action of men—personality, background, economic status—and not sex. Yet it is not enough to say that women when sitting as jurors neither act nor tend to act as a class. Men likewise do not act as a class. But, if the shoe were truly on the other foot, who would claim that a jury was truly representative of the community if all men were intentionally and systematically excluded from the panel? The truth is that the two sexes are not fungible [interchangeable]; a community made up exclusively of one is different from a community composed of both; the subtle interplay of influence one on the other is among the imponderables. To insulate the courtroom from either may not in a given case make an iota of difference. Yet a flavor, a distinct quality is lost if either sex is excluded. The exclusion of one may indeed make the jury less representative of the community than would be true if an economic or racial group were excluded.

This concern for the loss of "a flavor, a distinct quality" by excluding women would crop up later in the debate over picking individual jurors.

In *Taylor,* the Court extended its conclusion in *Ballard* to apply to state courts. Yet the justices continued to struggle with how equal representation on juries would affect a woman's ability to care for her home and family. For instance, it noted almost apologetically that "[t]here remains the argument that women as a class serve a distinctive role in society and that jury service would so substantially interfere with that function that the State has ample justification for excluding women from service unless they volunteer, even though the result is that almost all jurors are men." Accordingly, the Court reaffirmed the right of states to grant exemptions from jury service in cases of special hardship or incapacity, and to those "engaged in particular occupations the uninterrupted performance of which is critical to the community's welfare."

Under the Sixth Amendment's guarantee of a trial by "a fair cross section of the community," the Supreme Court held in 1946 that defendants in federal cases had the right to be judged by juries on which women were represented. The Court extended that ruling to cover state courts in the 1970s.

At the same time, however, the Court contrasted these kinds of special exemptions with a system that excludes all women. "It is untenable to suggest these days that it would be a special hardship for each and every woman to perform jury service or that society cannot spare any women from their present duties." To support this point, the Court offered evidence from the Department of Labor demonstrating that more than 50 percent of all women between the ages of eighteen and sixty-four were in the labor force, and nearly one third of mothers in family units with children under age three worked.

While these statistics perhaps speak more to the evolving nature of the structure of the family unit in American society than to the nature of the role played by women who happen to be members of a family unit, they certainly put to rest the suggestion that all women should be exempt from jury service based solely on their sex and the presumed role in the home.

In his dissent, Justice William H. Rehnquist challenged what he called the Court's "turnabout" since its decision in *Hoyt.* Such a change, he noted, encompassed "both our higher degree of sensitivity to distinctions based on sex, and the 'evolving nature of the structure of the family unit in American society.'" While acknowledging that "it may be fair to conclude that the Louisiana system is in fact an anachronism, and inappropriate for this 'time or place'" he suggested that it was improper for the Court to enforce "this Court's perception of modern life" against the states. He went on to challenge Justice Douglas's old notion that "a flavor" is lost if one sex is excluded. "This flavor," Rehnquist concluded, "is not of such importance that the Constitution is offended if any given is not so enriched. This smacks more of mysticism than law."

Duren v. Missouri, 439 U.S. 357 (1979)

The 8–1 decision in *Taylor* demonstrated that the Court was comfortable requiring a fair cross section, without systematic exclusion of women, in jury trials under the Sixth Amendment. But *Taylor* was more focused on the right of defendants to be tried by women jurors than on the right of women to serve at jury trials. The Court needed to be presented with a case that would allow it to examine whether women were being denied their equal protection rights by being excused from jury service. But the next jury selection case the Court heard, *Duren v. Missouri,* did not present such an opportunity, because, as in *Taylor,* the plaintiff was a man.

Jury selection in Jackson County, Missouri, commenced with an annual questionnaire mailed to people randomly selected from the voter registration list. The questionnaire included sections addressed to people in various categories, each offering a basis for exemption or disqualification from jury service. These categories included "any woman"; persons over age sixty-five; doctors; clergy; teachers; and persons who, if not at their regular place of employment, could adversely affect the public interest, health, safety, or welfare. Women could thus choose to "opt out" of jury duty. This was significantly different from the "opt-in" system of *Hoyt* and *Taylor.*

Attorneys for Billy Duren, led by litigator Ruth Bader Ginsburg, challenged the defendant's indictment and conviction for murder and robbery on the ground that while 54 percent of the adults in the county were women, and 26.7 percent of the individuals initially summoned for jury duty were women, less than 15 percent of Duren's potential jury pool was actually com-

prised of women. In fact, in Duren's case, the panel from which his jury was selected consisted of forty-eight men and five women. All twelve jurors ultimately chosen were men.

As in *Taylor,* Justice Byron R. White wrote the majority opinion. Here again he considered whether the plaintiff's case violated the Sixth Amendment's guarantee of a fair trial by an impartial jury. White discussed the three criteria required for someone to establish a violation of the "fair-cross section requirement," and concluded that Duren met each of them. First, the defendant had properly demonstrated that the group alleged to be excluded—women—was a "distinctive" group in the community. Second, he looked at the statistics relating to the number of women in the jury pool and concluded that their representation was "not fair and reasonable in relation to the number of such persons in the community." Third, the discrepancy in representation was regular, inherent even, in the particular jury-selection process that was used. It was, wrote White, a "disproportionate and consistent exclusion of women . . . quite obviously due to the system by which juries were selected."

But this was not the end of the inquiry. The case could be overcome if the state demonstrated a significant interest in having such a system. This was more demanding than the standard in *Hoyt,* where the state just had to prove its system was reasonable. In examining the state's justification for the statute, the Court found that the only interest advanced—"safeguarding the important role played by women in home and family life"—was not sufficient. While acknowledging that a state "may have an important interest in assuring that those members of the family responsible for the care of children are available to do so," and suggesting that an "appropriately tailored" exemption might survive such a challenge, the Court concluded that in this case no such justification existed.

Because *Duren* was so similar to *Taylor,* it was held applicable retroactively. That meant that the prosecutors, defense attorneys, and criminal court judges in Missouri had to redo the cases of all defendants who had challenged the opt-out system in the four years since *Taylor.*

Rehnquist again offered a solo dissent, reiterating his comments in *Taylor* and focusing on what he viewed as the fiction that these cases were not being decided on equal protection grounds.

Picking a Jury

J. E. B. v. Alabama ex rel. T. B., 511 U.S. 127 (1994)

As if confirming Rehnquist's observation on this latter point, in 1994 the Court finally recognized that the Equal Protection Clause fully protected the rights of women—and men—not to be discriminated against in jury selection. In *J. E. B. v. Alabama ex rel. T. B.,* the Court ruled that trial lawyers cannot exclude potential jurors because of their sex. This time, however, it was male jurors who had suffered the exclusion.

In 1988, Teresia Bible of Scottsboro, a small town in northern Alabama, had an affair with James Bowman, a married salesman from across the border in Tennessee. When she became pregnant he not only reneged on his promise to leave his wife and marry her but jilted her. After the child was born, Bible filed a paternity suit seeking child support. Bowman admitted to having had a sexual relationship with her but denied he was the father.

When jury selection began, there were thirty-six potential jurors in the pool: twelve men and twenty-four women. Three of the jurors were eliminated, leaving only ten men in the group of thirty-three potential jurors. The local prosecutor who was seeking child support for Bible used

nine of his ten peremptory challenges to remove all but one of the potential male jurors. (A peremptory challenge, or peremptory strike, is the practice of dismissing prospective jurors from the pool without the lawyers having to explain to the judge why they are unsuitable. This technique is often used to eliminate jurors the trial lawyers guess might be unfavorably disposed toward their client.) In response, the defense attorney used all but one of his strikes to remove potential female jurors, presumably because they would be more sympathetic to the mother.

Nonetheless, the final result was an entirely female jury. Bowman challenged this selection process, but the trial court ruled that it was not a violation of the Constitution. The trial proceeded and the jury eventually issued a decision against Bowman after a DNA test indicated a 99.92 percent probability that he was the father.

In reviewing the case on appeal from the Alabama court of appeals, the Supreme Court relied on *Batson v. Kentucky* (1986), a decision that prohibited peremptory strikes on the basis of race, and extended that prohibition to include gender. Justice Harry A. Blackmun, writing for a 6–3 majority, noted that the issue of whether women were unfairly stricken from jury pools was relatively new, given that for most of the nation's history women had either been forbidden or discouraged from participating in jury service at all.

Although the stated rationale for women's exclusion had been to allow them to stay home and take care of family responsibilities, there were also those who promoted this exclusion as a way to shelter women "from the ugliness and depravity of trials." "Women," Blackmun wrote, "were thought to be too fragile and virginal to withstand the polluted courtroom atmosphere." He cited a 1949 Arkansas case cautioning that "[c]riminal court trials often involve testimony of the foulest kind, and they sometimes require consideration of indecent conduct, the use of filthy and loathsome words, references to intimate sex relationships, and other elements that would prove humiliating, embarrassing and degrading to a lady."

Next Blackmun compared the Court's treatment of race and gender. He rejected the argument that discrimination against women had not been as severe as discrimination against African Americans, and was therefore less intolerable in the courtroom. "[W]ith respect to jury service," concluded Blackmun, "African-Americans and women share a history of total exclusion, a history which came to an end for women many years after the embarrassing chapter in our history came to an end for African-Americans." If lawyers can no longer exclude potential jurors on account of race, he reasoned, then they should not be allowed to do so on account of gender.

The only question remaining, Blackmun concluded, was whether permitting the exclusion of men or women jurors would "substantially" further the state's interest in achieving a fair and impartial trial. Blackmun quickly rejected the argument that the state's decision to strike all but one of the male jurors was based on the perception that they might be more sympathetic to the father in a paternity suit, while women jurors might be more sympathetic to the mother. "We shall not accept as a defense to gender-based peremptory challenges the very stereotype the law condemns," he insisted. Blackmun found that the state "offers virtually no support for the conclusion that gender alone is an accurate predictor of [jurors'] attitudes; yet it urges the Court to condone the same stereotypes that justified the wholesale exclusion of women from juries and the ballot box."

Blackmun reasoned that the litigants, jurors, and community are all harmed when jurors are "wrongly excluded from participation in the judicial process" because citizens lose confidence in the judicial system when they think the "deck has been stacked" in favor of one side. And "[s]triking individual jurors on the assumption that they hold particular views simply because of their gender," he continued, was damaging to the "dignity" of the jurors.

Justice Sandra Day O'Connor concurred in the majority opinion, but cautioned that men and women jurors may indeed judge some cases differently. "[O]ne need not be a sexist," she wrote, "to share the intuition that in certain cases a person's gender and resulting life experience will be relevant to his or her view of the case." She said the ruling should not be applied to criminal defendants or civil cases, but she acknowledged it probably would be.

In a dissent joined by Chief Justice Rehnquist and Justice Clarence Thomas, Justice Antonin Scalia denied that *J. E. B.* involved gender discrimination at all. Women were historically excluded from juries, Scalia recalled, "because of doubt that they were competent." Now women are "stricken from juries by peremptory challenges because of doubt that they are well disposed to the striking party's case." Thus, he concluded, "[t]here is discrimination and dishonor in the former, and not in the latter." Besides, he pointed out, it was men, not women, who were excluded from the jury panel in question.

Rehnquist added that peremptory challenges on the basis of gender were "generally not the sort of derogatory and invidious acts which peremptory challenges directed at black jurors may be." Echoing O'Connor, he wrote: "The two sexes differ, both biologically and, to a diminishing extent, in experience. It is not merely 'stereotyping' to say that these differences may produce a different outlook which is brought to the jury room."

3

SEX DISCRIMINATION

The Search for a Standard

INTERPRETING THE EQUAL PROTECTION CLAUSE

The Fourteenth Amendment to the Constitution, ratified in the wake of the Civil War, provides in part that "No state shall . . . deny to any person within its jurisdiction the equal protection of the laws." This simple phrase, known as the Equal Protection Clause, has spawned a complex body of judicial doctrine. But its original purpose was to ensure that the recently defeated Southern states did not infringe on the rights of the newly emancipated slaves.

Initially, it seemed as though the clause might be limited only to claims of racial discrimination. In its first interpretation of the Equal Protection Clause in *Slaughter-House Cases* (1873), the Supreme Court held that a group of Louisiana butchers could not rely on the clause to challenge a state monopoly. "We doubt very much whether any action of a State not directed by way of discrimination against [African Americans] as a class, or on account of their race, will ever be held to come within the purview of this provision," the Court said.

But in fact the Court soon began to expand the reach of the clause beyond its core requirement of equal treatment of the races, holding that it was essentially a directive that all persons "similarly situated" should be treated alike. The issue then became how to determine which groups were in fact similarly situated. A general "rationality" requirement was read into the provision: in order for legislation to pass muster, any distinction it drew between groups of people—any "classification," in legal parlance—had to be rationally related to the legislation's purpose. In other words, for the law to treat one group of people differently than another its defender simply had to show that there was a reason for the discrepancy that went beyond mere hostility to the targeted group.

A similar requirement was read into another provision of the Fourteenth Amendment, the Due Process Clause: "Nor shall any state deprive any person of life, liberty, or property, without due process of law." From the turn of the century through the 1930s, a conservative Supreme Court frequently used the Due Process Clause—and to a lesser extent the Equal Protection Clause—to strike down economic legislation and social reforms on the ground that they were "unreasonable." In the most groundbreaking of these cases, *Lochner v. New York* (1905), the Court ruled that a state law setting a daily ten-hour limit on the working hours of bakers was an unreasonable interference with the freedom of workers and employers to enter into contracts.

After 1937, a reaction against the so-called *Lochner* era set in. The Supreme Court began to apply the rationality requirements of both the Equal Protection and Due Process Clauses so leniently as to render them virtually meaningless. "State legislatures are presumed to have acted within their constitutional power despite the fact that, in practice, their laws result in some inequality," the Court said in 1961, in a fairly typical formulation. "A statutory discrimination will not be set aside if any state of facts reasonably may be conceived to justify it."

But while this permissive attitude prevailed in the context of social and economic legislation, the Equal Protection Clause had not been rendered completely powerless. In 1938, a footnote in an otherwise unremarkable case called *United States v. Carolene Products Co.* laid the groundwork for much of the Supreme Court's later elaboration of the Equal Protection Clause. Justice Harlan Fiske Stone, writing for the Court, observed that a more searching equal protection review might be appropriate when "legislation appears on its face to be within a specific prohibition of the Constitution, such as those of the first ten amendments." Similarly, the Court might want to take a harder look at "statutes directed at particular religious . . . or national . . . or racial minorities." The theory behind this approach was that the Court might need to step in when the ordinary political process was not adequate to ensure justice—either because the legislation interfered with rights that were central to that process, or because it discriminated against "discrete and insular minorities" who were likely to be victims of prejudice and lacked sufficient power to protect their rights in the political arena.

Under the liberal Warren Court of the 1960s, the split approach outlined in *Carolene Products*

solidified into a rigid "two-tier" system of evaluating equal protection claims. The Court reviewed ordinary, run-of-the mill challenges to social and economic legislation under its low-level "rationality" test. Those claims only had to pass the easy, reasonableness standard. But two kinds of claims warranted "strict scrutiny": claims that legislation infringed on a "fundamental right," such as the right to vote, the right to interstate travel, or the right to appeal in a criminal case; and claims that legislation had created a "suspect classification." A classification was "suspect" if it was based on a group's race, ethnicity, or religion—essentially the "discrete and insular minorities" of the *Carolene Products* footnote. Discrimination premised on these characteristics, the Court said, was so unlikely to be related to a legitimate state objective that it was in effect presumed to be the product of prejudice and hostility. In order to pass the strict scrutiny test, a legislative classification had to be "narrowly tailored" to achieve a "compelling state interest." This standard proved so difficult to meet that the strict scrutiny test was sometimes referred to as "strict in theory and fatal in fact."

After Warren E. Burger succeeded Earl Warren as chief justice in 1969, discontent with the two-tier standard surfaced both on and off the Court. Both Justices John Paul Stevens and Thurgood Marshall criticized the Court's equal protection jurisprudence, with Stevens declaring that there was "only one Equal Protection Clause," and Marshall advocating a "sliding scale" approach. "A principled reading of what this Court has done reveals that it has applied a spectrum of standards in reviewing discrimination allegedly violative of the Equal Protection Clause," Marshall wrote in a 1973 dissent. "This spectrum clearly comprehends variations in the degree of care with which the Court will scrutinize particular classifications, depending, I believe, on the constitutional and societal importance of the interest adversely affected and the recognized invidiousness of the basis upon which the particular classification is drawn."

While the Court failed to embrace either Stevens's or Marshall's views, it did begin to tinker with its two-tier approach so as to render it more flexible. In some cases, the Court applied the rationality test in a relatively rigorous fashion, occasionally using it to strike down legislation as unconstitutional. The justices also expanded the range of closely reviewed classifications beyond race and ethnicity to include illegitimacy and gender. For these last two categories, the Court devised an intermediate equal protection test, falling between rationality and strict scrutiny: legislation that discriminated against women or those of illegitimate birth had to be "substantially related" to achieving "an important governmental objective."

This intermediate standard has been developed primarily in cases of discrimination against women. But women do not fit neatly into the *Carolene Products* mold of "discrete and insular minorities": they are not discrete or insular, nor are they a minority. In order to justify giving them the benefit of heightened scrutiny, the Court has had to rely on another strand of the equal protection doctrine: the idea that people should not be subjected to discrimination on the basis of characteristics that are "immutable"—distinctions, like gender or race, over which they have no control—and that bear no relation to ability. Women, like racial minorities, have historically been subject to severe restrictions on such activities as voting, attending college, and working as lawyers—restrictions that were based on stereotype rather than on the actual capabilities of individual members of the group.

The four cases that follow are landmarks in the development of the Court's gender discrimination doctrine. As the Court grappled with the appropriate method of evaluating this category of equal protection claim, the justices first tried applying the rationality test in an unusually rigorous way (*Reed v. Reed*); then came to the brink of adopting gender as a full-fledged suspect classification (*Frontiero v. Richardson*); and finally settled on an intermediate standard that appeared to represent a workable compromise (*Craig v. Boren*). In the eyes of some Court watchers, the final case, *United States v. Virginia* (1996), appeared to raise the standard to the highest level. In any event, the decision has left some questions about the Court's future course in this area.

FOUR TURNING POINTS

Breaking New Ground

Reed v. Reed, 404 U.S. 71 (1971)

When the Supreme Court handed down its opinion in *Reed v. Reed* in November of 1971, the decision made headlines across the country. For the first time since the Fourteenth Amendment had gone into effect in 1868, the Court had struck down a state law on the ground that it discriminated against women in violation of the Equal Protection Clause.

The law in question—enacted in Idaho in 1864—required that when the father and mother of a deceased person both sought appointment as administrator of the estate, the man had to be preferred over the woman. When Richard Lynn Reed died intestate (without a will) at the age of sixteen, each of his divorced parents—Sally and Cecil—filed a petition seeking to be appointed administrator of their son's estate. The probate court, relying on the language in the 1864 statute, chose the father.

In a terse and unanimous opinion, the Idaho Supreme Court rejected Sally Reed's contention that the statute's preference for men over women was "arbitrary and capricious." The court ruled

When Sally Reed learned that an Idaho statute automatically favored her ex-husband as administrator of her deceased son's estate, she was, she recalls, "a little bit surprised. I felt a little bit angry that women would be stepped on like that." Her anger—which was strong enough to propel her case all the way to the Supreme Court—was a mixture of the political and the personal. A middle-aged housewife, she had never considered herself a feminist, but she had been brought up to believe that "a woman had just as much right as a man."

But it is clear that her stormy relationship with her ex-husband, and her closeness to her son, were mostly responsible for spurring her to action. As Sally Reed tells it, Cecil Reed—a machinist who died in 1996—was a difficult husband and father. Sally, who had suffered two miscarriages, had adopted the child over her husband's objections. And when Richard—nicknamed "Skip"—was three or four years old, Cecil deserted the family, leaving his wife to support herself and their son by caring for disabled veterans in her home.

Skip was "a lovely person," Reed recalls, and—like herself—musically inclined. He learned to play a variety of instruments, eventually composing his own music and forming a band that performed at high school dances. Skip hoped to go to college, and from the age of seven had saved money he earned by mowing lawns and doing other odd jobs for neighbors.

By the time Skip was sixteen his father had remarried and had two grown stepsons. Sally Reed recalls that Skip was reluctant to go to his father's house for weekend visits, especially for his last visit, which—at his father's request—was to be for an entire week. After two or three days Skip called his mother, asking to come home. But she persuaded him to stay, reminding him that his father had visiting rights.

Then, on Wednesday night, the police called. Skip had been found dead in the basement of his father's house, apparently having shot himself with a hunting rifle that was part of his father's gun collection.

Like most sixteen-year-olds, Skip did not leave much behind—just a few personal effects and the

After sixteen attorneys turned her down, grieving mother Sally Reed (right) finally persuaded Allen Derr (left) to appeal her case challenging a law that automatically appointed her ex-husband administrator of their deceased son's estate. In its first ruling striking down a law as sex discrimination under the Equal Protection Clause, the Supreme Court found in favor of Reed in 1971.

money he had been saving for college, the combined value of which was less than a thousand dollars. But when she heard that her ex-husband had applied to be appointed administrator of the estate, Reed resolved to challenge him in court.

After her initial defeat, Reed asked her lawyer to appeal the ruling. He turned her down, as did the sixteen other attorneys she consulted. They all told her she did not have a chance.

But at last she reached Allen Derr, a Boise attorney with a general practice. He was quiet for a long time after she explained her case. "He didn't laugh, but he did hesitate," she remembers. "Probably wondering if I was off my rocker." Derr explained that the case would probably have to go all the way up to the Supreme Court, and that it was unlikely that Reed would win. Nor, given the amount of money involved, was the case economically viable. "But I told her that the principle was viable," Derr says now, "and she felt very strongly."

Derr did take the case to the Supreme Court, with no more compensation than the small amount Reed could afford to pay. Although the ACLU took primary responsibility for writing the brief, Derr remained counsel of record and traveled to Washington, D.C., at his own expense to argue the case. And four years after her son died, Reed got the ruling for which she had been fighting: the Supreme Court declared the Idaho statute unconstitutional. But instead of going back to probate court for a hearing on the merits, she opted to enter into an agreement with her ex-husband to serve as coadministrators of Skip's estate.

"I didn't want Skip's things or his money," she says. "I just felt that a woman should have the privilege of asking."

that the legislature might have reasonably concluded that, in general, "men are better qualified to act as [administrators] than are women." In addition, the mandatory preference for men served the legitimate purpose of "curtailing litigation over the appointment of administrators."

The U.S. Supreme Court's opinion was also brief and unanimous, but it came to the opposite conclusion. Chief Justice Warren E. Burger, writing for the Court, formulated the question as "whether a difference in the sex of competing applicants for letters of administration bears a rational relationship" to the state's objective of reducing expensive probate litigation. Burger noted that Idaho did not deny letters of administration to women altogether; in fact, a woman whose spouse died intestate was given preference over any male relatives of the decedent. In a passing glance at society as a whole, Burger observed that—probably as a result of women's greater longevity—many estates were administered by surviving widows.

Without much further discussion, the Court held that the Idaho statute violated the Equal Protection Clause. "To give a mandatory preference to members of either sex over the other, merely to accomplish the elimination of hearings on the merits," Burger wrote, "is to make the very kind of arbitrary legislative choice forbidden by the Equal Protection Clause of the Fourteenth Amendment."

Although *Reed* has been hailed as a landmark decision, it is almost as remarkable for what it did *not* do as for what it did do. Sally Reed's attorneys in the Supreme Court (including Ruth Bader Ginsburg, then a volunteer attorney for the American Civil Liberties Union [ACLU]) had focused on the need to subject gender classifications such as the one at issue to strict scrutiny under the Equal Protection Clause: their brief devoted forty-six pages to the strict scrutiny standard, as compared to only seven pages arguing the fallback position that the statute should be invalidated under a rational basis test. But the Court's opinion simply applied the rationality standard without mentioning the possibility of adopting anything more stringent.

The advantage of this silence, for women's rights advocates, was that the Court did not explicitly reject the idea of designating gender a "suspect classification," thus leaving the issue open for another day. And given the Court's prior tolerance of similar discriminatory statutes, *Reed* clearly signaled a shift in attitude: state legislatures no longer would be able to assume that women could be excluded simply on the ground of administrative convenience. The Court, it seemed, was catching up to the rest of society, where—as the ACLU's brief pointed out—women were entering the workforce in unprecedented numbers, and statutes such as Idaho's were beginning to look like quaint artifacts of an outdated era. (In fact, by the time *Reed* reached the Supreme Court, the discriminatory Idaho provision was about to be effectively repealed.)

But the Court's use of the reasonableness test created uncertainty about what might come next, and was seen by some as hypocritical. After all, one feminist commentator pointed out, was it really so unreasonable—in 1971—for the Idaho legislature to conclude that men, in general, had more business expertise than women? Clearly the Court was not applying the reasonableness test in the traditional deferential manner—the way it had applied it, for example, in *Williamson v. Lee Optical*, a much-quoted 1955 case. There the Court had stated that, to satisfy the demands of the Equal Protection Clause, "the law need not be in every respect logically consistent with its aims to be constitutional. It is enough that there is an evil at hand for correction, and that it might be thought that the particular legislative measure was a rational way to correct it."

Had the Supreme Court adopted strict scrutiny in *Reed,* it would have sent an unmistakable signal to the lower courts that any legislation that discriminated on the basis of gender—even legislation intended to protect women—was invalid. But because the reasonableness test was so malleable, challenges to discriminatory legislation would now have to be resolved on a case-by-case basis.

Believing that more fundamental change was necessary, some women's rights advocates pinned their hopes on the Equal Rights Amendment, then pending in Congress. While the *Reed* decision was heartening, it seemed that only through a constitutional amendment could gender equality be firmly secured.

A Double Standard for Benefits

Frontiero v. Richardson, 411 U.S. 677 (1973)

The uncertainty engendered by the Court's opinion in *Reed v. Reed* surfaced the very next term in a case called *Frontiero v. Richardson.*

Sharron Frontiero, an air force lieutenant, sought an increased housing allowance after she married, as well as dental and medical benefits for her husband, Joseph, a full-time college student. Under federal law, a married man in the armed forces was automatically entitled to such perquisites, whether his wife earned a lot or a little, but a married woman was unable to obtain them unless she could prove that her husband was dependent on her for more than one-half his support. Although Sharron earned more than Joseph's monthly veteran's stipend, he did not receive more than half his support from her. Sharron was therefore denied the additional benefits.

The Frontieros sued in federal court, arguing that the difference in treatment of men and women violated the Constitution: the same benefits available to married men in the "uniformed services" should extend to married women, without a showing of actual dependency. (Because the Fourteenth Amendment's Equal Protection Clause applies only to action taken by a state—not by the federal government—the Frontieros had to invoke the Due Process Clause of the Fifth Amendment, which does apply to federal action. However, the Court has interpreted the Due Process Clause to require equal protection from the federal government as well.) Normally, a federal case goes through three levels of review: the district court, the court of appeals, and the Supreme Court. But because this case presented a constitutional challenge to a federal statute, it came before a three-judge district court whose decision could be appealed directly to the Supreme Court.

To begin with, the district court was not convinced that the difference in treatment here amounted to sex discrimination at all. While it was true that men were given an advantage over women in obtaining benefits for spouses, under the statutory scheme as a whole both women and men were entitled to an automatic presumption of dependency for their unmarried, minor children. And both sexes were required to prove dependency when seeking benefits for adult children and parents.

But, the district court held, even assuming that sex discrimination had occurred, it did not rise to the level of a constitutional violation. The government certainly had a rational basis for its action: the numbers of married men in the armed forces were so vast—more than a million—that requiring proof of dependency from each of them would impose a "substantial administrative burden." While it was true that men whose wives were not in fact dependent on them received, in the court's words, a "windfall," the mere fact that Sharron Frontiero had been denied this "windfall" did not "so unreasonably burden [her] that the administrative classification should be ruled unconstitutional." Under the rational basis test, the fact that a classification resulted in some in-

equality did not render it invalid. The court never discussed the fact that in essence Sharron was being paid less for her work than a man whose spouse had the same income as Joseph.

Judge Frank Johnson of the district court dissented on the grounds that *Reed v. Reed* had clearly rejected "administrative convenience" as a justification for unequal treatment of men and women.

In the Supreme Court, the appropriate standard of review—rational basis or strict scrutiny—became an issue for the first time. In the district court, the Frontieros' lawyers, Joseph Levin and Morris Dees, had not raised the question of strict scrutiny, believing that it was inappropriate in sex discrimination cases. "Our view was that it should be reserved for race," Levin says now. In a footnote, the district court had addressed the matter on its own initiative and concluded that *Reed* had rejected the use of strict scrutiny in sex discrimination cases.

But once the appeal was taken to the Supreme Court, the ACLU stepped in, and strict scrutiny for sex discrimination cases was very much at the top of its agenda. The Supreme Court briefs for the Frontieros (filed by both Levin and Dees and the ACLU) argued that the statutes should be struck down under either standard. But—as with the ACLU's brief in *Reed*—the bulk of the argument was directed to the need for strict scrutiny. *Reed* had caused widespread confusion in the lower courts, the ACLU argued. Some courts had regarded it "as a major precedent marking a new direction in judicial review of sex-based classifications." Others, like the district court in this case, had seen it as either breaking no new ground or else implicitly rejecting a strict standard of review.

The justices initially agreed in conference to hold the statutes unconstitutional without reaching the question of strict scrutiny. Justice William H. Rehnquist was the lone dissenter. But Justice William J. Brennan Jr., who had been assigned to

Sharron Frontiero remembers her initial reaction when she received her first air force paycheck after she had gotten married in December 1969. She opened it up, saw that it was the same amount as it had been before her marriage, and walked back to the clerk who had just handed it to her.

"Hey, wait a minute," said the twenty-three-year-old lieutenant, "you made a mistake."

As a physical therapist at Maxwell Air Force Base Hospital in Montgomery, Alabama, Frontiero knew that her colleagues—all men—had received increased housing allowances when they had gotten married. So when she and her husband, Joseph, returned to Montgomery after their wedding in their hometown of Gloucester, Massachusetts, she had expected the same treatment. When she did not get it, she honestly thought that the personnel office had made a mistake.

It was only after consulting the base legal office and filing a formal complaint that she began to realize what she was up against: a system of statutes and regulations that automatically granted dependency benefits to male members of the armed forces who got married, but denied them to females unless they could prove that they were actually supporting their husbands.

Joseph Frontiero, then twenty-four, was a full-time student at Huntingdon College in Montgomery, having followed Sharron there while she served out her four-year commitment in the air force. The regulations required that Joseph had to rely on his wife for more than one half his support in order to be considered her "dependent." Joseph's living expenses, including his share of household costs, totaled approximately $354 a month. A navy veteran, Joseph received educational benefits of $205 a month under the G.I. Bill, and he earned another $30 a month working part time as a night watchman in a vinegar factory. It was clear, then, that Joseph was not sufficiently dependent on Sharron. She furnished only $119 per month of his expenses, not the $178 or more that would have comprised more than half his support.

Since Maxwell Air Force Base had no on-base housing for married officers, the Frontieros had no choice but to live off base. And, although they could manage without the increased housing allowance, the additional money would have come in handy. More important, though, was the principle at stake.

"They had different rules for men and women," says Joseph now. "It was just wrong."

"Our idea," says Sharron, "was that men don't depend on women and women don't depend on men. Men and women depend on each other."

For about a year, Lieutenant Frontiero used internal air force channels to press her complaint, but without success. Then a local attorney named Joe Levin came to one of Joseph Frontiero's college classes to speak about civil rights. After the talk, Frontiero approached Levin and told him he had a case in which Levin might be interested.

Levin, a civil liberties lawyer—who, along with his partner Morris Dees, was soon to establish the Southern Poverty Law Center—immediately grasped the potential impact of the case. He felt sure they had a winner. The Frontieros expressed some concern about negative repercussions if they filed suit. "We were afraid she might get transferred to Alaska," Joseph recalls, but Levin assured them that the air force would be too concerned about appearances to retaliate.

Sharron Frontiero (left) was working as a physical therapist at Maxwell Air Force Base in Montgomery, Alabama, when she charged the air force with sex discrimination. Although married servicemen received on-base housing, Lieut. Frontiero was required to live off base at her own expense, and her husband, Joseph (right), a college student, was not entitled to medical facilities routinely available to wives of servicemen.

When the Frontieros lost in the district court, Levin was not discouraged; they had gotten a good dissent, and he felt sure they would prevail in the Supreme Court. But Sharron was stunned.

"I thought the three-judge court would just say, oh yeah, this is an oversight," she says. When the decision came down, "it was like the sun had come up on the wrong side of the world and I just couldn't fathom it. I was very naive."

Once the case reached the Supreme Court and the ACLU got involved, the Frontieros found that their role was essentially over. "Once the case got going no one had to talk to me," Sharron says. "It was like being the patient after whom the disease is named, or maybe the operation. I got wheeled in completely anesthetized."

But there was one group of people who very much wanted to talk to the Frontieros: the press. Sharron recalls that most of her knowledge about what was happening in the case came from reporters who called to ask for her comments. Repeating the story grew tedious.

Even as the federal courts pondered the legal implications of the Frontieros' marriage, their union was breaking up. Within a year of the Supreme Court's 1973 decision, the two were divorced. "We were a very young couple with the kinds of problems young couples have," says Sharron. "Only in terms of the legal decision were we a good match."

Both have since remarried. Joseph and his second wife now own a jewelry business in Charleston, South Carolina, and Sharron Frontiero Cohen still lives in Gloucester with her husband and has a son in college. These days she drives a bookmobile—a job that she says "combines being a truckdriver with being a librarian"—but she has also been a community activist and a writer. She has pushed for increased funding for local schools, and her writing has included a local newspaper column on children, and a set of mysteries—*The Mysteries of Research*—designed to teach research skills to kids.

Before *Frontiero v. Richardson*, she says, she had not considered herself a feminist. Partly as a result of the lawsuit, she came to see herself as one—although she is careful about the definition of the word, pointing out that her husband supported her for a number of years while she stayed home with their son. "There were expectations people had of women," she says, "and then I found out that there were expectations people had of feminists—and they were just as unreal. . . . I don't feel you have to be a CEO to be a feminist."

The lawsuit also provided her with the heady experience of winning a major Supreme Court victory while still in her twenties. "I started off in life thinking you can beat City Hall," she says. "It's taken me a long time to find out you can't always do it."

write the majority opinion, was sympathetic to the ACLU's position: in a case decided earlier that term, he had dropped a footnote stating that *Reed* had simply left open the question of the appropriate standard of review in sex discrimination cases. Brennan did circulate a draft opinion that accorded with the cautious decision reached in conference. But he attached a note indicating that he felt *Frontiero* would "provide an appropriate vehicle for us to recognize sex as a suspect criterion," and wondered whether a majority of the Court would agree.

Three other justices—William O. Douglas, Byron R. White, and Thurgood Marshall—responded favorably. That meant that Brennan was only one vote short of a majority for a more radical approach. But neither of the other two justices most likely to join the opinion—Lewis F. Powell Jr. and Potter Stewart—was willing to sign on.

In the end, rather than retreating to his original draft, Brennan decided to go ahead with a plurality opinion (one not signed by a majority of the Court, and therefore lacking the force of law) ruling that sex should be a suspect classification. *Reed v. Reed,* Brennan said flatly, had constituted a departure from the usual rational-basis analysis, and moreover, one that was clearly justified. Drawing heavily from the fact-laden brief filed by the ACLU, Brennan reviewed the United States' "long and unfortunate history of sex discrimination"—discrimination that was "rationalized by an attitude of 'romantic paternalism' which, in practical effect, put women, not on a pedestal, but in a cage."

The position of women and African Americans was similar in key respects: both had been barred from holding office, serving on juries, or suing in their own names—and African American men had won the right to vote and sit on juries when these rights were still denied to women of all races. Sex, like race, was a characteristic people were born with and were powerless to

alter. And, unlike intelligence or physical disability, it was one that usually bore no relationship to ability. Any legislation that used such a characteristic to group people for unequal treatment merited strict scrutiny.

Once Brennan applied that scrutiny, it took only a few paragraphs to demonstrate that the statutes were unconstitutional. The government's defense was essentially "administrative convenience"—probably not a sufficient argument under a rational basis test after *Reed,* and certainly not under strict scrutiny.

Stewart merely concurred in the judgment (that is, in the holding that the statutes were unconstitutional but not in Brennan's reasons for reaching that conclusion) and cited *Reed.* Powell also concurred in the judgment, but he filed a short separate opinion that was joined by Chief Justice Burger and Justice Harry A. Blackmun. It was unnecessary, Powell wrote, for the Court to add sex to the very restricted list of suspect classifications when the same result could have been reached under *Reed.* Besides, the Equal Rights Amendment (ERA) had been approved by Congress and been submitted for ratification by the states. "It seems to me," Powell wrote, "that this reaching out to pre-empt by judicial action a major political decision which is currently in process of resolution does not reflect appropriate respect for duly prescribed legislative processes." Indeed, at the time of the decision, thirty states of the required thirty-eight had ratified the ERA.

Rehnquist, still in dissent, simply stated that he agreed with the reasoning of the district court.

One commentator, writing in the *American Bar Association Journal,* wrote that Brennan's opinion would "endear him to Mses [Gloria] Steinem, [Betty] Friedan, [Bella] Abzug, et aliae, because of its wholehearted espousal of the cause of women's lib." The opinion did indeed establish Brennan as a hero to many women's rights advocates, and it fired up their hopes for a definitive judicial pronouncement that sex discrimination warranted strict scrutiny. All that was needed, it seemed, was one more vote.

Justice for Beer Drinkers

Craig v. Boren, 429 U.S. 190 (1976)

Although hopes had been raised in *Frontiero*, the Supreme Court's next pronouncement regarding gender discrimination proved that it was not yet ready to embrace strict scrutiny. Instead, the Court settled on a third standard that was something of a compromise between ordinary scrutiny (the rational basis standard) and strict scrutiny. The case it chose as its vehicle was surprising. It involved nothing more substantial than the right to buy beer, and supposedly nonintoxicating beer at that. Furthermore, the victims of the discrimination were not women, but men.

The case involved two sections of an Oklahoma statute regulating the sale of beer with an alcohol content of 3.2 percent, about half the level found in ordinary beer. Women were allowed to purchase such beer at age eighteen, but men were barred from doing so until they turned twenty-one. (Neither men nor women could purchase harder liquor until they were twenty-one.) The age differential in the beer statute was a remnant of a general distinction in ages of majority for men and women that dated back to territorial days, before Oklahoma became a state. In 1972 the Oklahoma legislature, taking heed of *Reed v. Reed* and other equal protection decisions, had equalized the age of majority for most purposes, setting it at eighteen for both sexes. However, pressure from anti-liquor forces prevented the legislature from extending the equalization to the purchase of 3.2 percent beer.

Shortly after the legislature's action, a twenty-year-old freshman at Oklahoma State University named Mark Walker decided to challenge the beer statute in federal court as a denial of equal protection. Because the law imposed penalties on the person who sold the beer rather than on the

The owner of the Honk-N-Holler convenience store in Stillwater, Oklahoma, teamed up with a college student to challenge a state law setting the age for purchasing 3.2 "nonintoxicating" beer at eighteen for women and twenty-one for men. The Supreme Court ruled in 1976 that the law was discriminatory, introducing a tougher standard for reviewing laws that treat men and women differently.

young man who purchased it, Walker's attorney, Fred Gilbert, advised him to add a beer vendor as a coplaintiff. Otherwise, Gilbert feared, the court might throw out the case on the ground that Walker did not have standing—that is, he was not the one who was actually injured by the statute. Walker found a licensed beer vendor, Carolyn Whitener, who shared his views on the unfairness of the state law, and added her as a plaintiff. While the case was still bogged down in pretrial hearings, Walker's twenty-first birthday came and went, making the case moot as to him. In order to circumvent that problem, an eighteen-year-old male, Curtis Craig, joined the case as a third coplaintiff.

The initial complaint in the case, filed in December 1972, was dismissed by a district court judge the following February on the ground that the state law was "a valid exercise of the State's power pursuant to the Twenty-First Amendment of the United States Constitution," which authorizes the states to regulate commerce in liquor. Gilbert successfully appealed that decision to the circuit court and brought the case before a three-judge district court.

The case finally proceeded to trial in 1974. Gilbert, whose legal writing style favored many exclamation points and italicizations, took a somewhat muddled position on the appropriate standard of review in the district court. He alleged in his complaint that the discrimination was "arbitrary, irrational, and capricious," implying that he was invoking the rational basis test. But he also argued that the legislative distinction was based "solely upon the . . . constitutionally impermissible and inherently suspect classification of . . . biological sex and reproductive anatomy."

Instead of explaining the legislature's original intent in retaining the age-sex differential in the beer law, the state offered a traffic safety justification. Relying heavily on statistical evidence, the state argued that more males than females between the ages of eighteen and twenty-one were arrested for drunk driving and were injured or killed in traffic accidents.

The three-judge panel ruled unanimously in favor of the state. At the outset, the court noted that it faced "the recurring problem of the proper standard of review." After surveying the Supreme Court's recent pronouncements in the area, the court settled on *Reed v. Reed* as the applicable precedent—which the court interpreted as a rational basis test, but with the burden of proof placed on the defendant. While the state's evidence certainly was not airtight (not least because much of the data related to a period after the statute was passed), it was sufficient to prove the state's rationality. "We conclude," the court wrote, "that the classification made has a fair and substantial relation to apparent objectives of the legislation."

At this point Ruth Bader Ginsburg, who as counsel to the Women's Rights Project at the ACLU had already been in correspondence with Gilbert, stepped in to offer assistance. "Delighted to see the Supreme Court is interested in beer drinkers," she wrote to Gilbert after the Supreme Court agreed in January 1976 to hear the case. Gilbert gladly accepted the ACLU's offer to file an amicus curiae brief (filed by someone not a party to a case but interested in the legal doctrine at issue).

As in *Frontiero*, the question of standard of review moved to the forefront once the case reached the Supreme Court. In his jurisdictional statement—a preliminary filing arguing that the case was substantial enough to warrant Supreme Court review—Gilbert used as one of his subheadings, "The Unsettled Question of the Relevant Test." In his brief on the merits, he argued that the statute should fall even under a rational basis standard. But Gilbert also put forward a novel argument for heightened (or increased) scrutiny: if the only reason sex had not been treated with stricter scrutiny was because of "organic differences" between the sexes, then why not apply strict scrutiny in cases like this one, where the discrimination had nothing to do with those biological differences?

Ginsburg's brief for the ACLU was virtually silent on the appropriate standard of review. Instead, it focused on the argument that the Oklahoma statute reflected outdated stereotypes about the differences between men and women. But the brief did seize upon one phrase in the Supreme Court's decision the year before in *Stanton v. Stanton*, which had struck down an Idaho age-of-majority statute on the ground that it discriminated on the basis of sex. It was a phrase that had also been mentioned by the district court and by Gilbert in his jurisdictional statement: the statute must fall, Justice Blackmun had written for the Court in *Stanton*, "under any test—compelling state interest, or rational basis, or something in between." The idea of "something in between" had also been bandied about by a number of legal commentators, who argued that the Court was in effect using an intermediate standard in gender discrimination cases.

At oral argument in the Supreme Court, however, it seemed that the Court might never reach the question of discrimination because of the threshold issue of standing. Like Mark Walker before him, Curtis Craig had now turned twenty-one—a mere ten days before the October 5, 1976, oral argument—and could no longer claim to be a victim of the statute's discrimination. Anticipating this development, Gilbert had asked the Court for permission to add yet another, younger male plaintiff. The Court had denied this request, leaving the beer vendor, Carolyn Whitener, as the only plaintiff who arguably had standing.

Although Whitener had originally been recruited as a plaintiff because of doubts about Mark Walker's standing to challenge a law that penalized vendors, the Court now expressed doubts about her standing. Several justices seemed skeptical of Whitener's ability to assert the equal protec-

tion claims of eighteen-to-twenty-year-old males. Another issue that troubled the justices was the relationship between the Fourteenth Amendment's Equal Protection Clause and the Twenty-first Amendment's guarantee of state regulation of liquor: could the Twenty-first Amendment override the equal protection guarantees of the Fourteenth?

In his opinion for the Court, William J. Brennan Jr. swept aside both sets of doubts. Vendors like Whitener had been "uniformly permitted to resist efforts at restricting their operations by acting as advocates of the rights of third parties who seek access to their market or function," he said. As for the Twenty-first Amendment, it was primarily aimed at interstate commerce in alcohol, not at individual rights: "[T]he Court has never recognized sufficient 'strength' in the Amendment to defeat an otherwise established claim of invidious discrimination in violation of the Equal Protection Clause."

Brennan boldly formulated the applicable standard of review as follows: "To withstand constitutional challenge, previous cases establish that classifications by gender must serve important governmental objectives and must be substantially related to achievement of those objectives." The classification at issue in *Craig*, he concluded, did not pass this test. The previous cases Brennan cited included both *Reed v. Reed* and *Frontiero v. Richardson*, and he noted that the district court in this case had recognized that *Reed* was controlling. This standard, Brennan seemed to be saying, was nothing new.

In fact—as various concurring and dissenting opinions stated explicitly—the *Craig* standard was something quite new. At first glance, it seemed that its most innovative element was the requirement that a governmental objective be "important"—apparently a compromise between the strict scrutiny standard of "compelling" and the rational basis one of "legitimate"—and beyond mere "administrative convenience." But since a state could frequently come up with an "important" objective (as Oklahoma had in this instance with its rationale of traffic safety), the significance of that aspect of Brennan's formulation was unclear.

More crucial, it seemed, was the Court's demand that the means employed by the state be "substantially related" to the achievement of the objective. But this part of the standard was, on its face, supported by rational-basis precedent. The word "substantial" had first appeared in a much-cited 1920 Supreme Court case called *Royster Guano v. Virginia,* which held that a classification "must be reasonable, not arbitrary, and must rest upon some ground of difference having a fair and substantial relation to the object of the legislation." The Court in *Reed* had in fact quoted this "fair and substantial" language in support of its decision. But most courts that cited *Royster Guano*—including the district court in *Craig*—did so in the course of denying, rather than allowing, an equal protection claim.

It was only when the *Craig* standard was placed in context that its novelty was truly apparent. As numerous commentators and lower courts observed, the Court had clearly been treating gender differently from other "non-suspect" classifications such as citizenship or income, which Brennan's linkage of his standard to "classifications by gender" seemed to acknowledge. Also significant was Brennan's use of the words "important" and "substantially related," rather than "legitimate" and "rationally related," without any tempering by a phrase such as "not arbitrary." And when it came to applying the standard, the Court's analysis was clearly more searching than traditional rational basis review.

Accepting for purposes of discussion that the state's objective was the clearly important one of traffic safety, the Court went on to subject the state's statistical evidence to rigorous examination.

Even the most persuasive of the statistical surveys showed only that .18 percent of females and 2 percent of males in the eighteen-to-twenty age group had been arrested for alcohol-related driving offenses. "Certainly," Brennan wrote, "if maleness is to serve as a proxy for drinking and driving, a correlation of 2% must be considered an unduly tenuous 'fit.'" It was unfair to punish the 98 percent of the young men who did not get arrested for the sins of the 2 percent who did. (And the Court did not comment on the unfairness of allowing beer to be purchased by the .18 percent of young women who get arrested, the same logic applies.) In any event, the state's traffic safety justification was seriously undercut by the fact that the statute barred young men from purchasing 3.2 percent beer but not from consuming it. In sum, "the relationship between gender and traffic safety becomes far too tenuous to satisfy *Reed*'s requirement that the gender-based difference be substantially related to achievement of the statutory objective."

Brennan's opinion was joined by four other justices, but the case nevertheless spawned a multiplicity of opinions: in addition to the majority opinion, there were several concurrences and two dissents. Most of these opinions at least implied that the Court had crafted a new, intermediate equal protection standard for gender discrimination cases. Some stated it explicitly.

Justice Lewis F. Powell Jr.'s concurring opinion endorsed *Reed* as the relevant precedent but criticized what he characterized as the majority's broad reading of that opinion. "As has been true of *Reed* and its progeny," he wrote, "our decision today will be viewed by some as a 'middle-tier' approach. While I would not endorse that characterization and would not welcome a further subdividing of equal protection analysis, candor compels the recognition that the relatively deferential 'rational basis' standard of review normally applied takes on a sharper focus when we address a gender-based classification."

The winning team behind *Craig v. Boren* posed for a photo on the occasion of that landmark decision's twentieth anniversary in 1996: Fred Gilbert, the Tulsa criminal defense attorney who argued the case against the state of Oklahoma before the Supreme Court; coplaintiff Carolyn Whitener, then a convenience store proprietor and now the owner of a computer equipment business; Ruth Bader Ginsburg, then a litigator for the Women's Rights Project of the American Civil Liberties Union and now a Supreme Court justice; and plaintiff Curtis Craig, then a college student and now general counsel of the Explorer Pipeline Company.

Justice John Paul Stevens also took issue with the Court's implication that a third equal protection standard now existed, but he went beyond that to declare that even a double standard was objectionable. "There is only one Equal Protection Clause," he wrote. Although the classification in this case was not totally irrational, it was hard for him to believe that traffic safety was the state's true objective. And since the state's evidence showed that only about 2 percent of young men had violated its alcoholic beverage laws, imposing sanctions on the remaining 98 percent was impossible to justify. Most likely, Stevens concluded, the statute was simply the product of stereotypical assumptions about the relative maturity of young men and women.

Justices Harry A. Blackmun and Potter Stew-

art's concurrences were brief. Blackmun's consisted of one sentence disagreeing with the Court's discussion of the Twenty-first Amendment, but signing on to the rest. Stewart was the only member of the Court who believed that the statute was unconstitutional because it was totally irrational.

Chief Justice Warren E. Burger wrote a brief dissent focusing primarily on the question of standing. There was no precedent, he argued, that would allow Carolyn Whitener, "a saloonkeeper," to assert the constitutional rights of her customers. Justice William H. Rehnquist's dissent was lengthier and more vehement.

Rehnquist first assailed the idea that men, as a class, were entitled to any form of heightened scrutiny. The Court had not suggested that the men in this case were the victims of "a history or

During his freshman year at Oklahoma State University (OSU), Mark Walker stopped off at a store to buy beer on his way to a party. Like many young men in Oklahoma before him, he discovered that state law allowed his date, but not him, to purchase the beer. Unlike those other young men, Walker decided to do something about a situation that struck him as patently unfair.

In the spring of 1972, around the time Walker became aware of the beer statute, the air in Oklahoma was thick with talk of equal rights and sex discrimination. In a widely publicized decision called *Lamb v. Brown*, a federal appeals court had struck down an Oklahoma statute that set the age at which criminal defendants were to be tried as adults at eighteen for females and seventeen for males. Almost simultaneously, the Oklahoma legislature, after a lively debate, became the first in the country to refuse to ratify the Equal Rights Amendment. That same spring, the legislature established eighteen as the age of majority for both men and women for almost all purposes.

But the statute governing the purchase of 3.2 percent, "nonintoxicating" beer was one with which the legislature had particular trouble. Oklahoma had a history of hostility toward alcohol: the state had retained Prohibition until 1959, and liquor by the drink was still unavailable in 1972. The drinking age was twenty-one, but state law set the age for purchasing 3.2 percent beer at eighteen for women and twenty-one for men. The legislature was divided between those who wanted to lower the beer purchase age to eighteen for both men and women, and those who wanted to raise it to twenty-one for both. By the end of March, the legislature had reached a compromise that left the law unchanged.

The legislative debate had received wide coverage in the press, and college students in particular had shown a keen interest in the issue. Walker de-

cided to research the question as part of a project for his American government class, and he complained vigorously about the law to his teaching assistant, Michael Graham. Graham, now a professor of political science at San Francisco State University, explained that the statute was probably constitutional under existing equal protection doctrine. But, he added, if Walker felt so strongly about it he should consult an attorney.

Walker died in a car accident at age twenty-five in 1976—just six months before the Supreme Court finally vindicated his objections to the Oklahoma statute—but those who knew him remember him as someone who would not take no for an answer. His stepfather, Monty Camp, recalls that, despite Walker's unathletic build, he became the first tenth-grader in his high school to qualify for the varsity football and wrestling teams. At around the same time that he decided to challenge Oklahoma's beer statute, he became a licensed lay reader in the Episcopal church—the youngest ever in his Oklahoma diocese.

Walker, who later graduated among the top ten in his class, was clearly not the type to let a matter like this drop. Picking up on his teaching assistant's offhand remark, he got in touch with Fred Gilbert, the Tulsa attorney who had recently won the much publicized equal rights victory in *Lamb v. Brown*. Gilbert, who at the time was primarily a criminal defense attorney, was more than receptive: he assured Walker that he had a winning case. Gilbert recommended filing a lawsuit in state court to have the statute declared unconstitutional, but Walker insisted on filing in federal court. Since the statute penalized the beer vendor rather than the beer purchaser, Gilbert advised Walker to find "a vendor desirous of selling 3.2% beer to males 18–21" to join the case as a coplaintiff.

In November 1972 Walker visited a Stillwater

As a freshman at Oklahoma State University, Mark Walker (left) decided to challenge the 3.2 percent beer law after reading about the statute in his American government class. He signed on beer vendor Carolyn Whitener (middle) as coplaintiff, and, when Walker turned twenty-one and was no longer subject to the statute's restrictions, he recruited his freshman fraternity brother Curtis Craig (right) as third coplaintiff. Sadly, Walker was killed in a car accident six months before the Supreme Court handed down its decision.

convenience store, the Honk-N-Holler, that sold 3.2 percent beer. There he met thirty-one-year-old Carolyn Whitener, who owned the store with her husband, Dwain. Whitener recalls that Walker spent several hours talking with her about the beer law.

"He said exactly the same thing I had said," she remembers. "Why were the laws like that?" Whitener did not see the beer law as a gender discrimination issue, but simply as "something that was unfair and didn't make sense." Coming from South Texas, her attitude toward alcohol was more relaxed than that of many Oklahomans. "You'd go into a grocery store there [in South Texas], and everyone had beer rolling around in their baskets," she says. "I never could understand what the big deal was about beer."

Still, Whitener never exactly consented to join Walker's suit. At first she believed that Walker was merely doing research for a term paper. Even when he returned to the store with Gilbert, Whitener thought their efforts were strictly on the local level. It was not until she read about the case in the newspaper in December 1972 that she realized Walker was filing a lawsuit—and that she was a named plaintiff. Whitener was none too pleased, and her husband, who had been out of town on business when Walker had approached Whitener and knew nothing about the case, even less so.

The Whiteners, who now run a business in Oklahoma City distributing computerized equipment used in selling cattle, had always kept a low profile. Many of their acquaintances did not even know they owned the Honk-N-Hollers, of which there were eleven at one time. Dwain had lost his beer vendor's permit after making a sale to a twenty-year-old man—the permit was now in Carolyn's name—but that did not incline him to challenge the law. At the time, he was trying to get out of the convenience store business altogether. And he was personally acquainted with a number of the state officials who were named in the suit as defendants.

Whitener did not, however, attempt to have her name removed from the case. She was busy with other things—running a business and raising two children. She also trusted Walker and supported *(continued)*

(continued)

what he was doing. Besides, she assured her husband, it would all be over soon.

In fact, the case—known as *Walker v. Hall,* with then-governor David Hall as the lead defendant—dragged on for the next four years, attracting far more attention than Whitener or anyone else had anticipated. During that time the Whiteners had to keep their store open and their beer permit current so that the lawsuit would remain viable. "It wasn't a happy time," she recalls.

Walker must have been equally dismayed at the delay in resolving the case. In November 1973, while the lawsuit was still in pretrial hearings, he turned twenty-one. No longer able to claim discrimination under the beer statute, he recruited an eighteen-year-old college freshman named Curtis Craig as an additional plaintiff. Craig, Walker's high school friend and OSU fraternity brother, speculates that Walker approached him because he knew Craig was planning to attend law school. Also, Craig says half jokingly, "he knew that, being a fraternity brother, I had a desire to drink 3.2 beer."

As with Whitener, Craig's participation in the lawsuit created some family tension. "I came from a non-drinking family," Craig says. "So for my name to be on it—yes, there was some concern there. But it was also a situation where my family supported the bigger issue."

Craig's involvement in the case consisted primarily of visiting several stores in Stillwater that sold 3.2 percent beer and having the store clerks sign documents certifying that they had refused to sell the beer to him because he was under age. And, at Gilbert's request, Craig—along with Whitener—traveled to Washington to attend the oral argument in the Supreme Court.

A somewhat jocular atmosphere prevailed after the first few words of Gilbert's opening argument. The challenged statute, he informed the justices in emphatic, outraged tones, "says that *all* females—even those that are the most drunk, the most alcoholic, the most immature, and the most irresponsible, may purchase 3.2 percent beer at age eighteen in absolutely unlimited quantities. . . ."

"The law doesn't say it in quite those words, does it?" one of the justices interrupted dryly, and the courtroom dissolved in laughter.

The newspapers played up this aspect of the case—now styled *Craig v. Boren,* because Gov. David Hall had been succeeded by David Boren—with headlines including "Justices Hear Sex Bias Case Amid Sarcasm, Laughter," and "Fun Foams As Top Court Talks Beer." But what struck Whitener, as she sat toward the back of the courtroom, was that she kept hearing the lawyers and justices saying her name. "I did not think my name would even be used," she recalls. In fact, because Craig had recently turned twenty-one, the viability of the lawsuit hinged entirely upon her.

Craig, now general counsel of the Explorer Pipeline Company in Tulsa, soon became all too aware of the importance of the precedent that bore his name. He entered the University of Tulsa Law School the year after *Craig* was decided, and he remembers the day his constitutional law class discussed the case as one of the most miserable of his life. He had expected the professor to call on him, but only to provide some behind-the-scenes factual information. Instead, the professor demanded detailed legal analysis. "He just grilled me," Craig says, still wincing at the memory. "And afterwards," he adds, "a number of us went out and consumed massive quantities of 3.2 beer."

pattern of past discrimination," and therefore in need of special protection from the Court. Rehnquist went on to accuse the majority of formulating its new equal protection standard "out of thin air." Its wording, he argued, was so vague as to invite judges to insert their own subjective views into the decision-making process: "How is this Court to divine what objectives are important? How is it to determine whether a particular law is 'substantially' related to the achievement of such objective, rather than related in some other way to its achievement?" The only redeeming feature of the Court's opinion, according to Rehnquist, was that it signaled a retreat from the plurality opinion in *Frontiero,* in which four justices had endorsed strict scrutiny for gender discrimination claims.

If Brennan had hoped to pass off the *Craig v. Boren* test as simply a reiteration of existing precedent, his effort was a dismal failure. The cat was out of the bag: a new equal protection standard had been born. The intermediate, or middle-tier, test was a compromise, and—as often happens with compromises—it left many dissatisfied. Surveying the plethora of concurring and dissenting opinions in *Craig* and other contemporaneous equal protection cases, one commentator wrote, "Surely we are near the point of maximum incoherence of equal protection doctrine." Another faulted the Court for failing "to articulate a decisionmaking process capable of consistent application."

But, whatever its faults, the *Craig* standard proved enduring. It has been cited routinely in constitutional sex discrimination cases ever since.

The Most Recent Standard

United States v. Virginia, 518 U.S. 515 (1996)

To most observers, it seemed that *Craig v. Boren* had written the final chapter in the saga of gender-based equal protection: claims of constitutional sex discrimination were to be judged under an intermediate scrutiny, or "middle tier," standard that fell somewhere between the strict scrutiny and rational basis tests. But in 1996—20 years after *Craig*—a Supreme Court case involving the all-male Virginia Military Institute (VMI) strongly suggested that the last word on the question had not yet been spoken.

VMI was a state-supported military college with a long and illustrious history. Founded in 1839, VMI prided itself on what it described as its unique "adversative" method of education, which emphasized physical hardship, mental stress, lack of privacy, and exacting regulation of behavior. First-year cadets, called "rats," had to endure seven months of harsh and demeaning treatment by upperclassmen in a boot-camp atmosphere (the "rat line"). The goal of the system was to mold character and produce leaders, and indeed many of VMI's alumni, bonded through adversity, had gone on to prominent positions in both military and civilian life.

Of the fifteen public institutions of higher education in Virginia, VMI was the only one that was still limited to one sex. Between 1988 and 1990, VMI received inquiries concerning admission from 347 young women. It responded to none of them. In 1990, a female high school student from Northern Virginia filed a complaint with the attorney general of the United States, alleging that VMI's male-only admission policy was a violation of the Constitution's guarantee of equal protection. Finding merit in her complaint, the Department of Justice filed suit in federal district court under the Civil Rights Act of 1964. (Adhering to case law developed under that statute, the Justice Department has kept the identity of the high school student a closely guarded secret, to protect her from retaliation.)

After a six-day trial that included expert testimony on both sides, the district court decided in favor of VMI in June 1991. The district court found the appropriate standard of review in *Mississippi University for Women v. Hogan,* a 1982 Supreme Court case involving a state-supported nursing school that refused to admit men. "Our decisions . . . establish," the Court had said in *Hogan,* "that the party seeking to uphold a statute that classifies individuals on the basis of their gender must carry the burden of showing an 'exceedingly persuasive justification' for the classification. . . . The burden is met only by showing at least that the classification serves 'important governmental objectives and that the discriminatory means employed' are 'substantially related to the achievement of those objectives.'"

The "important governmental objective" here, the district court held, was to promote diversity in higher education—specifically, to provide the choice of a single-gender educational environment. The evidence showed that such an environment could benefit many students, male or female: students at single-sex colleges of both sexes were more academically involved; interacted more frequently with faculty; and were more likely to be successful in later life, though this evidence was stronger for all-female schools than for all-male schools. And, clearly, there was a substantial relationship between the state's objective and the means employed to achieve it: the exclusion of women from VMI. Excluding one sex from a school was, in fact, not only substantially related to achieving the goal of providing a single-gender environment—it was the *only* way to achieve it.

The district court recognized that the state was offering young men a choice that was not available to young women. But, as the district court saw it, the dilemma was that if VMI were required to open its doors to women, the very experience they sought there would no longer exist. "[T]he evidence establishes," the district court ruled, "that key elements of the adversative VMI educational system, with its focus on barracks life, would be fundamentally altered, and the distinctive ends of the system would be thwarted, if VMI were forced to admit females and to make changes necessary to accommodate their needs and interests." While some women might in fact thrive in the VMI environment, the vast majority would not—"and educational systems are not designed for the exception but for the mean." Perhaps the real problem was not that VMI was all male, the district court suggested, but that Virginia did not maintain even one all-female insti-

tution of higher education. That issue, however, was not before the court.

When the case reached the court of appeals the following year, that very issue moved to the forefront. The court of appeals agreed with the district court that providing single-sex education was a worthy goal, and that VMI's system would be substantially changed by the admission of women. But if the state was going to provide a diversity of educational options for men, it needed to figure out some way to provide it for women as well. Therefore, the court ruled that Virginia had violated the Equal Protection Clause by offering VMI's method of citizen-soldier education to men only. But rather than dictating a specific remedial course of action, the court of appeals suggested three options: the state might choose to admit women to VMI, it might establish a parallel institution for women, or it might turn VMI into a private college. This last option would free the school from the constraints of the Equal Protection Clause, but also deprive it of state funding.

In response, Virginia convened a task force charged with the responsibility of designing a single-sex program for women that would, like VMI, seek to produce "citizen-soldiers." The result was a plan for the Virginia Women's Institute for Leadership (VWIL), a state-sponsored undergraduate program to be located at Mary Baldwin College, a private liberal arts school for women. The task force, composed of experts in women's education, concluded that VMI's "adversative" model would be inappropriate for most women. VWIL would rely instead on a cooperative method aimed at building up self-esteem rather than destroying it. There would be no rat line, no rigorous barracks life, and no uniforms. Instead, VWIL students would have training in self-defense and self-assertiveness, take courses in leadership, and receive military training through a preexisting ROTC program.

The next step was to return to court to secure approval of the program. In the district court, the Justice Department challenged the VWIL plan as inadequate, pointing out the substantial differences between VWIL and VMI. The average combined SAT score for entrants at Mary Baldwin was about 100 points lower than at VMI, its faculty held significantly fewer Ph.D.s and received lower salaries, and the women's college did not offer degrees in the sciences and engineering as did VMI. The recreation facilities at Mary Baldwin were minimal (two fields and a gym) compared to VMI's extensive competition-level fields tailored to different sports and its vast indoor facilities. Nor did Mary Baldwin have the history, reputation, and influential alumni network enjoyed by VMI, which included military generals, members of Congress, and business executives. VMI's distinguished alumni not only eagerly hired VMI graduates, but supported an endowment of $131 million compared to Mary Baldwin's $19 million. More fundamentally, VWIL, with its "cooperative" program, was an inadequate substitute for those women who wanted to attend VMI precisely in order to experience its "adversative" educational system.

The district court rejected these arguments. Establishing a new institution that was truly equal to VMI would be an impossible task, the court said, and it would be unrealistic to think that the court of appeals intended to impose such a requirement. The VWIL plan, the court held, "takes into account the differences and the needs of college-age men and women," based on expert recommendations. "If VMI marches to the beat of a drum," the court concluded metaphorically, "then Mary Baldwin marches to the melody of a fife and when the march is over, both will have arrived at the same destination."

The three-judge Court of Appeals affirmed this district court judgment, with one judge dissenting. In the process, the court sharply lowered the *Craig v. Boren* standard, applying what it called a "special intermediate scrutiny test for classifications based on homogeneity of gender in the context of higher education." Turning to the first prong of the *Craig* test—the "important" government objective—the court reasoned that it should take a cautious and deferential approach, so as to avoid simply substituting its own values for those of the government. The government objective itself, the court ruled, need only be legitimate as in the old "anything goes" rational basis test, not "important" as *Craig* decreed. As long as the state's purpose was not "pernicious," the court would defer to the state. The focus of the analysis should instead be entirely on whether the means chosen by the state "substantially and directly" furthered that objective.

Here, in the lower court's view, the government's objective—providing the option of single-sex education—was legitimate and certainly not pernicious. And the means chosen to achieve that goal—the exclusion of women from VMI and men from VWIL—was not only substantially related, but absolutely essential. The exclusion of women from VMI was also "directly related to achieving the results of an adversative method in a military environment. . . ." The court also had other concerns. "If we were to place men and women into the adversative relationship inherent in the VMI program, we would destroy . . . any sense of decency that still permeates the relationship between the sexes."

But the court also recognized that, in these circumstances, employing the two-pronged equal protection test risks "bypass[ing] any equal protection scrutiny": if the government's objective is to provide a single-gender environment, the exclusion of the other gender will always be a "substantially related," indeed necessary, method of achieving it. To ensure that the challenged gender classification did not entirely escape equal protection scrutiny, the court went on to add a third prong: the alternatives offered to men and women must be "substantively comparable." Applying the test to the facts of this case, the court concluded that the separate VMI and VWIL programs, while clearly not identical, were sufficiently comparable to pass muster.

When the Justice Department and Virginia sought review in the Supreme Court in 1995, it triggered an avalanche of amicus briefs from women's rights organizations denouncing the Court of Appeals' second decision. Not only was the newly devised test less protective than the established intermediate scrutiny standard, it was even more lax than the "separate but equal" doctrine discredited by the Court more than forty years before in the context of school desegregation. Both the Justice Department and the amicus briefs seized on a phrase the Court had used in a case called *Mississippi University for Women v. Hogan* to describe the intermediate scrutiny test: the government must show an "exceedingly persuasive justification" for the gender classification at issue (see p. 55).

But women's rights groups, and later the Justice Department, did not just call for a reaffirmation of the *Craig v. Boren* standard. Drawing on criticism of the intermediate scrutiny test that had been brewing for some time, they invited the Court to announce that gender discrimination, like race discrimination, would henceforth be subject to the strict scrutiny test. The briefs revived the arguments for strict scrutiny that had been offered by the plurality in *Frontiero v. Richardson*: sex, like race, was an immutable characteristic that bore no relation to ability, and women had been the victims of a long and unfortunate history of sex discrimination. Moreover, the intermediate scrutiny standard had simply proved too vague to be workable. The lower courts were rife with instances of its misapplication—with the case at hand offered as a prime example.

The Supreme Court had adhered to the intermediate scrutiny test in gender discrimination cases that had come before it since *Craig v. Boren*. But the Justice Department and others who argued for strict scrutiny pointed to footnotes in two Supreme Court decisions—one in the aforementioned *Hogan,* and another in a 1994 case called *J. E. B. v. Alabama ex rel. T. B.*—where the Court indicated that strict scrutiny for gender classifications was still a live possibility: it was not necessary to reach the question of strict scrutiny, the Court had said, because the challenged classifications could not even pass intermediate scrutiny. And several commentators concluded that, in the cases since *Craig,* the Supreme Court had been subtly ratcheting up the level of scrutiny for gender-based classifications—primarily through the phrase "exceedingly persuasive justification."

Some commentators also argued that the case for applying strict scrutiny to gender classifications had been strengthened by the Supreme Court's recent affirmative action decisions permitting preference in hiring and college admissions to groups that had previously been subject to discrimination. A traditional justification for heightened scrutiny under the Equal Protection Clause was that "discrete and insular" minorities, who could not defend their rights in the political arena, were in need of special protection from the courts. Since women are not a minority, the argument had gone—comprising, in fact, 53 percent of the population—they were not in need of the kind of heightened scrutiny reserved for racial and ethnic minorities. But in cases decided in 1989 and 1995, the Court had ruled that governmental affirmative action programs giving preferences to minorities were subject to strict scrutiny. While the Court's application of the strict scrutiny standard in this area was less stringent than usual, it was still exacting. And it was now being applied to discrimination against white males—clearly no one's idea of a discrete and insular minority.

As a practical matter, it would be difficult to apply the new strict scrutiny to race-based affirmative action programs without also applying it to gender-based programs, because most affirmative action programs used both categories. And retaining the two different standards would appear inequitable. Affirmative action plans for African Americans could be struck down under the stricter race standard while those for women could be upheld under the more lenient gender standard. All these factors gave the Court strong reasons for increasing the gender standard to strict scrutiny.

A number of feminists and some private women's colleges argued strongly against application of strict scrutiny. Such a ruling might threaten the existence of private single-sex schools, because it could jeopardize federal financial aid and tax breaks. More broadly, they said, strict scrutiny would bar the government from taking into account the legitimate differences between men and women, and—by requiring equal treatment across the board—force women into a male mold.

The advocates of strict scrutiny appeared to suffer a setback at oral argument when Deputy Solicitor General Paul Bender, arguing for the Justice Department, came under sharp questioning from Justice Sandra Day O'Connor (the author of the majority opinion in *Hogan*). "Couldn't this case be decided under the intermediate scrutiny standard?" she asked Bender. "Yes, absolutely," he replied. "Why then," O'Connor wanted to know, "had the government chosen this case to argue the issue of strict scrutiny?" Bender started to answer that on several occasions the Court had indicated that the standard of scrutiny was still an open question. "Well, it's not exactly an open question," O'Connor shot back, "in the sense that the Court has decided a

number of cases . . . applying . . . intermediate scrutiny. . . . If you look at *Mississippi University for Women v. Hogan,* the Court certainly tried to articulate a standard."

"[In] *Craig v. Boren* [we] said that was the standard," Chief Justice William H. Rehnquist interjected.

Justice Ruth Bader Ginsburg, who as a litigator had been the prime champion of strict scrutiny for gender classifications, remained silent during this exchange.

But it was Ginsburg who announced the opinion from the bench on June 26, 1996. Writing for a six-person majority, which included Justice O'Connor, Ginsburg ruled that the lower courts had erred in holding that VMI did not have to admit women. She did not squarely address the question of strict scrutiny, but she did leave the door open for further discussion. Ginsburg noted that the Court had not equated gender classifications, "for all purposes," to classifications based on race or national origin—the classifications for which strict scrutiny had "thus far" been reserved. She also applied the gender standard with the same rigor traditionally seen in strict scrutiny cases, as dissenting justice Antonin Scalia pointed out in great detail.

But while Ginsburg relied on the Supreme Court's prior intermediate scrutiny cases, the phrase that leapt to the forefront of her opinion was "exceedingly persuasive justification." The "core instruction" of the Court's previous cases, she wrote in beginning her analysis, was that "[p]arties who seek to defend gender-based government action must demonstrate an 'exceedingly persuasive justification' for that action." And the justification for the government action "must be genuine, not hypothesized or invented post hoc [afterward] in response to litigation."

Applying that standard, Ginsburg first viewed with skepticism Virginia's stated objective of providing educational diversity. No such purpose was evident at the time of VMI's founding in 1839, when the state excluded women from all higher education because "[h]igher education was considered dangerous for women," and subsequent history was equally unconvincing. Providing a variety of educational choices was not the state's true purpose, Ginsburg concluded, but was invented later. The state's next argument was that admitting women would undermine VMI's adversative system. It was undisputed, however, that at least some women would be capable of engaging in VMI's demanding program and would actually prefer it to a methodology such as VWIL's. And the question was not whether VMI would be suitable for most women; it was probably not suitable for most men. Rather, "the question is whether the commonwealth can constitutionally deny to women who have the will and capacity, the training and attendant opportunities that VMI uniquely affords."

The fear that the admission of women would destroy the adversative system and the school itself was "a judgment hardly proved, a prediction hardly different from other 'self-fulfilling prophecies' . . . once routinely used to deny rights or opportunities." Ginsburg offered some telling examples: an 1876 state court that ruled women could be prevented from being lawyers in order to "grade up" the profession; medical faculties that barred women from their schools for fear of such evils as women and men jointly displaying "the secrets of the reproduction system"; and police resistance to women on the force because their presence would "undermine male solidarity," deprive the men of "adequate assistance," and "lead to sexual misconduct." She pointed out how successfully women had performed once the federal military academies and services were opened to them. In short, she concluded, Virginia had "'fallen far short of establishing the "exceedingly persuasive justification"' . . . that must be the solid base for any gender-defined classification."

Turning to the adequacy of the state's remedy—the establishment of VWIL—Ginsburg found it sadly lacking. Virginia's claim that the dissimilarity between the two schools was justified by "real" differences between the sexes, and not by stereotypes, once again ignored the fact that some exceptional women would prefer the VMI approach. The VWIL program was hardly a match for VMI in many ways: faculty, curriculum, military program, student body, facilities, endowment, and prestige. In applying its newly devised, three-pronged test for examining the state's purpose, the Court of Appeals had engaged in circular reasoning and had gravely erred. "Women seeking and fit for a VMI-quality education," Ginsburg concluded, "cannot be offered anything less, under the State's obligation to afford them genuinely equal protection."

Chief Justice Rehnquist and Justice Scalia filed their own opinions, one concurring in the judgment and one dissenting. (Justice Clarence Thomas did not participate in deciding the case because his son, Jamal, was attending VMI.) The chief justice, while agreeing with the Court's conclusions, took issue with its analysis. Having dissented vigorously in *Craig v. Boren* two decades before, Rehnquist now found himself in the position of defending the precedent. The majority's reliance on the phrase "exceedingly persuasive justification" had introduced "an element of uncertainty respecting the appropriate test." The terms of the *Craig* test—"important governmental objective" and "substantially related"—were "hardly models of precision," but they had more content than the phrase on which the Court had now seized.

Rehnquist agreed that the state's proffered justification of educational diversity was unconvincing. But—unlike the majority—he based that conclusion only on the state's actions since the Supreme Court's decision in *Hogan*, which he said "placed Virginia on notice that VMI's admissions policy possibly was unconstitutional." Even

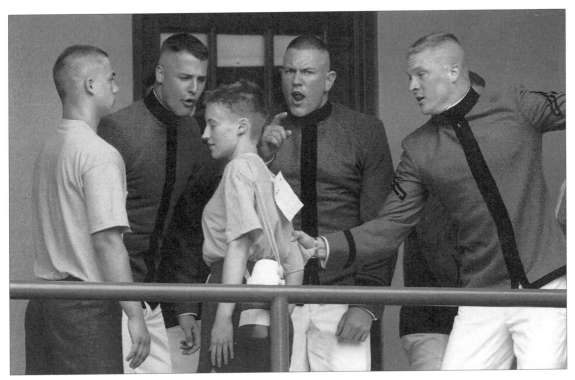

On the first day of classes after the Supreme Court's landmark decision forcing the all-male Virginia Military Institute to open its doors to women, Megan Smith braved the traditional verbal abuse inflicted on freshmen (called "rats") by returning cadets. She was one of 30 women and 428 men to undergo hazing in the school's traditional "rat line" in September 1997.

accepting the state's justification, Virginia's argument was flawed because it had failed to provide educational diversity for women as well as men. VMI would not necessarily have to admit women to satisfy the demands of the Constitution, but the state would at least have to create two single-sex institutions that "offered the same quality of education and were of the same overall calibre."

Scalia filed a scathing forty-page dissent. He had no problem, he said, with the Court's three-tiered system of equal protection standards, although he criticized the Court for applying them "whenever we feel like it." But those tests could not "supersede—and indeed ought to be crafted so as to reflect—those constant and unbroken national traditions that embody the people's under-

standing of ambiguous constitutional texts." One of those traditions was the all-male, government-supported military college.

But leaving aside the question of tradition, Scalia continued, the Court had not even honestly applied its own well-established intermediate scrutiny test. Like Rehnquist, Scalia viewed the majority's reliance on the phrase "exceedingly persuasive justification" as a departure from past practice. The Justice Department had argued for strict scrutiny, and the Court, "while making no reference to the Government's argument, effectively accepts it" (a point Ginsburg's opinion never denied).

Under the intermediate scrutiny standard, Scalia maintained, the question was not whether

The development of the equal protection standard in gender discrimination cases in the 1970s was in large part driven by the litigating strategy of Ruth Bader Ginsburg. Her aim was to persuade the Supreme Court to strike down laws that relied on outdated stereotypes about men and women and that unfairly penalized individuals who did not conform to traditional gender roles. "[G]eneralizations about 'the way women are,'" Ginsburg would later write when she herself had become a member of the Court, "estimates of what is appropriate for most women, no longer justify denying opportunity to women whose talent and capacity place them outside the average description."

As counsel to the Women's Rights Project of the ACLU, Ginsburg was the principal author of most of the briefs filed in the major Supreme Court sex discrimination cases of the 1970s. Ginsburg's goal was gradually to guide the Court to a position of heightened scrutiny for gender-based equal protection claims by bringing a series of cases that were clear winners. Often these cases involved plaintiffs who did not conform to the sex-role stereotypes on which the legislation at issue was based. And often, whether by statutory structure, accident, or design, the plaintiffs alleging discrimination were male. That fact underscored Ginsburg's argument that stereotypes cut both ways: neither men nor women should be required to conform to assumptions about what most men or most women were like.

Reed v. Reed (1971), the first gender discrimination victory, was also the first link in the chain Ginsburg helped to forge. The Women's Rights Project did not yet exist, and Ginsburg—who had been working as an ACLU volunteer attorney— became involved only after the Supreme Court had agreed to review the case. But *Reed* fit right in with her strategy of bringing clear winners. The facts

were sympathetic: a grieving mother sought to become administrator of her son's estate, but a clearly anachronistic Idaho law mandated an absolute preference for a male in such a role. Nor would the Court have to worry about upsetting people's expectations or costing the government a lot of money: because the Idaho statute had been repealed before oral argument, the immediate impact of the decision would be extremely limited.

In writing the brief, Ginsburg made an unusual choice. Usually a lawyer presents the court with the most conservative legal argument first, and introduces a more radical argument only as a fallback position. Ginsburg reversed that method: she first argued that the Court should apply strict scrutiny, and then—seemingly as an afterthought—took the position that the statute should be struck down even under the traditional rational basis test. Ginsburg had no expectation that the Court would actually adopt strict scrutiny at this stage. But, given the strength of the case, she saw little risk in trying to accustom the justices to the idea.

So, despite the fact that the Court decided to apply a rational basis test in *Reed*, Ginsburg was delighted with the opinion. The Court had picked up on Ginsburg's citation of a 1920 equal protection case, *Royster Guano v. Virginia*, that had used a relatively tough formulation of the rational basis standard: a classification "must be reasonable, not arbitrary, and must rest upon some ground of difference having a fair and substantial relation to the object of the legislation, so that all persons similarly circumstanced shall be treated alike." *Royster Guano* dated from a now discredited era when the Supreme Court used the Equal Protection Clause to invalidate economic reforms, and Ginsburg had been reluctant to rely on a case that was probably wrongly decided. But because the *Royster* language could serve as a building block on the road to strict scrutiny, she decided to use it. In the wake of *Reed*, the ACLU launched its Women's Rights Project, with Ginsburg at its head. At the time, Ginsburg was working simultaneously on two Supreme Court cases involving sex discrimination in the military: *Struck v. Secretary of Defense*, and *Frontiero v. Richardson*. Although *Frontiero* would ultimately make headlines and *Struck* would be consigned to the ash heap of history, at the time Ginsburg saw *Struck* as the more promising case. *Struck* involved an unmarried female air force officer who had been threatened with an involuntary discharge when she became pregnant. No adverse action had been taken against the father of the child, who was also an officer in the air force. But before the Court could hear the case, the air force decided to waive the female officer's discharge, and the case became moot.

As counsel to the Women's Rights Project of the American Civil Liberties Union, Ruth Bader Ginsburg was the architect of a comprehensive litigating strategy to end sex discrimination in the law.

That left *Frontiero* as the only hope for a major sex discrimination ruling during the 1972 Supreme Court term. But here Ginsburg ran into some disagreement with the local counsel who had litigated the case in the district court, Joe Levin of the Southern Poverty Law Center. The center's lawyers, busy with other matters, had asked the ACLU to prepare the jurisdictional statement—the filing that requests the Court to take the case. The ACLU had agreed, Ginsburg later said, on condition that the Women's Rights Project take charge of the litigation if the Court agreed to hear the case. But when Ginsburg sent Levin a draft of her brief on the merits, he objected to her emphasis on strict scrutiny. Believing that strict scrutiny was actually inappropriate for gender-based claims, Levin filed a brief that relied primarily on the rational basis argument, and Ginsburg ultimately filed her draft as an amicus curiae brief.

But Ginsburg's amicus brief had an impact that was more dramatic than even she had expected: four members of the Court, led by Justice William J. Brennan Jr., embraced her argument for strict scrutiny. Ginsburg had thought "that Brennan might wait—might hold back until there were about four cases—and maybe the fifth time around would say, 'Yes, now we have had a procession of cases, and

can see from the collection that sex indeed should be openly declared a suspect classification.'" By that time, Ginsburg hoped, a majority of the Court would be ready to join Brennan. But it was now apparent that the crucial fifth vote for strict scrutiny was lacking, and Ginsburg adjusted her strategy accordingly. Rather than hammering away at the need for strict scrutiny, Ginsburg focused on exposing the stereotypes that often underlay legislation that treated men and women differently.

Ginsburg alerted local ACLU affiliates to look out for promising cases, primarily Social Security and jury selection, in which women could argue discrimination. In these types of cases, she felt, the stereotyping that had entered into legislative judgments was easily exposed.

While still at work on *Frontiero*, Ginsburg had agreed to bring the Social Security case that would ultimately become *Weinberger v. Wiesenfeld*. As in *Reed*, the facts were sympathetic, and the discrimination stark: a father whose wife had died in childbirth was unable to stay home with his newborn son because Social Security regulations provided

(continued)

(continued)

survivors' benefits only for mothers. "[I]f there ever was a case to attract suspect classification for sex lines in the law," Ginsburg later said, "[*Wiesenfeld*] was the one."

But Ginsburg did not have mastery over the order in which cases reached the Supreme Court. Before *Wiesenfeld* could get there, a local ACLU affiliate in Florida—without first obtaining clearance from the national office—sought Supreme Court review for a case called *Kahn v. Shevin*. In Ginsburg's view, *Kahn* should never have gone to the Supreme Court at all, and certainly not during the 1973 term. The facts of the case were hardly as compelling as those in *Reed, Frontiero,* or *Wiesenfeld:* a widower was challenging a Florida statute that granted a small tax break to widows (as well as to the blind and totally disabled) who owned property. This was a statute that could be seen as an effort to compensate poor widows for past inequities, and might well survive rational basis review. In addition, Ginsburg was aware that the widowed mother of Justice William O. Douglas had had a difficult time financially, a fact that might incline him to be sympathetic to the state.

Nevertheless, Ginsburg offered to take charge of the litigation after the Supreme Court agreed to hear the case. Avoiding the question of strict scrutiny, her brief merely relied on *Reed* and *Frontiero* for the proposition that the Equal Protection Clause did "not tolerate legislative line-drawing on the basis of sex stereotypes." When the Court ruled against her—with Douglas writing the majority opinion—Ginsburg was not surprised. But her decision not to raise the issue of strict scrutiny at least left the question open for another day.

When *Wiesenfeld* reached the Court the following term, it was clear that that day had not yet come: Ginsburg again skirted the strict scrutiny issue, merely calling for "heightened scrutiny without further labeling." And Brennan, writing for the Court in striking down the Social Security legislation, did seem to be applying something stronger than traditional rational basis review. He argued

that the government could not shield its discriminatory actions by "the mere recitation of a benign, compensatory purpose"—something that, under a low-level equal protection standard, the government was in fact often allowed to do. After the setback of *Kahn,* the Court was now at least back to the sort of test it had applied in *Reed.*

One result of the ACLU's victories in *Reed* and *Frontiero* was that private attorneys began to jump on the sex discrimination bandwagon, bringing cases that would advance the interests of their particular clients but not necessarily of the women's rights movement as a whole. This development made further inroads into Ginsburg's influence over the Supreme Court's docket. In a 1975 case brought by a private attorney, *Schlesinger v. Ballard,* a male navy lieutenant challenged regulations regarding promotion that appeared to favor women. Ginsburg later observed that she could have presented an argument that the regulations actually disfavored women, but at the time the ACLU had neither the time nor resources to file even an amicus brief. The Court upheld the navy's regulations, with four dissenters arguing for the application of strict scrutiny.

Another case brought by a private attorney and heard two terms later, *Craig v. Boren,* had quite different results. *Craig* arrived at the Supreme Court simultaneously with *Califano v. Goldfarb,* an ACLU Social Security case that represented the culmination of Ginsburg's careful litigation strategy. *Goldfarb* concerned regulations that favored male workers by automatically granting survivors' benefits to their widows, but granted them to the widowers of female workers only if the men could prove that they had actually been financially dependent on their wives. *Craig,* brought by an attorney and litigants who did not consider themselves feminists, involved an Oklahoma statute that allowed young women to purchase 3.2 beer at age eighteen but required young men to wait until they were twenty-one.

Ginsburg later wrote that *Craig* "has been described as a gossamer case in view of the nonweighty interest pressed by the thirsty boys." Perhaps she would not have chosen to bring the case herself; clearly, she felt that *Goldfarb* was more substantial. But once the Supreme Court agreed to hear *Craig,* Ginsburg immediately offered her services to the local attorney, Fred Gilbert. Although she filed a separate amicus brief rather than helping to write the main brief, she advised Gilbert on strategy. "We don't have 5 votes for suspect classification so play that down," she wrote to him. "Urge instead 'heightened scrutiny' as evidenced in *Reed, Frontiero, Wiesenfeld,* and *Stanton* [*v. Stanton*]."

Although *Craig* and *Goldfarb* were argued the same day, it was *Craig* that came down first—and that had the stronger majority, 7–2 as compared to 5–4. And it was in *Craig* that six members of the Court subscribed to a new, intermediate standard of scrutiny for gender-based equal protection claims, thus cementing in place the heightened scrutiny for which Ginsburg had been striving.

Ginsburg was surprised, not by the outcome in *Craig,* but by the fact that the Court would make so historic a pronouncement in a case with such trivial subject matter. But Ginsburg herself later suggested that the Court had had a more difficult time with *Goldfarb* because it carried a substantial price tag: the government claimed that a decision in favor of the plaintiff would cost $500 million.

With the decision in *Craig,* Ginsburg achieved much—if not quite all—of what she had sought. In recent years, however, her litigating strategy has come under criticism. Some feminists have argued that by focusing on equal treatment for men and women, Ginsburg has forced women into a male mold. While Ginsburg has maintained that virtually all legal distinctions between men and women are the product of stereotypes, these "second wave" feminists believe that some differences between the sexes should be recognized and accommodated by the law—most notably in the areas of pregnancy and childrearing. Since most existing law is based on a male model, these critics argue, "equal" treatment often means, in practice, that women are treated like men. They suggest that the law recognize general differences between the sexes and give

preferential treatment to women in childrearing and other settings.(Ginsburg's supporters also point out that her approach allows men to assume traditional female roles, as evidenced by Stephen Wiesenfeld when he won the right to stay home with his newborn son.)

In *United States v. Virginia,* some feminists raised "second wave" arguments in amicus briefs presented to a Court that included now-justice Ruth Bader Ginsburg. To force the all-male VMI to admit women, they said, would jeopardize the existence of all-female schools, both public and private. The innate differences between men and women, they maintained, justified methods of education that were tailored to those differences. Men were suited to aggressive and competitive educational methods, women to cooperative models. Justice Ginsburg and the Court majority were unmoved. As had been the case when she was a litigator, Ginsburg's concern was primarily with the individual who did not conform to society's gender-based expectations.

Responding to her critics in 1988, when she was a federal circuit court judge, Ginsburg emphasized the pervasive discrimination that had existed against women in the early 1970s. "An appeal to courts at that time could not have been expected to do much more" than to unsettle commonly held conceptions of men's and women's separate spheres, she maintained. Now, the logical progression from the litigation of the 1970s was to shift the arena from the courts—"with their distinctly limited capacity"—to the legislature.

Most importantly, Ginsburg pleaded for tolerance within the feminist community, deploring "the tendency to regard one's feminism as the only true feminism, to denigrate rather than to appreciate the contributions of others." Feminism today, she urged, was "a house of many gables, with rooms enough to accommodate all who have the imagination and determination to think and work in a common cause." And—as even Ginsburg's critics would agree—much of the foundation of that many-gabled house was laid by Ginsburg herself.

some women (or perhaps only one) were interested in attending VMI and capable of participating in its program. Ginsburg's approach required a "perfect fit" between ends and means; in Scalia's view, a system that was unfair to a few nonconformists would nevertheless satisfy the "substantial relationship" requirement of the intermediate scrutiny standard. For example, in *Rostker v. Goldberg,* a 1981 case, the Court had ruled that selective service registration could constitutionally exclude women, even if some women were fit for noncombat roles, because the purpose of registration was to supply a pool of combat troops and Congress had passed laws barring all women from combat. "There is simply no support in our cases," Scalia said, "for the notion that a sex-based classification is invalid unless it relates to characteristics that hold true in every instance." In fact, given the choice, he thought the "stronger argument" was to reduce the gender standard to the old rational basis review.

Scalia then identified Virginia's "important" governmental interest as "providing effective college education for its citizens." Single-sex instruction was a means substantially related to that interest, because of its proven benefits. While the adversative method was not appropriate for everyone, providing the choice of such a method was also substantially related to the government's

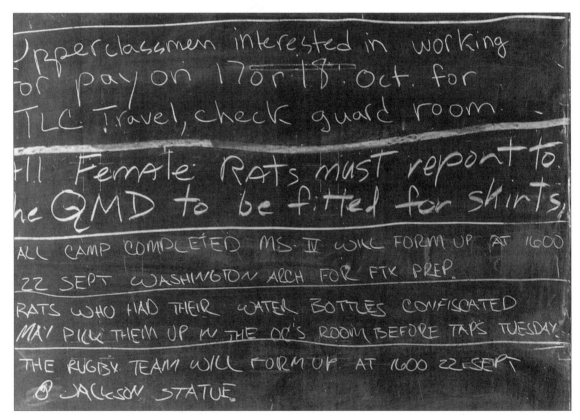

Female rats may be issued skirts as part of their dress uniform but they are still expected to undergo the rigorous adversative training system for which Virginia Military Institute is famous.

objective. And it had been found as a fact by the district court that if VMI were required to admit women, it "would eventually find it necessary to drop the adversative system altogether." While the best possible approach would be for the state to provide both adversative schools and traditional ones, in all three possible variations—all male, all female, and coed—Virginia did not have enough money to provide six schools. Given these realities, Virginia's exclusion of women from VMI was "substantially related to the Commonwealth's important educational interests."

Scalia concluded his dissent elegiacally, with a lengthy quotation from a booklet distributed to all first-year VMI students. Listing the characteristics of "a gentleman," the booklet admonished, among other things, that a gentleman must never discuss "the merits or demerits of a lady," "hail a lady from a club window," or "so much as lay a finger on a lady." It was "powerfully impressive," Scalia said, that "a public institution of higher education still in existence" sought to hold its students to such standards, and he doubted that "any of us, women included, will be better off for its destruction."

Outside the Court, some commentators—while agreeing with Rehnquist and Scalia that the VMI opinion signaled a departure from previous gender-discrimination precedents—saw this as a welcome development. "[T]he VMI decision may well be the final stepping stone on the path to a destination envisioned by feminist advocates, including Justice Ginsburg, decades ago," a law review author exulted. "That destination is strict scrutiny for gender classifications."

At VMI itself, the mood was grim. "This is everything that is good in our culture," said Superintendent Josiah Bunting III while the case was pending in the Supreme Court, "and it's going to change irretrievably if they bring in women." After the ruling, VMI's Board of Visitors considered buying the school from the state

in order to maintain its all-male status. But ultimately, in September 1996, the board voted 9–8 to open VMI to women.

The VMI administration made it clear that women would be held to the same standards as men, and did its best to prepare for their arrival: the school hired female staff, required all students and employees to attend seminars on sexual harassment and fraternization, and installed women's bathrooms and new shades on the barracks windows. In the fall 1997 thirty women enrolled as first-year cadets; seven months later, twenty-three of them were still around to perform the traditional crawl up a muddy twenty-foot hill that marks the end of the rat line. Five of those women made the rank of corporal for their sophomore year, and in May 1999 two women who had transferred to VMI in 1997 became the school's first female graduates.

The transition to coeducation has not been entirely smooth. Some alumni have complained that standards have been diluted, and feminist groups have remained skeptical of VMI's commitment to equality. Several students have been disciplined or expelled for sexual misconduct—including the school's top-ranking cadet, who was thrown out for allegedly using his position to pressure freshman women into having sex. Despite these hurdles, it is clear that coeducation at VMI is there to stay, and even appears to be a success. By August 1999, when the third crop of women cadets took their places on VMI's rat line, Superintendent Bunting told the *Washington Post* that standards had actually toughened since women had arrived on campus.

"What we are beginning to see is a certain type of young woman who is attracted to VMI," he said. "They are young women who have something to prove to themselves and to their friends. They want to take the road less traveled and flourish in a system that measures success in many different ways, not just in academics."

WOMEN IN THE FAMILY

From Subordinates to Equal Partners

When the United States was founded, the law made married women the subjects and servants of their husbands. He was the head and master of his wife and children under both common-law rules imported from England and civil-law rules from France and Spain (see p. 6). While women were citizens, their subordinate status in the family could not be reconciled with equal and full citizenship rights. Because a woman's role was simply to live in the world of the family and to be provided for and protected by her husband, she was not accorded economic or political rights.

While feminists began challenging these rules in state legislatures with partial success in the mid-nineteenth century, the final breakup of this legal regime did not occur until the last quarter of the twentieth century. Married women did gain the right to own their own wages by the turn of the twentieth century (previously their wages belonged to their husbands), but women still earned less than men for the same work or were segregated into low-paying jobs. Women's wages were not needed to support their families, the theory went, so they could be paid less than men. The law did not consider the possibility that husbands might need their wives' financial support, because men were expected to be the breadwinners. As "head and master," the husband was also responsible for making the financial decisions for the family, such as selling the family home.

Similarly, the law continued to expect women, not men, to care for children. For example, some legislatures saw no need to send girls to college because, unlike boys who would become heads of household and provide for their families, they were simply expected to grow up and raise new families.

Central to most of the cases that follow is women's economic role in the family. These decisions show the demise of the family-law system, with the Supreme Court saying "no" to the last vestiges of the old order. Today, the law makes married women full and equal partners with their husbands.

UNEQUAL BENEFITS FOR WIDOWS VERSUS WIDOWERS

Weinberger v. Wiesenfeld, 420 U.S. 636 (1975)

Califano v. Goldfarb, 430 U.S. 199 (1977)

Wengler v. Druggists Mut. Ins. Co., 446 U.S. 142 (1980)

Weinberger v. Wiesenfeld challenged a provision of the Social Security Act that was built on the premise that only male workers financially support their families and only women take care of young children. The law provided that when a male worker died, his widow was entitled to a government payment to enable her to stay home and care for the children rather than having to find a paid job. But when a female worker died, her widower was not entitled to this benefit. Congress simply assumed widowers neither needed the money nor wished to stay home to care for their offspring.

When Paula Polatschek Wiesenfeld died in childbirth in 1972, her husband, Stephen, applied for Social Security survivors' benefits for himself and their infant son, Jason. Although the boy received children's benefits, Stephen was told that he was not eligible for any himself because survivors' benefits were available only to women. This was true even though Paula, a high school mathematics teacher, had been her family's principal wage earner, and had made the maximum required Social Security contributions for more than seven years.

Wiesenfeld sued in federal court, claiming that the provision of the Social Security Act that denied benefits on the basis of gender violated the Due Process Clause of the Fifth Amendment. As in *Frontiero,* because the case challenged the constitutionality of a federal statute, it was heard by a three-judge federal district court panel. The district court acknowledged that the Supreme Court had not yet extended strict scrutiny to gender-based classifications. Perhaps, the court speculated, that was because the Supreme Court had not yet been confronted with a case that would pass constitutional muster under the traditional rational basis test, but not under the higher strict scrutiny standard.

As the district court saw it, that was precisely the situation in *Wiesenfeld.* If the case were judged under the traditional test, the three-member panel would accept the government's argument that the statute's provision of benefits to widows but not widowers was "rationally related" to the

After his wife died in childbirth, Stephen Wiesenfeld challenged a provision of the Social Security Act granting survivor's benefits to widows but not to widowers. The Supreme Court overturned the law in 1975, allowing Wiesenfeld to stay home part time and raise his son, Jason.

"valid public purpose" of rectifying the effects of past employment discrimination against women. Since women could not earn as much as men, it was necessary to protect women and families who had lost the male head of the household by giving them extra government financial payments. However, following Justice William J. Brennan Jr.'s reasoning in *Frontiero,* the court instead held that laws based on gender distinctions are "inherently suspect" and should therefore be subject to strict judicial scrutiny. Under that test, the court ruled that the provision of the Social Security Act denying surviving spouse benefits to widowers was unconstitutional because, despite helping some women, it actually increased employment discrimination against other women—those who were wage earners.

When the case reached the Supreme Court in 1975, it appeared that the justices would finally have to confront squarely the question of whether the rational basis test or the strict scrutiny standard applied to gender-based classifications. However, the Court sidestepped the issue; it found that the statutory distinction providing survivor's benefits to widows but not widowers did not withstand the *Frontiero* heightened level of scrutiny. The reason, the Court held, was that it was based on the same kind of "archaic and overbroad" generalizations about the importance of women workers' wages to the support of their families that were present in the statute in *Frontiero*.

[I]n this case Social Security taxes were deducted from Paula's salary during the years in which she worked. Thus, she not only failed to receive for her family the same protection which a similarly situated male worker would have received, but she also was deprived of a portion of her own earnings in order to contribute to the fund out of which benefits would be paid to others. . . . [T]he Constitution forbids the gender-based differentiation that results in the efforts of female workers required to pay social security taxes producing less protection for their families than is produced by the efforts of men.

To try to support its claim that the discriminatory provision was different than that in *Frontiero,* the government argued that the statute was intended to compensate widows for the difficulty widowed women typically encountered because of economic discrimination when they sought to support their families with their earnings. But the Court rejected this explanation, noting that the statute did not provide benefits to all widows who had been out of the workforce, but only to widows with minor children. Indeed, middle-aged widows who stayed home to raise their now grown children were denied such benefits even though they were the most likely victims of employment discrimination because they had been

out of the workforce for so long. Therefore, the Court reasoned, the primary purpose of the provision must have been to enable a widow to remain at home to care for her young children, and not to correct past discrimination.

Turning to the actual purpose of the statute, the Court then concluded that, since the statute's intent was to enable a parent to remain at home to care for a child, the gender-based distinction was "entirely irrational." As the majority opinion explained, the "fact that a man is working while there is a wife at home does not mean that he would, or should be required to, continue to work if his wife dies. It is no less important for a child to be cared for by its sole surviving parent when that parent is male rather than female. And a father, no less than a mother, has a constitutionally protected right to the 'companionship, care, custody, and management'" of his children.

The Court's decision reflected a growing intolerance of gender-based distinctions grounded in outdated stereotypes that harm women—in this case, that "male workers' earnings are vital to the support of their families, while the earnings of female workers do not significantly contribute to their families' support." However, the Court's decision also reflected a concern for the fathers and children whose rights are violated by such arbitrary gender-based distinctions.

Like Sally Reed and Sharron Frontiero, Wiesenfeld was represented before the Supreme Court by Ruth Bader Ginsburg, counsel to the Women's Rights Project of the American Civil Liberties Union (ACLU). Ginsburg later joked that while the Court was unanimous in agreeing that the statute was unconstitutional, the justices were somewhat divided in their reasoning. "The majority thought it was discrimination against the women as wage earner, because she paid the same Social Security taxes but her family received different benefits. A few thought it was discrimination against the man, because he didn't have the same opportunity to give personal care to the baby as the woman would have. And one thought it was discrimination against the baby."

Indeed, the members of the Court differed slightly in their focus. Brennan, writing for the seven-person majority, considered that the entire family—deceased female wage earner, widower father, and child—was disadvantaged by the provision. Justice Lewis F. Powell Jr. and Chief Justice Warren E. Burger joined Brennan's opinion but also wrote separately to focus primary attention on the discrimination against the female wage earner and "less significance" on the discrimination against stay-at-home fathers. Justice William H. Rehnquist concurred that the statute was unconstitutional but based his decision solely on the fact that the discriminatory provision was not rationally related to the statute's purpose of enabling the children of deceased contributing workers to have the personal care of the surviving parent.

The ultimate significance of *Wiesenfeld* came in the Court's strong recognition of the harm in what Ginsburg has called the "double-edged" nature of gender-based classifications based on outdated stereotypes about women's roles in society. As more women entered the workforce in the 1970s and participated significantly in providing for their families, laws that had been enacted to provide for women who stayed home but not for women wage earners (because legislatures believed most women should be or were dependent on their husbands) were proving to be destructive not only to the growing number of working women but also to their families. And the harm to their families included the fathers' loss of the regular companionship of their children, and the children's loss of their fathers' loving care.

The issue of wage discrimination against working women and their surviving husbands arose again two terms later in another case involving a different discriminatory provision of the Social Security Act. The provision in *Califano v. Goldfarb* allowed all male workers to leave survivors' benefits to their widowed spouses, but gave that right only to a tiny group of female workers—those providing 75 percent of the family's income (all of her share of the family budget and half of his). Only 2.4 percent of all working women met this test.

Leon Goldfarb, a retired federal worker, challenged the constitutionality of the provision when he was denied widowers' benefits upon the death of his wife, Hannah, because he failed to meet the statute's requirement that he be providing less than a quarter of the family's income. A secretary in the New York public schools for twenty-five years, Hannah had paid Social Security taxes at the same rate as her male colleagues, he argued, and she expected herself and her husband to be fully protected from the economic consequences of old age, disability, and death. Leon's job was not covered by the Social Security system, so he could not collect in his own name.

"I walked into the Social Security office . . . a week after my wife passed away. They told me I was ineligible under the law and then I went back every six months to see if the law had changed," the Russian-born Goldfarb told the *New York Times*. "I knew it wasn't fair. We earned that money. We gave it in every month, there shouldn't have been strings attached to it." His two children urged him to challenge the law, but it was not until he read about a suit by another widower— Stephen Wiesenfeld—that he finally took action.

The district court declared the provision unconstitutional on the basis of *Frontiero* and *Wiesenfeld*. The Supreme Court agreed, although this time—because it carried a high price tag— the decision was far from unanimous. In a plurality opinion for four members of the Court, Brennan again wrote that burdening a widower but not a widow with the task of proving dependency upon a deceased spouse was unconstitutional. He

When Paula and Stephen Wiesenfeld learned that Paula was expecting a baby in 1972, like most expectant parents they began to make plans. Paula was a high school mathematics teacher who was also working toward a Ph.D. in preparation for a career in education administration. Stephen was starting a consulting business out of their New Jersey home. Since Stephen worked at home, and Paula was the couple's primary breadwinner, they decided that Stephen would stay home with the baby. The Wiesenfelds' decision was an example of the new flexibility in family life made possible by the increasing opportunities for women in the workplace. Families were now beginning to reexamine the allocation of roles based on their particular circumstances.

When Paula died in childbirth, the Wiesenfelds' circumstances changed dramatically. The question was no longer which parent, but whether any parent would be the child's primary caregiver. For Stephen, the decision was simple: he would stay home with their son, Jason, as he and Paula had planned. To help him afford to quit working and raise the boy, Stephen applied for Social Security survivors' benefits. But his request was turned down. Although Jason was eligible for children's benefits, Wiesenfeld was told that he was not eligible for benefits himself, because this particular survivors' benefit was available only to women. This was true even though Paula had been her family's principal wage earner, and had made the maximum required Social Security contributions for more than seven years.

Wiesenfeld knew that the law was unfair. "It was the early '70s, the beginning of the women's movement. I saw the inequities in the law, and knew that it shouldn't be there," he said. Testifying years later before the Senate Judiciary Committee about the case, he recounted the injustice that resulted from the commonly held presumption, both in society and in the law, that men, and not women, were the family breadwinners: "Women not only earned less money than men for the same work, they were also forced to contribute to a Social Security system that did not insure them with [the] equal [degree of] protection."

Still, Wiesenfeld assumed that there was not much he could do about it. "You know the saying, 'You can't fight city hall,'" he said. "I believed that." But when he read an article in the local *New Brunswick Home News* about families pursuing alternative lifestyles, he wrote a letter to the editor describing his experiences. He wanted to bring attention to the discriminatory provisions of the Social Security Act that he felt posed a barrier to nontraditional family arrangements.

When Phyllis Zatlin, a language professor at Rutgers University, read Stephen's letter, she called him to ask whether he was interested in pursuing his case. When he replied that he was, Zatlin put him in touch with a friend of hers who was a law professor at Columbia University. The law professor, who was also counsel to the Women's Rights Project of the American Civil Liberties Union, was Ruth Bader Ginsburg. She wrote to Wiesenfeld

reasoned that the provision deprived female wage earners of the same degree of protection for their spouses that men receive as a result of their employment, while taxing women at the same rate as men who received the same salary. As in *Frontiero*

and *Wiesenfeld*, such a result was impermissible, at least when it was based on "archaic and overbroad" assumptions regarding the financial roles of men and women. Newly appointed justice John Paul Stevens concurred in the judgment but

Twenty-three years after arguing Stephen Wiesenfeld's case before the Supreme Court, Justice Ginsburg (left) copresided over his son's wedding ceremony. A graduate of Ginsburg's alma mater, Columbia University Law School, Jason (right) attributes his success to his father (center) having stayed home to parent him.

offering her assistance, telling him that she believed that his case raised important constitutional issues and would go to the Supreme Court.

The letter was prescient. The case was not only heard by the Court but resulted in a unanimous decision ruling the gender distinctions in the federal law unconstitutional. That outcome permitted Wiesenfeld to collect the survivor's benefits that helped him to stay home and raise his then three-year-old son.

Wiesenfeld's and Ginsburg's efforts paid off, and not only by establishing one of the most important decisions in the area of sex discrimination. Jason Wiesenfeld, who received a law degree from

Ginsburg's alma mater, Columbia University, and is now a lawyer in New York City, cites his father and Ginsburg as two of the most influential people in his life. "The decision enabled my father to stay home and raise me," he says. "He was there when I came home from school. He helped me do my homework, and would chaperone trips with other children's mothers. He was there for me, and I guess that is why I am where I am today."

The bonds forged between the father, son, and lawyer as a result of the case are still strong. When Jason was married in 1998, Justice Ginsburg, who had stayed in touch with Stephen and Jason over the years, copresided at the ceremony.

argued that the provision discriminated against the surviving male spouses rather than the deceased female wage earners because he did not consider Social Security benefits to be part of the working women's compensation.

Four justices dissented on the ground that the provision in *Goldfarb* was related to a valid governmental interest in administrative convenience. Indeed, the government claimed that a decision in favor of Goldfarb would cost the government

$500 million in the first year in payments to men like Goldfarb. The dissent also noted that, unlike the provision in *Wiesenfeld*—which unconditionally denied all benefits to surviving fathers with minor children based solely on the father's gender—the provision at issue in *Goldfarb* merely placed a requirement of proof of dependency on widowers that it did not impose on widows.

For the dissent, the issue in *Goldfarb* was no longer whether female wage earners were denied the same benefits as males as held in *Wiesenfeld*, because now they refused to see Social Security benefits as a form of compensation for work. Instead, the dissenters focused on whether the government was justified in dispensing with the administrative burden of determining financial need in the case of widows but not widowers. According to the dissent, "the dependency test was not imposed on widows, apparently on a . . . belief that the actual rate of dependency was sufficiently high that a requirement of proof would create more administrative expense that it would save in the award of benefits."

Justice Brennan's plurality opinion held, however, that under the intermediate scrutiny standard of review adopted by the Court that term in *Craig v. Boren*, saving the government the time and expense of determining dependency by widows was not a sufficiently important government interest to justify a gender-based distinction. And in his concurrence Justice Stevens did not believe Congress had any such purpose of saving money. He pointed out that the government actually paid $750 million per year extra to widows who had not depended on their husbands and that this cost was much higher than any money the government saved by not screening women for dependency. As he put it, the government "has paid a truly staggering price for a relatively modest administrative gain."

Nor did Stevens believe that Congress intended to redress past economic discrimination

against widows, because the widows who got a break compared to the widowers were those women who had not depended on their husbands. Financially independent widows automatically got the Social Security payments that were denied to financially independent widowers. Stevens summed up: "It is fair to infer that habit, rather than analysis or actual reflection, made it seem acceptable to equate the terms 'widow' and 'dependent surviving spouse.' . . . I am therefore persuaded that this discrimination against a group of males is merely the accidental byproduct of a traditional way of thinking about females."

Three years after *Goldfarb*, the Court decided yet another case involving a statutory provision that discriminated between working women and men in awarding benefits to their surviving spouses. In *Wengler v. Druggists Mutual Insurance Co.*, the Court struck down a Missouri workers' compensation statute that denied a widower benefits upon a working wife's death unless he proved dependence on his wife's earnings, but granted benefits to widows even when they had not depended on their husbands. Applying the intermediate scrutiny standard, a more unified Court held that the discriminatory provision was unconstitutional. The Court again rejected the claimed justification for the provision's disparate treatment of men and women—that it was more efficient to presume dependence in the case of wives because many more wives were dependent than were husbands—as unsubstantiated.

This time, the Court returned even more strongly to the theme it announced in *Wiesenfeld*, and at which even the dissenters hinted in *Goldfarb*. The Missouri statute, it held, constituted both "discrimination against working women" and "discriminat[ion] against men who survive their employed wives dying in work-related accidents." Because the *Wengler* benefits were "workers' compensation," three of the four *Goldfarb* dissenters who had not viewed the Social Security benefits in that case as work compensation could return to their *Wiesenfeld* position. Therefore this time seven justices voted against sex-based laws that harmed both working wives and their survivor husbands.

Stevens again concurred in the judgment that the law was unconstitutional, but reasoned that it discriminated only against men. Rehnquist, the lone dissenter this time, again said that the legislative distinction between widows and widowers was a permissible exercise of administrative economy.

Like *Wiesenfeld*, the results in *Goldfarb* and *Wengler* revealed that even when a statutory provision appeared to favor some women, it would not pass constitutional muster if it arbitrarily distinguished between husbands and wives on the basis of unsubstantiated assumptions about their financial dependency on one another. The cases again illustrated that both working women, whose tax dollars did not procure for them the same amount of protection as those of male workers, and surviving husbands, who did not receive the same benefits as surviving widows, could be harmed by gender-based distinctions designed to "protect" women (but that did not take into account the many different lives women could lead).

COMPENSATING WOMEN FOR PAST DISCRIMINATION

Kahn v. Shevin, 416 U.S. 351 (1974)

Califano v. Webster, 430 U.S. 313 (1977)

Clearly, the Court was becoming increasingly less tolerant of gender-based classifications that disadvantaged female wage earners, even when the statutes had originally been intended to protect women who were financially dependent on men. But, at the same time, the Court also showed a tolerance for so-called "benign" distinctions intended to benefit financially dependent women, as long as they posed no disadvantage to working women. This was particularly true in cases involving laws that could be characterized as "compensatory" in nature, because they were intended to, or had the effect of, remedying past economic discrimination against women.

Kahn v. Shevin and *Califano v. Webster* are examples of what are sometimes referred to as "remedial" or "compensatory" cases. In the former, the Court upheld a Florida state tax law provision that provided a $500 property tax exemption for widows (as well as for the blind and totally disabled), but not for widowers.

When Mel Kahn, a widower, applied for and was denied the exemption because he was a man, he challenged the constitutionality of the provision under the Equal Protection Clause of the Fourteenth Amendment. The lower state court, citing the Supreme Court's decision in *Frontiero*, held that the provision—which had existed in some form since 1885—was unconstitutional because it discriminated on the basis of sex. The Florida Supreme Court, applying the minimal rational basis test, reversed the lower court's decision, finding the provision valid because it was fairly related to its purpose of reducing the economic disparity between men and women that results from women's lower wages in the workforce. (The lower wages made it more difficult for women to pay taxes.)

Ginsburg, then counsel to the ACLU's Women's Rights Project, argued Kahn's case before the Supreme Court. She criticized the assumption that all widows were in need of tax relief on the ground that "labeling any group, racial, ethnic, or sexual, as needy persons" created harmful stereotypes. "An income test," she argued, "is readily available to a Legislature that wishes to distinguish on the basis of need, and an immutable birth characteristic should be irrelevant for general law

Dade Widower's Tax Plea Rejected by Supreme Court

Mel Kahn

Florida widower Mel Kahn lost his 1974 sex discrimination suit against the state for denying widowers a $500 property-tax exemption extended to widows, the blind, and the totally disabled. The law was intended to cushion the financial impact on wives of losing a husband.

purposes." The Court, however, decided to affirm the Florida Supreme Court's decision.

In writing the majority opinion, Justice William O. Douglas, who was raised by a widowed and impoverished mother, backed away from the heightened review for which he had voted in *Frontiero*, in part because he thought the lowest standard of review should apply to tax law. He also distinguished *Kahn* from *Frontiero* by noting that the earlier case had involved a statute that denied female workers benefits received by male workers, and had even relied on past discrimination as a justification for heaping an additional economic disadvantage on working women. In contrast, the justice described the tax law in *Kahn* as intended to cushion the impact of spousal loss for "the sex for which that loss imposes a disproportionately heavy burden." He also emphasized that the government had denied benefits in *Frontiero* "solely" for administrative convenience, and that there had been no remedial purpose for rectifying past discrimination in that case.

Douglas began his opinion by affirming that "[t]here can be no dispute that the financial difficulties confronting the lone woman in Florida or in any other State exceed those facing the man. Whether from overt discrimination or the socialization process of a male-dominated culture, the job market is inhospitable to the woman seeking any but the lowest paid jobs." Noting the statistical evidence of women receiving substantially lower compensation (57.9 percent of the median for men in 1972), Douglas agreed with the Florida Supreme Court that the statute in question had a "fair and substantial" relation to the "object of the legislation," which the justice presumed to be the redress of such inequities. The fact that the statute had been enacted almost a hundred years earlier, and was more likely intended to protect women from their inability to provide for themselves than to repay them for the injustices they had suffered as women, did not enter into the Court's analysis.

Kahn was decided before the Court announced its intermediate level of scrutiny for gender-based classifications in *Craig v. Boren*. The dissents, which argued for a higher level of review than the minimal rational basis test applied by the majority, thus reflected the still unsettled state of the law at the time. Justice Brennan, joined by Justice Thurgood Marshall, found the intent to redress past economic discrimination in *Kahn* to be a compelling governmental purpose, but did not endorse the way the Florida legislature had chosen to achieve it. His dissent intimated that if the statute had limited the tax break only to widows who actually suffered financial hardship when their husbands died, they would have found the connection more compelling. By giving the break to "financially independent heiress[es]," the law was overinclusive as to its purpose of helping needy widows, and was therefore unfair. Justice Byron R. White, in a separate dissent, agreed with Ginsburg's arguments and expressed his disapproval of legislating by sex classification rather than by determining who, widow or widower, was poor enough to warrant tax relief.

In *Reed* and *Frontiero,* the Court had demonstrated a growing intolerance of statutes that disadvantaged women: an attitude brought about, no doubt, by the dramatic changes in society caused by the large numbers of women entering the workforce (see p. 39). In *Kahn,* the Court showed a reluctance to abandon the gender-based classifications that benefited, rather than disadvantaged, women. But, in its readiness to ascribe progressive purposes to a ninety-year-old statute, the Court was grasping at ways to distinguish laws based on debilitating paternalistic attitudes from those based on a genuine desire to recognize past injustice against women and to help integrate them into the larger society on equal terms with men.

By the time the Court decided *Califano v. Webster* three years later, intermediate scrutiny of gender-based classifications had taken hold, and the Court had invalidated several more laws that were detrimental to female wage earners. Nonetheless, in *Webster,* the Court again upheld a statute that benefited women on the ground that it was compensating them for past economic discrimination, and, unlike the laws in *Wiesenfeld v. Goldfarb,* did not penalize any women wage earners. Nor did the Court find any evidence in *Webster* of "casual assumptions that women are 'the weaker sex' or are more likely to be child-rearers or dependents."

The case involved a provision of the Social Security Act that permitted female wage earners to exclude three more of their low-earning years than male wage earners from the calculation of their "average monthly wage," upon which old-age benefits would be based. This permitted female workers to have a slightly higher average monthly wage than they otherwise would, and than did male workers with the same wage history. In turn, that gave women higher old-age benefits than men with the same salary received.

Ironically, Congress did not choose the more favorable benefit formula as a way to raise women's old-age benefits, but instead was concerned that employers would not hire older women. (Congress would not outlaw sex discrimination in employment until 1964.) So in 1956 Congress simply lowered the retirement age at which women could collect old-age benefits from age sixty-five (until then the age for both men and women) to sixty-two, thus allowing women at least to collect a government benefit if employers discriminated against them by refusing to employ them. Because the formula for calculating benefits was based on "retirement age," the new age in turn produced the three-year difference between men and women in low-earning years that could be excluded from the calculation of their benefits, giving women the higher-retirement benefit.

Even more ironically, the Court did not mention that in 1956 some women's organizations actually opposed lowering the retirement age for women. They feared that employers would use the reduction as an excuse to refuse to hire women at age sixty-two, or to force them into retirement. Forced unemployment deprived them of salaries that men their age could earn and also reduced the amount of their monthly Social Security check from what it would have been if they could have worked for another three years.

As in *Kahn,* the Court found the statute to be remedial in nature, and therefore permissible. The Court noted that the legislative history of the provision, which was adopted in 1956, unambiguously reflected that its purpose was to "compensate for past employment discrimination." The majority distinguished the clearly defined remedial purposes of the provision in *Webster* from the "accidental byproduct" of stereotypes about women and their role in society that had characterized the provisions the Court struck down in *Wiesenfeld* and *Goldfarb.* The Court cautioned that "the mere recitation of a benign, compensatory purpose is not an automatic shield which protects against any inquiry into the actual purposes underlying a statutory scheme." In other words, schemes that had not actually been enacted to remedy past discrimination, or schemes that in practice penalized women wage earners, would be struck down.

Chief Justice Warren E. Burger, in a concurrence joined by Justices Potter Stewart, Harry A. Blackmun, and William H. Rehnquist, argued that the distinction between the "offensive" provisions struck down in cases such as *Wiesenfeld,* and the "benign" provisions upheld in cases such as *Kahn,* was overly subjective. Instead, the concurring justices based their decision to uphold the statute in *Kahn* on the same administrative convenience rationale made by Rehnquist in his dissent in *Goldfarb.*

It is worth noting that Congress had already revoked the different retirement age provision in question in 1972, five years before the Court decided *Webster.* To the Court, the fact that Congress had determined that the provision was no longer necessary did not undermine the argument that the provision had been related to the important governmental interest of redressing past discrimination, and may have in fact strengthened it. The Court suggested that Congress may have decided that, in light of other, more direct legislative reforms prohibiting sex discrimination against women in the workforce, the provision at issue had become unnecessary.

HARMFUL STEREOTYPES

Stanton v. Stanton, 421 U.S. 7 (1975)

Orr v. Orr, 440 U.S. 268 (1979)

Califano v. Westcott, 443 U.S. 76 (1979)

Kirchberg v. Feenstra, 450 U.S. 455 (1981)

In the late 1970s, the Court struck down a number of statutes that reflected and reinforced stereotypical attitudes about men as wage earners and women as care givers. In particular, laws that codified the role of men as economic heads of the family were increasingly suspect, whether they pertained to age-of-maturity laws, payment of alimony, unemployment benefits, or control over marital property such as the family home. These stereotypes were damaging to women because they effectively kept them in an inferior economic "caste" or class. And even the laws that seemed to benefit some women actually reinforced stereotypes, harming them further.

Age of Majority: Twenty-one for Boys, Eighteen for Girls

In *Stanton v. Stanton,* the Court was confronted with a Utah coming-of-age statute that not only reflected society's long-held belief that women were financially dependent on men, but also made that dependence more likely. When Thelma and James Stanton divorced in 1960, James was ordered to pay child support for their two children, eight-year-old Sherri and five-year-old Rick. When Sherri turned eighteen, James canceled his child support payments for her, although he did not stop supporting Rick when he turned the same age. He argued that his financial obligations to his daughter had ceased, citing a Utah law that provided that girls became adults at age eighteen, but boys not until age twenty-one.

Sherri's mother, Thelma, challenged the constitutionality of the Utah statute that provided different ages of majority for men and women. She asked the court to order Sherri's father to continue supporting his daughter until she turned twenty-one. The Utah Supreme Court upheld that statute, stating that there was a rational basis for the classification: namely, that men are generally required to provide for their families, and therefore young men need more education than young women—who, the court said, tend to mature faster and marry earlier.

Thelma Stanton appealed to the U.S. Supreme Court in 1975. Justice Harry A. Blackmun wrote the majority opinion for the Court striking down the law specifying a greater age of majority for boys than for girls as a violation of the Equal Protection Clause of the Fourteenth Amendment. Justice Rehnquist dissented, reasoning that it was not necessary to reach the issue and better to avoid deciding it.

The Court did not disagree with the Utah Supreme Court that, in general, men were more likely to be the main providers for their families and therefore needed a college education, or that women tended to mature and marry earlier. However, while that may still have been generally true, the Court acknowledged that times were changing: "No longer is the female destined solely for the home and the rearing of the family, and the male only for the marketplace and the world of ideas." The Court took notice of the "presence of women in business, in the professions, in government and, indeed, in all walks of life where education is a desirable, if not always a necessary, antecedent." The Court concluded that "[i]f a specified age of minority is required for the boy in order to assure him parental support while he attains his education and training, so, too, it is for the girl."

Furthermore, the Court recognized not only that stereotypes exist and can be unfair, but also that the law itself can play a role in creating and perpetuating the conditions that underlie the stereotypes: "To distinguish between [the genders] on educational grounds is to be self-serving: if the female is not to be supported so long as the male, she hardly can be expected to attend school as long as he does, and bringing her education to an end earlier coincides with the role-typing society has long imposed." The Court left for the Utah state courts the question of whether eighteen or twenty-one was the appropriate age of majority, but held that it must be the same for both boys and girls.

Alimony for Men, Too

Four years later, the Court was again confronted with legislation based on the same stereotypes about the respective economic and social roles of men and women, but this time the legislation at least nominally benefited, rather than hurt, women. In *Orr v. Orr*, the Court confronted an Alabama law that required husbands, but not wives, to pay alimony to a needy spouse in the event of a divorce.

An ex-husband who had fallen more than $3,000 behind in his alimony payments, William Orr challenged the Alabama statute in 1976 when he found himself dragged into court by his former wife, Lillian, in a contempt proceeding. When they divorced two years earlier, Orr, a business executive, had agreed to pay his ex-wife $1,240 a month in alimony.

When the case reached the Supreme Court in 1979, the justices ruled in William's favor: "There is no question but that [he] bears a burden he would not bear were he female." A six-vote majority by Justice Brennan held that " 'the old notion' that 'generally it is the man's primary responsibility to provide a home and its essentials,' can no longer justify a statute that discriminates on the basis of gender." Clearly, the law "carries with it the baggage of sexual stereotypes."

On its face, the statute discriminated against men, not women, because it required them to support their financially needy ex-wives, while women were not expected to do the same for their financially needy ex-husbands. The statute took no note of the individual circumstances of a particular marriage, but instead categorically designated men as economic providers and women as economic dependents. Referring to *Stanton v. Stanton* and *Craig v. Boren*, the Court held that the purpose of designating and reinforcing men as financial heads of households, and women as financial dependents, was constitutionally impermissible.

U.S. Supreme Court declares alimony law discriminatory

The Court then considered two other possible objectives of the state. It accepted as an important goal the compensation of women for the past discrimination they had suffered in the context of their marriages. This discrimination, Lillian's attorney argued, has "left [women] unprepared to fend for themselves in the working world following divorce." The Court also agreed with Alabama that the statute fulfilled another important objective: protecting "needy" spouses.

But instead of analyzing whether "female sex" was an accurate proxy for "needy spouse" or for "persons who had suffered discrimination," the Court took a different approach. Because Alabama already held individualized hearings to determine the extent, if any, of a woman's financial need or past discrimination, it could easily expand the inquiry at such hearings to cover both spouses. Such a gender-neutral scheme, the Court suggested, would accomplish the goal of protecting needy or discriminated against women without presupposing that all women are dependent on their husbands. It would also enable Alabama to protect financially dependent men. Finally, it would not help women who were the least needy—those who could afford to pay alimony to their husbands.

Once again, the Court cautioned that laws can both reflect and perpetuate stereotypes. Brennan concluded his majority opinion by noting that "[l]egislative classifications which distribute benefits and burdens on the basis of gender carry the inherent risk of reinforcing stereotypes about the 'proper place' of women and their need for special protection." Therefore, he said, "even statutes

Businessman William Orr refused to pay alimony to his ex-wife, Lillian Orr (pictured), on the ground that Alabama law discriminated against men in providing for alimony payments to women only. The Supreme Court overturned the law in 1979, holding that ex-husbands have alimony rights as well.

purportedly designed to compensate for and ameliorate the effects of past discrimination must be carefully tailored."

The Court's opinion in *Orr* recalled the struggle the Court had faced earlier when it confronted other gender-based statutory distinctions that seemed to benefit at least some women. In *Kahn v. Shevin* and *Califano v. Webster,* the Court upheld such statutes; in *Weinberger v. Wiesenfeld* and *Califano v. Goldfarb,* it struck them down. Now the Court seemed more assured than in the past in reaching the conclusion that despite the fact that such laws might nominally benefit some women, the outdated stereotypes upon which they rested could not support the use of gender-based distinctions because of their harmful effects.

As with some of those earlier cases, *Orr* provoked a backlash among women's rights groups who argued that women were losing their privileges. But others were proud of the recognition that many women were capable of earning superior wages. As a practical matter, the Court's ruling had widespread repercussions in moving the law to a gender-neutral position. Ten other states that maintained divorce laws similar to Alabama's were forced to change their laws as a result of the Court's decision. Now courts can require both financially able husbands and wives to pay alimony to needy spouses at divorce. And laws concerning child custody, attorney's fees, and child support arrangements were also considerably affected by the decision as they were reshaped to recognize the new economic and caretaking roles of both men and women in the American family.

Unemployed Fathers, Unemployed Mothers

One of the last cases in which the Court confronted a law premised on the notion that men, rather than women, were likely to be the main wage earners in a family was *Califano v. Westcott.* That case tested the constitutionality of a federal statute enacted in 1968 that provided welfare benefits to families when a father, not a mother, became unemployed.

The Westcotts and Westwoods were two Massachusetts families with infant sons when they sought Aid to Families with Dependent Children, Unemployed Father (AFDC–UF) benefits for their children. Both families were denied aid because wives Cindy Westcott and Susan Westwood, rather than their husbands, had been the family breadwinners before they lost their jobs. Both women's husbands were also unem-

ployed, but neither had sufficient work history (having a job at least one year out of the last four) to entitle them to AFDC benefits. Cindy and Susan met the work history requirements, and were unemployed, but the statute did not provide for benefits to families where the mother, rather than the father, was an unemployed wage earner. In all other respects, both families qualified for aid under the program.

The district court held that the program was unconstitutional to the extent that it denied benefits to the families based solely on the fact that the women, rather than the men, were the otherwise eligible unemployed parents. The federal government appealed to the Supreme Court, which unanimously held the program to be unconstitutional. (The Court was split, however, on the issue of remedies. The majority ruled that the government should immediately grant benefits to the families of unemployed mothers like Westcott and Westwood. Four dissenters argued that it was preferable to stop these financial payments to families with an unemployed father rather than extending them to families with an unemployed mother.)

The government offered two defenses of the statute. First, it insisted that the statute did not discriminate against women as a class because the families that lost benefits each had one wife and one husband, thereby impacting men and women equally. The Court rejected this argument on the basis of *Frontiero, Wiesenfeld,* and *Goldfarb.* In all those cases women wage earners lost benefits for their families. Just as those laws discriminated "against one particular category of family—that in which the female spouse is the wagearner," so too did this law.

Next, the government argued that the statute was related to the important government interest of discouraging fathers from abandoning their children in order to make them eligible for benefits. This problem arose because part of the 1939

AFDC statute provided financial assistance to needy families when a parent deserted the family but not when a parent became unemployed. Out-of-work fathers sometimes deserted their families so that they would have enough money to live on by getting this payment. To counteract those kinds of desertions, Congress started a new program in 1961 for families with an unemployed *parent*. In 1968 Congress changed the law again, this time to limit the benefit specifically to families with an unemployed *father*. When the case came to the Supreme Court in 1979 the government now argued that, because most mothers were not likely to desert their families, there was no need for an AFDC–Unemployed Mother program; such mothers would stay with their children whether their families got the financial payment or not.

The Supreme Court rejected this argument for two reasons. First, it noted that there was no evidence that the gender-based distinction was originally tied to the goal of keeping families together. Rather, it found evidence that the distinction, which was added in 1968, was intended to restrict eligibility and save money. Congress explained that the original purpose of the 1961 law had been to help families whose father had lost his job. But because the 1961 version was gender neutral, it allowed families with a working father and an unemployed mother to receive the government payment. Congress clearly felt that such families did not need benefits, so it changed the law to save money by giving them only to families whose *father* lost his job. The Court noted:

From all that appears, Congress, with an image of the "traditional family" in mind, simply assumed that the father would be the family breadwinner, and that the mother's employment role, if any, would be secondary. In short, the available evidence indicates that the gender distinction was intended to reduce costs and eliminate what was perceived to be a type of superfluous eligibility for AFDC–UF benefits.

It had nothing to do with encouraging fathers not to desert, the Court ruled, and therefore the government's argument to uphold the law because it achieved that purpose had to be rejected.

But even if the law did intend to prevent a father's desertion, it would not achieve that purpose, the Court further held. Why? Because if a working mother lost her job, and the family did not have enough money based on the father's income, he would still have the same incentive to desert the family. Hence, the gender classification was not "substantially related to the achievement of any important and valid legislative goals."

Husband as "Head and Master" of Household

In 1981 the Court was confronted with yet another statute that not only reflected, but also codified, the stereotype of men as "head and master" of their households—this time in the form of a challenge to a Louisiana law that permitted husbands, but not wives, to unilaterally dispose of property owned jointly by the couple. This rule was just like the old coverture laws that gave the husband the sole right to manage or sell his wife's share of any real property, such as a family home her father might have given her. While most states had gradually abolished these rules in the nineteenth and twentieth centuries, Louisiana gave husbands this power into the 1970s.

The case began in 1974, when Joan Feenstra filed criminal charges against her husband, Harold, alleging that he had molested their young daughter. While he was in jail, Harold hired a lawyer, Karl Kirchberg, to help him fight the charges. To guarantee payment of Kirchberg's $3,000 fee, Harold took out a second mortgage on the house he owned with Joan, without telling her. He did not have to; under Louisiana law a husband had exclusive control over the disposition of joint property.

Harold was eventually released from prison after the charges against him were dropped, and after officially separating from his wife he left the state without paying Kirchberg his legal fees. Joan remained in the house. Several months later, Kirchberg informed her of the second mortgage on the house, and threatened to foreclose unless she paid the $3,000 her husband owed him. She refused, and he obtained an order authorizing the local sheriff to seize and sell her home so he could use the profits to obtain his legal fee.

At the same time Kirchberg filed a lawsuit to confirm the legality of the sheriff's order. Joan responded by challenging the constitutionality of the Louisiana law that gave her husband exclusive control of property they owned together.

The district court rejected her complaint, calling the right of husbands to dispose of joint property a "bedrock" of Louisiana property law. The theory behind such statutes, which were still in place in at least eight states, including California, in the mid-1970s, was that if more than one person could sell joint property, the title to the assets could become hopelessly tangled. But there was no question that that one person should be the man; according to the stereotypes underlying the statute, he not only probably paid for the property, but was also best able to make business decisions.

It was a sign of the times that while Joan's appeal was pending, the state legislature repealed the provision. Beginning in 1980 Louisiana required the consent of both spouses to sell or mortgage family homes. However, because the second mortgage had been obtained while the old law was in effect, the change in the law did not help her.

The Fifth Circuit Court of Appeals reversed the district court, and the state of Louisiana, having already repealed its "head and master" statute, decided not to appeal that decision to the Supreme Court. Kirchberg, however, did appeal the decision, which the Court unanimously affirmed.

Applying what was by now a familiar analysis, the Court stated that "[b]y granting the husband exclusive control over the disposition of community property, [the statute] clearly embodies the type of express gender-based discrimination that we have found unconstitutional absent a showing that the classification is tailored to further an important governmental interest." The Court rejected Kirchberg's argument that, because the statute permitted a woman to prevent the unilateral mortgage of her property by her husband by filing a declaration that her consent was needed with the state before the mortgage occurs, the statute was not unconstitutionally discriminatory. Instead, it focused on the fact that Kirchberg could not offer an "exceedingly persuasive justification" for the statute that would overcome the presumption that gender-based distinctions are impermissible. Moreover, the Court noted, the state of Louisiana had withdrawn from the litigation and did not even attempt to defend the already obsolete provision.

With this momentous decision, the long era of women's subjugation in marriage was finally over and women were now fully citizens. The last vestiges of the old male-dominated model of the family had given way to the new, egalitarian family.

 ### The Equal Rights Amendment

Following the voting rights victory of 1920 some former suffragists, particularly from the National Woman's Party, saw full equality before the law as the next battle. They introduced the first Equal Rights Amendment (ERA) to Congress in 1923, providing that "Men and women shall have equal rights throughout the United States and every place subject to its jurisdiction." The bill eventually passed the Senate in 1950 and again in 1953. However, both times it contained the so-called Hayden Rider, which stated that "the provisions

In 1969 members of the National Organization for Women demonstrated outside the White House in support of the Equal Rights Amendment. The House of Representatives passed the proposed amendment in 1971, and the Senate the following year, but the three-quarters majority of the states necessary for ratification was never achieved.

of this article shall not be construed to impair any rights, benefits or exemptions now or hereafter conferred by law upon persons of the female sex." Suspicious of this language, the women's rights movement opposed the bill and it never passed in the House.

Some women's groups also opposed the ERA because they feared it might jeopardize existing labor laws protecting blue-collar women from performing jobs requiring night work, heavy lifting, or long hours. Once these laws began to be invalidated under Title VII of the Civil Rights Act of 1964, which prohibited employment discrimination on account of sex, women's groups and unions changed their minds.

In October 1971 the House finally passed the ERA by a vote of 354–24. On March 22, 1972, the Senate accepted the House version by a vote of

84–8. Its key provision now declared that "equality of rights under the law shall not be denied or abridged by the United States or by any State on account of sex." Hawaii ratified the amendment within hours of Senate approval, and over the next three months nineteen more states followed suit.

Two years later North Dakota became the thirty-fourth state to ratify the ERA. Both political parties endorsed the amendment in the 1976 presidential election. But it was not until the following year that ERA proponents managed to persuade a thirty-fifth state, Indiana, to ratify the amendment. The ERA now needed only three more states to achieve the three-quarters majority necessary for ratification, but its March 1979 deadline was closing in.

Meanwhile, opposition to the ERA had coalesced in the form of an organization, headed by

Phyllis Schlafly, known as STOP ERA. The acronym "STOP" stood for Stop Taking Our Privileges. STOP ERA contended that, rather than providing equality to women, the Equal Rights Amendment would deny them the privileges they enjoyed under current state and federal laws. Schlafly speculated in a 1975 interview with *U.S. News and World Report* that

ERA would take away the right of a young woman to be exempt from the draft and from military-combat duty. It would take away the right of a wife to be supported by her husband and provided with a home by her husband. It would take away the right of a mother to have her minor children supported by the children's father. It would take away the right of a woman who does manual labor to have the benefit of protective labor legislation.

ERA will take away our right to attend single-sex colleges because, by definition, such colleges discriminate [by sex]. It would take away the right to maintain fraternities or sororities on college campuses, because they discriminate on the basis of sex. ERA will most probably legalize homosexual marriages too, and enable these couples to file joint income-tax returns, adopt children and get other rights that now belong to husbands and wives.

In 1977 the National Organization for Women (NOW) led a boycott of states that had not ratified the ERA. Nearly fifty national groups supported this boycott at its peak, but no new states ratified as a result. Missouri, hurt by economic losses stemming from the boycott, responded by suing the organization under federal and state antitrust laws. NOW ultimately prevailed, but the suit drained resources and disrupted its focus.

With ratification stalled at thirty-five states, Rep. Elizabeth Holtzman (D-N.Y.) introduced legislation that would extend the ERA's deadline. Some supporters opposed this move, fearing the momentum for ratification could be lost. Rep. Robert McClory (R-Ill.), an ERA sup-

porter, complained, "It is as if we are in the eighth inning of a baseball game and we are behind. This proposal says we want to add three extra innings. I think that's unwise, because we still may win in the ninth inning." But others felt that, after six years, the momentum for ratification was already gone. In fact, of the twenty-six amendments added to the Constitution between 1791 and 1971, none had required more than four years between submission to the states by Congress and final ratification by three-fourths of the states.

In October 1978, Congress voted to extend the deadline by three years and three months. Idaho and Arizona immediately challenged the constitutionality of this extension. Meanwhile, four states, including Idaho, had rescinded their earlier ratification. A federal court held that the extension was unconstitutional and that Idaho's rescission was valid. The Supreme Court stayed this judgment pending review, and then dismissed the case (*Idaho v. Freeman* [1982]) as moot once the deadline for ratification passed.

Despite the extension, not one more state ratified the ERA, and on June 30, 1982, it died. In November 1983, an attempt to begin the ratification process anew failed by six votes in the House of Representatives.

In their book, *ERA: Postmortem of a Failure*, Edith Mayo and Jerry K. Frye concluded, "The primary failure of the ERA's supporters throughout was their inability to devise effective persuasive appeals that made a clear distinction in the public mind between 'political and legal equality' and 'sexual sameness.'" A typical fear, expressed by one observer, was that the ERA raised "the specter of a halfback sipping tea at a sorority party and a homecoming queen chug-a-lugging at a fraternity beer bust." Arguments that the ERA amounted to an assault on the family, marriage, and children also succeeded. Many states nonetheless passed their own equal rights laws.

SINGLE-SEX SCHOOLS

When Harvard College was founded in 1636 it opened its doors only to male students. For the next two hundred years all colleges and universities in the United States were closed to women. By 1848, when women convened the first Women's Rights Convention in Seneca Falls, New York, they protested this injustice: "[Man] has denied [woman] the facilities for obtaining a thorough education, all colleges being closed against her."

As part of the new women's rights movement, women began to press for the right to receive a college education. But they faced considerable opposition. Some opponents were influenced by Charles Darwin's theory that women's brains were not as advanced as those of men. Dr. Edward H. Clarke, a retired member of Harvard Medical School, wrote a best-selling book in 1881 explaining that girls who studied hard and competed academically with boys would not develop adequate reproductive organs.

In this climate it was not possible to persuade most existing colleges to allow women students. Nor were there any constitutional provisions or laws women could use to force the schools to stop their discrimination. In order to provide women with access to a college education, some women's rights advocates started new and separate higher educational institutions for girls—seminaries at first, and then colleges.

In Mississippi, for example, Sally Reneau started campaigning for a women's college in 1856. By 1870 Mississippi provided some higher education to both sexes, but not until 1882 did the University of Mississippi finally open its doors to women. Two years later, the state established the Mississippi Industrial Institute and College for the Education of White Girls by the State of Mississippi. From the beginning, far more women attended its courses than those of the university, specializing in subjects such as kindergarten teaching, stenography, painting, and needlework—all courses that the school's charter deemed "necessary or proper" for the "girls of the state."

One hundred years later the school became the subject of an important Supreme Court case, *Mississippi University for Women v. Hogan.* By then, however, the educational landscape had greatly changed, thanks to the women's movement of the late 1960s and 1970s. New laws prohibited sex discrimination in education programs, and the Supreme Court had ruled that the Constitution required equal protection for women and men. By the 1970s even all of the Ivy League universities and the U.S. military service academies admitted women on a nondiscriminatory basis. By 1982, when the Court considered the *Hogan* case, very few single-sex schools were still in existence.

A NURSING SCHOOL FOR WOMEN ONLY

Mississippi University for Women v. Hogan,
    458 U.S. 718 (1982)

After the Supreme Court held in the 1950s that racially segregated public schools and universities were inherently discriminatory, another question was still unanswered: Were the remaining single-sex schools unconstitutional as well, or would the Court treat gender differently because gender seg-regated schools, unlike racially segregated schools, were of educational value? Could the doctrine of separate but equal, discredited in the context of race, have validity in the context of gender? Were there innate differences between the sexes that warranted educational methods tailored to their different needs? Or were single-sex schools simply an anachronism, surviving only because of blind adherence to tradition? It took the Court two decades to hold that, while theoretical arguments about the merits of single-sex schooling might be persuasive, in practice the vestiges of publicly funded single-sex education did not provide equal opportunities to men and women.

The first single-sex education case to reach the Supreme Court was brought—like several other landmark gender discrimination cases—by a male plaintiff. In 1979 Joe Hogan, a twenty-five-year-old registered nurse, decided to further his career by earning a bachelor's degree in the field. Luck-ily for him, there was a state-sponsored nursing school right in the town where he lived, Colum-bus, Mississippi. Unluckily, though, the school was part of the Mississippi University for Women (MUW). Established in 1884 and affectionately known as the "W," MUW was the only public

The Mississippi University for Women, established in 1884, was the first state-sponsored all women's university. By the time the Supreme Court forced it to admit male applicants in 1982, the school had become the last of its kind.

single-sex institution in the state. The university rejected Hogan's application to its School of Nursing on the ground that he was a man.

With the help of a young civil rights lawyer named Wilbur O. Colom, Hogan filed suit in district court, arguing that MUW's women-only admissions policy violated the Equal Protection Clause. MUW argued that the state offered two coeducational nursing schools—one in Jackson and one in Hattiesburg—and that Hogan could simply attend one of them. Hogan countered that both of them were over 150 miles away, and that he would have to quit his job, sell his house, and move his family in order to attend.

Four years earlier, the Supreme Court had ruled in *Craig v. Boren* that constitutional gender discrimination claims must be reviewed under a heightened equal protection standard: plaintiffs had to show that the state's discriminatory policy was "substantially related to an important governmental objective." But, for some reason the district court ignored the *Craig* standard, and relied on earlier cases involving single-sex schools that had applied the lenient rational basis test, which merely demanded that the claim be reasonable.

Six months later, the Fifth Circuit Court of Appeals had little difficulty reversing the district court's decision. Noting that the district court had erred in applying the rational basis test, the court of appeals pointed to an even more fundamental problem with the lower court decision. The state could not justify its exclusionary admissions policy with the explanation that, as the district court had phrased it, it was "providing . . . educational opportunities for its female student population." Rather, the state's objective must be to provide educational opportunities for *all* its citizens. "To justify gender-based discrimination in this case," the appeals court concluded, "Mississippi cannot advance a reason that is based on gender."

The appeals court acknowledged that its decision would upset those "who hold dear the continuation of the 'W' as a place for educating the 'girls of the state.'" But "the maintenance of MUW today as the only state-supported single-sex collegiate institution in the State cannot be squared with the Constitution." Although Hogan had asked only that the School of Nursing be opened to men, the appeals court seemed to be saying that the entire university must become coeducational—or that the state must establish an equivalent institution for men.

Armed with the court's order, Hogan enrolled at MUW on August 29, 1981—two days after the university asked the Supreme Court to reverse the appeals court's decision. In its Supreme Court brief, the university raised a new argument: that the maintenance of MUW was "nothing more than educational affirmative action for females."

(Affirmative action in education is the policy of giving preference in university admissions to women and minorities because those groups had previously been restricted from access to higher education.) Thus, the state's objective in operating a single-sex school was not merely to broaden the range of educational opportunities for women: it was to compensate them for past discrimination. Citing "recent scientific studies," the university argued that women who attended all-female colleges were more likely to speak out in class, develop high aspirations, and attain positions of leadership in society. Women's colleges provided female role models because their faculty and administrations were predominantly female, and their curriculums could be tailored to women's special needs and ambitions.

The university also raised the startling argument that Congress, in exempting historically single-sex schools from the reach of Title IX, which was passed by Congress in 1972 to enforce gender equity in schools receiving federal funds—had shown its intent to permit MUW to continue to exclude men. At oral argument, the lawyer for the university, Hunter M. Gholson, explained that he was not actually arguing that Congress had the authority to limit the reach of the Constitution—an argument that had, in any event, been rejected by the Supreme Court in *Marbury v. Madison* in 1803. Rather, he was suggesting that the Court might choose to defer to the views expressed by Congress when interpreting the Constitution.

By five votes to four, the Supreme Court ruled in favor of Hogan. Justice Sandra Day O'Connor—only recently appointed as the first woman justice, and widely perceived as the swing vote in the case—delivered the Court's opinion. Focusing narrowly on the School of Nursing, O'Connor found the university's affirmative action argument unconvincing. Considering that in 1971, when the School of Nursing opened, 98 percent of all registered nurses were female, affirmative action hardly seemed necessary to assist women in gaining entry into the field. On the contrary, the exclusion of men from the nursing school tended to perpetuate the stereotype of nursing as a female profession and keep nurses' wages low. Nor was there any evidence that affirmative action was the actual motivation behind the school's founding, given that the school's 1884 charter defined its purpose as providing "the girls of the state" training in such traditionally female occupations as teaching, bookkeeping, photography, stenography, painting, and needlework.

Furthermore, the university had failed to show that its policy of excluding men was substantially related to its purported goal of compensating women for past discrimination. The fact that MUW permitted men to audit classes, O'Connor wrote, "fatally undermines its claim that women, at least at the School of Nursing, are adversely affected by the presence of men."

In footnotes, O'Connor was careful to limit the reach of the Court's holding. Since Mississippi maintained no all-male college or university, the Court was not faced with the issue of whether "separate but equal" schools would be permissible. And the Court was striking down the single-sex policy only at the School of Nursing, not at the university as a whole.

O'Connor gave short shrift to the university's Title IX argument. She maintained that it was far from clear that Congress had intended to exempt MUW from any constitutional obligation, as opposed to the obligations imposed by Title IX itself. In any event, although the Court sometimes did defer to congressional interpretation, she wrote, "neither Congress nor a State can validate a law that denies the rights guaranteed by the Fourteenth Amendment."

Chief Justice Warren E. Burger and Justice Harry A. Blackmun entered short dissenting opinions, with Burger noting that the Court's ruling would not necessarily apply to an all-female program in a traditionally male field, such as business. Justice Blackmun argued that although the Court purported to write its decision narrowly, it would inevitably jeopardize any public single-sex institution.

Justice Lewis F. Powell Jr., who often wrote the Court's opinions in the area of education, filed a lengthy and vigorous dissent. He characterized the case as one in which an honored tradition—that of single-sex education—was being jettisoned to serve the personal convenience of one man. "[T]here is, of course, no constitutional right to attend a state-supported university in one's home town," he wrote.

It was coeducation, Justice Powell argued, that was the novel idea: single-sex schooling had been the norm throughout much of the country's history. Thousands of women had voluntarily chosen such an environment, Powell maintained, and research showed that students at single-sex colleges exhibited greater academic involvement and self-esteem. This case involved no sex discrimination, Powell said. The state was simply seeking to expand women's choices, and Hogan could gain the education he sought elsewhere in the state. "The Equal Protection Clause," he concluded, "was never intended to be applied to this kind of case."

The practical impact of the *Hogan* decision was slight: while there were, at the time, 118 private women's colleges in the country, only public institutions are subject to the strictures of the Constitution. And the only public women's college other than MUW—Texas Woman's University—had a nursing school that was already coeducational. But O'Connor's opinion was hailed by feminists, who had feared that the Court might use the case to weaken the *Craig v. Boren* standard—or to articulate it in such a way that it could be used to justify policies favoring men. If anything, *Hogan* supported the *Craig* standard by characterizing it as a test that required the state to

In September 1979 twenty-four-year-old Joe Hogan's career seemed to be on a steady uphill climb. Since moving to Columbus, Mississippi, from his home state of Tennessee, he had worked his way up from nursing-home orderly to surgical supervisor at the Golden Triangle Regional Medical Center. In 1974 Hogan had earned a certificate in licensed practical nursing from a local vocational-technical center. After that he had attended Itawamba Junior College, commuting sixty-two miles each way while continuing to hold his full-time job. In May 1979

Hogan received an associate's degree in nursing.

He knew that certain options in the field of medicine were closed to him. His original plan of medical school was not a possibility because of the cost, and the military, where he might have obtained some lesser medical training, was also unavailable because he was blind in one eye. But it was clear that, if he wanted to continue to rise in the nursing profession, further education would be necessary. The trend, he said later, was "to eliminate the two-year nurse and make the four-year degree

Civil rights lawyer Wilbur O. Colom (left) filed a sex discrimination suit on behalf of Joe Hogan (right) after the Mississippi University for Women rejected Hogan's application for admission to its nursing program. Once enrolled, Hogan faced ostracism and ridicule by students and teachers, but he did not drop out until the Supreme Court issued a ruling in the case.

the only professional nurse." Ultimately, he hoped to become a nurse-anesthetist.

The logical next step—and the one that many of his colleagues were taking—was to enroll in the four-year state nursing program that was located right in Columbus. In fact, Hogan had called the school back in 1976, asking about admission. He was told then that his application would be rejected—not because he was not qualified, but because of his gender. The nursing school was part of Mississippi University for Women (MUW), the oldest—and virtually the only remaining—state university in the country that was exclusively for women. So while Hogan's colleagues (almost all of them female) were able to further their careers by attending classes there before or after work, Hogan could not.

Hogan could have enrolled in one of the two co-educational state nursing programs in Mississippi—one in Jackson and one in Hattiesburg—but both were at least 150 miles away. Already having gone through a grueling commute to obtain his associate's degree, he did not relish the idea of another, even more arduous one, not to mention moving. "I'm well known," he said at the time. "I'm respected. I like where I work. And I just don't see the need in having to go 150 miles or more to attend a nursing program when there's one right in my town. . . . I'd have to sell my house. I'd have to move my whole family, my wife, to Jackson. That would be a real extreme hardship on me to have to do that."

So on September 13, 1979, Hogan applied to MUW's School of Nursing. Six days later the university sent him a rejection notice, accompanied by a printed sheet advising him that the school accepted only women and that its exclusionary policy had been approved by the courts. At that point, Hogan began looking for a lawyer.

After discovering that the lawyers were asking for fees he could not afford, he turned to the American Civil Liberties Union, which put him in touch with Wilbur O. Colom, a young lawyer in Columbus who had done some civil rights work. The ACLU agreed to pay Colom's expenses, and Colom—thirty years old and only four years out of

law school—agreed to take the case on a contingency basis. At the time, Colom had no idea whether the case was a winner. Nor did he imagine it was going to the Supreme Court.

Although Hogan lost in the district court, the Fifth Circuit Court of Appeals agreed with him that the university's admissions policy was unconstitutional. MUW immediately appealed the ruling to the Supreme Court, but the university was ordered to admit Hogan pending the high court's decision. On August 24, 1981, amid abundant press coverage, Hogan—accompanied by Colom—arrived at the MUW admissions office and began the process of registering as a student in the School of Nursing. "I feel like I've corrected a great injustice," Hogan told the local newspaper shortly before registering.

He added that he had nothing against single-sex education in principle; he just did not believe it should be state supported. "It's not just women's taxes that are supporting it," he said, "it's men's taxes, too." Nor was he interested in changing any of MUW's cherished traditions, or even its name. "All I care is what the diploma is in," he said. "I don't care what the name of the university on it is."

But fierce defenders of the "W" remained adamantly opposed to Hogan's admission. Even before enrolling, he had been subjected to what the *New York Times* characterized as "bitter ridicule" by students and alumnae of the school.

The president of the alumnae association declared that Hogan's admission was "diametrically opposed to what, for nearly a century, Mississippians have calmly and quietly done well, and that is educate women." The president of the university said that the admission of men "would have a definite adverse impact on what the students who come here can expect."

A traditional ditty at the university (which had been called Mississippi State College for Women, or MSC, until 1973), was rewritten. Called "The Old Maid's Song," the original version had been

(continued)

(continued)

Oh, I'm from MSC, oh, pity me
There's not a boy in the vicinity
And every night at 9 they lock the door
I don't know what the heck I ever came here for.

In a reflection of the prevailing mood on campus, the new rendition was

Oh, I'm from MSC, oh, pity me
There's only Joe in the vicinity
And every day in class he's such a bore
I don't know what the heck he ever came here for.

The ridicule did not abate once Hogan started classes. Hogan (who did not respond to a request for an interview for this book) told Colom that when he sat down in class all the other students would move at least four seats away from him. Even some of the instructors ignored him, he said. Hogan was miserable, but he knew that if he dropped out of MUW before the Supreme Court issued its decision, his case would be thrown out as moot.

"He told me, 'The minute this case comes down, I'm out of here,'" Colom recalls.

Meanwhile, Colom was readying himself for his first Supreme Court oral argument. He had secured the support of the NOW Legal Defense Fund and other feminist groups, arguing that—even though the plaintiff was male—the *Hogan* case could mean "the death of VMI, the Citadel, all those male military schools." Now those groups were trying to persuade Colom, who became eligible to argue in the Supreme Court only one month before the Court heard the case, to step aside and let a more experienced advocate take over. Colom left the decision to Hogan, who insisted that Colom handle the argument.

By this time Colom was well aware of the significance of the case. He "felt that an enormous backlash was under way against women's rights," he later wrote in a *New York Times Magazine* article, and that the Court might undermine constitutional protection against gender discrimination by ruling in favor of the university. What he hoped, he says now, was to push the Supreme Court to be even less tolerant of such discrimination than it had been in the past.

Even so, he says, he "wasn't terribly nervous." While a student at Antioch Law School in Washington, D.C., he had worked as an intern in the Office of the Administrative Assistant to Chief Justice Warren E. Burger, and so had some inkling of what went on behind the scenes. "I'd heard the justices complain about lawyers just reading their notes," he says, so his strategy was to be as conversational as possible—while also being so well prepared that he could cite a specific page number in the record in answer to a justice's question.

When the decision came down on July 1, 1982—just one day after the time limit for the passage of the Equal Rights Amendment had expired—Colom and his associates brought out champagne and "toasted the women of the feminist movement." Hogan celebrated in his own way: he dropped out of MUW after completing his first year there. Now reportedly working as a nurse in Louisiana, he has avoided any publicity associated with the case.

"I did not go after this to make a name for myself," he told the Columbus newspaper at the time of his enrollment at MUW. "I just wanted an education."

As for MUW, immediately after the Supreme Court issued its decision President Strobel announced that the school would abide by the Court's decision. Nevertheless, he said, MUW would continue "its central mission of providing excellence in educational opportunities for women." Although the Court's opinion was confined to the nursing school, ultimately the entire university was opened to men. In 1999 the nursing school remained overwhelmingly female, with only 15 male students out of a total enrollment of 221. But many young men have benefited from Hogan's courageous lawsuit: the student population at the university as a whole was almost one fifth male. Nevertheless, the name of the school remains unchanged.

show an "exceedingly persuasive justification" for discrimination on the basis of gender.

WOMEN AS CITIZEN-SOLDIERS

United States v. Virginia, 518 U.S. 515 (1996)

(This case is also discussed at length in Chapter 3, p. 55.)

In the wake of the Supreme Court's decision in *Mississippi University for Women v. Hogan*, at least one other public single-sex institution undertook an internal review to determine whether to open its doors to all applicants, regardless of gender. The Board of Visitors of the Virginia Military Institute (VMI)—an all-male institution that turns out tough citizen-soldiers—appointed a Mission Study Committee in October 1983, a little over a year after the *Hogan* decision came down. The committee finally concluded in May 1986 that VMI should continue the admissions policy—excluding women—it had maintained since its founding in 1839. Although the committee revealed little about how it reached the decision, its report focused primarily on the supposed difficulty of attracting female applicants.

But the committee misread the tenor of the times. Between 1988 and 1990 the school—while keeping its all-male policy—received inquiries about admission from 347 young women. Ultimately, in 1990 the United States Department of Justice sued VMI on behalf of one young woman who alleged that VMI's male-only admissions policy was in violation of the Equal Protection Clause of the Constitution.

In some respects, the case was strikingly similar to *Hogan*. Just as MUW and its School of Nursing had reflected a traditional, stereotypical view of "women's work," opponents argued, so too was VMI rooted in a stereotypical conception

of toughness, physical stamina, and military ability as exclusively male traits. The school's argument against admitting women was that the unique benefits for men of its demanding military-style "adversative system" would be lost if women were included. The adversative approach included demeaning treatment, lack of privacy, physical harassment, and exercises such as scaling a muddy twenty-foot hill.

From the founding of the University of Virginia in 1819 until well after the Civil War, the state had excluded women from all its universities and colleges; by the mid-1970s all of Virginia's fifteen institutions of higher learning except VMI were coeducational. Thus, as in *Hogan*, Virginia offered no parallel institution that was exclusively for women. That situation, however, was soon to change. When the case reached the Fourth Circuit Court of Appeals, the court held that VMI's exclusion of women did violate the Constitution. But the court suggested that the state could choose among three options: require VMI to open its doors to women, let the school go private and thus forgo state funds, or establish an equivalent institution for women.

After consulting with experts in the field of women's education, Virginia chose the last option and established the Virginia Women's Institute for Leadership (VWIL). The institute, housed at the private, all-female Mary Baldwin College, made no attempt to duplicate the VMI experience. Instead, the experts—drawn from Mary Baldwin faculty and staff—created a more nurturing, cooperative environment that they said was more appropriate for the education of women and the development of their self-esteem. Instead of living in barracks, VWIL students were housed in ordinary Mary Baldwin dorms. And, although the program was supplemented with an ROTC program, self-defense and self-assertiveness training, and leadership courses, the curriculum consisted primarily of regular Mary Baldwin classes.

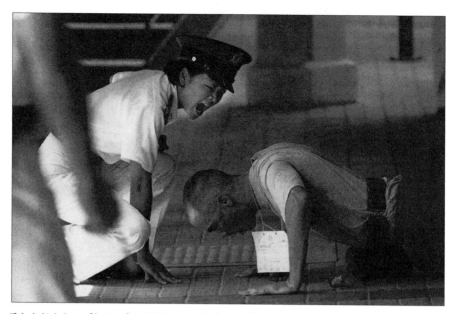

"I don't think the rats [freshmen] are thinking about the fact that I'm a woman," remarked Mia Utz, one of two women to transfer to Virginia Military Institute in 1999 and join the elite upperclass. "They are thinking that I'm an upperclassman and I'm getting in their faces."

The lower courts accepted VWIL as an appropriate substitute for VMI, but the Supreme Court was unconvinced. In a decision written by Justice Ruth Bader Ginsburg, seven members of the Court held that VMI's male-only policy violated the Equal Protection Clause, and that the establishment of VWIL did not remedy the violation. The state had failed to demonstrate an "exceedingly persuasive justification" for its discrimination, Justice Ginsburg wrote—elevating a phrase highlighted in *Hogan* to what Justice Antonin Scalia, in dissent, claimed was a new constitutional standard.

VMI argued that single-sex education provided important benefits, and that its objective in limiting enrollment to men was to diversify educational approaches within the state. But—employing an even more skeptical analysis than it had trained on MUW's affirmative action justification in *Hogan*—the Court found that history did not support VMI's diversity argument. Rather, at the time of VMI's founding, "higher

education . . . was considered dangerous for women" and women were barred from admission based on notions about their "proper place." And while VMI might have broadened the educational choices open to men, it did nothing to expand the choices for women.

VMI also argued that admitting women would inevitably lead to the dismantling of its adversative system, since most women would neither choose, nor thrive under, such a system. But Justice Ginsburg dismissed this argument as one in a long series of "self-fulfilling prophecies" used to deny women access to such professions as law and medicine. The question was not whether most women would choose to attend VMI, but whether it was constitutionally permissible to exclude those women—however few—who were willing and able to undergo the rigors of its traditional system.

As for VWIL, its cooperative, nurturing approach did nothing for those women who wanted to attend VMI precisely in order to experience its adversative method. More important, VWIL was vastly inferior to VMI in terms of faculty, student body, course offerings, military program, facilities, alumni contacts, endowment, and prestige. Much of the history of the Constitution, Justice Ginsburg concluded, "is the story of the extension of constitutional rights and protections to people once ignored or excluded." Just as the country had learned to broaden its comprehension of "We the People," so VMI would have to adjust its conception of the "citizen-soldiers" it strove to produce to include women. (African American cadets had gained admittance in 1968.)

In a vehement echo of now retired justice Lewis F. Powell Jr.'s dissent in *Hogan,* Justice Scalia denounced the majority opinion as a death sentence for the tradition of single-sex education. Not only did it signal the end of public single-sex institutions, Justice Scalia wrote, but even private single-sex schools were now threatened. In Justice Scalia's view, the majority opinion had declared gender discrimination to be as "suspect" as discrimination on the basis of race. The Court had already held that governmental support of racially segregated schools violated the Constitution. Justice Scalia could see no way to distinguish single-sex schools, under the terms of the majority opinion. And, because government support of private education is so pervasive, the withdrawal of government support from single-sex private schools would inevitably lead to their extinction.

Justice Scalia found the majority opinion "especially regrettable" because, in recent years, experts had been increasingly supportive of the view that single-sex education provided significant benefits for both sexes. He cited the case of Detroit, where the school board had announced a program to establish three boys-only schools for inner-city youth—only to abandon the plan after it was met with a lawsuit. "Today's opinion," Justice Scalia wrote, "assures that no such experiment will be tried again."

While the Detroit schools opened their doors to both boys and girls, just a few months after the VMI decision was announced an experimental school for girls began operation. In the fall of 1996 the Young Women's Leadership School (YWLS)—a public school in the East Harlem section of New York City—enrolled its inaugural class of fifty seventh-grade girls. Conceived by private philanthropists but funded by the city, the school's objective was to provide disadvantaged black and Hispanic girls with a supportive environment in which they could flourish academically and emerge as self-confident, independent learners and potential leaders. The curriculum emphasized math and science—fields in which females have historically lagged behind males—and the teachers used strategies that have been shown to work well with girls.

As in Detroit, the school was challenged almost immediately: the New York chapters of the National Organization for Women and the American Civil Liberties Union filed an administrative complaint with the United States Department of Education, charging that the school's gender-based admissions policy violated both Title IX and the Fourteenth Amendment. With the complaint still under consideration, YWLS has continued operation and has expanded to the twelfth grade.

Legal commentators are already speculating about how the Supreme Court would rule on the case. Because YWLS has a true compensatory purpose and is not rooted in nineteenth-century gender stereotypes, the Court might distinguish it from both VMI and MUW and allow the school to continue operation. Or, following its logic in VMI, the Court might rule that because some boys might benefit from the educational methods employed by the school, boys cannot be categorically excluded. Similarly, the Court might rule that there is a nondiscriminatory way to achieve the goal of educating girls in math and science—such as training teachers and boys in coeducational classes to encourage girls to speak up more. On the other hand, the Court might also be swayed by recent research showing that girls, but not boys, benefit from single-sex education. Alternatively, the Court might reason that YWLS is simply creating a new stereotype of girls unable to stand up to male competition, and that upholding single-sex schooling for girls but not boys violates the principle of equal treatment established by the Court in the 1970s.

In any event, it seems that the last word has not yet been spoken on the issue of single-sex education. The YWLS case—or something like it—will most likely test the limits of the Court's pronouncements in this area at some point in the future.

Gender Equity in Education: Title IX of the Education Act Amendments of 1972

The primary statutory tool for enforcing gender equity in education is Title IX of the Education Act Amendments of 1972, commonly referred to simply as Title IX. Enacted at a time when women were seeking to replicate some of the gains that African Americans and other minorities had achieved through the civil rights movement, Title IX was closely modeled on Title VI of the Civil Rights Act of 1964. Title VI had banned racial or ethnic discrimination by any program receiving federal financial assistance. In 1970, when the House Special Subcommittee on Education and Labor began holding hearings on discrimination against women, the original proposal was simply to add the word "sex" to the list of discriminatory criteria prohibited by Title VI of the 1964 act. But because testimony at the subcommittee's hearings focused largely on the prevalence of sex discrimination in education, the proposal that emerged—and which ulti-

mately became Title IX—was limited to education. The statute provides that "[n]o person . . . shall, on the basis of sex, be excluded from participation in, be denied the benefits of, or be subjected to discrimination under any education program or activity receiving Federal financial assistance."

The Equal Protection Clause of the Constitution also prohibits gender discrimination in education, but the Constitution applies only to actions taken by the government itself—in this case, to public or state schools. Title IX covers private educational institutions as well. But because the federal government has no constitutional authority to regulate education directly, Title IX's ban on discrimination is tied to the provision of federal funds: if a school discriminates on the basis of sex, it risks losing any federal financing it receives. And if a school receives no federal money, Title IX does not apply. But federal aid to education is so pervasive that only a small number of schools fall outside the reach of the statute. In a 1984 case, *Grove City College v. Bell,* the Supreme Court held that even federal grants to individual students constitute aid to the college they attend.

Congress placed the responsibility for enforcing Title IX with the Department of Education's Office of Civil Rights (OCR). The OCR resolves complaints from individuals, reviews compliance plans submitted by institutions, and seeks termination of federal funds to noncomplying schools. The statute expressly gives the federal government authority to bring legal actions against such schools. In addition, the Supreme Court has interpreted the act to allow private individuals to sue, and not just for the termination of federal funds but for damages and injunctive relief.

The area of education where Title IX has clearly had the largest impact is athletics. The effect of the statute was immediate and dramatic: while only 7.4 percent of high school athletes were female in 1970, by 1978 that number had risen to almost 32 percent. Title IX has required schools to equalize the resources they devote to girls' and boys' teams, and in some cases to create new girls' teams or integrate existing all-boys' teams. So close is the identification between the statute and the idea of gender equity in sports that a women's athletic wear company has chosen to call itself "Title IX Sports."

Regulations implemented by the Department of Education under Title IX have also barred discrimination against pregnant students, requiring schools to include them in regular classes if that is where they desire to be. Originally, the department also promulgated a regulation prohibiting discriminatory dress codes, but only one case—brought by a boy who objected to a hair-length rule—was decided under the regulation before it was rescinded by the Reagan administration. More recently, the Supreme Court has held that Title IX encompasses sexual harassment claims, and that in certain circumstances a school board may be held liable when a teacher or fellow student sexually harasses a student.

As for discrimination in admission to educational institutions, the major Supreme Court cases have been decided under the Equal Protection Clause. While Title IX has some application in that area, the reach of the statute is specifically limited to the admissions policies of "institutions of vocational education, professional education, and graduate higher education, and to public institutions of undergraduate higher education"—thereby exempting elementary and secondary schools and private colleges.

The statute also provides an exemption for any public undergraduate institution "that traditionally and continually from its establishment has had a policy of admitting only students of one sex." As the Supreme Court pointed out in *Mississippi University for Women v. Hogan,* however, Congress cannot authorize a discriminatory practice that violates the Constitution. And as a result of the Supreme Court's constitutional rulings on public single-sex colleges, this last exemption has turned out to be an empty one: there are no longer any traditionally single-sex public colleges to take advantage of it.

6

DIFFERENT TREATMENT OF MEN AND WOMEN

As previous chapters have shown, since 1971 the Supreme Court has struck down a host of state and federal laws that discriminated against women and men in violation of the Equal Protection Clause. At the same time, however, the Court has also permitted the unequal treatment of men and women in three key areas: the military, parenting outside marriage, and consensual sexual relations among teenagers.

According to the laws that the Court upheld as constitutional, women have fewer military obligations than men, unwed fathers have weaker rights to their children than unwed mothers, and only teenage boys, not teenage girls, can be prosecuted for consensual sex with a minor.

Perhaps because each of these areas reflected long-standing and deeply entrenched views of appropriate behavior for men and boys versus women and girls, the Court has allowed certain laws to stand without applying serious scrutiny. In cases dealing with these issues, the Court employed an altogether different test than the heightened scrutiny standard adopted in *Craig v. Boren* in 1976 (see p. 45) and further advanced by the Virginia Military Institute decision in 1996. Justices who wrote majority decisions in cases striking down sex-discriminatory laws under the

Craig v. Boren standard often became dissenters in these other cases, and vice versa.

At the beginning of the twenty-first century, however, important new developments signal that even in these last holdouts for an older world view, the law may again adjust to societal changes. Expanded roles for men and women may bring about full equality, without reservation, under the law. Chief among the signals of change: the Court's 1996 ruling in *United States v. Virginia;* the military's acceptance of women in combat; fathers' greater willingness to care for their children; and a more clear-eyed view of older teenage girls' sexual interests and younger teenage boys' vulnerability to sexual exploitation.

WOMEN AND THE ARMED FORCES

Historically, the law has barred women from military service. Women who managed to fight in early U.S. wars did so only by disguising themselves as men. The armed forces did not let women in until the twentieth century: as nurses and clerks during World War I, and in temporary, all-women, noncombat units during World War II. In 1948, a new federal law allowed women into permanent military service for the first time, but still under very limited terms. Only 2 percent of the military could be female, and those few women permitted to serve were barred from combat and from holding high command positions above the rank of lieutenant colonel/commander (except for one "temporary" woman colonel/captain in each service).

It was not until 1967 that Congress allowed women to comprise more than 2 percent of military personnel or to serve in the highest command positions or on draft boards. Women broke other barriers in the 1970s, when the nation's military service academies finally took down the "men only" admission signs. For the first time, too, women were allowed to command both male and female troops. When women served successfully in the Persian Gulf during Operation Desert Storm in 1991, Congress at last ended the total ban on women's service in combat. (The Pentagon had tried as early as 1979 to limit women's exclusion from combat.) In 1994 President Bill Clinton's administration permitted women to serve in many, but still not all, combat positions. Ultimately, in 1996 the Supreme Court invalidated the male-only admission policy at a state military college, the Virginia Military Institute (VMI), using a tough standard for judging the constitutionality of single-sex laws, even in a military setting.

The ramifications of laws limiting women's presence in the military and excluding women from combat duty have been the subject of three notable cases before the Court. *Schlesinger v. Ballard* questioned the navy's double standard for promotion of male and female officers, *Rostker v. Goldberg* reviewed the government's male-only draft registration requirement, and *Personnel Administrator of Massachusetts v. Feeney* examined the discriminatory impact on women employees of a government program giving veterans an absolute preference in hiring over better-qualified nonveterans.

Combat Ships and Sea Duty

Schlesinger v. Ballard, 419 U.S. 498 (1975)

Navy lieutenant Robert Ballard was faced with dismissal from the armed forces because, in a span of nine years, he had been passed over twice for promotion. According to the navy's "up or out" policy, however, had he been a female officer he would have had thirteen years to achieve promotion before being terminated. With those thirteen years, plus a previous seven years of enlisted service, he could have earned retirement benefits based on twenty years of service. Not having served long enough to earn this retirement pay, Ballard challenged the navy's policy as an impermissible sex-based classification.

When Ballard's case reached the Supreme Court in 1975, a year before *Craig v. Boren,* Justice Potter Stewart wrote the majority opinion upholding the navy's different treatment of male and female officers. Stewart reasoned that the law Congress had passed dictating this policy did not rely on "archaic and overbroad generalizations" about gender because women and men in the navy were "*not* similarly situated with respect to opportunities for professional service." Stewart cited Congress's instructions that "women may not be assigned to duty in aircraft that are engaged in combat missions nor may they be assigned to duty on vessels of the navy other than hospital ships and transports." As a result of this ban, when male and female lieutenants competed with each other for promotion, the women's records showed no service at sea, thereby reducing the women's chances for promotion. Using the lenient rational basis test, the Court upheld Congress's sex-based differential as legitimately remedial.

This holding resembled the Court's reasoning in *Kahn v. Shevin,* which upheld against an equal protection challenge a Florida property tax ex-

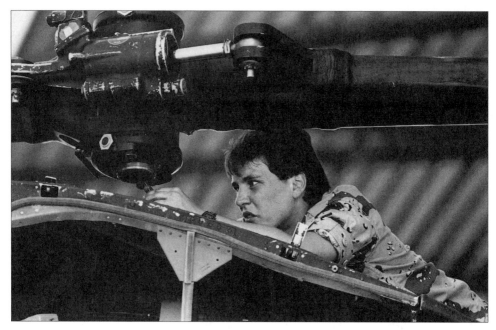

In 1991 a female American soldier assembled the rotor blades on a newly arrived helicopter at the airport in Saudi Arabia in preparation for the Persian Gulf War. The integral role women played in that war led Congress to lift the ban on women flying jets and helicopters in combat missions.

emption for widows, along with the blind and the totally disabled. The Court accepted, uncritically, Florida's assertion that the exemption compensated widows for past discrimination. As he had in *Kahn*, Justice William J. Brennan Jr. dissented. He questioned whether one discrimination (against women) should in turn excuse another (against men). In Brennan's view, compensating women was not in fact the legislation's purpose. He therefore concluded that the statute must fall.

By the time Ballard's case reached the Supreme Court in 1975, the Defense Department had already submitted a bill to eliminate the difference in the time period men and women could serve without promotion. And in 1978 U.S. District Court judge John J. Sirica held unconstitutional Congress's ban on assignment of female personnel to sea duty. In *Owens v. Brown* he wrote that the legislative background of the law

"tends to suggest a statutory purpose more related to the traditional way of thinking of women than to the demands of military preparedness." Consequently, Judge Sirica ordered the navy to begin the process of opening opportunities for sea duty to qualified navy women. A few months after Judge Sirica's decision, Congress passed a law permitting the navy to send its women to sea in ships, but on noncombatant vessels only. Finally, in 1991 Congress permitted navy women to be assigned to sea duty on combat ships and to fly aircraft in combat situations.

Registering Women for the Draft

Rostker v. Goldberg, 453 U.S. 57 (1981)

Justice William H. Rehnquist continued Justice Stewart's "not similarly situated," low-level review in *Rostker v. Goldberg*, a 1981 decision in which the Court divided 6–3. Rehnquist ruled that Congress's exclusion of women from registering for the draft was "not invidious" discrimination, "but rather realistically reflects the fact that the sexes are not similarly situated" with regard to the maintenance of a ready military force. The primary purpose of a draft would be to select combat troops, Rehnquist reasoned, so it made no sense to register women for the draft if they were precluded by law from serving in combat. "The Constitution," Rehnquist wrote, "requires that Congress treat similarly situated persons similarly, not that it engage in gestures of superficial equality."

The case was a holdover from 1971, when a group of men from Philadelphia protested the Vietnam War draft on the ground that women did not face the same obligation. They claimed that this unequal treatment violated the equal protection principle implicit in the Fifth Amendment's Due Process Clause. Ironically, the draft resisters initially had urged the unconstitutionality of the draft for a host of political and moral reasons, sex discrimination being their argument of last resort.

The case went into legal limbo when the draft expired in 1973 during the waning months of the Vietnam War. All but one of the original litigants dropped out of the suit because they felt that arguing the case solely on the ground of gender discrimination was, in essence, conceding that the draft was acceptable if it included women. This was contrary to their belief that drafting young people to kill against their will was immoral. Their lawyers recruited a new lead plaintiff,

In 1971 a group of men protested the Vietnam War draft on the ground that women did not face the same obligation. The case lost momentum when the draft expired in 1973 but was revitalized in 1980 when President Jimmy Carter reactivated registration, although not an actual draft, in the face of the Soviet Union's invasion of Afghanistan.

Robert Goldberg, a medical student who believed in the gender discrimination argument. "They didn't have to talk me into it. . . . I had no idea how big this thing would get, but it was what I was feeling. So I became part of it," Goldberg told historian Linda Kerber in 1993.

The case was revitalized in January 1980 when President Jimmy Carter reactivated registration, although not an actual draft, in the face of the Soviet invasion of Afghanistan. Iran had seized the American embassy and was holding American hostages; Carter worried that the United States looked impotent. He wanted to send a signal that the U.S. military was prepared to take measures against Soviet aggression. Carter called for compulsory registration of both men and women, although he promised to retain women's exemption from combat duty. "There is no distinction possible, on the basis of ability or performance," he said, "that would allow me to exclude women from an obligation to register."

When Congress debated Carter's proposal, it paid a lot of attention to the issue of drafting women to serve, as opposed to merely registering them for the draft. In its report, Congress expressed the traditional concerns about who would take care of the home and family if women went to war. Historically, women had been exempted from the draft for a variety of reasons. Some thought that men should "provide the first line of defense" while "women kept the home fires burning." Others thought that only men, not women, should put their lives at risk. Still others thought that if women fought the nation would undoubtedly be defeated.

Congress calculated that only 6 percent of enlisted skills were closed to women during peacetime as a result of the exclusion from combat, but during wartime 42 percent of the skills required by the military related to combat. Therefore, Congress concluded, it was unnecessary to draft women because they could not meet the Pentagon's wartime needs for combat troops. As to

whether combat restrictions should be lifted, Congress continued to question women's ability to perform combat roles. Did women possess the necessary physical strength and psychological mettle? Were they too nurturing and not aggressive enough? What about pregnancy? Could women bond with a group of men?

After intense debate, Congress voted to authorize a male-only registration. Goldberg's case was quickly revived as a class-action suit, on behalf of himself and all males facing registration. Bernard Rostker, the director of Selective Service (the government's draft program), was the defendant.

On July 18, 1980, only three days before the registration requirement was to go into effect, a federal district court found it unconstitutional. The government instantly appealed; the costly sign-up program it had developed was now in jeopardy. The very next day, however, Justice Brennan, the member of the Court responsible for stay applications from federal courts in Philadelphia and the rest of the mid-Atlantic region, granted a stay pending appeal. Registration began on time.

When the Supreme Court heard the case on March 24, 1981, it did not consider whether women could or should perform combat roles. Instead, government lawyers argued that the Court should use the lowest level of scrutiny in judging the men-only registration law, asking only whether the "distinction drawn between men and women bears a rational relation to some legitimate government purpose." Donald Weinberg, Goldberg's attorney, argued that an even higher level of scrutiny should be used than the intermediate level established in *Craig v. Boren*. Justice Rehnquist's opinion for the Court took a different approach.

Observing that the primary purpose of raising troops is to engage in combat, Rehnquist stated for the Court's majority that excluding women from registration for the draft was closely related to the government objective of military readiness. Should the nation switch from registration to an actual draft, having women draftees would create administrative burdens and hinder flexibility because only 80,000 women could be used in noncombat positions. Military flexibility, he wrote, was a matter of national security and justified any sex discrimination in the underinclusive law. Rehnquist also felt strongly that the judiciary should defer to the authority of Congress.

In a dissent joined by Justice Brennan, Justice Thurgood Marshall criticized the exclusion of women "from a fundamental civic obligation" based on notions of their "proper role." He pointed out that if the military services drafted men and women in proportion to the number of positions each could fill, the administrative burdens and lack of flexibility would not exist. He also disagreed with the majority's deference to Congress in military matters: "Congressional enactments in the area of military affairs must, like all laws, be *judged* by the standards of the Constitution."

In a separate dissent also joined by Justice Brennan, Justice Byron R. White wrote that women played an important role in the military and that not every position need be "filled with combat-ready men." Although he did not see anything unconstitutional about barring women from combat, White agreed that it was unconstitutional to exclude them from registration. Like Marshall, he thought the nation could not count on recruiting enough women volunteers to staff noncombat jobs. White also criticized the Court majority's reliance on an "administrative convenience" rationale: "[T]he number of women who could be used in the military without sacrificing combat-readiness is not at all small or insubstantial, and administrative convenience has not been sufficient justification for the kind of outright gender-based discrimination involved in registering and conscripting men but no women at all."

In the 1990s Congress modified its laws governing the combat exclusion of women, who in 1999 made up 14 percent of the armed forces. This change was partly in response to the vital role women played in the 1991 Gulf War, in which thirteen female soldiers were killed. Although women continued to be excluded from ground combat and the special forces, Congress permitted women to be assigned to sea duty and to combat aircraft in all branches of the military. For the first time, women were allowed to fly jets into combat from the decks of aircraft carriers and to pilot helicopters in combat situations. In 1994 the Clinton administration opened up 250,000 positions previously closed to women because they were considered combat-related. In 1998 the navy approved five women to command combatant ships.

In the wake of the Supreme Court's 1996 ruling in the Virginia Military Institute case, it is now uncertain whether the Court would allow a law to stand that treated military men and women unequally if such a case presented itself. Could the military show an "exceedingly persuasive justification for women's categorical exclusion [from any combat position], in total disregard of their individual merit," an exclusion encompassing even "women who have the will and capacity" to do the job? The Court so focused the inquiry regarding women cadets in *United States v. Virginia*. In the event of another military draft, would the Court find an exceedingly persuasive justification for drafting only men to fight and risk injury, capture, and death? Are only men to be liable for the ultimate civic responsibility of U.S. citizens? These are questions the Court could face in the twenty-first century.

Giving Veterans Job Preferences

Personnel Administrator of Mass. v. Feeney, 442 U.S. 256 (1979)

Perhaps more limiting than the historic exclusion of women from combat jobs was the 2 percent ceiling on women's participation in the military that was in effect until 1967. This restriction discouraged women from pursuing careers in the military and from availing themselves of its generous benefits, including training and educational subsidies. Nor were women able to gain the prestige military service garnered for some male politicians, most notably Presidents John F. Kennedy and Dwight D. Eisenhower. Thus women's unequal status in the military spilled over to civilian life—especially in the area of civil service employment, where preference in hiring and promotions was given almost exclusively to male veterans.

In *Personnel Administrator of Mass. v. Feeney,* the Supreme Court faced a constitutional challenge to one such veterans' preference program. The courts had been confronted with challenges to veterans' preference schemes before, but only from men; in this case, the plaintiff—Helen B. Feeney—was not only a nonveteran but also a woman. And the Massachusetts statute under attack was far more generous to veterans than most states' preference systems: rather than merely allotting veterans extra points on civil service exams or allowing them to win in the case of a tie, the Massachusetts system gave veterans an absolute, lifetime advantage in the competition for civil service jobs. The statute provided that any veteran with a passing score would automatically be placed at the top of a list of eligible applicants, no matter how low the veteran's score or how high that of the nonveterans. The hiring agency was then required to choose a candidate from a small group at the top of the list.

In practice, this system resulted in the virtual exclusion of women from a broad range of high-paying civil service jobs. Feeney's experience was a telling example. During the twelve years that she worked for a Massachusetts state agency, she took a number of civil service examinations in an effort to secure a better job. Not only did she pass these examinations, she often did quite well. But in each case, veterans with lower scores were placed

ahead of her on the eligible list. On a 1971 exam she received the second-highest score but was placed sixth on the list, behind five male veterans. On a 1973 exam she received the third-highest score but was listed fourteenth, behind twelve male veterans, eleven of whom had lower scores. And in 1974 her score would have tied her for seventeenth on the list, but instead she was ranked seventieth, behind sixty-four veterans, sixty-three of whom were men. Fifty of those men had lower scores than Feeney. Nor was Feeney's experience an aberration: on each of fifty sample eligible lists placed in evidence, at least one woman had been displaced by veterans with lower scores.

The case was first heard before a three-judge federal district court, which found that the state's purpose in enacting the legislation had been to aid veterans, not to penalize women. Nevertheless, the court found the discriminatory impact of the statute so severe as to render it unconstitutional.

When the case first reached the Supreme Court, the justices sent it back to the district court for reconsideration in light of the Court's 1976 decision in *Washington v. Davis.* The Court held in that case—which involved race discrimination—that discriminatory impact alone did not render a statute unconstitutional. Instead, the Court ruled, it was the plaintiff's burden to prove that those who enacted the statute actually intended to discriminate. On reconsideration, the district court adhered to its prior disposition. The discriminatory consequences of the legislation were so inevitable, the court held, that they could not be said to have been "unintended."

Once again, the state appealed to the Supreme Court. Justice Stewart, writing for the majority, acknowledged that the "impact of the veterans' preference law upon the public employment opportunities of women has . . . been severe." But, the Court said, impact served merely as a starting point in the analysis. The ultimate issue was intent. The statute was gender-neutral on its face, drawing a distinction between veterans and nonveterans, not between men and women. And the group that benefited from the statute—veterans—included some women, while the group disadvantaged by the preference—nonveterans—included many men. (Justice Stewart's reasoning here is reminiscent of his 1974 opinion in *Geduldig v. Aiello* (see p. 168), where the Court held that legislation discriminating on the basis of pregnancy was gender-neutral because, as he put it, the law differentiated between "pregnant women" and "nonpregnant persons," not between women and men.)

Feeney argued that the Massachusetts veterans' preference policy was inherently gender-biased because, historically, it had been far more difficult for women to become veterans. Not only had federal law limited women's participation in the armed forces to no more than 2 percent until 1967, but eligibility requirements for women were more stringent than those for men, and opportunities for career advancement were more limited. But, said Stewart, if this argument were to be accepted, then any veterans' preference scheme would be discriminatory—and Feeney had acknowledged that less sweeping "points added" schemes were legitimate. In any event, he asserted, "the history of discrimination against women in the military is not on trial in this case."

Finally, Stewart addressed the argument that had convinced the district court: foreseeability. "Where a law's consequences are that inevitable," the district court had asked rhetorically, "can they meaningfully be described as unintended?" Yes, answered Stewart, they can. Obviously, the legislature must have foreseen, and therefore intended, that women would be adversely affected by the statute. But that sort of intent did not rise to the level of a "discriminatory purpose" that would render a law unconstitutional. Rather, it was incumbent on the plaintiffs to show that the legislature "selected or reaffirmed a particular course of action at least in part 'because of,' not merely 'in spite of,' its adverse effects upon an identifiable group." That showing, Stewart concluded, was absent here.

Marshall, joined by Brennan, dissented. The legislature's primary objective may have been to benefit veterans, but that fact did not exclude the possibility that it also intended to disadvantage women. Because a legislature is a collective entity where many individual purposes may be at work, Marshall wrote, determining the sole or even the dominant purpose behind a given statute is often impossible. Given this difficulty, "the critical constitutional inquiry is not whether an illicit consideration was the primary cause of a decision, but rather whether it had an appreciable role in shaping a given legislative enactment."

Furthermore, because direct evidence of discriminatory purpose is rarely available, courts have no choice but to rely on circumstantial evidence, principally, discriminatory impact. Here the impact of the preference system on women was drastically disproportionate: 47 percent of Massachusetts men were veterans, as compared to less than 1 percent of the state's women. Marshall also pointed out that, until 1971, the state had exempted from the preference scheme any jobs "especially calling for women"—which, because of stereotypical assumptions about women's roles, in practice meant low-paying secretarial or clerical jobs. The veterans' preference system, he wrote, thus rendered upper echelon state civil service employment "an almost exclusively male prerogative."

The bias inherent in the Massachusetts scheme was particularly apparent, Marshall observed, when it was "viewed against the range of less discriminatory alternatives available to assist veterans." For example, the state could limit the absolute preference for veterans to a brief period of time or provide veterans with tax breaks. "Unlike these and similar benefits," Marshall wrote, "the costs of which are distributed across the taxpaying public generally, the Massachusetts statute exacts a

By the time Helen B. Feeney's phone rang one summer afternoon in 1975, she knew all too well that the Massachusetts veterans' preference system rendered it virtually impossible for nonveterans to obtain the most desirable civil service jobs.

Hired in 1963 as a senior clerk stenographer for the state Civil Defense Agency—a job for which there had been little or no male competition—Feeney had been able to advance to federal funds and personnel coordinator for the agency four years later. But that promotion had come as a result of her score on an exam on which veterans received only two bonus points. On the numerous other civil service exams Feeney took—exams on which veterans with passing scores were automatically placed at the top of the list—she was repeatedly bumped from competition by veterans with lower scores.

"After a while, the civil service exams were a cinch for me," Feeney told historian Linda Kerber. "I took every one I could get; that let me know the structure of the exams. On one exam I got a 96 and the person who got the job got a 70."

In March 1975 Feeney was laid off as part of a governmental reorganization. A few months later came a phone call from a lawyer named Betty Gittes, one of a group of women attorneys who had initiated a lawsuit challenging the Massachusetts veterans' preference system. Now she had a problem: just before the case was to go to trial the state legislature had changed the law so that veterans' preference no longer applied to the hiring or promotion of lawyers. Because all the plaintiffs in the

After being repeatedly passed over for promotion despite good scores on civil service exams, Helen B. Feeney challenged a Massachusetts statute that automatically placed veterans with a passing score at the top of a list of eligible applicants for a civil service job. Feeney argued that the 2 percent ceiling on women's participation in the armed forces—in effect until 1967—had made it difficult for women to become veterans and that veteran preference programs therefore had a discriminatory impact on women.

pending case were lawyers, it was possible that the court would throw out the suit as moot—unless the women could find a nonlawyer who was willing to join as a plaintiff. Gittes had combed through the civil service lists, looking for women with high scores who had been displaced by veterans. She had already approached a number of women who had

substantial price from a discrete group of individuals who have long been subject to employment discrimination, and who, 'because of circumstances totally beyond their control, have [had] little if any chance of becoming members of the preferred class.'"

Veterans' groups were delighted with the Court's decision: the National Commander of the declined to participate because they feared repercussions. Now she was on the phone with Feeney, asking if Feeney would be willing to add her name to the suit.

Feeney felt it was a strange coincidence. "There I was, sitting at home on a Sunday afternoon minding my own business," she says now, "and this was something I had thought of all along, that I can't be promoted because I'm not a veteran."

But Feeney had never considered bringing a lawsuit herself, for two reasons. One was the cost. The other was her husband, who "would not have wanted me sticking my neck out." Now, however, Feeney was recently widowed. And the cost of the lawsuit—which, according to one of the lawyers, Rick Ward, would have amounted to at least half a million dollars—was being borne by the ACLU and a large Boston law firm, Ropes & Gray.

Even before she traveled from her home in Dracut, Massachusetts, to Boston to meet with the lawyers, Feeney had made up her mind to sign on as a plaintiff. "On the drive in to Boston, and then looking for a parking place," she recalls, "I was saying to myself, surely you will, Helen, surely you will."

But, she adds, "I thought there would be quite a few other women involved." It came as a shock when—just as the lawyer-plaintiffs had feared—the district court ruled in 1976 that the case was moot as to all plaintiffs save Feeney. "I felt like the cheese in the nursery rhyme," Feeney told Linda Kerber; "you know, 'the cheese stands alone.'"

Not only was Feeney alone, she was the sole target of a barrage of hate mail and nasty phone calls. "I am a disabled veteran," one note read. "You are not a veteran, but you could be disabled." Every time a development in the case made the news, she received calls with messages like, "Have somebody else start your car tomorrow."

Feeney had known public criticism before: a longtime Democratic activist in Dracut, she had once been burned in effigy at a town meeting there. But, she said, she hadn't thought the furor over the veterans' preference case would be so intense. "At times I thought, why am I doing this?" she added. But she knew that if she withdrew from the case, all the lawyers' hard work would be for naught.

And Feeney also had her supporters. Even Massachusetts governor Michael Dukakis was on her side: after the district court ruled in Feeney's favor, the governor urged the state attorney general, Francis X. Bellotti, not to appeal the decision. When Bellotti made it clear that he was determined to go ahead, Dukakis took the highly unusual step of asking the Massachusetts Supreme Judicial Court to prevent Bellotti from doing so. The state's highest court ruled that the decision whether or not to appeal was up to Bellotti. This difference of opinion was echoed at the federal level: Solicitor General Wade McCree filed an amicus curiae brief in the U.S. Supreme Court in support of Massachusetts, over the opposition of President Jimmy Carter and four federal agencies (Office of Personnel Management, Department of Defense, Department of Labor, and Equal Employment Opportunity Commission).

Feeney was surprised and disappointed by the Supreme Court's decision upholding the Massachusetts veterans' preference, but she got on with her life. She found a non–civil service job as executive director of the Dracut Council on Aging, and in 1989, after her retirement, she earned a Masters in gerontology from the University of Massachusetts. She now lives in North Andover, Massachusetts, not far from one of her two daughters, and does volunteer work.

American Legion called it a "restatement of allegiance to the veteran population by a grateful nation." But feminists, predictably, were gravely disappointed. And the *Boston Globe* editorialized that the ruling was an "unnaturally static" one in which "past errors [were] rigidly to be preserved." The only way for women to beat the veterans' preference system, it seemed, was to join it—that is, to enlist in the armed forces in greater numbers, and to push for an expanded role for women in the military.

UNWED FATHERS AND THEIR CHILDREN

Another area of law in which the Supreme Court has sometimes allowed legislatures to classify men and women differently are cases involving unwed fathers and their children. Unlike the old family-law rules that made the husband head and master of his wife and children, laws pertaining to fathers and mothers who did not marry took a different approach. In terms of duties, a husband was obligated to support his children. But unwed fathers were not so obligated (though eventually this rule changed). Similarly, in terms of legal rights, if the husband and his wife divorced, under an unyielding "head and master" rule the husband would keep custody of their children. But the law gave no such legal rights to unwed fathers: they had no right to the custody and care of their children (though eventually they sometimes gained the right to visit their children), nor could they block the adoption of their children by others. The unwed mother alone had both duties and rights regarding the children she bore.

Not surprisingly, since historically the law absolved unwed fathers of legal obligations, many of them responded in turn by acting less than responsibly. As a result, many states also passed other laws presuming that if the father had not legitimated his son or daughter then he had no real relationship with that child. For example, some statutes denied children any inheritance or benefits based on their unwed father's property or earnings unless the father formally acknowledged his paternity. By contrast, children of an unwed mother need not be "legitimated" in order to inherit from their mother, because she unquestionably is the children's parent and it is assumed that mothers bond closely with their children.

Consequently, unwed fathers pursued lawsuits, some of them ultimately decided by the Supreme Court, protesting laws that denied them equal parental status. While the Court was sometimes sympathetic to unwed fathers, more often it relied on stereotypes about irresponsible and uncaring fathers, as opposed to connected and loving mothers, and ruled against the fathers' pleas. Ironically, the very fathers who were trying to be responsible and caring, who wanted the law to recognize their ties to their children, often saw both legislatures and courts turn a deaf ear to their pleas.

Child Custody

Stanley v. Illinois, 405 U.S. 645 (1972)

In the earliest of these cases to reach the Supreme Court, *Stanley v. Illinois* (1972), the Court ruled that the father of children born out of wedlock was entitled to a hearing to prove his fitness as a parent before his children could be removed from his custody upon the death of their mother. The father had lived with his two children all their lives and had supported them financially until their mother died. But under Illinois law, "parents" were defined to include married parents and unwed mothers, *not* unwed fathers. So when the mother died, the state declared that their children now had no "parent," were wards of the state, and should live with court-appointed guardians, who would make all the legal decisions about their lives.

The law, however, did not allow the state to do this either to unwed mothers or to widowed parents. Indeed, these parents had a right to a hearing to determine whether they were fit parents if the state ever sought to take their children away. If they were deemed fit, the state could not remove the children from their care. The father sued, asserting as one of his claims that he was the subject of unfair sex discrimination.

The state responded that "most unmarried fathers are unsuitable and neglectful parents," and that it could therefore treat them differently from both unwed mothers and married parents. Justice White, writing for the Court's majority, disagreed: "all unmarried fathers are not in this category; some are wholly suited to have custody of their children." He concluded that administrative convenience was not a sufficient reason for denying the unwed father's due process and equal protection rights.

The Right to Veto an Adoption and to Sue for Wrongful Death

Caban v. Mohammed, 441 U.S. 380 (1979)

Parham v. Hughes, 441 U.S. 347 (1979)

Lehr v. Robertson, 463 U.S. 248 (1983)

In *Caban v. Mohammed* (1979), a five-member majority of the Court struck down a New York state law that gave an unwed mother, but not an unwed father, the right to veto their child's adoption. In this case the father, Abdiel Caban, had lived with and supported his children and their mother, Maria Mohammed. When the children were two and four, she left with them and married another man. Abdiel likewise married another woman, who eventually tried to adopt his children, but Maria withheld her consent. By contrast, Maria's husband was permitted to adopt the children because Abdiel, as an unwed father, had no power under New York law to block his children's adoption.

Justice Lewis F. Powell Jr. concluded that New York's law was "another example of 'overbroad generalizations'" that could not survive inspection under *Craig v. Boren*'s heightened scrutiny test. "The effect of New York's classification," he

wrote, "is to discriminate against unwed fathers even when their identity is known and they have manifested a significant paternal interest in the child." New York's adoption law, he continued, "both excludes some loving fathers from full participation in the decision whether their children will be adopted and, at the same time, enables some alienated mothers arbitrarily to cut off the paternal rights of fathers."

Justice Stewart dissented, maintaining that unwed fathers and unwed mothers are not "similarly situated" with respect to their relationship with their children.

Justice John Paul Stevens, himself an adoptive father, also dissented, joined by Chief Justice Warren E. Burger and Justice Rehnquist. Stevens thought that unwed fathers, like Abdiel, who had a "substantial relationship" to their children and admitted their paternity, were "relatively rare." In contrast, "in the more common adoption situations, the mother will be the more, and often the only, responsible parent, and . . . a paternal consent requirement will constitute a hindrance to the adoption process." The "mere fact that an otherwise valid general classification appears arbitrary in an isolated case," Stevens said, "is not a sufficient reason for invalidating the entire rule."

In *Parham v. Hughes,* a case decided the same day as *Caban v. Mohammed,* the Court rejected a sex discrimination challenge to a Georgia law denying an unwed father (but not the unwed mother) the right to sue for his child's wrongful death. Both mother and child had been killed in an automobile accident. The father who brought suit for the child's wrongful death had signed his son's birth certificate, continually contributed to the child's support, and maintained a close relationship with the child, seeing him on a daily basis. But because the father had not formally legitimated his son—something no unwed mother had to do—Georgia law disallowed the suit.

The Court divided 5–4. Justice Stewart wrote a plurality opinion, joined by Chief Justice Burger and Justices Rehnquist and Stevens, that took an approach reminiscent of his opinion in *Schlesinger v. Ballard.* He first asked, is the Georgia law "invidiously discriminatory"? A law would fit that description if it relied on "overbroad generalizations based on sex which are entirely unrelated to any differences between men and women or which demean the ability or social status of the affected class." But "where men and women are not similarly situated . . . and a statutory classification is realistically based on the differences in their situations," Stewart reasoned, no "invidious discrimination" is at work.

Justice Stewart next explained why men and women were not "similarly situated" with regard to suits by unwed parents for the death of a child and why, in his view, the Georgia law did not discriminate against "men as a class."

[T]he conferral of the right of a natural father to sue for wrongful death of his child only if he has previously acted to identify himself, undertake his parental responsibilities, and make his children legitimate, does not reflect any overbroad generalizations about men as a class, but rather the reality that in Georgia only a father can by unilateral action legitimate an illegitimate child.

Once again, the Court used the existence of one discriminatory law (against women) to excuse another (against men), just as it had done in *Rostker v. Goldberg,* the draft registration case.

The critical fifth vote in *Parham* was provided by Justice Powell, who wrote a separate concurring opinion. The Georgia law "is substantially related to the State's objective of avoiding difficult problems of proof of paternity" after the death of a child, he asserted. By requiring the unwed father "to declare his intentions at a time when both the child and his mother are likely to be available to provide evidence," Powell maintained, Georgia

could settle paternity questions more easily. "The marginally greater burden placed on fathers," he concluded, "is no more severe than is required by the marked difference between proving paternity and maternity."

Justice White dissented, joined by Justices Brennan, Marshall, and Harry A. Blackmun. The dissenters protested the "startling circularity" of the idea that one discrimination justifies another, and found Georgia's sex-based classification both under- and over-inclusive. If the state was interested in promoting "a legitimate family unit" and "setting a standard of morality," then allowing unwed mothers to sue encouraged women whose marital status did not support those interests. If the state wanted to avoid "potential problems of proof of paternity," it was wrong to bar as suitors "many who are capable of proving their parenthood, solely because they are fathers." White's dissenting opinion was most biting when he analyzed the state's final argument that "more often than not" the unwed father "suffers no real loss from the child's wrongful death." He considered that "such a legislative conception about fathers of illegitimate children is an unacceptable basis for a blanket discrimination against all such fathers. Whatever may be true with respect to certain of these parents, we have recognized that at least some of them maintain as close a relationship to their children as do unmarried mothers." Applying the standard announced in *Craig v. Boren* (which the plurality declined to do), White concluded that unjustifiable sex discrimination infected Georgia's law.

Just five years after *Caban* and *Parham* were handed down the Court upheld, 6–3, a New York law that denied an unwed father who failed to take certain steps not required of an unwed mother the right to notice and hearing prior to the child's adoption. Although New York had modified its adoption law since *Caban,* the different outcome in *Lehr v. Robertson* resulted primarily from the father never having established a substantial relationship with his child. This time the Court ruled that New York's unilateral unwed-mother adoption veto, as revised in response to *Caban,* was constitutional and did not discriminate impermissibly against unwed fathers on the basis of their sex. Writing for the Court this time, Justice Stevens said that "[if] one parent has an established custodial relationship with a child and the other parent [has] never established a relationship, [equal protection] does not prevent the state from according the two parents different legal rights." Such parents are not "similarly situated."

Justice White dissented, joined by Justices Marshall and Brennan. He pointed to the father's version of events, on which he had tried, unsuccessfully, to be heard. The father asserted that he persistently tried to establish a relationship with his child, but was thwarted when the child's mother concealed their whereabouts. He further alleged that the child's mother refused his offer of financial assistance. Justice White concluded: "It makes little sense to me to deny notice and hearing [of an adoption proceeding] to a father who . . . has unmistakably identified himself by filing suit to establish his paternity and has notified the adoption court of his action and interest."

Children Born Outside the United States

Lorelyn Penero Miller v. Madeline K. Albright,
  523 U.S. 420 (1998)

This same disagreement among the justices affected the Court's decision in 1998 to uphold a 1940 federal immigration law allowing all unwed mothers, but only some unwed fathers, to transmit their citizenship to their children. The law in question granted citizenship to children born out of wedlock in a foreign country to a U.S. citizen and a foreigner if the mother was a U.S. citizen, but placed several conditions on an unwed father's transmission of U.S. citizenship to his child.

Miller v. Albright was brought by twenty-eight year-old Lorelyn Penero Miller, born out of wedlock to a Filipina mother and a U.S. citizen, a serviceman stationed at an Air Force base in the Philippines at the time of Lorelyn's conception. Lorelyn Miller applied for citizenship in 1992, while she was living with her father, Charlie Miller, in Texas. Her application was rejected because her father had not, as was required of fathers by law, either legitimated her, acknowledged he was her father under oath, or had a court establish his paternity before Lorelyn turned twenty-one. (The law now requires that paternity be established by age eighteen.)

Lorelyn claimed that the sex differential violated the equal protection principle. Lower courts had rejected this argument on the ground that Congress enjoys broad discretion in granting citizenship. Before the Supreme Court, the government urged that unwed mothers and unwed fathers are not similarly situated in relation to their children. A mother is always present at a child's birth, the government reasoned, so she naturally develops a bond with her baby. A father not married to the mother may lack a similarly strong commitment to the child, and should therefore be required to establish paternity and show that he would support the child financially in the United States.

The Court decided the case 6–3, but there was no majority opinion and no ruling for the Court on the sex classification question. Justice Stevens, joined only by Chief Justice Rehnquist, voted to uphold the law and relied on the same approach he had earlier taken in *Lehr v. Robertson.*

[It cannot] be denied that the male and female parents are differently situated in this respect. The blood relationship to the birth mother is immediately obvious and is typically established by hospital records and

Lorelyn Penero Miller (wearing white jacket) spoke with reporters outside the Supreme Court after hearing arguments for her 1998 case challenging a federal law that granted citizenship to children born out of wedlock in a foreign country to a U.S. citizen and a foreigner if the mother was a U.S. citizen, but placed several conditions on an unwed father's transmission of U.S. citizenship to his child. Miller's mother had met her father, Charlie Miller (standing behind her left shoulder), when he was stationed in the Philippines by the U.S. Air Force.

birth certificates; the relationship to the unmarried father may often be undisclosed and unrecorded in any contemporary public record. Thus, the requirement that the father make a timely written acknowledgment under oath, or that the child obtain a court adjudication of paternity, produces the rough equivalent of the documentation that is already available to evidence the blood relationship between the mother and the child.

Mothers "typically will have custody of the child immediately after the birth," Stevens reasoned, thus they naturally have a closer connection to their children than do fathers. An unwed father can play a very fleeting role in his child's life; indeed, he may not even be aware of the existence of the child. A U.S. serviceman who fathers a child on tour of duty might well resist any responsibility for the child. Thus, Stevens concluded (speaking only for himself and the chief justice), the separate rule for unwed mothers and fathers is "eminently reasonable" and passes muster under the rational basis test. That test was in order, Stevens believed, because of the large deference due to Congress "in the area of immigration and naturalization." In a separate opinion, Justice Antonin Scalia, joined by Justice Clarence Thomas, agreed with this deference rationale.

In a differently oriented concurring opinion, Justices Sandra Day O'Connor, joined by Justice Anthony M. Kennedy, asserted that Lorelyn Miller did not have the right to sue on behalf of her father, Charlie Miller, and had no standing to sue in her own right. According to O'Connor, the father was the real victim of discrimination, the one penalized because of his sex. If Charlie Miller had remained a party to the suit along with his daughter, the decision might have been 5–4 to overturn the law. (Charlie Miller initiated the suit, but had been dismissed by the district court and did not appeal the dismissal.) With regard to Stevens's use of the rational basis test, O'Connor wrote: "It is unlikely, in my opinion, that any gender classifications based on stereotypes can survive heightened scrutiny, but under rational scrutiny, a statute may be defended based on generalized classifications unsupported by empirical evidence."

Justices Ruth Bader Ginsburg, Stephen G. Breyer, and David H. Souter would have allowed Lorelyn Miller to assert her father's equal protection claim, particularly in view of the questionable dismissal of Charlie Miller as a party. They vigorously maintained that the sex classification could not withstand constitutional scrutiny. The law "treats mothers one way, fathers another, shaping government policy to fit and reinforce the stereotype or historic pattern," wrote Ginsburg in her dissent. She critically observed that Stevens's opinion pervasively relied on generalizations, "on what 'typically,' or 'normally,' or 'probably' happens 'often.'" The Court had repeatedly cautioned, she stated, "that when the Government controls 'gates to opportunity,' it 'may not exclude qualified individuals based on "fixed notions concerning the roles and abilities of males and females".'" Only an "exceedingly persuasive justification," she asserted, one that does "'not rely on overbroad generalizations about the different talents, capacities, or preferences of males and females,' will support differential treatment of men and women."

In a separate dissent, Breyer questioned Stevens's assumption that mothers are more likely to care for their children and to develop strong bonds to them. "What sense does it make to apply these [citizenship barriers] only to fathers and not to mothers in today's world," he asked, "where paternity can readily be proved and where women and men both are likely to earn a living in the workplace?" Ginsburg made a direct appeal to Congress for legislative action to "restore . . . impartiality [to our immigration and nationality law] before the century is out."

The outcome of the case had little practical effect on Lorelyn Miller because she had married a U.S. citizen and had become a legal resident of the United States before the Supreme Court issued its decision. With no opinion for the Court in *Miller,* it will be left to future cases to settle the question of whether men should have equal parental rights with women outside marriage now that women have gained equal rights with men in marriage.

TEENAGE SEX

Michael M. v. Superior Court of Sonoma Cty.,
 450 U.S. 464 (1981)

Control of women's sexuality has long been a preoccupation of the law. Justice Ginsburg's opinion in *United States v. Virginia* (1996) recalled Thomas Jefferson's views about women, sex, children, and democracy in early America.

Were our State a pure democracy . . . there would yet be excluded from their deliberations . . . women, who, to prevent depravation of morals and ambiguity of issue, should not mix promiscuously in the public meetings of men.

The underlying idea was once widely held. So that fathers might know for certain that their children were genetically theirs, it was considered best to keep women away from the public sphere, thereby preventing them from meeting other men and seducing them!

Today, few in the United States would give voice to such views. Yet in some states the law still endeavors to stop teenage girls, and only girls, from having sex. If girls choose to do so anyway, the law blames not them, but the teenage boys or men who are their sexual partners. The law calls this kind of consensual sex "statutory rape" and punishes the male participant as a criminal. It is not rape as historically defined by the law—sex forced on a female without her consent and which she resisted. Calling it rape is a fiction the law has justified on the ground that teenage girls are "incapable of consent." By this, the law does not mean that they are actually unable to consent, but only that they should not be able to consent—that is, that they should remain chaste. Under this same theory of statutory rape it was permissible for teenage boys to have sex with impunity as long as their female partners were older than the statutory age of consent.

In 1980 the Supreme Court confronted a statutory rape law from the state of California. By then, reflecting the trend to rewrite such laws in gender-neutral terms, thirty-seven states had statutory rape laws that applied equally to males and females. "Although most of these laws protect young persons (of either sex) from the sexual exploitation of older individuals," explained Justice Brennan, "the laws of Arizona, Florida, and Illinois permit prosecution of both minor females and minor males for engaging in mutual sexual conduct. In addition, eight other States permit both parties to be prosecuted when one of the participants to a consensual act of sexual intercourse is under the age of 16." But California retained a law that punished only men and boys for having consensual sex with girls seventeen and younger.

Originally, California's law, passed in 1850, applied only to girls nine and under. The California legislature moved the age line up to thirteen in 1889, fifteen in 1897, and seventeen in 1913. That was the law seventeen-year-old Michael M. (minors' surnames and identities are concealed) faced in 1978, when he was prosecuted for having "illegal sexual intercourse" with a sixteen-year-old named Sharon.

When Michael M.'s case came before the Supreme Court, the justices again splintered on the appropriate test for the sex-based differential, just as they had in the cases involving military service and unwed parents. Justice Rehnquist's plurality opinion (joined by Chief Justice Burger, Justice Stewart, and Justice Powell) explicitly relied on the *Parham v. Hughes* standard, that a sex-based law will be upheld "where the gender classification is not invidious, but rather realistically reflects the fact that the sexes are not similarly situated." As in *Parham*, the plurality in *Michael M.* did not take into account the statute's underinclusiveness—its failure to penalize female participants in consensual sexual acts. For the *Parham* test does not require invalidation of under- or overinclusive laws, as does the more difficult *Craig v. Boren* test. Under *Parham*, once the Court determines that the sexes are not "similarly situated," it switches to rational basis review to uphold the statute if the state merely offers a rational justification for it, thus sliding over the question of unfair generalizations about the sexes.

The justification offered by the state in *Michael M.* for punishing males but not females was the prevention of out-of-wedlock teenage pregnancy. The Court considered the dramatic increase in such pregnancies in the 1970s, and the corresponding social, medical, and economic consequences for the mother, child, and the state, and found this state purpose satisfactory. (Teenage girls disproportionately resort to abortions, their children are more likely to become wards of the state, the risk of maternal death is much higher, and teenage mothers drop out of school more often.) The plurality accepted this justification despite the fact that the California legislature had originally enacted the law to protect girls' chastity, not to prevent teenage pregnancy.

Justice Rehnquist's plurality opinion first stated that teenage girls and boys are not "similarly situated" with respect to the problems and risks of sexual intercourse. "Only women may become pregnant," he wrote, "and they suffer disproportionately the profound physical, emotional, and psychological consequences of sexual activity. The statute at issue here protects women from sexual intercourse at an age when those consequences are particularly severe." He thus concluded that the law was "sufficiently related to the state's objectives to pass constitutional muster."

Rehnquist explained why punishing young men but not young women for the same act was justified.

Because virtually all of the significant harmful and inescapable identifiable consequences of teenage pregnancy fall on the young female, a legislature acts well within its authority when it elects to punish only the participant who, by nature, suffers few of the consequences of his conduct. It is hardly unreasonable for a legislature acting to protect minor females to exclude them from punishment. Moreover, the risk of pregnancy itself constitutes a substantial deterrence to young females. No similar sanctions deter males. A criminal

In 1981 a plurality of the Supreme Court upheld the constitutionality of a California law (since rewritten) that punished the boy but not the girl when two teenagers engaged in consensual sex. The plurality justified this double standard on the ground that women suffer disproportionately the consequences of sexual activity because only they can become pregnant.

sanction imposed solely on males thus serves roughly to "equalize the deterrents on the sexes."

In his view, California's statutory rape law promoted equality by equalizing male and female inhibitions: punishment of young men compensated for young women's fear of unwanted pregnancy. Rehnquist and the other three members of the Court's plurality accepted California's argument that broadening the statute to punish both men and women would make it less effective because it would be more difficult to enforce. Presumably, women would be afraid to report statutory rapes if they were at risk of being prosecuted themselves.

Justice Blackmun provided the decisive fifth vote for the plurality. His concurrence compared *Michael M.* to *H.L. v. Matheson* (1981), a Supreme Court decision invalidating a Utah statute requir-

ing that a minor's parents be notified before an abortion procedure. Both cases, he wrote, involved attempts to control and curtail young people's sexual activities. Although Blackmun supported privacy rights for minors in the abortion context, he reasoned that California's goal of preventing teenage pregnancy warranted a privacy invasion in the consensual sex context. He was also influenced by the fact that Michael M.'s conduct involved force (he had slapped Sharon in the face), so that the liaison may not have been truly consensual.

The specifics of the sexual encounter indicated to Blackmun both Sharon's initial willingness and her subsequent change of mind. At midnight on June 3, 1978, Michael M. and two friends had approached Sharon at a bus stop at Rohnert Park in Sonoma, California, where she was waiting with her sister. Michael quickly persuaded Sharon, who had been drinking, to walk with him to the railroad tracks. They began kissing and hugging, lying down in nearby bushes. Sharon then declined her sister's invitation to go home with her. After her sister left, the couple moved to the park where they continued kissing on a bench. According to Sharon, however, their eventual sexual intercourse on the bench was not consensual. Michael hit her in the face when she tried to resist him and she refused to take off her pants. "I said 'No,' and I was trying to get up and he hit me back down on the bench and then I just said to myself, 'Forget it,' and I let him do what he wanted to do," she recalled in her testimony.

Justice Brennan, writing a dissent joined by Justices White and Marshall, objected that the plurality had not shown that California's goal of preventing teenage pregnancy was "substantially" related to the statute in question, the test that the Court had established in *Craig v. Boren*. His dissent addressed the statute's underinclusiveness. The state had not demonstrated that a gender-neutral law (under which the underage girl would be punished as well) of the kind other states had adopted would be any more difficult to enforce or any less effective. Indeed, a gender-neutral illegal-sex law might actually discourage young women from having sexual relations more than the current law, because they too would risk punishment.

Brennan went on to note that the law's original purpose had nothing to do with preventing pregnancy and everything to do with protecting a young woman's "virtue." The law did not protect young men because, unlike young women, they were considered legally capable of consenting to sex. "It is perhaps because the gender classification in California's statutory rape law was initially designed to further these outmoded sexual stereotypes, rather than to reduce the incidence of teenage pregnancies," concluded Brennan, "that the State has been unable to demonstrate a sub-stantial relationship between the classification and its newly asserted goal."

In a separate dissent, Justice Stevens echoed Brennan's doubt that a statutory rape law could significantly reduce teenage sexual activity. "Custom and belief," rather than law, he wrote, have a greater impact on teenage behavior. Nevertheless, Stevens declared that venereal disease and teenage pregnancy were such scourges that a gender-neutral law prohibiting all teenagers from engaging in sexual intercourse was warranted. If a teenage girl is at greater risk from sex because pregnancy is more of a burden to women, then that is all the more reason, he argued, to apply the law to her. In his view it is irrational to exempt the most endangered from punishment, because then they are essentially being permitted to harm themselves; more logical would be to punish the aggressor but not the victim. But is it valid, Stevens asked, to assume that the aggressor is always the man? Or would such an assumption be based on "traditional attitudes toward male-female relationships" and irrational prejudices? And if both participants are equally willing, is it fair that "one, and only one, of two equally guilty wrongdoers be stigmatized by a criminal conviction?"

The dissenters apparently influenced the California legislature, which in 1993 amended its statutory rape law to become a gender-neutral illegal intercourse law. The new law prohibits sex with anyone under eighteen, but does not send the offender(s) to prison if the two partners are within three years of each other in age. (Under this version, Michael M. could not have been sentenced to jail because he was seventeen and Sharon was sixteen.) But if one person is under sixteen, and the other is over twenty-one, the older person can be imprisoned for up to four years. Under the new law, adult women who pressure teenage boys into sex fall within the statute's ambit.

7

DISCRIMINATION IN THE WORKPLACE

As women made headway in terms of securing their civil rights (the right to practice a chosen profession) and political rights (the right to vote or to serve on a jury), they then turned to address another important issue: economic rights. The rapidly increasing presence of women in the paid workforce during the 1960s spurred a greater demand for employment equality. In the mid-1960s women's rights groups emerged to press for improving the status of women in the workplace by ending hiring and pay discrimination. Women's groups forced legislatures and courts to confront the fact that laws and employer practices based on the traditional model of men as breadwinners and women as homemakers were not only increasingly out of date but were damaging to women and their families. Whatever might have been true in the past, such laws and practices now effectively consigned women to a subordinate economic class they were no longer content to occupy.

In the 1950s women married earlier than in previous decades, had more children, and were expected to devote themselves full time to home and family. But while some women—pushed out of wartime jobs to make way for returning World War II veterans—retreated to the home, others quietly moved into "pink-collar" office and service jobs. By the mid-1960s women accounted for 60 percent of the growth in the paid labor force and comprised more than one third of all workers. And instead of dropping out when they got married or had children, women remained on the job or returned to the workforce when their children reached school age. Mothers of children under eighteen comprised almost a third of all women workers in the 1960s. By 1970 less than half of all U.S. women were full-time homemakers.

These trends accelerated in the 1970s. Mothers of pre–school age children became, for the first time, the fastest growing segment of the female workforce. Women still outnumbered men among part-time workers, and still predominated in low-paying secretarial, sales, and service jobs. Women who sought jobs in the more lucrative fields traditionally dominated by men found that they faced widespread discrimination. The time-honored belief that working women did not need substantial paychecks because they were not the ones supporting their families proved hard to eradicate.

In the third quarter of the twentieth century women were also still prevented from earning higher wages by protective laws that barred women from working at night, lifting heavy weights, or working in dangerous places like mines, supposedly because they were too vulnerable or weak, but also to protect men's jobs. Especially harmed by such state legislation and employment discrimination were poor women who worked out of dire necessity and women of color who faced economic barriers because of their race as well as their sex.

Passage of the Civil Rights Act of 1964, which included a chapter subdivision called Title VII that prohibited employment discrimination on account of race, creed, national origin, or sex, put an end to these protective laws and provided women with a powerful tool for challenging employment inequalities. Among the earliest casualties under Title VII were state laws passed to "protect" working women. Lower federal courts in the late 1960s and early 1970s were virtually unanimous in condemning the laws as mandating discrimination against women and therefore conflicting with Title VII. Laws that limited the number of hours women could be employed, banned night work, and set limits on the weights women were allowed to lift on the job—laws initially supported by many women's groups—came to be perceived as barriers rather than protections as individual working women came forward to litigate these cases.

By 1980 women had at least gained a toehold in many traditionally male occupations. Their representation in skilled professions such as medicine and law was growing rapidly, but they were still vastly underrepresented in blue-collar jobs involving manual labor. The advent of employer affirmative action programs in the 1970s, designed to increase the participation of women and minorities in jobs from which they had long been absent, helped women to advance. In *Johnson v. Santa Clara Transportation Agency* (1987), the Supreme Court condoned affirmative action for women when it upheld an employer's affirmative action plan setting goals and timetables for in-

creasing the presence of women in certain traditionally segregated blue-collar jobs.

The women who, backed by Title VII, gained a sure footing on the corporate ladder now encountered a new problem: bumping their heads against a "glass ceiling" that kept them out of the highest levels of management. As recently as 1998 women composed only 3.8 percent of high-ranking corporate officer positions in Fortune 500 companies. Lack of mentoring, prejudice, second-rate or dead-end assignments, family choices and responsibilities, exclusion from informal "old boy" networks, and the fact that it takes decades for a previously excluded group to rise to the top of a field have all been cited as factors keeping women from reaching the top level in their jobs. Advancement to the highest echelon of some businesses, such as law and accounting firms, requires that individuals, after serving for a number of years as an employee, either be admitted to partnership (which is an ownership share in the firm) or terminated from employment. The Supreme Court decided two cases in the 1980s that extended Title VII's reach to include partnership decisions.

Even as women's ranks in the paid workforce swelled, their pay continued to lag well behind that of their male colleagues. In 1960 women earned on average only sixty cents for every dollar earned by men. This wage gap was partly remedied by passage, a year before Title VII, of the Equal Pay Act of 1963. The act required that men and women be paid equal wages for equal work. But that law, which applied only to situations where men and women were doing the same or very similar jobs, did not reach the large number of segregated "women's jobs," which were typically low-paying, dead-end positions. And it did not apply to situations where women and men, working in admittedly different jobs, could show that the duties nonetheless required similar levels of skill, effort, and responsibility.

By the 1990s the wage gap had narrowed: women were earning on average more than seventy-five cents to every dollar earned by men. But the economy had changed since the 1950s. Women's increased earnings had for most families become essential to maintaining a middle-class lifestyle or just to keeping out of poverty. The notion of the man providing the family income while the woman earned spending money for herself had all but vanished. In part because of an increasing divorce rate, many women found themselves providing all or most of the support of children. And in two-wage-earner families, the old male-breadwinner, female-homemaker division had given way to an economic partnership. Although women's earning power in general continued to lag behind that of men in 1999, in nearly one out of three families wives were earning more than their husbands.

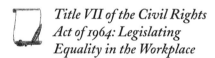

Title VII of the Civil Rights Act of 1964: Legislating Equality in the Workplace

Title VII, the most comprehensive and powerful of all federal laws prohibiting sex discrimination in employment, got off to a rocky start. In 1963 Rep. Emmanuel Celler (D-N.Y.) introduced in Congress an omnibus civil rights bill prohibiting race discrimination in a number of realms, including voting rights, public accommodations, public facilities, and federally assisted programs. Title VII of the bill barred discrimination in employment based on an employee's "race, color, creed, or national origin." A handful of women's rights activists quickly lobbied for the addition of "sex" to the list. They persuaded Rep. Howard W. Smith (D-Va.) to introduce a floor amendment adding what proved to be a very controversial provision outlawing employment discrimination on account of sex.

Although he was a longtime supporter of the Equal Rights Amendment, Smith was also a member of a coalition of white southern conservatives opposing the civil rights bill. Many liberals hesitated to support the "sex" provision because they feared it would sink the whole bill, jeopardizing the opportunity to advance civil rights for African Americans. While Smith later denied that he had ulterior motives when he introduced the amendment, he cracked a joke trivializing women's rights when he endorsed it in the House of Representatives. With one exception, every male representative who voted for the women's amendment voted against the Civil Rights Act. But their strategy backfired, and the whole bill, including the prohibition against sex discrimination, was passed as the landmark Civil Rights Act of 1964.

Title VII's core antidiscrimination provision states:

It shall be an unlawful employment practice for an employer—(1) to fail or refuse to hire or to discharge any individual, or otherwise to discriminate against any individual with respect to his compensation, terms, conditions, or privileges of employment, because of such individual's race, color, religion, sex, or national origin; or (2) to limit, segregate, or classify his employees or applicants for employment in any way which would deprive or tend to deprive any individual of employment opportunities or otherwise adversely affect his status as an employee, because of such individual's race, color, religion, sex, or national origin.

Title VII prohibits discrimination by private employers of more than fifteen workers, as well as labor unions, employment agencies, and training or apprentice programs. Federal government employees have been protected under a separate section of Title VII from the outset, but state and local government employers and educational institutions were not bound by the act until a 1972 amendment to Title VII closed that loophole. Congress finally imposed antidiscrimination prin-

In 1964 President Lyndon B. Johnson signed an omnibus civil rights bill that included a subchapter, known as Title VII, outlawing discrimination in hiring and promotion on the basis of race, color, creed, national origin, or sex. The sex category was an afterthought, added after vigorous lobbying by women's rights activists.

ciples on itself when, in 1995, it passed the Congressional Accountability Act.

Title VII also created a federal agency, the Equal Employment Opportunity Commission (EEOC), to investigate and conciliate employment discrimination complaints and, where appropriate, to bring suit against employers in federal court. (The U.S. Justice Department prosecutes suits against state and local governments.)

The victims of discrimination may also bring suit in federal court, but only if they have first filed a "charge" with the EEOC. Title VII provides for various forms of judicial relief for winning plaintiffs, including hiring, reinstatement, and back pay with interest, as well as attorneys fees and court costs. Since 1991 compensatory and punitive damages can be awarded as well.

Three broad categories or "theories" of discrimination can be asserted in Title VII discrimination suits. First is "disparate treatment," where the employer treats persons of different races or sexes differently, and the question is whether it did so because of the person's protected trait (i.e., sex or race) or for some other reason. In such cases the employee claims that the treatment was discriminatory, while the employer offers a "legitimate, nondiscriminatory" reason for what it did. The employee then tries to prove that the reason the employer gave was a "pretext," or cover, for discrimination.

While these cases are by far the most common, they mostly turn on their individual facts, and rarely reach the Supreme Court. The disparate treatment cases involving sex discrimination that the Court has decided have been used to establish general principles applicable to all categories of employees, not just men and women. (One significant exception is the Court's sexual harassment cases, discussed in Chapter 8.)

In some disparate treatment cases courts are faced with a situation where the employer was partly motivated by sex discrimination and partly by a "legitimate, nondiscriminatory reason." The Supreme Court chose a sex discrimination case, *Price Waterhouse v. Hopkins* (1989), to announce a general approach to these so-called "mixed motive" cases and to say some important things about what constitutes sex discrimination as well.

But if most disparate treatment cases apply to all different groups of employees, the other two theories of Title VII violation have presented interesting problems specific to gender cases. The most straightforward is "facial" discrimination, meaning that it is overt or intentional, and the term is used when the employer has a policy that is explicitly based on sex. Unless the employer can defend its policy by showing that a person's sex is a "bona fide occupational qualification" (BFOQ) for the particular job, the court will declare the employer's policy illegal under Title VII. The question of whether a policy discriminating on the basis of pregnancy constituted facial discrimination based on sex proved so contentious in the courts that Congress finally amended Title VII to address it explicitly (see Chapter 9, p. 170).

Finally, Title VII can be used to reach beyond intentional discrimination to employment practices that were not adopted in order to discriminate but that in fact select applicants for hire or promotion in a "significantly discriminatory pattern." This type of discrimination is called "disparate impact" or "discriminatory impact" discrimination. If the employer can show that such a policy is truly "job related" and is a "business necessity," then it is permitted to continue using the policy. But if the employee can show that there is another way for the employer to serve its interests without such an undesirable, discriminatory effect, then it is considered a violation of Title VII.

GETTING HIRED

Mothers with Pre-School Age Children

Phillips v. Martin Marietta Corp., 400 U.S. 542 (1971)

The first sex discrimination case under Title VII to reach the Supreme Court involved Martin Marietta Corporation, a defense contractor whose policy was to refuse to hire women with pre-school age children. The employer's assumption was that the mothers of young children made less reliable employees than fathers because they bore primary responsibility for childcare and would therefore be more likely than fathers to take time off to tend to their children's needs. Thus, under the policy even mothers who did not face such problems were excluded, while fathers who were divorced or widowed and had sole custody and responsibility for their children faced no such barrier.

When Ida Phillips answered an ad in her local Florida newspaper for assembly trainees at Martin Marietta the company turned her down, citing its policy of not hiring mothers with young children. Needing the decent wages offered by the defense contractor to support her children, Phillips sued under Title VII, claiming that the policy was facially discriminatory. The company defended itself, showing that 70 to 75 percent of applicants for the advertised position—but an even larger percent of its hires (75–80 percent)—were women. It claimed that this meant that its policies did not discriminate against women.

The district court and the Court of Appeals for the Fifth Circuit were persuaded by the company's arguments. The appeals court held that when another element (in this case having pre–school age children) was added to a person's sex, the policy could not be said to facially discriminate against women. "Ida Phillips was not refused employment because she was a woman nor because she had pre–school age children," the court reasoned. "It is the coalescence of these two elements that denied her the position she desired."

When a rehearing was requested and denied, Chief Judge John R. Brown of the Court of Appeals wrote a scathing dissent to the majority's refusal to rehear the case. "The case," he declared, "is simple. A woman with pre-school children may not be employed, a man with pre-school children may. . . . It is the fact of a person being a mother—i.e., a woman—not the age of the children, which denies equal employment opportunity to a woman which is open to a man." Calling the court's double element rationale the "sex plus" standard, the chief judge condemned it for blunting Title VII's power. "If 'sex plus' stands, the Act is dead," he warned. "Free to add non-sex factors, the rankest sort of discrimination against women can be worked by employers." Employers could evade a charge of sex discrimination by simply adding to a gender-based limitation another factor—such as minimum educational or aptitude requirements. Brown also argued that working mothers were precisely whom Congress was trying to protect in its civil rights employment legislation, because their earnings had become essential to the economic needs of their families.

In 1971 the Supreme Court unanimously overturned the decision of the Court of Appeals, holding that Martin Marietta's policy did indeed discriminate on the basis of sex: "The Court of Appeals erred," it declared, "in reading [Title VII's prohibition of sex discrimination] as permitting one hiring policy for women and another for men—each having pre-school-age children."

Nonetheless, the Court sent the case back to the lower court for trial. In doing so it suggested that the employer might be able to justify treating mothers and fathers differently under its policy by invoking a loophole to Title VII's prohibition of sex discrimination, the bona fide occupational qualification exception. The BFOQ exception allows for hiring or promoting on the basis of sex (or age, religion, or national origin) if it can be shown that such a discriminatory practice is a "bona fide occupational qualification reasonably necessary to the normal operation of that particular business or enterprise." In *Phillips* the Court speculated that "[t]he existence of . . . conflicting family obligations, if demonstrably more relevant to job performance for a woman than for a man, could arguably be the basis for a distinction under [the BFOQ exception]."

In a concurring opinion Justice Thurgood Marshall strenuously objected to the Court's suggestion that a BFOQ defense could be established for a policy such as Martin Marietta's. Even if it were true that the "vast majority" of women shouldered greater responsibility for their pre–school age children than did men, the solution consistent with Title VII was to require *parents* to meet minimum performance standards and provide for the care of their children so that job performance would not suffer, not to exclude *mothers* from jobs.

The BFOQ defense would not be used before the Supreme Court in a sex discrimination case for another six years. The case that presented it was *Dothard v. Rawlinson* (1977), and once again Justice Marshall would find himself in disagreement with the Court's approach to that defense.

Height and Weight Requirements

Dothard v. Rawlinson, 433 U.S. 321 (1977)

Height and weight requirements to be an Alabama prison guard, or "correctional counselor," in the 1970s meant an applicant had to be at least 5′2″ and weigh more than 120 pounds. This ruled out twenty-two-year-old Dianne Kimberly Rawlinson, a slim college graduate who had majored in correctional psychology and who aspired to a job as a prison guard. Rawlinson brought a class action suit against the height and weight requirements under the "disparate impact" theory of Title VII violation. "Disparate impact" discrimination means the employer has a policy that does not officially or intentionally discriminate against men or women, yet in practice that policy has a disproportionately adverse effect on one sex. In this case the height and weight requirement would filter out 41 percent of women and only 1 percent of men, judged by national height and weight statistics.

After Rawlinson filed her suit Alabama passed a new regulation requiring that guards being assigned to maximum security prisons for "contact positions," that is, positions requiring "continual close physical proximity to inmates," be of the same sex as the prisoners. In Alabama there were four maximum security men's penitentiaries, and one such prison for women. This meant that roughly one quarter of the state's correctional counselor jobs were open to women. So even if Rawlinson passed the height and weight requirements, she could not compete for about 75 percent of prison guard jobs in the state. She amended her complaint to include a challenge to this new regulation that segregated the assignment of guard jobs by sex.

The district court found in favor of Rawlinson, saying that the requirements created an arbitrary barrier to equal employment for women. The state appealed directly to the Supreme Court, claiming

that sex, height, and weight were valid occupational qualifications given the nature of the job.

In an opinion written by Justice Potter Stewart, the Court ruled 8–1 that the height and weight requirements were discriminatory. Although the requirements were facially neutral they selected applicants for hire in a significantly discriminatory pattern. Moreover, the employer had not proven that its height and weight standards were necessary for effective job performance. Although the state argued that the requirements had "a relationship to strength, a sufficient but unspecified amount of which is essential to effective job performance as a correctional counselor," it had produced no evidence at trial establishing that relationship. Besides, said Stewart, if strength is what is required for the job, the state should adopt and validate a test that measured strength directly.

Justice William H. Rehnquist wrote a concurring opinion, joined by Justice Harry A. Blackmun and Chief Justice Warren E. Burger. Although Rehnquist agreed that the defendant failed to present evidence to support its "strength" defense of the height and weight rules, he suggested that the state could perhaps have made the case that the *appearance* of strength (i.e., *looking* tall and heavy) could in fact be crucial to maintaining security. "I would think," he said, "that Title VII would not preclude a state from saying that anyone under 5′ 2″ or 120 pounds, no matter how strong in fact, does not have a sufficient appearance of strength to be a prison guard."

Justice Byron R. White wrote a dissent arguing that, although women made up more than a third of Alabama's general labor force but less than 13 percent of its "correctional counselor" workforce, there was no proof that the height and weight restrictions were responsible for the gap.

On the issue of whether women could fill close contact jobs in men's maximum security prisons, the Court acknowledged that the policy discrimi-

Dianne Kimberly Rawlinson hired Pamela Horowitz—the lawyer who would argue her case before the Supreme Court—in, of all places, a beauty salon. In fact Rawlinson, who was turned down by the Alabama prison system to be a prison guard in 1974 because she did not meet their minimum height and weight requirements, was shampooing Horowitz's hair. Like many of the salon's clients, Horowitz worked at the Southern Poverty Law Center in downtown Montgomery. One day she asked Rawlinson why someone with her obvious intelligence was stuck in such a menial job. "Actually," replied Rawlinson, "I'm having a problem. Are you a lawyer?"

When Rawlinson explained her situation to Horowitz, a native Minnesotan who had come to Alabama to do poverty litigation after graduating from Boston University Law School, she was immediately interested. The Southern Poverty Law Center was already preparing a case on behalf of Brenda Mieth, who had been rejected for a job as a state trooper because of the same height and weight requirements. When Horowitz heard Rawlinson's tale, she knew she had found an even better case to challenge the regulation that indirectly kept many women from pursuing their chosen careers.

Rawlinson, whom everyone calls Kim, was born in Montgomery, Alabama, in 1953. Her parents owned their own real estate office. When Rawlinson entered the University of Alabama she thought she would major in psychology and become a counselor. But during her senior year she was awarded a stipend to work for three professors who were conducting studies on criminal behavior and the correctional system. One had a grant to study juvenile justice, another to analyze inmates' letters, and the third to conduct psychological tests on male prisoners. Rawlinson was fascinated by their work. She promptly switched her major and earned

Kim Rawlinson was five pounds too light to qualify for a prison guard job under Alabama's regulation requiring a minimum height and weight for certain jobs. She successfully challenged the regulation as sex discrimination because it ruled out a disproportionately high number of women applicants.

a B.S. in correctional psychology. With the encouragement of her professors, she decided on a career in corrections.

Despite her college experience, which included a stint in the Tuscaloosa police department's juvenile division, she was turned down for several jobs because she lacked prison experience. Then one day she received a letter from the personnel director rejecting her application to be trained as a prison guard, or "correctional counselor," because she did not meet the state's height and weight requirement to hold that kind of a job. She was 5'3" and weighed

115 pounds, and the regulation required her to be at least 5'2" and weigh 120 pounds.

"It was so arbitrary, it didn't make sense to me," recalls Rawlinson. She wrote back asking for clarification. The personnel director sent her a copy of the regulations, adding that he could not waive them. So Rawlinson traveled to Birmingham to file a complaint with the state's Equal Employment Opportunity Commission. Unable to find work, she began washing hair in the salon where she had her fortuitous encounter with Horowitz.

Horowitz and Morris Dees, the head of the Southern Poverty Law Center, filed a class action suit against the Department of Public Safety and the Department of Corrections. Rawlinson became the main plaintiff in the case, which was enlarged to challenge a new regulation barring women from working in "close contact" positions in all-male maximum security prisons. Her parents were horrified, and tried to dissuade her from going ahead with the suit. They worried it would hurt their business.

Horowitz and Dees had trouble finding examples of women prison guards performing their jobs effectively, because there were so few women working in corrections in the 1970s. They did get testimony from female guards in Chicago, although they were not working in a maximum security prison. When the state's attorneys questioned Rawlinson to prepare their side of the case, they passed her gory pictures of male prison guards stabbed to death by inmates. When she failed to be intimidated they kept insisting that she look more closely at a photo of a slain guard. "I don't get their argument," Rawlinson finally said to her attorneys. "Being a man, being big didn't help him. . . . Why are they sharing this with me?" Based on her limited experience, she had found working with inmates interesting, not threatening. "Maybe it's naive if you do not have any fear," she explained, "but where I come from if you treat people like human beings they treat you well."

Rawlinson's attorneys won in district court, but the state appealed the case directly to the Supreme Court, bypassing the appeals court. Horowitz learned that the justices had agreed to hear the case when she got a call from a *Wall Street Journal* reporter. At first Horowitz whooped with joy, but then she began to worry. It was great to have the opportunity to argue before the Supreme Court, but she thought perhaps the justices might rule against her.

She was half wrong. The Court found that the height and weight requirement did indeed discriminate against women, but the justices let stand the other regulation barring women guards from working in all-male maximum security prisons. Their reasoning—that women were too vulnerable to sexual attacks in Alabama's notoriously violent prisons—surprised Horowitz. After all, Judge Frank Johnson, a member of the three-judge court that had ruled in Rawlinson's favor, knew the conditions in Alabama's prisons first hand and had not had reservations about allowing women to work there.

Rawlinson did not attend the oral argument and heard about the Court's decision from a contact at the Southern Poverty Law Center. Horowitz had left the center to work for the American Civil Liberties Union in Washington, D.C., where she now is in private practice. Rawlinson was happy with the outcome, although the importance of her case did not hit her until years later, when she was invited to speak about it at her graduate school. The decision had little direct impact on her career because by then she had already gotten what she wanted: a job in corrections.

During the appeals process Judson Locke, Alabama's prison commissioner, had gotten to know Rawlinson. He liked her and told personnel to find her a job. She worked as a counselor at a juvenile diagnostic center for almost a year. Then, in 1976, the state prison hired her as a correctional counselor trainee in an all-male minimum security prison. The youthful prisoners were first-time offenders and were in minimal custody—no bars or fences, and no weapons on the guards. She enjoyed the work immensely.

(continued)

(continued)

Rawlinson did not fear for her safety. She believed that inmates do not tolerate abuse toward women and children among themselves, so she never felt personally threatened. "Having a woman in the prison made them more civil, they would protect me," she recalled. She also found that women seemed to have a better rapport with the inmates, listened to them more, and were sometimes better able to gain their cooperation. Many of the prisoners told her that having women guards made prison seem more normal, more tolerable. She did encounter a few problems: "Once I gave a major disciplinary [punishment] and the inmates didn't like it and they slashed my tires. Another time they stole my car in an escape."

Rawlinson wrote a poignant letter to the editor of the Alabama *Journal* explaining her case and describing her interest in criminal justice. She took exception to the notion that guarding prisoners was merely a question of physical force. "Physical standards for prison guards are irrelevant," she wrote, "except that guards should be in excellent health." "However," she continued, "there should not be so much focus on how big and mean a person is, as on how able he or she is to handle the job, mentally as well as physically. And this, dear public, has nothing to do with inches, pounds or sex!"

After starting her new corrections job Rawlinson took on an added challenge. Auburn University had just opened up a graduate program in criminal justice and, interested in recruiting women, offered her a full scholarship. She obtained her master's degree in 1980.

Rawlinson had always wanted to be more of a counselor than a guard. In 1977 she was able to switch to a prison where inmates were evaluated and classified before being assigned elsewhere. As a classification specialist, she tested and evaluated all kinds of prisoners, even those on death row. But less than three years after taking the assignment she quit—not just the job, but prison work entirely.

Rawlinson was engaged to a fellow correctional officer, and under nepotism rules (forbidding family members from working together) they could not both remain in their jobs. But she also left because she was placed under official investigation and therefore was unable to earn raises or win promotions. No charges were ever filed against her and authorities have declined to provide a reason for the investigation.

The period that followed was a dark one for Rawlinson. She was diagnosed with cancer of the uterus and, at age twenty-seven, underwent a hysterectomy. Her body went into instant menopause, sending her hormones on a roller-coaster ride. Her doctors tried to stabilize her with various prescription drugs, including lithium. She developed a substance abuse problem from her medications. Her marriage collapsed after only six months.

After several years Rawlinson got treatment, began weight-lifting competitively, and turned her life around. She remarried and discovered she had a talent for sales. Rawlinson sold Mary Kay cosmetics, earning a director title and a red Grand Am sportscar. She is now a sales representative in Montgomery for a telecommunications company, and she continues to work in prisons as a volunteer.

Although Rawlinson was awarded $16,000 in back pay as part of the settlement, she received only about $3,000 after her lawyers got their share. Still, she believes that justice was done: "I was hired, although not under ideal circumstances, but I was hired." At the time of the Supreme Court decision Rawlinson had met a woman who was "100 pounds soaking wet and barely five feet tall" and who was just embarking on a career in corrections. Rawlinson knows that her friend, who has proven to be a talented and dedicated guard, would never have been hired as a correctional counselor if Rawlinson had not filed her suit. She is proud to have helped her and other women like her. "When you stick your neck out for something," Rawlinson insists, "maybe it's going to get stomped on but at least you know what you are doing is right."

nated on the basis of sex. But the justices voted 6–3 that women could legitimately be excluded because the Board of Corrections had proved in this case that being a man was a BFOQ for guarding male prisoners in a maximum security prison. The reason: women were more vulnerable to male sexual attack. Alabama's maximum security prisons were described as jungles marked by "rampant violence" where sex offenders constituted one-fifth of the population and were not segregated from the other prisoners. Justice Stewart reasoned that "a woman's relative ability to maintain order . . . could be directly reduced by her womanhood."

There is a basis in fact for expecting that sex offenders who have criminally assaulted women in the past would be moved to do so again if access to women were established within the prison. There would also be a real risk that other inmates, deprived of normal heterosexual environment, would assault women guards because they were women. In a prison system where violence is the order of the day, where inmate access to guards is facilitated by dormitory living arrangements, where every institution is understaffed, and where a substantial portion of the inmate population is composed of sex offenders mixed at random with other prisoners, there are few visible deterrents to inmate assaults on women custodians.

Justice Marshall, joined by Justice William J. Brennan Jr., dissented from the majority's interpretation of the BFOQ exception. The Alabama prison system's exceptional barbarity did not, they asserted, justify discriminating against women. Rather, Alabama should act "with all possible speed" to remedy prison conditions so bad that another federal court had already ruled that they violated the Constitution. Marshall also took issue with the notion that female guards would be more susceptible to inmate attack than male guards, reminding the Court that "invisible deterrents are the guards' only real protection."

No prison guard relies primarily on his or her ability to ward off an inmate attack to maintain order. Guards are typically unarmed and sheer numbers of inmates could overcome the normal complement. Rather, like all other law enforcement officers, prison guards must rely primarily on the moral authority of their office and the threat of future punishment for miscreants. As one expert testified below, common sense, fairness, mental and emotional stability are the qualities a guard needs to cope with the job. Well qualified and properly trained women, no less than men, have these psychological weapons at their disposal.

Marshall suggested that each woman should assess for herself whether she wanted to expose herself to the dangers of the job. He also pointed out that there was no evidence that women guards would unwittingly invite sexual assaults. "With all respect," he wrote, "this rationale regrettably perpetuates one of the most insidious of the old myths about women—that women, wittingly or not, are seductive sexual objects." "The proper response to inevitable attacks on both male and female guards," Marshall admonished, "is not to limit the employment opportunities of law-abiding women who wish to contribute to their community, but to take swift and sure punitive action against inmate offenders." In other words, he concluded, if it is men's illegal sexual aggression that threatens prison security, then women should not have to pay the price by being excluded from the job.

Dothard had widespread impact because it struck down a criterion that was used in many occupations to exclude women. For decades, height and weight requirements had kept women from becoming police officers, firefighters, and prison guards—all traditional pathways to advancement for working-class men because they provided a good salary, a pension, and job stability. And *Dothard* was so focused on the unusually violent atmosphere of Alabama's prisons that courts later found that women in other states could indeed work as prison guards in all-male facilities that were more adequately structured and staffed and more soundly managed than Alabama's.

MAKING PARTNER

In the late 1960s and early 1970s, when Title VII was new legislation and many employers still had official policies discriminating against women, cases of facial discrimination flooded the federal courts. Those courts found that only the narrowest of situations allowed a company to claim the BFOQ exception to Title VII. Employers nationwide thus learned to avoid policies that explicitly discriminated against women. Consequently, sex discrimination went "underground," which meant that the majority of plaintiffs now brought cases against policies where the discrimination was more difficult to determine. These cases challenged the courts to decide whether the "real" reason employers took an adverse action against a job applicant or employee was the employee's sex, or whether to believe there was some other, legitimate explanation offered in court for the employer's actions.

In one such case, the trial court found that the employer acted both for discriminatory *and* nondiscriminatory reasons when it rejected a woman employee's bid for partnership in one of America's premier accounting firms. The Supreme Court's resolution of this case, *Price Waterhouse v. Hopkins,* involved both important general questions of Title VII doctrine and special rulings on what constitutes evidence of sex discrimination. But first, the Court had to decide whether partnership decisions were even covered by Title VII, which it did in *Hishon v. King & Spalding.*

Hishon v. King & Spalding, 467 U.S. 69 (1984)

Price Waterhouse v. Hopkins, 490 U.S. 228 (1989)

Among the most sensitive employment decisions are those concerning admission to partnership.

Unlike an ordinary promotion, a conferral of partnership entails a change in status from "employee" to "employer." Because partners generally govern a firm by consensus, a successful candidate for partnership must be someone whose judgment the existing partners trust. And once an individual has been made a partner, the decision is virtually impossible to reverse. "[W]hen a businessman selects a partner," one senator remarked during the debate on Title VII of the Civil Rights Act of 1964, "he comes dangerously close to the situation he faces when he selects a wife." But despite that expression of concern, Congress did not explicitly exempt partnership decisions from the scope of the statute.

In *Hishon v. King & Spalding,* the justices confronted the partnership issue in the context of their own profession, the law. Generally, large law firms hire many associates fresh out of law school each year and impose heavy workloads on them. After five or six years the firm's partners invite some, but rarely all, of those associates to join the partnership. Those who are not asked to become partners are generally expected to find employment elsewhere.

Elizabeth Anderson Hishon had worked as an associate at King & Spalding, a large Atlanta law firm, for six years when her name first came up for partnership in 1978. The firm rejected her that year, and then again the following year. Hishon filed a lawsuit under Title VII in 1980, pointing to the fact that no woman had ever served as a partner at the firm. But the lower courts did not reach the question of discrimination: they dismissed the case on the ground that Title VII simply did not apply to the selection of partners. "[W]e are unwilling to dictate partnership decisions under the guise of employee promotions protected by Title VII," the Court of Appeals for the Eleventh Circuit held. "The very essence of a partnership is the voluntary joinder of all partners with each other."

In a unanimous opinion written by Chief Justice Warren E. Burger, the Supreme Court brought Hishon's case back to life, and in doing so set an important Title VII precedent. In her complaint Hishon had alleged that, after a five- or six-year apprenticeship, consideration for partnership was "a matter of course" for associates who had received satisfactory evaluations. If this allegation was true, Burger said, then fair consideration for partnership was one of the "terms, conditions, or privileges of employment" covered by Title VII—and Hishon should be given a chance to prove her case.

The law firm argued that applying Title VII to its partnership decisions would infringe on its constitutional rights of free expression and free association. Burger acknowledged that lawyers make a "distinctive contribution" to society, but said that the firm "had not shown how its ability to fulfill such a function would be inhibited by a requirement that it consider petitioner for partnership on her merits." And although invidious discrimination by private individuals and firms was not prohibited by the Constitution, it had "never been accorded affirmative constitutional protection."

In a separate concurring opinion Justice Lewis F. Powell Jr. underscored that, while decisions as to who should be admitted to partnership were covered by Title VII, the decisions made with respect to persons who already *were* partners were not similarly covered. In this case, Powell said, Hishon alleged that the firm had induced her to accept employment by promising that she would be considered for partnership on a "fair and equal basis." If that allegation was true, then the firm had assumed a contractual obligation to consider Hishon for partnership without regard to her sex.

Five years later, in *Price Waterhouse v. Hopkins,* the Court moved beyond the threshold question of whether Title VII applied to partnerships and delved into the substance of a partnership deliberation. At Price Waterhouse, one of the "Big Eight" accounting firms, partnership decisions involved input from a large number of people. Once a candidate's name had been submitted by partners in the candidate's local office, all the other partners in the firm were invited to submit written comments. Then, after a review of all comments and interviews with the partners who had submitted them, the firm's admissions committee would make recommendations to its policy board. In turn the policy board would decide whether to submit the candidate's name to the entire partnership for a vote, "hold" the candidacy for later consideration, or reject the candidate.

Ann Branigar Hopkins had worked in a Washington, D.C., office of Price Waterhouse for five years when the partners in that office submitted her name for partnership in 1982. At the time, only seven of the firm's 662 partners were women, and Hopkins was the lone woman among the eighty-eight individuals under consideration for partnership. Of the thirty-two partners who submitted comments about Hopkins, thirteen recommended that she be admitted to the partnership, pointing out that she had a stellar record in bringing in business and praising her "strong character, independence, and integrity." Eight partners voted to reject Hopkins, three recommended that she be placed on hold, and eight did not have an informed opinion. In the end the policy board recommended that Hopkins's candidacy—along with nineteen others—be held for reconsideration the following year.

As part of the evaluation process, a number of partners—even some of those supporting Hopkins—criticized her interpersonal skills, calling her overly aggressive, harsh, and difficult. Some of these negative comments reflected a perception that Hopkins was not sufficiently feminine. One partner described her as "macho," another suggested that she take "a course at charm school," and several objected to her use of profanity. And when one of the partners informed Hopkins of the

When Ann Hopkins got the news that she would not be making partner at Price Waterhouse—the huge accounting firm where she was a senior manager—she was "in shock." She had consistently irritated the firm's senior partners, she was told. But she was unable even to remember meeting any of the senior partners. "I could offer no explanation," she recalls in her book, *So Ordered: Making Partner the Hard Way.* "Five years of long hours, hard work, and remarkable results were down the tubes."

A tough-talking army brat with Texas roots, Hopkins was a computer specialist with a background in mathematics. She had thrown herself into her work at Price Waterhouse, traveling overseas and pulling all-nighters to win accounts. One of those accounts was a $25 million contract to design a worldwide financial management system for the U.S. Department of State. None of the other candidates for partnership had brought in anything comparable.

Despite the fact that she was the only woman among the eighty-eight individuals proposed for partnership in 1982, it barely occurred to Hopkins that her rejection had anything to do with her gender. The question came up during a grim postmortem conversation with a couple of female colleagues, but, Hopkins writes, "We found unimaginable any notion that gender influenced business decisions." Even when Tom Beyer—a partner with whom Hopkins had worked closely—advised her that she could improve her chances for reconsideration if she walked, talked, and dressed more femininely, Hopkins simply dismissed his counsel as "nonsense." And when Hopkins reluctantly consulted a lawyer, she told him, in response to his question, that she could not recall any "overt sexist comments." But then, she added, "I infrequently recognized sexist comments."

Ann Hopkins was denied partnership at Price Waterhouse because she was considered overbearing, arrogant, and abrasive—which made some view her as insufficiently feminine. Arguing that such traits could be seen as an asset in a male employee, Hopkins filed a sex discrimination suit. A divided Supreme Court ruled that sex stereotyping was gender discrimination and that unless the firm could prove it would have fired her for other reasons it must admit her as a partner.

It was only during the trial of her lawsuit against Price Waterhouse in 1985, Hopkins told the *New York Times,* that she finally began to understand what had happened to her. Listening to Dr. Susan Fiske, a psychologist who had been retained by her own lawyers as an expert witness, Hopkins learned that the likelihood of stereotyping is greatest when an individual is one of a small minority—for example, the only female in a group of eighty-eight candidates for partnership. Price Waterhouse was arguing that it had rejected Hopkins because she was overbearing, arrogant, and abrasive. But, Fiske testified, the very same behavior might well have been viewed in a positive light had it been exhibited by a man. It was only because the Price Waterhouse partners were expecting Hopkins to conform to a nurturing and demure feminine stereotype that they objected to her personality.

But understanding that sexual stereotyping had entered into—or even caused—the firm's decision to reject her did not make it any easier for Hopkins to listen to witnesses for Price Waterhouse repeatedly catalogue the perceived flaws in her character. "I felt as if my personality were being dissected like a diseased frog in the biology lab," she writes in her book.

During the six-year life of the lawsuit, Hopkins had to cope with a number of personal crises that may well have been caused, or exacerbated, by the litigation itself. With her husband self-employed and earning an uncertain income, it was essential that Hopkins find another lucrative job after leaving Price Waterhouse: she had three children in private schools, and mounting legal bills. What she would have liked was a job similar to the one she had left, with one of the other major accounting firms. But, because of the lawsuit, she writes, "I was a pariah in the Big Eight." After starting her own consulting business, she eventually secured a job as a budget planner with the World Bank.

Other problems were not so easy to solve. Her husband announced that he wanted a separation and moved out of the house; on May 10, 1989—nine days after the Supreme Court's decision in Hopkins's lawsuit against Price Waterhouse—their divorce became final. One of her children was diagnosed as severely dyslexic, and the other two developed behavior problems.

But at least Hopkins kept winning in court; after every victory she threw a huge party, and her children grew to be on intimate terms with the staff of a local caterer. ("How many times do we have to win this thing?" one of Hopkins's sons asked at one point.) And there was one battle Hopkins did not have to fight herself: when Elizabeth Hishon won her victory against the law firm

of King & Spalding in the Supreme Court in May 1984—a few months after Hopkins filed her suit in the D.C. district court—it became settled law that Title VII applied to partnerships. Hopkins tracked down Hishon's phone number to offer congratulations and to tell her "that I was next in the legal line behind her," she writes. Later, when Hopkins's case was pending in the Supreme Court, the two women got together for drinks when Hishon happened to be visiting Washington. "We glibly referred to each other as 'Landmark One' and 'Landmark Two,'" Hopkins recalls. (After the Supreme Court decision in *King & Spalding*, Hishon herself had settled out of court.)

After two trials, two appeals, and one trip to the Supreme Court, Hopkins at last achieved her goal of making partner at Price Waterhouse. At the second trial, district judge Gerhard Gesell had expressed some qualms about conferring partnership by judicial fiat. "I'm just talking to you as a person and trying to understand," he told Hopkins during the trial. "[Y]ou're an intelligent woman. . . . You've shown you [can] make a living on your own. You've probably shown they were wrong, so what is the point of wanting to put yourself into a position of future friction?"

But Hopkins and her lawyers made it clear that partnership was the remedy they wanted, with her lawyers arguing that Title VII would be seriously weakened if courts refused to issue such orders in partnership cases. On May 14, 1990, when Judge Gesell handed down his order requiring Price Waterhouse to admit Hopkins to the partnership, gleeful pandemonium erupted at the office of Hopkins's lawyers. "A wedding reception would have been glum by comparison," Hopkins recalls in her book.

But after the celebrating was over, Hopkins found that—as Judge Gesell had feared—she still had more difficulties to overcome. "The circumstances under which I became a partner were less than ideal," she points out dryly in her book. Relegated to a sleepy suburban outpost of the firm, with no mentor and no clients, Hopkins began to

(continued)

(continued)

wonder if she could get back her old job at the World Bank. But after a couple of years Hopkins was able to return to Price Waterhouse's Office of Government Services, where she had worked before she embarked on what she jokingly refers to as her "sabbatical." By the spring of 1995, Hopkins writes, "I had all the client work I could handle."

Despite her recognition of the debt she owes to Hishon, Hopkins prefers to view her legal battle as more of a personal struggle than as part of a larger movement. While some of her supporters cast her as a feminist symbol, a friend told the *New York Times* that that "is not a cloak that she wears easily."

In a 1999 interview with the *Times*, she attributed her decision to sue to a value system that places a high priority on bringing about change when necessary. "It's important to how my children see themselves," Hopkins told the *Times,* explaining her motivation for bringing the lawsuit. "It's important to how a whole lot of people I may not know very well see me."

In the 1999 interview Hopkins described herself as "very comfortable" at the firm, now known as PricewaterhouseCoopers. When she rejoined the firm in 1991, about 5 percent of the partners were women; eight years later the figure was closer to 10 percent. Hopkins predicted that in another fifteen years there might be enough women at the firm to make the question of gender a nonissue.

Hopkins's own daughter, Tela, is one woman who is doing her part to achieve that goal: in September 1998, after graduating from college, she took a job with PricewaterhouseCoopers. Hopkins's only comment on her daughter's decision was, "I think it's a good profession."

---

decision to place her candidacy on hold, he advised her that in order to improve her chances she should "walk more femininely, talk more femininely, dress more femininely, wear make-up, have her hair styled, and wear jewelry." Before the time for reconsideration came, the firm informed Hopkins that she was, in fact, no longer a candidate for partnership. Hopkins left the firm and sued.

The district court ruled that although Price Waterhouse had legitimate concerns about Hopkins's interpersonal skills, the firm had also relied on impermissible gender stereotypes in rejecting her candidacy. The firm thus had "mixed motives"—a legitimate, nondiscriminatory one as well as a discriminatory one. The question was whether the firm could prove, by "clear and convincing evidence," that it would have rejected Hopkins even in the absence of discriminatory motives on the part of certain partners. If so, the firm would still be liable for damages, but in such "mixed motive" cases the relief the court awarded Hopkins could be limited.

In this case, the district court held, Price Waterhouse had not been able to prove that it would have rejected Hopkins had it relied only on permissible considerations. Nevertheless, Hopkins was not entitled to a promotion: while she had argued that she had been "constructively discharged"—that is, that Price Waterhouse made her working conditions so intolerable that she had been forced to leave—the district court found that Hopkins had left voluntarily. Nor, because of the absence of evidence on the issue, was she even entitled to any back pay.

On appeal, the circuit court affirmed the crux of the district court's decision, with one adjustment: had Price Waterhouse been able to prove that it would have reached the same decision without considering the biased comments, the firm would have been able to avoid all liability under Title VII. But the appeals court also reversed the district court on another point that worked in Hopkins's favor: the firm's decision to deny her partnership, coupled with its decision not to reconsider her the following year, amounted to a "constructive discharge."

In the Supreme Court, Justice Brennan wrote a plurality opinion—that is, an opinion that drew more votes than any other but failed to win a majority—in which Justices Thurgood Marshall, Harry A. Blackmun, and John Paul Stevens joined. Essentially endorsing the approach of the lower courts, Brennan argued that in passing Title VII Congress meant to condemn not only employment decisions made *solely* on the basis of illegitimate discrimination, but also "mixed motive" cases such as this one. Once the plaintiff has proved that discrimination affected the employer's decision, Brennan said, the burden should then shift to the employer to prove that it would have reached the same decision had it relied only on legitimate considerations.

A decision based on a belief that a woman cannot or must not be aggressive, Brennan held, was a decision made on the basis of sex stereotyping and therefore on the basis of gender. "An employer who objects to aggressiveness in women but whose positions require this trait places women in an intolerable and impermissible Catch-22," Brennan wrote, "out of a job if they behave aggressively and out of a job if they do not."

In this case, it was clear that this sort of sex stereotyping had entered into the comments of a number of partners. That was enough to shift the burden to the employer to show that it would have made the same decision in the absence of discrimination. And, while agreeing with the circuit court that an employer could avoid all liability by making this showing, Brennan concluded that Price Waterhouse had not been able to do so. But the lower courts had erred in one particular: instead of requiring the employer to prove this by "clear and convincing evidence," they should have applied the more lenient "preponderance of the

evidence" standard that was the general rule in noncriminal cases.

Two justices filed opinions concurring in the judgment—that is, supporting the result, but not entirely agreeing with the reasoning of the plurality. Justice Byron R. White disagreed with the plurality's apparent requirement that the employer submit objective evidence that it would have taken the same action for legitimate reasons alone. If the employer "credibly testifies" to that effect, White wrote, that should be sufficient.

In a much lengthier concurrence Justice Sandra Day O'Connor emphasized that the plurality's framework of proof—shifting the burden to the employer to show that it would have made the same decision absent discrimination—was only applicable in a certain subset of Title VII cases: those in which a plaintiff could show "by direct evidence" that an illegitimate criterion not only played a role in the decision, but was a "substantial factor" contributing to it. (Brennan had altered his opinion in an attempt to win O'Connor's vote and thereby secure a majority, but O'Connor had remained unsatisfied by the changes.)

Justice Anthony Kennedy, joined by Chief Justice William H. Rehnquist and Justice Antonin Scalia, dissented. Shifting the burden of proof to the employer, Kennedy stated, was a marked departure from the usual practice in Title VII cases, in which the burden of proof remains on the plaintiff at all times. And although the Court's holding should apply only to a limited number of cases, Kennedy predicted that it would cause widespread confusion in the lower courts. Examining the evidence under the usual Title VII standard, Kennedy concluded that Hopkins had failed to prove that gender discrimination was the reason the firm had rejected her.

But the Supreme Court's decision did not resolve the case. The district court now needed to reevaluate Price Waterhouse's defense under the "preponderance of the evidence" standard and—if the firm was unable to meet it—to determine an appropriate remedy. Ultimately, the court not only awarded Hopkins $371,000 in back pay, but also ordered the firm to admit her as a partner.

Reacting to *Price Waterhouse* and other Supreme Court decisions interpreting Title VII, Congress passed the Civil Rights Act of 1991 in an attempt to ease the burden on plaintiffs claiming discrimination. Under *Price Waterhouse,* an employer has been able to avoid all liability in a "mixed motives" case by showing that it would have made the same decision in the absence of discrimination. This meant that even if an employer admitted that it did not want to hire women, it would have been absolved of liability under Title VII for rejecting a female applicant if it could persuade the judge that it had another, nondiscriminatory motive for not hiring her. The 1991 amendment to Title VII changed this rule by providing that the company will be held liable if discrimination is "a motivating factor" in the employer's decision.

Even so, the employer still has a good reason to try to persuade the judge it would have made the same hiring decision in the absence of discrimination. If it manages to do so, the employer can dramatically limit the relief that the court can order it to provide to the plaintiff. The 1991 Civil Rights Act provides that if the employer makes such a showing, it will not be required to pay damages or back pay or to hire, promote, or reinstate the plaintiff. All the court has the power to do is to order the employer to pay the plaintiff's attorney's fees, and to declare that it discriminated against the plaintiff and must refrain from engaging in further discrimination.

AFFIRMATIVE ACTION

With passage of the Civil Rights Act of 1964, companies were no longer allowed to hire or promote workers based on their race, religion, sex, or national origin. But civil rights activists argued that merely outlawing discriminatory employment practices was not enough to increase the presence of nonwhites and women in the workplace. To compensate for a history of racism and sexism something more aggressive was called for, especially to combat the more subtle barriers that exclude women and minorities from accessing the better, higher paying jobs.

The idea was for employers to give special consideration to members of minority groups against which they had previously discriminated. This policy, known as "affirmative action," called for the government to give priority to members of formerly excluded groups in awarding government jobs or contracts and in granting admissions to federally funded universities.

In 1965, the year Title VII went into effect, President Lyndon B. Johnson signed the first executive order requiring that businesses that have contracts with the federal government implement affirmative action by hiring and promoting racial minorities. He cautioned that recruitment "goals may not be rigid and inflexible quotas. . . , but must be targets reasonably attainable by means of applying every good faith effort to make all aspects of the entire affirmative action program work." There was no mention of gender in the executive order, even though women—although not a minority in terms of their numbers—also had a long history of employment discrimination.

This oversight was remedied two years later, when Johnson amended his order to include women as a category that companies with federal government contracts were required to include in their affirmative action plans. This meant these companies had to keep statistics on women in all job categories and, where women were "underutilized," establish goals and timetables to increase their representation. In 1969 President Richard Nixon extended the reach of affirmative action to include all jobs in the federal government.

But the notion of affirmative action encountered, and continues to encounter, significant opposition. Affirmative action policies remain highly controversial because they focus on equality in results over equality in opportunity. In other words, achieving a more diverse, representative workforce or student body is emphasized over treating workers or students equally through unbiased hiring or admissions practices. Some opponents believe that affirmative action reinforces gender and racial stereotypes. And even those who support the notion of affirmative action often disagree on specific program issues such as whether general goals or specific quotas are more appropriate, whether affirmative action policies should cover promotions, and what to do about those who lose out on school and work opportunities because they do not qualify for preferred status.

During the 1970s the Supreme Court articulated and legitimated the concept of affirmative action in a series of cases dealing with race. As a result of these decisions, private and public employers began giving preference to racial minorities to avoid charges of discrimination. As these voluntary affirmative action plans were put into widespread effect, white males filed lawsuits under Title VII, claiming that they had been subjected to racial discrimination.

The first important "reverse discrimination" suit decided by the Supreme Court involved a white male applicant who challenged a University of California–Davis Medical School program that set aside 16 of 100 slots for minority students in order to achieve a more racially diverse student body. A divided Court (the nine justices issued six separate opinions) ruled in *Regents of the University of California v. Bakke* (1978) that race could be a factor in admissions programs among qualified applicants but that the U.C. Davis program's use of specific quotas was illegal. The following year the Court decided *United Steelworkers of America v. Weber*, in which it upheld, this time under Title

VII, an affirmative action plan. In an industry with a long history of racial exclusions from skilled jobs, a private company and its union created a training program to promote unskilled workers into skilled positions. Half the slots were to be reserved for African Americans until the percentage of African American skilled workers approximated the percentage of African Americans in the local labor force.

During the 1980s the Reagan administration tried to discourage affirmative action by challenging the legality of quotas. But in several decisions the Supreme Court upheld the use of quotas to achieve racial balance in the workplace. The Court did, however, preclude the use of affirmative action when the result was that senior nonminority workers would be laid off while junior minority workers were retained. In 1987 the Court confirmed its support for affirmative action when it heard its first and only affirmative action case that dealt with gender. *Johnson v. Santa Clara Cty.* marked the first time the Court had recognized women as a group eligible for affirmative action.

Johnson v. Transportation Agency, Santa Clara Cty., 480 U.S. 616 (1987)

In 1978 the Santa Clara Transportation Agency adopted a temporary affirmative action plan to remedy past discrimination against women and racial minorities by setting goals for hiring and promotion of members of previously excluded groups. The county's Board of Transportation had stated that the goal of the plan was the "attainment of a County work force whose composition . . . includes women, disabled persons and ethnic minorities in a ratio in all job categories that reflects their distribution in the Santa Clara County [California] area work force." Although women composed 36 percent of the area's labor force, they constituted only 22 percent of the agency's employees. And three quarters of those female agency employees held low-paying clerical jobs. No woman had ever held a highly paid "skilled crafts worker" position at the agency.

Diane Joyce was a thirty-three-year-old single mother trying to raise four children after the death of her husband. She worked for the county's road maintenance arm for four years as an account clerk. When a road dispatcher job became available in 1974, promising higher wages because it was a "skilled crafts worker" position, Joyce applied for it. The dispatcher duties included assigning road crews, equipment, and materials and maintaining records of the road work to be done.

The agency told Joyce she was not eligible for the dispatcher position because she had never served as a road maintenance worker. So she applied for one of ten openings on the road maintenance crews. Of the 110 road maintenance positions, none had ever been held by a woman. Joyce was given the position—the first woman in the county to hold such a job.

The experience proved to be both trying and fulfilling for Joyce. The county was slow to provide the standard coveralls provided to male workers, producing them only after Joyce, having ruined several pairs of her own pants, filed a formal grievance with her union. Her coworkers were hostile and wrote obscenities on her truck. She nonetheless loved her work, which entailed everything from maneuvering trucks up mountains to shoveling tar. "You know," she said, "women pay $50 a month to join a health club and here I was getting in great shape."

During the nearly five years she worked as a road maintenance crew member, she also filled in as needed as a road dispatcher. When, in December 1979, another position as road dispatcher became available, she again applied for it. Of the applicants, nine were considered "well qualified" for the position. Joyce was among those nine, along with a coworker named Paul Johnson.

Johnson had joined the Santa Clara Transportation Agency three years before Joyce. Like Joyce, he had unsuccessfully applied for the road dispatcher opening in 1974. At fifty-five, Johnson had prior experience as a dispatcher in a previous job but had worked only two years on road crews, as opposed to Joyce's five years of road crew experience. Yet Johnson had the inside track because he had been temporarily assigned to the position of road dispatcher for the previous three months.

The nine "well qualified" candidates were interviewed by a two-person review board. The board rated the candidates, giving them scores between seventy and eighty. Johnson scored seventy-five, tying him for second with another applicant, while Diane Joyce scored seventy-three, placing her third. The candidates were then interviewed by a three-person board of transportation agency supervisors, two of whom had been antagonistic toward Joyce in the past. One had called her a "rebel-rousing, skirt-wearing person." The other was the road maintenance supervisor who had refused to provide her with coveralls. Not surprisingly, the three-person board recommended the promotion of Johnson to the dispatcher position.

Prior to the second interview, Joyce called Helena Lee, the county's affirmative action officer. Lee contacted the agency's affirmative action coordinator, who recommended to the director of the Transportation Agency, James Graebner, that Joyce be selected. Graebner, authorized under county rules to choose among the "eligibles," selected Joyce. Johnson sued the agency, arguing that he had been discriminated against on the basis of sex, in violation of Title VII.

Johnson initially won his case in district court but lost before the Court of Appeals for the Ninth Circuit. The appeals court held that the Santa Clara plan "falls on the permissible side of the line" regarding affirmative action plans.

In its landmark 1987 decision the Supreme Court agreed in a 6–3 vote that the county's affirmative action plan permitting the agency to remedy the "manifest imbalance" of men and women in "traditionally segregated job categories" was legal. Writing for the majority, Justice Brennan said the plan "provides assurance both that sex or race will be taken into account in a manner consistent with Title VII's purpose of eliminating the effects of employment discrimination, and that the interests of those employees not benefitting from the plan will not be unduly infringed."

Specifically, Brennan approved of the plan because it "represents a moderate, flexible, case-by-case approach to effecting a gradual improvement in the representation of minorities and women in the Agency's work force." In other words it established flexible promotional goals and did not impose strict quotas. The plan also required women to compete for skilled jobs against other qualified applicants and did not close off male workers' possibilities for advancement. Brennan hailed the plan as a temporary measure designed to achieve a balanced workforce that would presumably be abandoned once that goal was met.

But the Court's six-justice majority was not unified, a lack of consensus that perhaps reflected the ambivalence of society in general toward affirmative action. Justice Stevens wrote a concurrence saying that it was not necessary for a company to focus on past discrimination in order to give preference to members of underrepresented groups. Employers should, he thought, be free to consider other legitimate reasons to give preferences to members of underrepresented groups. In a separate concurrence, Justice O'Connor contended that evidence of such past discrimination was indeed necessary. In this case she thought the statistics on the underrepresentation of women in nontraditional jobs were sufficient.

Justice White dissented on the ground that a statistical imbalance between men and women in a certain job category was not necessarily evidence of intentional or systematic discrimination. White also joined most of Justice Scalia's vigorous dissent (which Chief Justice Rehnquist joined entirely), accusing the majority of unfairly reaching beyond the goal of eliminating past discrimination to achieving "proportionate representation by race and sex in the workplace. . . ." Scalia argued that women were underrepresented in traditional male jobs involving manual labor not because they had been excluded but because they were either not interested in performing physically challenging work or did not have the necessary qualifications.

Scalia also pointed out that unskilled persons such as Johnson were "members of the nonfavored groups least likely to have profited from societal discrimination in the past." "A statute designed to establish a color-blind and gender-blind workplace," he reasoned, "has thus been converted into a powerful engine of racism and sexism. . . . The irony is that these individuals—predominately unknown, unaffluent, unorganized—suffer this injustice at the hands of a Court fond of thinking itself the champion of the politically impotent."

Johnson established that voluntary affirmative action plans, if properly designed to increase the numbers of women in traditional male job categories, are legal under Title VII for public sector employment. The decision thus extended the reach of *Weber* beyond the private sector. *Johnson* also acknowledged that the aim of affirmative action policy can extend to the achievement of racial and gender balance in the workforce based solely on proof of statistical imbalance rather than on proof of actual prior discrimination. And in *Johnson* the Court allowed for a great deal of flexibility in determining the need for such plans and in the details of how they are implemented.

It is difficult to measure how much affirmative action has helped women advance in the workplace because their increasing success can be at-

When Paul Johnson applied for a job promotion to become a road dispatcher in California's Santa Clara County, he never imagined that he would become the lightning rod in the controversy over affirmative action. For fifty-five years Johnson had lived an ordinary existence, working hard and believing that life in America was just and equitable—a faith that would be tested and eventually broken.

It seemed like a reasonably straightforward proposition for Johnson, to apply for a job for which he was eminently qualified. What he did not anticipate was that a qualified woman would also apply for the road dispatcher position, or that his employer would use the job opening as an opportunity to implement its affirmative action plan, adopted only a year earlier. When the County Transportation Agency chose to hire Diane Joyce as dispatcher, Johnson took action, a decision that would take him out of the quiet anonymity that had been his life.

Johnson had wrestled with his share of life's challenges, but he had always persevered through hard work and common sense. He was born to poor Kansas farmers. When he was eight his father died, and Johnson was sent to Texas to be raised by relatives. After serving in a submarine during World War II he worked as a roughneck in the oil fields. Then came marriage, and a move in 1948 to San Jose, where the climate was warm, the economy booming, and road jobs plentiful.

After working at a construction company for seventeen years, Johnson came to work for Santa Clara County in 1967. He started out as a clerk in the road yard and easily fit into the male camaraderie of the job. Johnson was described as "the kind of guy you like to have for a neighbor—quiet, industrious, and decent." Indeed he was a firm believer in the notion that you work hard, you get rewarded—it was as simple as that. So much so that he resented those

who questioned that belief, and was the leader of the antiunion faction at his road unit.

By the time Johnson applied to become dispatcher, he had had his eye on that higher paying job for six years, and had been acting as dispatcher in the incumbent's absence. Johnson was confident that the dispatcher's job was his to claim: "I knew there was no one else taking the test that was anywhere near qualified as I was." Out of twelve original applicants, nine scored over the qualifying seventy in an oral test. Under the county's personnel policies, the hiring supervisor was free to choose any one of those in that final pool. Johnson had tied for the second highest score of seventy-five. Although not the highest score, he was told by the superintendent that he was going to get the job.

Meanwhile, Joyce—who had ranked right behind Johnson with a score of seventy-three—put in a phone call to the county's affirmative action officer. A thirty-three-year-old widow with four children, Joyce was desperate for a raise. She had been passed over for higher paying jobs all her working life, and this time she was not taking any chances. After all, she too had coveted the dispatcher's job for six years, and had worked hard toward that goal: she had taken night classes and passed a test in order to work as road maintenance worker—experience she was told was prerequisite for dispatchers.

With diehard unionists as parents, Joyce grew up knowing the importance of standing up for one's rights. Like her parents, Joyce had become a union activist, and was a leading figure as shop steward for the local union. She was known to fight back against acts of harassment by coworkers and supervisors by effectively filing grievances. Joyce was considered a "skirt-wearing rebel rouser" by some at the road unit, which had an old boy's network that was described as nearly impenetrable by outsiders.

When presented with an opportunity to imple-

In 1987 the Supreme Court ruled that Santa Clara County had the right to promote Diane Joyce to a road dispatcher job over Paul Johnson, an arguably more qualified male applicant, as part of its affirmative action program.

ment the county's affirmative action plan, the head of the Transportation Agency overrode his subordinate's decision and appointed Joyce. It was not a difficult decision for the director, given that, of the 238 "skilled crafts worker" positions in his agency, none was, or had ever been, held by a woman.

Incredulous, Johnson "felt like tearing something up." Determined to fight, he first went through internal channels. It was the brother of his equally outraged wife who referred the Johnsons to a local law firm that had successfully sued in court on behalf of another victim of affirmative action. Thus Johnson found the lawyer who would lead his suit against Santa Clara County, claiming under Title VII that he had been discriminated against on the basis of his gender.

Johnson initially won his case at the district court level in the summer of 1982. By the time it reached the Court of Appeals, the case had assumed its own momentum. Johnson wanted to call it quits when the appeals court overturned the district court's decision in 1984, but the case had now ceased to be about Johnson as an individual: it had been hijacked in the service of a much larger political debate raging across the nation. Johnson reluctantly agreed to let a public interest law firm take his case to the Supreme Court. Interested parties

from both sides of the affirmative action debate feverishly pushed their agenda as the case became a political platform. After all, *Johnson v. Transportation Agency* was the first (and to this date, the only) Supreme Court case to deal specifically with gender in affirmative action.

Forty public interest groups submitted amicus curiae briefs to the Court, of which only two supported Johnson. The justices debated whether, for an affirmative action plan to be valid, evidence of prior discrimination was required, or if statistical imbalance was in itself justification. In the end, the Santa Clara plan was deemed valid, and Joyce won, exulting in victory: "The case will have an impact on all women, and I'm very happy for them."

Johnson denounced the ruling as "a gross miscarriage of justice," and remained bitter for years. Aside from his mother and his wife, he had been surrounded by men all his life. He was one of five sons and himself had three sons. All his colleagues were men. Although his own mother had worked side by side with his father on their 180-acre farm and had kept it going on her own for a while, Johnson did not think most women were suited for manual labor. Yet he was not a knowing perpetrator of the original discrimination that affirmative action was intended to reverse. Johnson himself described his plight most succinctly: "If they're going to make a change, why should I be the goat?"

In 1984 Johnson took early retirement and retreated to the small seaside town of Sequim in northern Washington state. He played a lot of golf and cribbage and had time to reflect on his ordeal. In 1989 he sent newspapers an "Open Letter to the White Males of America," which was ghostwritten by his wife, Betty, who had supported the family during the litigation with money she earned as a bank teller. The editorial bitterly denounced the Supreme Court for ruling "that the White Male is to be the SCAPEGOAT for all the past discrimination in our history" and suggested organizing to prevent the erosion of further rights. Johnson continues to receive letters from those who feel left behind in the push for affirmative action.

tributed to many different factors. Yet there is no doubt that women's pay and presence in the labor force have increased greatly in the era of affirmative action. For example, less than 5 percent of lawyers and 10 percent of doctors were women in 1970; by the end of the century more than 20 percent of both those professions were women. Similarly, in 1970 full-time women workers earned 60 percent of the wages earned by men with similar schooling; that figure exceeded 75 percent by the end of the century.

But despite these successes, the number of women being hired for skilled craft positions has remained low. Only 10 percent of precision, production, crafts, and repair jobs were held by women in 1998, and only 3 percent of mechanics and 1.5 percent of construction workers were women. White males still held most of the skilled jobs at the Santa Clara Transportation Agency, but a few more women and minorities joined the ranks after *Johnson*. Among these was Joyce's daughter, Donna, who worked on the road crew.

The Equal Pay Act of 1963: A Remedy for Women

Women worked in different jobs and earned less money than men from the very beginning of the Industrial Revolution. In the first mechanized mills of New England in the 1830s, female textile workers labored long hours and made half of what male employees in the carefully segregated male jobs earned. The first Women's Rights Convention, held in Seneca Falls, New York, in 1848, listed among the "repeated injuries and usurpations on the part of man toward woman," the fact that "[h]e has monopolized nearly all the profitable employments, and from those she is permitted to follow, she receives but a scanty remuneration."

By the early twentieth century blue-collar women were still confined to unskilled jobs, working an average of twelve hours per day for pay that was not enough to support the women themselves, let alone their families. Even when women performed the same work as men, men's wages were one and a half to three times higher than women's. The turn-of-century reformers first responded to the dire circumstances of working women by securing laws limiting the hours women could work. In 1908 the Supreme Court held that restrictions on women's hours (but not on men's) were constitutional (see p. 17). Then, when hours laws deepened women's economic distress by reducing the time they could spend earning wages, reformers advocated that states set minimum wages for women in various industries.

As early as the 1880s, the American Federation of Labor had called for equal pay for equal work regardless of sex. But the union acknowledged that enforcement of the principle would probably help men more than women, since many women workers were hired only because they could be paid lower wages than men. Indeed, over the years unions sometimes called for equal pay for equal work as a tactic to eliminate women from the trades, as experience showed that when employers were required to pay women the same wages as men, they stopped employing women.

World War I broadened women's opportunities, but a War Labor Board policy of equal pay for equal work had little practical effect. The Great Depression of the 1930s inspired a second government policy statement in favor of equal pay for equal work: the National Recovery Administration declared that paying women less than men for equal work constituted an unfair labor practice. But again, men were the intended beneficiaries, since the policy was meant to discourage employers from replacing higher paid males with lower paid females.

When the United States entered World War II, most firms still did not pay their employees "irrespective of sex." However, due to labor shortages and the need to attract women workers,

Labor shortages during World War II forced many companies to pay women (such as these workers putting the finish on transparent bomber noses) the same rates as men. Although the war experience led to the introduction of the first federal equal pay bill in 1945, Congress did not actually pass the Equal Pay Act until 1963.

many firms switched to a one-rate-for-the-job wage policy. The National War Labor Board, which strictly controlled U.S. labor relations during the war, issued its famous General Order No. 16 in 1942, which encouraged (but did not require) employers to pay women as much as men "for comparable quality and quantity of work on the same or similar operations." As a result, more than two thousand companies had voluntarily equalized their pay scales by the end of the war.

In the years after World War II, industrial employers' increasing use of job evaluation programs to set wages also encouraged greater pay equality between the sexes because those programs generally provided for one pay rate regardless of who was performing the job. In 1939 only 13 percent of firms surveyed based their pay scales upon professional job evaluations, but by 1947 more than half did so. However, job evaluation only equalized pay rates in career paths shared by the sexes and was ineffective in fields dominated by women.

The war experience helped bring about the introduction of the first federal equal pay bill in 1945. That bill, and others like it, failed to become law. Yet the number of women in the workforce continued to grow. In 1945 women made up one fourth of the paid labor force. By 1963, the year the Kennedy administration successfully introduced its equal pay bill, that figure had climbed to one third.

Earlier equal pay bills would have guaranteed equal pay for "comparable work" rather than "equal work." Several members of Congress insisted that the word "comparable" be removed and replaced with "equal," for the express purpose of limiting the Equal Pay Act's scope to different pay for the same basic jobs. But even the 1963 act's requirement of equal pay for "equal work on jobs the performance of which requires equal skills" drew criticism. As the Supreme Court later told the story in *Corning Glass Works v. Brennan* (1974):

In both the House and Senate committee hearings, witnesses were highly critical of the Act's definition of equal work. . . . Many noted that most of American industry used formal, systematic job evaluation plans to establish equitable wage structures in their plants. Such systems . . . took into consideration four separate factors in determining job value—skill, effort, responsibility and working conditions—and each of these four components were further systematically divided into various subcomponents. . . .

In comparison to the rather complex job evaluation plans used by industry, the definition of equal work used in the first drafts of the Equal Pay Act was criticized as unduly vague and incomplete. . . .

Congress, acting in response to these concerns, incorporated into the equal pay bill the "well-defined and well-accepted principles of job evaluation," adding to the equal skill requirement the additional job evaluation factors, "effort," "responsibility," and "working conditions."

The Equal Pay Act of 1963 (EPA) passed with little opposition. In his book *The Equal Pay Act: Implications for Comparable Worth,* Walter Fogel explained why.

The discussion of the Act in the House of Representatives (the Senate hardly debated it) before its passage was devoted largely to assuring the Act's few opponents that it was (1) narrow in scope, and (2) could not be used by the U.S. Department of Labor to harass business establishments. The bill's supporters went to some excesses on the first point, assuring the House members that equal pay would be required only when men and women were performing the "same job under the same working conditions," or "virtually identical" jobs. These adjectival criteria were more limiting than that of "equal" work, the adjective actually included in the Act.

As finally enacted, the EPA reads as follows.

No employer having employees subject to any provisions of this section shall discriminate, within any establishment in which such employees are employed, between employees on the basis of sex by paying wages to employees in such establishment at a rate less than the rate at which he pays wages to employees of the opposite sex in such establishment for equal work on jobs the performance of which requires equal skill, effort, and responsibility, and which are performed under similar working conditions, except where such payment is made pursuant to (i) a seniority system; (ii) a merit system; (iii) a system which measures earnings by quantity or quality of production; or (iv) a differential based on any other factor other than sex.

Most litigation involving the EPA has centered on how to apply it within the much more comprehensive scope of Title VII. The EPA has also served as a useful tool for workers suing companies with less than fifteen employees, which makes them too small to be covered under Title VII. The Equal Employment Opportunity Commission took over responsibility for the act's enforcement in 1979.

PAY AND BENEFITS

Working on the Night Shift

Most equal pay cases, particularly those involving simple wage discrepancies, have been decided easily at the state or lower court level and have never reached the Supreme Court. Consistent with the legislative history, lower federal courts interpreted "equal work" to mean the same, or substantially the same, work. The Supreme Court would not rule on an equal pay case until 1974, in *Corning Glass Works v. Brennan*. That opinion clarified the meaning of important concepts and terms used in the Equal Pay Act of 1963.

Corning Glass Works v. Brennan, 417 U.S. 188 (1974)

Corning Glass Works has long operated plants in Corning, New York, and Wellsboro, Pennsylvania. Prior to 1925, these plants operated only dur-

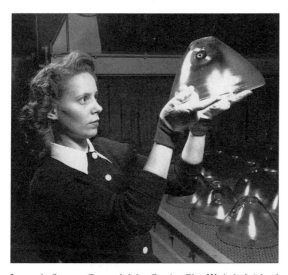

In 1974 the Supreme Court ruled that Corning Glass Works had violated the Equal Pay Act by paying a lower base wage to female day shift inspectors than to male night shift inspectors.

ing the day. Corning's jobs were segregated by sex: assembly workers were all men, the lower paid inspection workers all women. Then the company began installing automatic production equipment at the two plants, making night shifts feasible. New York and Pennsylvania had "protective" laws against women working at night, which meant that all night shift jobs, including night inspection jobs, had to be staffed by men. But Corning's male day workers who became night inspectors refused to work for the lower "women's wage." Moreover, the men viewed the inspection jobs as "demeaning," and "women's work." To attract men to work as night shift inspectors, the company decided to pay male night inspectors at roughly the male assembly workers' rates—about twice the hourly rate for the female day inspectors. (By contrast, the male assembly workers, whether they worked day or night shifts, received the same wage.) And so it remained, with the temporary exception of World War II, when the wartime labor shortage led to the temporary suspension of protective legislation restricting night work for women. In 1944 Corning's plants were organized by a labor union. The initial collective bargaining agreement established for the first time a plantwide "shift differential"—a premium for all night shift jobs. (It also required that wages be set using a professionally developed job evaluation plan.) But the new shift differential, instead of being *substituted* for the original pay premium given to male night inspectors, was simply *superimposed* on it, thus perpetuating the original base pay differential between male and female inspectors.

Pennsylvania partially repealed its prohibition against women working at night in 1947, as did New York in 1953. In Pennsylvania the night employment of women was allowed, with the approval of the state labor department, if public transportation was available or the employer itself provided it. Unfortunately, no public transportation was available in Wellsboro, and Corning did not consider providing it cost effective. In New York the night employment of women was legal where the state industrial commissioner found transportation and safety conditions to be satisfactory and granted approval. But Corning simply never sought approval for employing women at night in its New York plants. (In 1969 both New York and Pennsylvania completely abolished night work restrictions on women as woman-only protective laws came to be viewed, in the wake of passage of Title VII, as discriminatory on the basis of sex.)

It was not until 1966, two years after the Equal Pay Act became effective, that Corning opened up night shift positions to women. The company consolidated its male and female seniority lists and allowed women to exercise their seniority, on the same basis as men, to bid for the higher-paid night inspection jobs as vacancies occurred. As a result, some women were able to join the male night inspectors. In 1969 Corning, pursuant to its most recent collective bargaining agreement with its union, established a new job evaluation system for setting wage rates. The agreement abolished the separate base wages for day shift and night shift inspectors that originated in the 1920s (the plantwide premium for night work continued). The job evaluation produced a new base wage rate, applicable to all inspectors, that was higher than the old (female) day rate but lower than the old (male) night rate. But while the new rate would apply to inspectors hired after it went into effect, the wages of existing night inspectors were "red circled" at the old, higher rate. Thus the agreement locked in the original, half-century-old male premium that incumbent night inspectors received.

Secretary of Labor Peter J. Brennan, alleging that Corning had failed to comply with the Equal Pay Act in a timely manner, brought suits against the company in federal courts in New York and Pennsylvania. He sought back wages for the female day shift inspectors in an amount equal to the difference between their wages and the red circle rates received by the night shift inspectors. The cases were appealed to the Second and Third Circuit Courts of Appeals.

In its defense, Corning argued that the male night shift workers were paid more not because they were male, but rather because night work was inconvenient and unpleasant. The fact that the work was done at night rather than during the day meant that a "working condition" differed significantly, rendering the night and day jobs "unequal" and therefore not "equal work" warranting "equal pay." Secretary Brennan, on the other hand, argued that the time of day an employee worked was not a "working condition," in the standard usage of job evaluations, and thus the day and night jobs were "equal work." A pay differential might in theory qualify under the statutory exceptions as "any other factor other than sex," exempting the employer from liability even if the work was equal. But in Corning's case, Brennan argued, this particular pay differential was in fact based upon sex, and therefore the exception could not save Corning from liability.

Ironically, the 1963 testimony of Ezra G. Hester, Corning's former industrial relations director, before the House and Senate subcommittees considering the Equal Pay Act, weakened the company's working condition argument. In his testimony, Hester had successfully urged the inclusion of three additional criteria as determinants of job equality—effort, responsibility, and working conditions—into the language of the act, pointing out that these, along with skill, were standard criteria used in industrial job evaluations to create a rational wage structure. Unfortunately for Corning, Hester had never mentioned day versus night shift as being a "working condition," and for good reason—the definition of "working conditions" widely accepted in American industry did not include time of day worked. Consistent with the general practice, Corning's *own* job evaluations in 1944 and 1964 found no significant differences in the duties performed by day and night inspectors and gave to both the same point values on skill, effort, responsibility, and, significantly, working conditions.

The Second Circuit Court of Appeals noted this history of the act in concluding that the day and night inspection jobs were equal, and that Corning had violated the Equal Pay Act. The Third Circuit disagreed, concluding that time of day should be treated as a working condition, rendering the day and night inspection jobs unequal, and therefore held in favor of Corning. The Third Circuit's decision was largely based on a statement made by Rep. Charles Ellsworth Goodell during the 1963 debates on the proposed Equal Pay Act: "Finally, standing as opposed to sitting, pleasantness or unpleasantness of surroundings, periodic rest periods, hours of work, difference in shift, all would logically fall within the working condition factor."

On review, the Supreme Court consolidated the cases. Justice Marshall wrote the opinion for the five-justice majority, agreeing with the Second Circuit that Corning had violated the Equal Pay Act by paying a lower base wage to female day shift inspectors than to male night shift inspectors. He further held that Corning had not remedied its violations of the act by permitting women to work as night shift inspectors since 1966, nor even by equalizing wages in 1969, because it had also established a higher "red circle" rate for existing night shift employees. Had the employer raised the base wage for day inspectors to match that of the night inspectors when the Equal Pay Act became effective, the "red circle" rate would have applied to incumbent day shift workers as well as to the night shift workers. Justice Marshall also agreed with the Second Circuit

that the higher base pay paid to inspectors on the night shift was not based on "a factor other than sex"; the history of its adoption revealed that it was indeed because of the night inspectors' sex that the higher amount was paid. The three dissenting justices essentially agreed with the reasoning of the Third Circuit opinion.

Corning was required by the language of the EPA not only to provide immediate pay increases to its day inspectors, but also to pay the back wages owed to them.

Equal Pay for Comparable Worth

Twenty years after passage of the Equal Pay Act, working women still made only sixty cents to every dollar paid to men. This was in large part because 75 percent of working women held positions in occupations dominated by women, which almost always pay lower wages than male dominated jobs. Plainly, there was some pay discrimination that the Equal Pay Act, with its narrow focus on equal pay for the same or very similar jobs, could not reach. Title VII clearly prohibited the pervasive practice of earlier years of segregating the sexes into "men's jobs" and "women's jobs," but the pattern of sex stratification in the workplace, with its accompanying pay difference, persisted.

Moreover, some women's groups felt that the slogan "equal pay for equal work" should be replaced by "equal pay for work of comparable worth." What they sought was an end to the practice of undervaluing traditional female jobs (secretary, nurse, grade school teacher). Women in traditional female jobs, they contended, should be paid the same as men in traditional male jobs if the women's work required comparable (or more) skill, effort, and responsibility. For example, why should nurses, who held advanced degrees and had passed rigorous certification tests, be paid less than tree trimmers and sign painters? Failure of employers to pay nurses as much as or more than these less skilled male workers, they argued, should be considered discrimination against women on the basis of their sex. Since the Equal Pay Act was not up to the job of eradicating pay discrimination against women, they turned their attention to Title VII, which broadly prohibited sex discrimination in "compensation."

The argument that Title VII reached pay discrimination that the Equal Pay Act did not was complicated by an amendment to Title VII added shortly before its passage. Concerned that courts might interpret Title VII in a way that conflicted with the Equal Pay Act, passed just the year before Title VII, Sen. Wallace Bennett of Utah offered an amendment whose purpose was to prevent such conflicts. The Bennett Amendment provided:

It shall not be an unlawful employment practice under [Title VII] for any employer to differentiate upon the basis of sex in determining the amount of the wages or compensation paid or to be paid to employees of such employer *if such differentiation is authorized by the provisions of the Equal Pay Act.*

Lower courts disagreed on what the Bennett Amendment meant. Did it mean that the only pay discrimination that could be recognized under Title VII was the equal pay for equal work type claim created by the Equal Pay Act? Or perhaps it meant that equal pay for equal work cases under Title VII had to be interpreted just the way they would under the Equal Pay Act, but that other types of claims involving pay discrimination should also be permitted under Title VII? And if other types of claims could be recognized, were comparable worth suits among them? In *County of Washington v. Gunther* (1981), the Supreme Court resolved the first two issues but did not squarely address the third.

County of Washington v. Gunther, 425 U.S. 161 (1981)

In Washington County, Oregon, female guards in the women's section of the county jail, called "matrons," received 30 percent less in pay than their male counterparts, called "deputy sheriffs," who guarded the male prisoners. Because many more men than women were jailed in Washington County, matrons had considerably fewer inmates to contend with than did the deputy sheriffs. To fill out their time, the matrons were given clerical duties that the deputy sheriffs did not perform—tasks that made their jobs, while similar to the men's, not "equal work" in the Equal Pay Act sense. The county investigated the pay discrepancy and concluded that "the women deserved 95 percent of the men's salary." Despite this finding, no salary changes were made and the matrons continued to earn 70 percent of the deputies' wages, a difference of about $200 a month.

Alberta Gunther and three other matrons sued under Title VII. The County of Washington's defense raised a critical issue of interpretation of the Bennett Amendment to Title VII. That provision, maintained the county, precluded the plaintiffs' Title VII suit. The Bennett Amendment, it contended, was designed to harmonize the two acts in their treatment of sex-based pay inequalities. This meant, it argued, that a Title VII pay discrimination claim was limited only to those claims that would be recognized under the Equal Pay Act—in short, cases where women were paid differently even though performing the *same* work as men. Because the duties of matrons and deputy sheriffs differed significantly, with the deputies being responsible for ten times as many prisoners as the matrons and the matrons devoting a chunk of their time to lower value clerical tasks, the county argued that the "equal work criteria" of the Equal Pay Act were not met, and thus, because of the Bennett Amendment, the matrons' Title VII claim should be dismissed.

The Supreme Court ruled by a narrow 5–4 majority against Washington County and allowed the matrons to sue for pay discrimination. In writing for the majority, Justice Brennan held that a Title VII claim of wage discrimination did not have to meet the equal work requirements of the Equal Pay Act. In other words, a woman employee could sue her employer for gender-based pay discrimination even if her company did not employ a man to work the same job for higher pay. But while the decision opened the door slightly for women working in jobs not strictly equal to their male counterparts, it also specifically declined to authorize suits based on the theory of comparable worth.

In his dissent, Justice Rehnquist complained that the Court "conveniently and persistently ignores relevant legislative history and instead relies wholly on what it believes Congress *should* have enacted." He cited the Bennett Amendment to Title VII, which stated that a disparity in wages could be considered discriminatory under Title VII only if the women and men employees were performing equal work. Rehnquist also expressed his relief that the Court had not extended its opinion to situations involving comparable work.

After earning the right to proceed with its suit from the Supreme Court, the prison matrons decided to settle with Washington County out of court. But any pay increase they might have won through the courts could only have been ordered retroactively. In 1974, seven years before the case reached the Supreme Court, the matrons' jobs had been wiped out when Washington County closed down their jail and sent the inmates to a nearby prison.

Both before and after *Gunther,* comparable worth suits have not fared well in the lower federal courts. Reluctant to engage in evaluating the comparative worth of dissimilar jobs, courts claim

Washington County, Oregon, paid Alberta Gunther and three other female prison guards 30 percent less than it paid its male prison guards. Although the women had fewer inmates to guard and rounded out their time performing clerical duties, a narrow Court majority ruled in 1981 that they were entitled to sue for pay discrimination.

lack of expertise and cite the dangers of interfering with the economic realities of supply and demand. On the other hand, some unions have been able to bargain for increases in the wage of employees working in traditional women's jobs and a few states have enacted comparable worth statutes in an effort to insure pay equity for women. A much larger group of states has reviewed state jobs and made some comparable worth pay adjustments for state employees.

Discrimination in Fringe Benefits

While the Equal Pay Act clearly covers basic wages, an important aspect of an employee's overall compensation is the fringe benefit "package" that he or she receives. Health and disability insurance and retirement benefits, for example, can substantially increase the value of a job to the employee. When fringe benefits are not provided evenhandedly by gender, such practices may sometimes be challengeable under the Equal Pay Act, but for the most part such challenges are best pursued under Title VII, where coverage of benefits is more securely provided for. One very important type of fringe benefit is retirement or pension benefits, which provide support for workers after retirement. Traditionally, such benefits either cost women more or provided lower monthly payments to them. This practice was successfully challenged in two Supreme Court cases, *Los Angeles Department of Water and Power v. Manhart* (1978) and *Arizona Governing Committee v. Norris* (1983).

Los Angeles Department of Water and Power v. Manhart, 435 U.S. 702 (1978)

Arizona Governing Committee v. Norris, 463 U.S. 1073 (1983)

The life expectancy of the average American woman is seven years longer than that of the average American man. Armed with this knowledge, the Los Angeles Department of Water and Power required that its female employees make higher monthly contributions to the pension fund than its male employees. Since women as a class live longer, the Department reasoned, they would require more monthly pension payments than men, and thus, as a group, end up with more benefits. Because the pension contributions were automatically withheld from employee paychecks, the take-home pay of female employees was less than that of male employees with the same salary.

In 1973 Marie Manhart and others sued under Title VII on behalf of a class of women employed, or formerly employed, by the department, claiming that the employer had discriminated against them on the basis of sex. While the case was pending in the district court, the California

legislature enacted a law prohibiting the practice challenged by the plaintiffs. In compliance with the new law, the department amended its plan, effective January 1, 1975, to require the same pension contributions from male and female employees. Meanwhile, the district court held that the pre-1975 contribution differential violated Title VII and ordered that the department refund all excess contributions made by female employees before the 1975 amendment of the plan. This ruling was upheld by the Ninth Circuit Court of Appeals.

The department appealed to the Supreme Court, maintaining that the differential in take-home pay between men and women was not discrimination within the meaning of Title VII because the difference in the level of contributions was offset by the difference in the value of the pension benefits provided to the two classes of employees. In addition, the department argued that the differential was based on a factor "other than sex" within the meaning of the Equal Pay Act of 1963, and was therefore protected by the Bennett Amendment to Title VII which provided that a sex-based wage and compensation differential "authorized" by the Equal Pay Act was not an unlawful employment practice under Title VII. Finally, the department argued that even if requiring women to pay larger contributions to the pension fund violated Title VII, the district court order requiring it to refund the excess contributions to the affected women was inappropriate.

While it was well established by the mid-1970s that discrimination on the basis of gender stereotypes and assumptions about women or men as a group was prohibited by Title VII, *Manhart* presented a different question. Would an employer policy based on a "true generalization"—in this case, that women outlive men—also constitute facial discrimination? Writing the Court's 7–2 majority opinion, Justice Stevens concluded that the policy was, indeed, discriminatory. Stevens pointed to the language of Title VII that makes it unlawful "to discriminate against any *individual* with respect to his compensation, terms, conditions, or privileges of employment, because of such *individual's* race, color, religion, sex, or national origin." The statute, he said, thus "precludes treatment of individuals as simply components of a racial, religious, sexual, or national class. If height is required for a job, a tall woman may not be refused employment merely because, on average, women are too short." "Even a true generalization about the group," he concluded, "is an insufficient reason for disqualifying an individual to whom the generalization does not apply."

Applying this principle to the case at hand, Justice Stevens pointed out that while the Los Angeles Department of Water and Power could demonstrate that women *as a class* live longer than men, "there was no assurance that any individual woman working for the Department [would] actually fit the generalization. . . . Many of those individuals will not live as long as the average man. While they were working, those individuals received smaller paychecks because of their sex, but they will receive no compensating advantage when they retire."

On the question of whether the discrimination was, in the language of the Bennett Amendment, "authorized" by the Equal Pay Act, the Department argued that its policy came within the exception to the act that authorizes a "differential based on any other factor other than sex." This was so, it said, because the different contributions exacted from men and women were based on longevity rather than sex. To this, Justice Stevens responded that the record contained no evidence that any factor other than the employee's sex was taken into account in calculating the differential between the respective contributions by men and women.

As for fairness to men as a group, Stevens pointed to the fact that employee group insurance plans necessarily rely on the better risks to subsidize the poorer risks.

Healthy persons subsidize medical benefits for the less healthy; unmarried workers subsidize the pensions of married workers; persons who eat, drink, or smoke to excess may subsidize pension benefits for persons whose habits are more temperate. Treating different classes of risk as though they were the same for purposes of group insurance is a common practice which has never been considered inherently unfair. To insure the flabby and the fit as though they were equivalent risks may be more common than treating men and women alike; but nothing more than habit makes one "subsidy" seem less fair than the other.

Stevens noted that other persistent disparities in average longevity between groups other than men and women were not used to charge different rates to employees. As examples, he cited the 6.3 year gap in life expectancy between whites and nonwhites and a ten year gap between married and unmarried men. Most telling, perhaps, was the department's requirement that men and women pay equal contributions for death benefits even though the seven year gap in life expectancy meant in this situation that the *women* employees subsidized the *men*.

Chief Justice Burger and Justice Rehnquist dissented. They viewed the different treatment of men and women as valid because of the longevity factor.

Gender-based actuarial tables have been in use since at least 1843. . . . Employers cannot know in advance when individual members of the classes will die. Yet, if they are to operate economically workable group pension programs, it is only rational to permit them to rely on statistically sound and proved disparities in longevity between men and women.

Although the Supreme Court ruled that higher pension contributions could not be required of female employees, it refused by an 8–1 vote to award "retroactive" repayment (back pay reimbursement) to women workers who had contributed at the higher rate before 1975. The justices reasoned that such a repayment could be "devastating for a pension fund" and might jeopardize the pensions of all the employees. Justice Thurgood Marshall, the lone dissenter on the relief issue, pointed out that while the Court's reasoning might be appropriate "in some hypothetical case," the department had made no claim that the solvency of the retirement fund would be threatened by the relief ordered by the lower court. He argued that reimbursing the women for their earlier overpayments was the only way to vindicate Title VII's goal of "making persons whole for injuries suffered through past discrimination."

But if requiring women to make a larger contribution than men to the employer's pension fund violated Title VII, what about a plan that required equal *contributions* from the sexes, but paid women a lower *benefit* upon retirement? The Supreme Court addressed that question five years later in *Arizona Governing Committee v. Norris* (1983). The state of Arizona offered its employees the opportunity to enroll in a "deferred compensation" (retirement) plan. Employees could select a plan from any of several private insurance companies designated by the state and the state would withhold the appropriate sums from the employee's wages and channel them to the company chosen by the employee.

The amount of retirement benefits for this plan depended upon the amount of compensation deferred, the employee's age at retirement, and the employee's sex. Most employees chose plans that provided monthly annuity payments from retirement until the employee's death. All of the companies on the state's list used gender-based mortality tables to calculate monthly annuity benefits. Using these tables, a man would receive larger monthly payments than a woman who de-

ferred the same amount of compensation and retired at the same age. These tables did not incorporate other longevity factors such as smoking habits, alcohol consumption, weight, medical history, or family history.

Nathalie Norris, an employee of the state who had invested in an annuity plan, sued the state on behalf of herself and other women employed by the state in federal district court, alleging that the employer violated Title VII by administering an annuity plan that discriminated against these women in retirement benefits on the basis of sex. The district court agreed with the plaintiffs and held that the plan violated Title VII. Citing *Manhart,* the Court of Appeals upheld the district court's order directing the state to cease using gender-based actuarial tables and to pay retired female employees benefits equal to those paid to the men.

When the case reached the Supreme Court, the state of Arizona argued that no discrimination had occurred since the female employees had retirement options that provided equal benefits to men and women *as groups.* And, unlike in the case of *Manhart,* women were not required to pay more into a retirement plan.

The Court held that the state's retirement benefits arrangements for its employees "does constitute discrimination on the basis of sex in violation of Title VII, and that all retirement benefits derived from contributions made after the decision today must be calculated without regard to the sex of the beneficiary."

Justice Marshall explained in an opinion for five justices.

[T]he classification of employees on the basis of sex is no more permissible at the pay-out stage of a retirement plan than at the pay-in stage. We reject petitioners' contention that the Arizona plan does not discriminate on the basis of sex because a woman and a man who defer the same amount of compensation will obtain upon retirement annuity policies having approximately the same actuarial value. . . . This underlying assumption—that sex may properly be used to predict longevity—is flatly inconsistent with the basic teaching of *Manhart:* that Title VII requires employers to treat their employees as *individuals,* not "as simply components of a racial, religious, sexual or national class."

Nor was the Court impressed with the employer's argument that the discrimination problem was attributable to the private companies that administered and paid benefits under the plan, not to the employer itself. "Having created a plan whereby employees can obtain the advantages of using deferred compensation to purchase an annuity only if they invest in one of the companies specifically selected by the State," wrote Marshall, "the State cannot disclaim responsibility for the discriminatory features of the insurers' options."

Justice Lewis F. Powell Jr., who had voted with the majority in *Manhart,* now wrote on behalf of the dissenters. Unlike *Manhart,* which involved an employer-operated pension fund, Powell argued that the sex-based distinction that Norris challenged was a product of a private insurer's practice of providing sex-based annuities—a practice that was standard in the insurance industry. Title VII, he said, was never intended to "revolutionize the insurance and pension industries."

On the question of retroactive benefits, Justice Sandra Day O'Connor, who agreed with Justice Marshall that the deferred compensation plan discriminated against women, joined the dissenters to provide a fifth vote for denying the women plaintiffs equal retirement benefits derived from contributions they had made before *Norris* was decided. The appropriate remedy, these justices agreed, was to equalize only those future benefits supported by contributions made after the Court's decision, even if that meant that it would be years before women actually received the same benefits as men. Justice Powell estimated that Arizona's cost for equalizing benefits from the date of the Court's order would range from $817 million to $1,260 million annually for fifteen to thirty years. "There is no justification for this Court," wrote Justice Powell, "to impose this magnitude of burden retroactively on the public."

The dissenters on the retroactive relief issue—Justices Marshall, Brennan, White, and Stevens—would have been more generous to the plaintiffs. The state of Arizona, they pointed out, had been on notice since the *Manhart* case that the use of sex-based actuarial tables was unlawful under Title VII. The dissenters believed that relief for the plaintiffs should *at minimum* require that the state "ensure that [a woman employee's] monthly benefits are no lower than they would have been had her post-*Manhart* contributions been treated in the same way as those of a similarly situated male employee."

8

SEXUAL HARASSMENT

Since its first ruling on the subject in 1986, the Supreme Court has struggled to define different categories of sexual harassment and to determine precisely under which circumstances to hold an employer liable for an employee's sexual misconduct. Companies have responded by adopting a variety of anti–sexual harassment programs to protect themselves and their employees.

But sexual harassment is not exclusively an employment issue; it also affects students in their "workplace"—their schools. Students may face two types of sexual harassment: by teachers and administrators, and by peers. The Supreme Court has very recently tried to adapt the rules it set forth for harassment by professionals in the adult context of the workplace to harassment by students in the immature context of the schoolyard.

SEXUAL HARASSMENT ON THE JOB

Although there are state and local laws that explicitly prohibit sexual harassment in the workplace, there is no such federal law. Title VII is used by courts to prosecute sexual harassment on the job, yet its language only vaguely outlaws job discrimination "because of sex." Congress intended Title

VII to ban all gender discrimination in the workplace, but it did not consider whether sexual harassment constituted such discrimination when it drafted the legislation. It was a feminist legal scholar, Catharine MacKinnon, who asserted that unwanted sexual advances were a form of gender discrimination in her influential book, *Sexual Harassment of Working Women* (1979). This theory was adopted by the Supreme Court in 1986 in a case called *Meritor Savings Bank v. Vinson.* Now, in order for victims of sexual harassment to claim that their civil rights have been violated, they must show that the abuse was a form of gender discrimination. Thus the "sexual" in the term "sexual harassment" refers to the fact that the misconduct was directed at the victim because of his or her gender, and not to the sexual nature of the harassment.

It was not until the mid-1970s that women who had been subject to unwanted sexual advances on the job began suing their employers. Initially, the courts refused to recognize sexual harassment as a form of gender discrimination on the ground that the harasser was attracted to a particular woman and not trying to abuse her because of her gender. But soon, federal appeals courts began reversing those rulings.

The first successful lawsuits involved clear *quid pro quo* (Latin for "this for that") harassment, in which supervisors fired, demoted, or otherwise retaliated against employees who refused to go along with their sexual requests. Employers are "strictly liable" for quid quo pro harassment, which means they are liable even if they did not know the harassment was occurring and had an active antiharassment program in place. But the first sexual harassment suit to reach the Supreme Court did not involve an open-and-shut quid pro quo case but a more subtle claim of "hostile working environment" harassment: when a worker is not threatened with a job setback or promised a promotion by the harassing supervisor. In this first case the issue was further complicated by the victim having been coerced into a sexual relationship with her boss that lasted for several years.

Meritor Savings Bank, FSB v. Vinson, 477 U.S. 57 (1986)

In 1974 Mechelle Vinson was hired as a teller-trainee by Sidney Taylor, a vice president and branch manager at Meritor Savings Bank in Washington, D.C. Vinson was good at her job and was promoted to teller, head teller, and then assistant branch manger. In September 1978 she notified Taylor that she was taking sick leave for an indefinite period. When Vinson had not returned to work two months later, she was fired.

The reason Vinson could not face returning to work was because she believed that Taylor had sexually harassed her. Vinson claimed that as a result of his misconduct she suffered extreme physical and emotional stress that caused insomnia, nervousness, and hair loss. She sued Taylor and the bank for money damages.

Vinson said in her testimony that the harassment had begun when Taylor asked her out to dinner one night and then suggested they go to a motel. At first she refused, but, fearful of losing her job, finally agreed to go. They began a sexual relationship that continued over the next several years. At work, Taylor openly fondled her in front of other employees. He would also follow her into the women's restroom when she went there alone and expose himself to her; on several occasions he even forcibly raped her. When she told him she had a new boyfriend in 1977, Taylor finally left her alone. Vinson did not report the harassment to Taylor's supervisors or use the bank's complaint procedure because she said she was afraid of him. Taylor denied that he had engaged in a sexual relationship with Vinson. The bank also denied any knowledge of any misconduct by Taylor. Under Title VII it is the employer and not the alleged harasser who is liable for misconduct at work. So while Taylor and the bank were sued under local law only the bank was sued under Title VII in federal court. But before the courts could rule on the bank's liability, they first had to determine whether Taylor's conduct constituted sexual harassment.

The district court found that Vinson was not the victim of sexual harassment because the "relationship was a voluntary one." The Court of Appeals reversed, and the Supreme Court, in an opinion written by Chief Justice William H. Rehnquist, unanimously agreed to uphold the appeals court's decision. "When a supervisor harasses a subordinate because of the subordinate's sex," he wrote, "that supervisor 'discriminate[s]' on the basis of sex." Feminist legal scholar MacKinnon was a member of Vinson's victorious legal team and sat as co-counsel during oral arguments.

Despite Congress's language in Title VII prohibiting discrimination with respect to the "compensation, terms, conditions, or privileges" of employment, the Court found that harassment was not limited to economic "quid pro quos." Although there was no "tangible economic loss" to Vinson (such as being denied a raise or a promotion) as a result of the harassment, the Court held that she had indeed been sexually harassed because her employer had created a "hostile working environment" that violated Title VII.

The Court relied on the Guidelines on Discrimination Because of Sex, issued in 1980 by the Equal Employment Opportunity Commission (EEOC), which more broadly defined sexual harassment. The guidelines included under its definition "conduct [that] has the purpose or effect of unreasonably interfering with an individual's work performance or creating an intimidating, hostile, or offensive working environment." In writing the guidelines, the EEOC had drawn on previous cases where employees had successfully argued that they had been unlawfully discriminated against because of harassment on the basis of their race, religion, or national origin. In other words, being subjected to repeated sexual advances by a superior could be equated with being subjected to abusive racial or ethnic epithets.

Rehnquist's opinion also required that for the conduct to be discriminatory it had to go beyond simple acts of flirting, and must be "sufficiently severe or pervasive to alter the conditions of the victim's employment and create an abusive working environment." As to the district court's finding that Vinson's participation in the sexual relationship had been "voluntary," Rehnquist wrote that "the correct inquiry" was whether Vinson by her conduct "indicated that the alleged sexual advances were unwelcome, not whether her actual participation in sexual intercourse was voluntary." But what about the liability of the Meritor Savings Bank? Is an employer liable for a hostile work environment created by a supervisor's sexual advances? Did the fact that Vinson had neglected to report the harassment to management insulate the bank from liability? (The bank's grievance procedure required her to complain first to her supervisor—which would have been Taylor!) The EEOC suggested that a company should not be held liable if it had made available avenues of complaint to management for reporting sexual harassment, and if it responded to an employee's complaint. Nor should it be liable if a victim did not take advantage of such a procedure and the company did not know about the hostile work environment. If, however, the company had no way for a victim to report sexual harassment claims, or if it had knowledge of the harassment but ignored it, then it should be liable. A divided Court declined to issue a definitive ruling on the employer liability question.

Justice Thurgood Marshall wrote a concurrence, joined by Justices William J. Brennan Jr. and Harry A. Blackmun, as well as by Justice John Paul Stevens (who also joined the majority opinion, not finding them in contradiction). Marshall agreed with the majority's holding on sexual harassment but disagreed with their failure to find the employer liable. Marshall reminded the justices that under Title VII employers were automatically liable for the discriminatory actions of their supervisors. Why then, he asked, should sexual harassment involving "hostile environment" situations require that an employee have complained to management before an employer can be held liable? He argued against this special exception.

A supervisor's responsibilities do not begin and end with the power to hire, fire, and discipline employees, or with the power to recommend such actions. Rather, a supervisor is charged with the day-to-day supervision of the work environment and with ensuring a safe, productive workplace. There is no reason why abuse of the latter authority should have different consequences than abuse of the former. In both cases it is the authority vested in the supervisor by the employer that enables him to commit the wrong: it is precisely because the supervisor is understood to be clothed with the employer's authority that he is able to impose unwelcome sexual conduct on subordinates.

Harris v. Forklift Systems, Inc., 510 U.S. 17 (1993)

Lower courts generally resisted the standard established in *Meritor* as making it too easy for employees to win sexual harassment suits. In a notable case called *Rabidue v. Osceola Refining Co.* (1986), an appeals court found that in order for a victim to prove that she had been sexually harassed she not only had to prove that she personally suffered psychological damage from the harassment, but that any "reasonable person" would have suffered as well. And it was not enough for the victim to show that the harassment had injured her psychological well-being; she also needed to show that her work performance suffered as a result of the hostile work environment.

However, when the Supreme Court reconsidered sexual harassment in the 1993 case of *Harris v. Forklift Systems, Inc.*, it held unanimously that the victim did not need to show that she suffered serious psychological injury as a result of sexual harassment. Justice Sandra Day O'Connor wrote that Title VII's prohibition of sex discrimination "comes into play before the harassing conduct leads to a nervous breakdown," and that "[s]o long as the environment would reasonably be perceived, and is perceived, as hostile and abusive, there is no need for it also to be psychologically injurious." O'Connor's opinion did not, however, address the issue of whether the definition of conduct that a "reasonable person" perceives as sexual harassment can sometimes differ between men and women, and even among women themselves.

The suit was brought by Teresa Harris, who had worked as a manager at Forklift Systems, Inc., an equipment rental company in Tennessee. Her boss, Forklift's president Charles Hardy, constantly insulted her in front of others because she was a woman. On several occasions he told her, "You're a woman, what do you know," and, "We need a man as the rental manager." At least once,

he called her "a dumb ass woman." Again in front of others, he suggested that the two of them "go to the Holiday Inn to negotiate [Harris's] raise." Hardy occasionally asked Harris and other female employees to fish coins out of his front pants pocket. He made sexual innuendoes about Harris's and other women's clothing.

Harris complained to Hardy about his conduct. He said that he had been only joking, apologized, and promised to stop. But he soon resumed his old ways. While Harris was arranging a deal with one of Forklift's customers, he inquired, "What did you do, promise the guy . . . some [sex] Saturday night?" Humiliated, Harris quit in October 1987 after two and a half years on the job.

When Harris sued Forklift, the district court in Tennessee ruled against her. Although it conceded that Hardy's conduct "would offend the reasonable woman," the court held that it was not "so severe" as to create an "intimidating or abusive" work environment. The Court of Appeals affirmed that ruling, agreeing that Hardy's misconduct had not damaged Harris's psychological well-being. When the Supreme Court reviewed the case it reaffirmed *Meritor,* and expanded its interpretation of what kind of harassment violated Title VII. Even a work environment, wrote O'Connor, "that does not seriously affect employees' psychological well-being, can and often will detract from employees' job performance, discourage employees from remaining on the job, or keep them from advancing in their careers." In short, the test now became whether the victim suffered psychological injury or an adverse effect on work performance, but not necessarily both.

O'Connor acknowledged that "no single factor" was required to prove sexual harassment, but she did itemize four circumstances that would point to a hostile work environment: "The frequency of the discriminatory conduct; its severity; whether it is physically threatening or humiliating or a mere offensive utterance; and whether it unreasonably interferes with an employee's work performance."

In a brief concurring opinion, Justice Antonin Scalia complained that the terms "abusive" and "hostile" were not adequately defined. He thought juries and employers would be better guided by one simple and absolute test: whether the conduct unreasonably interfered with an employee's work performance. However, he conceded that he knew of "no test more faithful to the inherently vague statutory language" of Title VII than the majority's more complex and ambiguous test. Justice Ruth Bader Ginsburg also wrote a brief separate concurrence. She asserted that Harris did not have to show that the sexual harassment had interfered with her job performance in order to recover money damages from the company. (Harris eventually settled with the company out of court.) "The critical issue, Title VII's text indicates," Ginsburg observed, "is whether members of one sex are exposed to disadvantageous terms or conditions of employment to which members of the other sex are not exposed."

Sexual Harassment Gains National Attention

In the 1990s the public's awareness of the problem of sexual harassment exploded. This was in large part due to a Supreme Court–related incident that had occurred two years before *Harris*. In October 1991, during the Senate confirmation hearings of Clarence Thomas, the Supreme Court nominee was accused of sexual harassment. University of Oklahoma law professor Anita Hill alleged that Thomas had sexually harassed her when he was Assistant Secretary for Civil Rights at the Education Department and then Chair of the EEOC. Hill, like Thomas, was an African American and a Yale Law School graduate, and had been his special assistant. She was invited by the Judiciary Committee to outline her allegations in detail in nationally televised hearings. Thomas categorically denied the charges and was confirmed by the Senate.

But those 1991 hearings raised public awareness of the issue and gave new momentum to the women's movement's age-old efforts to combat sexual harassment. Congress passed a Civil Rights Act that expanded Title VII to include compensatory and punitive damages. Before passage of the act, sexual harassment victims could recover their out-of-pocket expenses, lost wages (if they were fired), back pay, and get a court order against future harassment. But there was no compensation for the pain and humiliation the victim had suffered. And employers had no financial incentive to try to prevent sexual harassment. Victims could and did use various state laws to recover damages in a piecemeal fashion. After passage of the act, victims of sexual harassment could receive up to $300,000 in damages, depending on the company's size. (Employees of companies with less than fifteen workers are not covered under Title VII and can only sue for sexual harassment under state and local laws.)

Sexual harassment suits of all kinds doubled between 1991 and 1998. By 1998 four such cases had made their way up the appellate courts and were chosen by the Supreme Court for review. The Court's opinions in these four cases went beyond unanimously announcing general principles and set about defining practical applications that dealt with the complexities of sexual harassment law.

Same-Sex Harassment

Oncale v. Sundowner Offshore Services, Inc., 523 U.S. 75 (1998)

The first of these 1998 cases was *Oncale v. Sundowner Offshore Services*, which brought a new twist to sexual harassment law because this time the victim and the harassers were all men. The case was an important one, because the lower courts had either rejected same-sex harassment cases or limited them to incidents in which a heterosexual employee complained of harassment by a homosexual coworker. The case also highlighted one of the weaknesses of defining sexual harassment as sex discrimination. Could sexual harassment be considered sex discrimination if both victim and harasser are the same sex?

The suit was brought by Joseph Oncale against the shipping company that employed him as part of an all-male crew on an oil rig off the coast of Louisiana. In 1991 he claimed to have been "sexually assaulted, battered, touched, and threatened with homosexual rape" by his two supervisors, John Lyons and Danny Pippen. When company officials refused to help, he resigned after three months on the job for fear of being raped. Oncale, a young man with a wife and two small children, sued for sexual harassment. The supervisors and the company denied that there had been any taunts or assaults.

Both the district court and the Court of Appeals for the Fifth Circuit ruled that Oncale could not sue under Title VII because that law prohibited sex discrimination and did not apply to same-sex harassment.

The Supreme Court, however, in a short and unanimous opinion by Justice Scalia, ruled that it was perfectly possible for a man to be guilty of discriminating against a man, or a woman against a woman. It was the conduct itself, and not the sex of those involved, that determined whether the sexual harassment constituted sex discrimination. The Court made it clear that neither sexual desire nor sexual orientation were necessary factors in determining sex discrimination, although they might be relevant. Victims needed only to show that they were targeted because of their sex. He offered a few examples of how a same-sex harassment claim might be shown to be discrimi-

Joseph Oncale claimed he was sexually pursued and harassed for several months by his male supervisors on an oil rig off the Louisiana coast, forcing him to quit his job. In 1998 the Supreme Court unanimously ruled that sex discrimination can include same-sex harassment.

nation. For instance, he cited evidence of "general hostility" to the presence of people of the victim's sex in the workplace, or "direct comparative evidence" of how the harasser treated members of both sexes. These examples did not apply in Oncale's case, however, because he worked with an all-male crew. At the same time, Scalia emphasized that the law only prohibited serious harassment that went beyond "male-on-male horseplay or intersexual flirtation." "We have never held," reminded Scalia, "that workplace harassment, even harassment between men and women, is automatically discrimination because of sex merely because the words used have sexual content or connotations." The misconduct must be so persuasive and offensive as to make it difficult for the victim to get his or her job done. Scalia voiced confidence that "Common sense, and an appropriate sensitivity to social context, will enable courts and juries to distinguish between simple teasing or roughhousing among members of the same sex."

Unfulfilled Threats

Burlington Industries, Inc. v. Ellerth, 524 U.S. 742 (1998)

Faragher v. City of Boca Raton, 524 U.S. 775 (1998)

On the last day of the same term in which the Supreme Court handed down *Oncale,* the justices also decided two companion cases addressing the issue of whether employees who reject their bosses' sexual advances and suffer no retaliation can still sue and win money damages for sexual harassment. Courts had earlier established that employers were automatically liable for quid pro quo harassment—when an employee suffers a job loss, demotion, or lack of promotion for resisting a supervisor's advances—because those reprisals represented official actions by the company. The question now was: Are companies also liable in instances where a supervisor makes an "unfulfilled threat," or bluffs, in demanding sexual favors from a lower-ranking employee who neither submits nor suffers adverse consequences on the job? In both of these cases the supervisor did not follow through on threats and the company did not know about the misconduct because the employee, being isolated from upper management, did not lodge a complaint.

The first case, *Burlington Industries, Inc. v. Ellerth,* stemmed from a suit filed by Kimberly Ellerth, a marketing representative at Burlington Industries, a large manufacturing company, in its Chicago division's two-person office. Ellerth claimed to have been sexually harassed by her New York–based supervisor, Ted Slowik, who was a mid-level manager for the company. According to Ellerth, Slowik made sexual comments, grabbed her knee, and urged her to wear shorter skirts. "You're gonna be out there with men who work in factories, and they certainly like women with pretty butts/legs," he admonished. On another occasion, when they were in a hotel lounge on a business trip, he said suggestively, "I could make your life very hard or very easy at Burlington." She did not submit, and was promoted anyway. Ellerth quit after a little more than a year for unrelated reasons. Her faxed letter of resignation did not mention sexual harassment. Ellerth had once told Slowik that a remark he made was inappropriate, but she did not inform the company or her office coworker (a superior) of the harassment until long after she quit, despite knowing that the company had a policy against sexual harassment.

Seven members of the Court held that a company is "vicariously liable" for a sexually hostile work environment, even if the victim suffered no job setback. Even an empty threat had a detrimental effect on a worker, reasoned Justice Anthony Kennedy, who wrote the majority opinion. However, he also insisted that the employer should have an opportunity to defend itself against the liability. If the company "exercised reasonable care to prevent and correct promptly any sexually harassing behavior," or if the "employee unreasonably failed to take advantage of any preventive or corrective opportunities provided by the employer," then it might not be liable.

Justices Scalia and Thomas both dissented because they saw no evidence of negligence on the part of the employer. In writing the dissent, Thomas criticized the new standard set by the majority because it could be applied "even if the employer has a policy against sexual harassment, the employee knows about that policy, and the employee never informs anyone in a position of authority about the supervisor's conduct." He argued that it was not always easy for a company to know when a supervisor has created a hostile work environment. In those situations the supervisor has not been acting in the best interest of the employer and would logically try to hide his misconduct. "Sexual harassment," Thomas wrote, "is simply not something that employers can wholly prevent without taking extraordinary measures—constant video and audio surveillance, for example—that would revolutionize the workplace in a manner incompatible with a free society." Therefore, he concluded, an employer should not automatically be held liable for a supervisor's misconduct, but only if it knew or should have known about the harassment and "failed to take remedial action."

Thomas sharply criticized the majority for its new employer liability rule, calling it "a whole-cloth creation that draws no support from the legal principles on which the Court claims it is based." He also lamented that the rule "provides shockingly little guidance about how employers can actually avoid vicarious liability" and "ensur[es] a continuing reign of confusion in this important area of the law."

The other case decided that day, *Faragher v. City of Boca Raton,* was brought by Beth Ann Faragher, who worked as an ocean lifeguard part time and during summers from 1985 to 1990 for the Parks and Recreation Department of the City of Boca Raton, Florida. She sued the city and two of her supervisors, Bill Terry and David Silverman, who she claimed had harassed her (and other female lifeguards) by patting her on the rear, talking about her breasts, tackling her, and making lewd comments. She also alleged that Terry once said that he would never promote a woman to the rank of lieutenant, and that Silverman once threatened, "Date me or clean the toilets for a year." Faragher and the other female lifeguards never complained to the city managers of the pool because they had no contact with them and were completely at the mercy of their super-

In 1998 the Supreme Court held in two separate cases that employers are liable for sexual harassment even in instances when a supervisor's threats are not carried out and the victim does not report the misconduct. Kimberly Ellerth (left) was a marketing representative in Chicago for Burlington Industries, and Beth Ann Faragher (right) was a summer lifeguard in Boca Raton, Florida, when they were allegedly subjected to unwanted sexual advances by their supervisors.

visors. In 1986 Boca Raton had adopted a sexual harassment policy, which was revised in 1990, but had failed to circulate it to the lifeguards or to their supervisors. Faragher sued for sexual harassment after quitting her job to attend law school. She then became a public defender in Denver.

In another seven-member opinion, this time written by Justice David Souter, the Court again held the employer liable despite its not having known about the harassment and the victim not having suffered any job-related retaliation. Souter reasoned, "When a fellow employee harasses, the victim can walk away or tell the offender where to go, but it may be difficult to offer such responses to a supervisor." But a supervisor's power to hire and fire, and to set work schedules and pay rates, does not disappear when the supervisor "chooses to harass through insults and offensive gestures rather than directly with threats of firing or promises of promotion." It is the company's responsibility to guard against misconduct by supervisors because it has a "greater opportunity and incentive to screen them, train them, and monitor their performance" than with ordinary workers.

As in the Burlington Industries case, Souter did permit the employer to defend itself against a liability charge if it could prove that it had taken active measures to prevent harassment at the company, by, for example, instituting an effective antiharassment policy. Or if the employer could prove that the employee had "failed to take advantage of any preventive or corrective opportunities provided by the employer." Since the city of Boca Raton had not properly promulgated its antiharassment policy, it was clearly liable under the Court's new rule. Justices Thomas and Scalia again dissented on the ground that the employer had not been proven negligent. "I disagree with the Court's conclusion," wrote Thomas, "that merely because the city did not disseminate its sexual harassment policy, it should be liable as a matter of law." The city should at least have a chance, he wrote, to show that Faragher could have made the city aware of the harassment through a "reasonably available avenue" or that it would not have learned of the harassment even if the policy had been properly distributed.

SEXUAL HARASSMENT IN SCHOOLS

Teachers Harassing Students

Franklin v. Gwinnett County Public Schools,
    503 U.S. 60 (1992)

Gebser v. Lago Vista Independent School Dist.,
    524 U.S. 274 (1998)

When sexual harassment occurs in schools that receive public funding, the federal law used to prosecute the school districts is not Title VII but Title IX of the Education Act Amendments of 1972—the federal law barring sex discrimination in all schools and colleges that receive federal aid (see p. 96). As in Title VII, the word "harassment" does not appear anywhere in Title IX, which was drafted by Congress to combat more conventional forms of discrimination, such as the unequal allocation of scholarship money or athletic opportunities. Very few sexual harassment cases have been filed under Title IX (as with Title VII the actual harassers are only prosecuted under state law) compared with the number prosecuted under Title VII.

The first school-based sexual harassment case to reach the Supreme Court turned on the question of whether a student may be awarded money damages when he or she has been harassed by a teacher. The 1992 case, *Franklin v. Gwinnett County Public Schools,* involved a Georgia high school student who contended that a teacher had on several occasions forced her to have sex with him. The school initially discouraged her from pressing charges against the teacher and then dropped its investigation of the matter when the teacher quit. When the girl sued the school district for money damages, a district court ruled that Title IX did not allow for monetary compensation. A unanimous Supreme Court adopted a broad view of Title IX, holding that since Congress had not spelled out specific remedies for violations of Title IX, then all appropriate relief—including money damages—should be made available to victims. And unlike Title VII, Title IX did not place damage caps on how much money a victim could receive. (Although in practice juries typically award students suing under Title IX very modest sums under $50,000, substantially less than they tend to award workers suing under Title VII.) But the ruling did not define the precise circumstances under which schools could be held liable, which led to conflicting interpretations in the lower courts.

The next Supreme Court test of sexual harassment under Title IX, *Gebser v. Lago Vista Independent School Dist.,* helped to clarify those circumstances six years later. Alida Star Gebser, a Texas high school student, and her mother, Alida

Jean McCollough, sued Lago Vista school district for damages stemming from young Alida's sexual relationship with her teacher, Frank Waldrop. Unlike in *Franklin,* however, the school district had known nothing about the relationship.

Gebser first met Waldrop when she enrolled in his book discussion group in eighth grade, but it was not until the following year, when she was assigned to his high school social studies class, that he made a sexual advance while visiting her home to drop off a book. A sexual relationship developed between them and continued for several semesters. Gebser did not report this development to her parents or to the school because she was afraid she would lose Waldrop as a teacher. Absent any formal antiharassment policy or grievance procedure, she was also not sure how to respond to the situation. Meanwhile, the school principal had received complaints from other students that Waldrop was making sexually suggestive comments in the classroom. The principal forced Waldrop to offer an apology to a group of parents, although the teacher maintained he had not made such comments. A few months later, Waldrop was caught by a police officer who found him having sex with Gebser in a car by a country road.

After being arrested and fired from his job, Waldrop eventually pleaded guilty to the criminal charge. Mrs. Gebser and her daughter filed a suit against Waldrop and the school board in both Texas and federal courts. The school board was protected from liability in state court under Texas law, so attention turned to the federal suit under Title IX. Gebser's case was thrown out by both the district court and the Court of Appeals for the Fifth Circuit. The appeals court interpreted the Supreme Court's decision in *Franklin* to mean that schools could not be held liable unless they knew of the harassment and had turned a blind eye. But other federal appeals courts had interpreted *Franklin* to mean that unless an educational institution had a procedure for dealing with sexual harassment complaints, it could not defend itself by saying it was not aware of the misconduct.

Gebser's lawyers argued that the school board was negligent in failing to provide students with information about what to do if they were being sexually harassed by a teacher. Counsel for the school board stressed that there was no way that the school could have known about the harassment because Waldrop engaged in sexual relations with Gebser off of school property. They also cautioned that a large damage award would sharply cut into the school district's $1.6 million budget, only $100,000 of which came from the federal funds that exposed the school to the Title IX suit.

Writing for the five-member majority, Justice O'Connor held that the liability standard for Title IX should be higher than for Title VII. This meant that a school district would be liable for sexual harassment of a student only if an individual "with authority to take corrective action" had been notified of the misconduct and had not taken steps to correct it. Under Title VII employers can be liable even if they were not notified about, or were not aware of, the harassment.

Justice Stevens wrote the dissent, which was joined by Justices David Souter, Ruth Bader Ginsburg, and Stephen G. Breyer. He argued that this standard was too high, and that few students would be able to prove that a school had been aware of the misconduct but had ignored it. Title IX's purpose was to protect individuals from discrimination, Stevens reasoned, and the best way to do that was to "provide a damages remedy." In a separate dissent Ginsburg, joined by Souter and Breyer, suggested that school districts should be able to defend themselves by showing that they had implemented an anti–sexual harassment policy.

While the decision effectively protected school districts from costly damage suits, it also gave schools little incentive to uncover and prevent the sexually crude taunting and harassment that some students must endure.

Students Harassing Other Students

Davis v. Monroe County School Bd. of Ed., 526 U.S. 629 (1999)

The following year a case came before the Court in which a school was aware of, and neglected to stop, the sexual harassment of a student. In *Davis v. Monroe County School Bd. of Ed.*, a sharply divided Supreme Court ruled that public schools can be sued and forced to pay damages if they fail to stop sexual harassment for which they have received notice. But this time the case involved a student being harassed by a peer, not a teacher. And now the Court was faced with trying to adapt the rules it had established for adults in the workplace to the often messy and awkward emotional lives of schoolchildren.

In her majority opinion Justice O'Connor also set the standard for peer harassment higher than that for adult employees accused of harassment. In her words, a school was only liable if it knew about the harassment and had been "deliberately indifferent" to it. And the misconduct had to be more serious than the traditional teasing and name-calling of schoolchildren. It was required to be so "severe, pervasive, and objectively offensive" as to prevent students from learning.

The harassment at issue in the case went beyond awkward acts of flirting. A fifth-grade boy (known only as G. F. in court filings to protect his identity) was accused of sexually taunting his classmate, ten-year-old LaShonda Davis, by trying to grab her breasts and rub against her in the halls, putting a doorstop in his pants, and whispering that he wanted to "get in bed" with her. Davis sat at the desk adjacent to G. F.'s in class and kept begging to have her seat changed.

Aurelia Davis (left) repeatedly complained to Georgia school officials to take action against the boy who sexually harassed her daughter, LaShonda (right), then only ten years old. The Supreme Court narrowly held in 1999 that public schools can be sued and forced to pay damages if they are made aware of such abuse but do nothing to stop it.

LaShonda's mother, Aurelia Davis, repeatedly complained to school officials at Hubbard Elementary School in Forsyth, Georgia, but they failed to discipline G. F. or take any action. LaShonda's grades dropped and she wrote a suicide note. Finally, after the abuse went on for five months, Mrs. Davis called the sheriff and had G. F. arrested. The boy eventually pleaded guilty to sexual battery.

In 1994, two years after the harassment started, Davis sued the local Board of Education. The school board won in lower courts, arguing that the drafters of Title IX had not spelled out that schools were obligated to stop peer harassment as a condition of receiving public money. The Supreme Court took the case because other courts had reached a different conclusion. O'Connor agreed that Congress should have been clearer about the responsibilities of schools in protecting students from peer harassment when it wrote Title

IX, but she argued that earlier lower court rulings, common law, and federal regulations had all sent some warning that schools were responsible.

Justice Kennedy, whose vigorous dissent criticized the Court for going too far, broke tradition by reading portions of his opinion from the bench. "The majority seems oblivious to the fact that almost every child, at some point, has trouble in school because he or she is being teased by his or her peers," he admonished. "After today," Kennedy further complained, "Johnny will find that the routine problems of adolescence are to be resolved by invoking a federal right to demand assignment to a desk two rows away." In an unusually direct rejoinder from the bench, Justice O'Connor replied that at least the majority opinion "assures that little Mary may attend class."

"The real world of school discipline," Kennedy's dissenting opinion continued, "is a rough-and-tumble place where students practice newly learned vulgarities, erupt with anger, tease and embarrass each other, share offensive notes, flirt, push and shove in the halls, grab and offend." He questioned whether immature behavior by children "who are just learning to interact with their peers" could be defined as sexual harassment or as sex discrimination. Kennedy also wondered whether schools should really be expected to control their students in the same way they control their paid teachers and administrators.

Kennedy and the other three dissenters, Justices Scalia and Thomas and Chief Justice Rehnquist, worried that the ruling would produce an onslaught of costly suits that would burden schools by cutting into their scarce resources. Kennedy also feared that the threat of lawsuits would inaugurate "a climate of fear that encourages school administrators to label even the most innocuous of childish conduct sexual harassment." But O'Connor's majority opinion stated firmly that in order for school boards to avoid being held liable they were not obliged to "purg[e]" schools of peer harassment, nor were administrators required to "engage in particular disciplinary action." The dissenters' overarching complaint was that the majority opinion gave too much power to the federal government to dictate the appropriate way for schools to supervise children "who are beginning to explore their own sexuality and learning how to express it to others." Decisions about how to handle this issue, Kennedy wrote, "are best made by parents and by the teachers and school administrators who can counsel them," not by the government. He did not believe that Congress, in writing Title IX, had intended for the government to play such an intrusive role.

PREGNANCY AND CHILDBIRTH

The question of how pregnancy should affect a woman's employability was not a burning public issue when the vast majority of married American women stayed at home rearing children while their husbands earned the family's financial support. Yet as early as 1908 the Supreme Court addressed the issue of whether motherhood and gainful employment outside the home were really compatible (see p. 17), and upheld a state law that provided women some special protection—a shorter work day—in large part because of the "burdens of motherhood" and the public's interest in keeping mothers healthy so that they would produce equally healthy, "vigorous" offspring. *Muller v. Oregon* created a special category of women in the workplace, that of the "potentially pregnant," and set the stage for years of debate on how employers should deal with potential and actual maternity of women workers.

Since *Muller,* women—especially mothers—have become a dramatically greater presence in the paid workforce. By the end of the century more than half the mothers of pre–school age children were employed. Yet it was not until the late 1970s that government and the courts forced employers to accommodate women in their dual role of workers and mothers. Before then, pregnant workers were either fired or forced to take long, unpaid maternity leaves with no guarantee of their seniority or even their job. And employers denied women disability and medical benefits to pay for the costs of delivering their babies on the theory that pregnancy was not a temporary work disability but instead a condition that signaled a woman's impending departure from the labor force for home and childrearing.

Childbearing surely has been the thorniest issue in sex discrimination in employment. How should courts employing gender equality principles approach women's unique reproductive role? Should women receive preferential treatment as a result of that role? Because obviously only women can carry, bear, and nurse babies, employers, legislators, and courts have had difficulty figuring out how to let them perform those functions without sacrificing their equality in the workplace. And the issue of maternity leave highlights another inequity: although women have made great strides in being accepted as full-fledged members of the workforce, they still shoulder a greater portion of childrearing responsibilities at home.

The first four cases regarding pregnancy and the workplace that the Supreme Court heard turned on three questions: Should women be required to take unpaid leave beginning in mid-pregnancy and extending well past childbirth?

Should employers' disability plans compensate the "normal" condition of pregnancy along with diseases, injuries, and surgical procedures? Can employers cancel the seniority women accrue before childbirth, treating them like new hires when they return to work? Both constitutional and statutory law came into play in the Court's consideration of these cases, sometimes with conflicting results.

SHOULD PREGNANT TEACHERS TEACH?

Cleveland Bd. of Ed. v. LaFleur, 414 U.S. 632 (1974)

Common sense dictates the necessity of maternity leave for working women so they can deliver their babies and recover from childbirth. What constitutes a reasonable and just employment policy on maternity leave, however, is less straightforward.

Jo Carol LaFleur and Ann Elizabeth Nelson were teaching junior high school in Cleveland, Ohio, when they became pregnant during the 1970–1971 academic year. Their employer, the Cleveland Board of Education, enforced a 1952 rule requiring the women to take unpaid maternity leave beginning five months before the expected date of childbirth. The rule also prohibited them from returning to work until the beginning of the first semester falling at least three months after they had given birth, and then only with written approval from a physician. Return to work did not mean return to their previous positions, however. Instead, the rule allowed only for teachers returning from maternity leave to have priority in assignment to vacancies for which they were qualified. Neither LaFleur nor Nelson wanted to take unpaid maternity leave, but both were forced to stop working in March 1971 or face dismissal from their jobs altogether.

During the same school year Susan Cohen, a pregnant teacher in Chesterfield County, Virginia, faced a similar situation. Her employer's maternity leave regulation required her to take unpaid leave starting four months prior to the expected birth of her child. (Unlike its counterpart in Cleveland, however, this regulation did not have a postpartum three-month waiting period for return to work.) Cohen's request to the school board to continue working until the beginning of her ninth month was rejected, as was her subsequent request to finish out the current semester, which would have taken her into the beginning of her sixth month of pregnancy, one month beyond the mandatory cutoff date.

LaFleur and Nelson in Ohio and Cohen in Virginia decided to challenge their respective employers' rules in court. Interestingly, the two cases reached the Supreme Court with opposite legal histories. LaFleur and Nelson had lost in district court and won on appeal, with a finding by the Sixth Circuit Court of Appeals that the Cleveland rule violated the Equal Protection Clause of the Fourteenth Amendment; Cohen had won in district court and lost when the Chesterfield County school board appealed to the Fourth Circuit Court of Appeals.

At the core of the Cleveland school board's argument was the presumption that pregnant women are less fit to handle the rigors of teaching and disciplining urban high school students. Although the board maintained that its primary purpose in enforcing the 1952 rule was to preserve the continuity of classroom instruction—a legitimate state interest—the petitioners' brief echoed the *Muller* case in its emphasis on the delicacy of pregnant women.

Children today, nurtured, as the evidence shows, by the violence of television programs and their reactions to the world around them, must be taught by able-bodied, vigorous teachers. . . . [A pregnant school teacher] experiences the three classic fears of pregnancy—miscarriage, agony in labor, and a deformed child. Her pregnancy in the environment in which she finds herself, full of active, demanding, disrespectful and, indeed, sometimes jeering young people, affects her ability to teach. . . . She is no longer able-bodied in the classroom.

Satisfied that it had established the need to protect pregnant women from the dangers of school life, the board said that the pregnant teachers' desires for individualized cutoff and return dates for their maternity leaves took no account of the school system's duty to preserve the well-being of students and to maximize administrative efficiency. Careful to cover every angle, the board also reminded the Court of its decision in *San Antonio School Board v. Rodriguez* (1973), in which it held that education is not a fundamental constitutional right. Thus, argued the board, it follows that there is no constitutional right to teach, as long as the teacher is not being deprived of freedom of speech or due process.

Attorneys for LaFleur retorted that the Cleveland rule involved classification based on sex and violated the Equal Protection Clause. But, even if the Court did not choose to see the rule as discriminatory on the basis of sex, they argued, it was still unconstitutional because it challenged the right to bear children and to work.

As for the medical evidence, they countered that the experts agreed that the temporary disability brought on by pregnancy should be evaluated *individually,* and that the second trimester (the twelfth through twenty-eighth week of the pregnancy), when the teacher was being forced to leave, was in fact the safest period in most pregnancies. When presented with the question of whether common conditions of pregnancy such as bladder pressure, weight gain, and swollen ankles would cause problems with job performance, expert witness and Georgetown University pro-

In 1952 the Cleveland Board of Education passed a rule forcing female teachers to take unpaid maternity leave beginning five months before the expected date of childbirth and ending at least three months after the child was born, with no guarantee of returning to the same position. Twenty years later, junior high school teacher Jo Carol LaFleur challenged the rule when she was pregnant with her son, Michael.

fessor of obstetrics and gynecology André E. Hellegers responded:

[Water retention in pregnancy totals about] seven pounds of water which is a heck of a sight less than is carried by most obese men. . . . I cannot ascribe any differences than from men who have had nephritis [a kidney disorder], to beer drinkers . . . or even salt eaters. . . . I don't know if any job specification goes to the circumference of ankles except in the chorus line.

Setting aside generalizations about the pregnant teacher's ability to do her job, what about the argument that a uniform rule was administratively necessary? In fact, the teachers' lawyers claimed, mandatory leave and return policies for pregnant teachers actually increased discontinuity of classroom instruction and created more confusion by introducing substitutes and disappointing students who were already experiencing a high rate of teacher turnover. Even the school board admitted that all the schools really needed was "adequate" notice of the date on which the teacher would begin her leave.

The Supreme Court found that both Ohio and Virginia denied pregnant teachers their constitutional right to due process by establishing arbitrary cutoff dates for maternity leave that served no legitimate state interest. As for postpartum reemployment eligibility, the Virginia rule was upheld because all it required was submission of a medical certificate, with reemployment guaranteed no later than the beginning of the next school year. This procedure served the state's interest (teacher fitness, continuity of instruction) without unduly burdening women. By the same reasoning, the Court found the three-month postpartum waiting period (plus medical certificate) of the Cleveland rule unconstitutional. Justice Potter Stewart, writing for the majority, issued a reminder that administrative efficiency and convenience do not stand above the Constitution's Due Process Clause. Thus, Cohen's judgment was reversed and the Sixth Circuit's decision in *LaFleur* was affirmed.

The Court's reasoning, however, departed from that of the Sixth Circuit in one key respect. Instead of seeing the Cleveland rule as a violation of the Equal Protection Clause, it interpreted the rule as violating the Due Process Clause by creating "irrebuttable presumptions" about a pregnant woman's ability to work and her fitness to return to work after giving birth. Such presumptions, Justice Stewart wrote, "unduly penalize a female teacher for deciding to bear a child, and [are] not administratively justified."

Justice Lewis F. Powell Jr., concurring in the result, backed the appeals court's application of the Equal Protection Clause rather than the Due Process Clause. He reasoned that not every regulation that "burdens" childbearing, such as placing an upper limit on welfare assistance to families with more than a designated number of dependent children, violates Due Process.

In his dissent, Justice William H. Rehnquist noted that classification (as opposed to case-by-case treatment) is a time-honored and necessary practice. He cited voting age, drinking age, and mandatory retirement age for government employees as examples: "All legislation involves the drawing of lines. . . . The Court's disenchantment with 'irrebuttable presumptions' . . . is in the last analysis nothing less than an attack upon the very notion of lawmaking itself."

Following on the heels of *LaFleur* was a similar case brought by Mary Ann Turner, a teacher from Utah. The twist was that she was unemployed. The Court did not require a full briefing or oral argument before issuing a decision per curiam in *Turner v. Department of Employment Security of Utah* (1975). It held that a Utah law that made pregnant workers ineligible for unemployment benefits for a period extending from twelve weeks before the expected date of childbirth until six weeks after the child was born was constitutionally invalid under the principles of *LaFleur* because it presumed that all women are unable to work during an eighteen-week period surrounding childbirth.

Although clearly a judicial breakthrough for pregnant working women, the *LaFleur* decision was somewhat overtaken by events. Months before the case was argued, Title VII of the Civil Rights Act of 1964 had been amended to include state agencies and educational institutions, and shortly thereafter, the Equal Employment Opportunity Commission (EEOC) issued guidelines indicating that mandatory leave and termination policies for pregnant women were unlawful under Title VII.

PREGNANCY IS NOT A DISABILITY

Geduldig v. Aiello, 417 U.S. 484 (1974)

Because the *LaFleur* decision rested on the Due Process rather than the Equal Protection Clause, the Court was able to sidestep the issue of sex discrimination in its decision on maternity leave. But it would not be able to avoid the equal protection issue five months later in the case of *Geduldig v. Aiello.*

In 1972 twenty-one-year-old Jacqueline Jaramillo was taking home $515 a month from her job with the Alameda County Legal Aid Society, a private non-profit group in California. Her husband was attending law school and receiving $205 a month in benefits under the G.I. Bill, all of which went to pay for his education. When Jaramillo became pregnant, the state disability insurance program, which required private employers to deduct contributions from employees' checks and turn them over to a state fund, refused her claim for temporary benefits because of a statutory exclusion for pregnancy-related disabilities. "In no case," the law stated, "shall the term 'disability' or 'disabled' include any injury or illness caused by or arising in connection with pregnancy up to the termination of such pregnancy and for a period of 28 days thereafter." Legal Aid did not provide any paid leave; nor was Jaramillo eligible for welfare since her husband was receiving G.I. benefits that would only increase by $25 per month when the child was born.

Jaramillo and three other pregnant women, all of whom had been paying into California's Unemployment Compensation Disability Fund and were "otherwise qualified" to receive disability benefits, challenged the state's pregnancy exclusion and won in district court. But in the meantime a state appellate court ruled in another case that the exclusion should apply only to "normal" pregnancies, effectively eliminating the challenge of three of the four women—Carolyn Aiello and Elizabeth Johnson, whose pregnancies were terminated because they were life threatening, and Augustina Armendariz, who had a miscarriage. Thus, the question that came before the Supreme Court on appeal was whether exclusion of the disability associated with *normal* pregnancy and childbirth from the state's disability coverage constituted discrimination against women.

According to California's 1974 Unemployment Insurance Code, an employment "disability" referred to mental and physical illnesses and injuries that prevented a person from performing his or her regular or customary work and defined a person as disabled "on any day in which, because of his physical or mental condition, he is unable to perform his regular or customary work." But the definition of disability, however broad, was not entirely inclusive. A worker became eligible for benefits only on the eighth day of disability (unless hospitalized) and continued only until the twenty-sixth week. Institutionalized alcoholics, drug addicts, sexual psychopaths, and women with pregnancy-related disabilities were not entitled to compensation. Without these exclusions, the state argued, the disability insurance program would become too expensive to maintain and would force lower-income employees to contribute more than they could afford to the Disability Fund.

Insurers routinely make policy decisions that exclude entire categories of risk. Was California then guilty in this case of anything more than serving the legitimate interests of the state? In fact, the affidavit of Betty Kidder, a disability insurance officer serving Alameda County, revealed an approach to compensation by the local office that was at once more liberal and more restrictive than that indicated by California's Unemployment Insurance Code. Kidder stated that she had paid out claims for sex change operations, alcohol and drug addictions, and circumcisions, but never for pregnancy-related disabilities. The most frequently compensated injuries and illnesses, she continued, were hernias and heart attacks, both of which were suffered in great majority by men. Not only had her department never compensated a pregnancy-related disability, it had also refused to compensate pregnant women for disabilities that did *not* relate to pregnancy or for disabilities that sounded like they were related to pregnancy (e.g., a hysterectomy) even when the woman was not pregnant.

General Electric (GE), which would itself become the petitioner in a similar case in 1976, offered in its amicus curiae brief this analysis of California's pregnancy exclusion.

The purpose of sickness and injury insurance is to soften the blow of an unexpected sickness or injury. A rational relationship between the pregnancy exclusion in the California statute and the statute's purpose is shown by the fact that pregnancy is not a sickness; rather it is a voluntarily induced condition.

In other words, whereas sex-change operations, circumcisions, hernias, and heart attacks were not preventable, pregnancy was. Witness, GE stated, the pill and the IUD—readily available, near-foolproof methods of birth control.

Six members of the Court agreed that the pregnancy exclusion did not constitute sex discrimination. The statutory exclusion, Justice Stewart held, was based on a physical condition, not on gender "as such"—it differentiated between "pregnant women and nonpregnant persons" and not between men and women. "While the first group is exclusively female," wrote Stewart, "the second includes members of both sexes. The fiscal and actuarial benefits of the program thus accrue to members of both sexes." Within

A champion of women's rights in his opinions, Justice William J. Brennan Jr. urged his fellow justices to make the connection between sex discrimination and pregnancy, reasoning that the exclusion of pregnancy disability from otherwise comprehensive benefit packages meant that only women suffered an uncompensated disability.

this framework, the policy of excluding pregnancy and childbirth, as well as "pregnancy-related disabilities" whether real or perceived, would be assessed by the Court under the traditional rational basis standard, which asks whether the distinction made by a statute serves a "legitimate," "reasonable" interest of the state, rather than the more rigorous test the Court had applied to sex-based laws since the early 1970s. California's claim that disability compensation for pregnant persons would create a financial burden heavy enough to destroy the program easily stood up to the test of ordinary, rational basis, judicial scrutiny.

The subtle distinction between a sex-linked characteristic (pregnancy) and a gender-based difference failed to persuade Justices William J. Brennan Jr., William O. Douglas, and Thurgood Marshall. Brennan's dissent argued that the exclusion was obviously based on gender and therefore should be subject to closer scrutiny.

[B]y singling out for less favorable treatment a gender-linked disability peculiar to women, the State has created a double standard for disability compensation: a limitation is imposed upon the disabilities for which women workers may recover, while men receive full compensation for all disabilities suffered, including those that affect only or primarily their sex. . . . Such dissimilar treatment of men and women, on the basis of physical characteristics inextricably linked to one sex, inevitably constitutes sex discrimination.

California's interest in keeping its disability insurance program operating within its current financial constraints (holding the employee contribution to 1 percent of wages; continuing benefits at the established level) may have been "legitimate," but it was, in the dissenters' view, insufficiently strong to justify this discrimination against women, especially since "California's legitimate interest in fiscal integrity could easily have been achieved through a variety of less drastic, sexually neutral means." Brennan also noted that the EEOC, the agency charged with enforcement of Title VII's prohibition on sex discrimination in employment, had issued guidelines interpreting that federal law to prohibit, as sex discrimination, exclusions from employers' disability insurance plans just like the one in the state law at issue in *Geduldig*. It would be as a test of the EEOC's interpretation of Title VII that the next major case involving pregnancy discrimination as sex discrimination would reach the Court.

General Elec. Co. v. Gilbert, 429 U.S. 125 (1976)

General Electric, like the state of California as well as many private companies, excluded pregnancy from its disability plan. Because GE had a private insurance plan that, unlike state plans, is not subject to constitutional constraints, it was challenged under Title VII. That federal law made it illegal for an employer to "discriminate against any individual with respect to his compensation, terms, conditions, or privileges of employment, because of such individual's race, color, religion, sex, or national origin," or to "limit, segregate, or classify his employees in any way which would deprive or tend to deprive any individual of employment opportunities or otherwise adversely affect his status as an employee because of such individual's . . . sex. . . ."

In 1972 Martha V. Gilbert, who worked for GE in Salem, Virginia, together with forty-two other employees from GE plants, filed a complaint with the EEOC charging that GE's pregnancy exclusion constituted sex discrimination under Title VII. The district court found for the employees, concluding that even normal pregnancy was disabling for six to eight weeks—a period encompassing labor, delivery, and recuperation—and that GE's health plan did not similarly exclude sex-related disabilities that affected only men. GE's actuarial defense (that the expenditures of the program were already as high or higher for women than for men), which had influenced *Geduldig*, was not persuasive. Title VII, the district court determined, was not intended to provide employers with a "cost differential defense" to charges of sex discrimination. The Fourth Circuit Court of Appeals affirmed, disregarding *Geduldig*, which had been decided in the meantime, because that case had turned on the Equal Protection Clause, not Title VII.

The force of Title VII comes from the fact that not only intentional discrimination but also a "neutral" (not sex-based) plan or policy can violate it if the *effect* of that plan or policy can be shown to discriminate against members of a class. In this sense, Title VII goes beyond the intentional discrimination standard of the Constitution's Equal Protection Clause. Thus plaintiffs believed they had an argument in *Gilbert* that they lacked in *Geduldig:* that even if a policy that discriminates on the basis of pregnancy does not *facially* discriminate on the basis of sex, it necessarily would have a discriminatory *effect* on women. Nevertheless, the relationship between federal statutes and constitutional law, between administrative guidelines and judicial interpretation, is not a hierarchy set in stone, a situation well illustrated by the justices' decision to reverse the appellate ruling in *Gilbert.*

Once again, the Court relied on the argument that "underinclusiveness" is not equivalent to discrimination, that pregnancy-related disabilities are significantly different from other, covered disabilities, and that insurers are free to exclude some risks. If this reasoning sounded identical to that used in *Geduldig,* it was because the Court decided to use that decision as a "starting point" for Title VII cases. Despite the absence of the words "equal protection" from Title VII, Justice Rehnquist wrote, the language was similar enough to that of the Equal Protection Clause to warrant close comparison, especially since Congress never defined "discrimination" in its statute. Rehnquist found no intentional discrimination against women because, unlike ovarian cancer, for example, pregnancy is not "a disease or disability comparable in all other respects to covered diseases or disabilities and yet confined to members of one race or sex." The Court did acknowledge that under Title VII intent to discriminate does not have to be proven, but disagreed with the lower court's view that GE's policy had a discriminatory "effect." The benefit package, the Court concluded, was not in the aggregate worth more to men than to women.

For all that appears, pregnancy-related disabilities constitute an additional risk, unique to women, and the failure to compensate them for this risk does not destroy the presumed parity of the benefits, accruing to men and women alike, which results from the facially evenhanded inclusion of risks. To hold otherwise would endanger the commonsense notion that an employer who has no disability benefits program at all does not violate Title VII even though the "underinclusion" of risks impacts, as a result of pregnancy-related disabilities, more heavily upon one gender than upon the other.

Having dispensed with the "unintended effects" argument, the Court criticized the 1972 EEOC guideline that specifically stated that disabilities due to pregnancy and childbirth should be compensated on the same terms and conditions as other temporary disabilities. Rehnquist wrote that despite previous exhortations by the Court to give the guidelines "great deference" in applying Title VII, such guidelines were not controlling upon the judiciary. They may be able to "persuade," but never to control. In this case the EEOC, with its then thin and inconsistent record on sex discrimination, failed to persuade.

Justice Brennan did not agree. In fact, he disagreed with the entire conceptual framework used to decide *Gilbert.* The Court had chosen to focus on actuarial equality of included risks, saying that there was no risk from which men were protected and women were not and vice versa. In Brennan's view, the appropriate framework had to be found in social context, not abstract, hypothetical reasoning in "a social or cultural vacuum devoid of stereotypes." Part of that social context was the history of GE's employment policies toward women. Like those of many other companies, GE's policies included denying benefits, scaling back women's wages because they could get pregnant, and forcing unpaid maternity leave. (The company did end its practice of forcing unpaid maternity leave when the *Gilbert* suit commenced.) Brennan rejected as "purely fanciful" the Court's notion that GE's process of assigning risks was gender neutral, given the company's poor track record in treating women fairly.

Brennan further argued that excluding pregnancy because it was voluntary and not a disease contradicted the inclusion of such items as sports injuries, attempted suicides, and elective cosmetic surgery, not to mention the exclusion of complications and illnesses arising from pregnancy. How could inclusion of such procedures as prostatectomies, vasectomies, and circumcisions keep the plan "gender neutral"?

Had General Electric assembled a catalogue of all ailments that befall humanity, and then systematically proceeded to exclude from coverage every disability that is female-specific or predominantly afflicts women, the Court could still reason as here that the plan operates equally: Women, like men, would be entitled to draw disability payments for their circumcisions and prostatectomies, and neither sex could claim payment for pregnancies, breast cancer, and the other excluded female-dominated disabilities. Along similar lines, any disability that occurs disproportionately in a particular group—sickle-cell anemia, for example—could be freely excluded from the plan without troubling the Court's analytical approach.

Justice John Paul Stevens's dissent briefly and plainly addressed the question of classification. If the risk of absence from work due to pregnancy was treated differently from any other risk of absence, does that discriminate against women, since only women can get pregnant? Because GE failed to present a justifiable defense for assessing the risk differently, it placed pregnancy in a category by itself and therefore placed women in a special category. Thus for Stevens there was no need to reach any further: the classification was not pregnant versus nonpregnant persons, but women versus men, and therefore discriminatory.

Clearly, the *Geduldig* and *Gilbert* decisions left some working women no better off than before. Some feared that the Court majority's reasoning actually left them worse off. If employers could deny disability benefits for pregnancy and childbirth without violating either the Constitution or Title VII, what would stop them from denying a wider range of rights to pregnant women? As a coalition pressing for pregnant workers' rights began to build, the Court decided one more case that reexamined Title VII and created yet another subcategory of working women—the formerly pregnant.

HAVING A BABY, LOSING SENIORITY

Nashville Gas Co. v. Satty, 434 U.S. 136 (1977)

Nora D. Satty was working for the gas company as an accounting clerk in Nashville, Tennessee, when she became pregnant in 1972. She began unpaid maternity leave in her eighth month and then attempted to return to work seven weeks after she gave birth, only to find that her job had been eliminated in a cutback. In its stead, the company placed her in a temporary, lower-paying position. During her temporary employment Satty applied for three permanent positions, each of which she would have gotten had it not been for the company's pregnancy policy, which provided that women who took maternity leave lost all of their pre-leave seniority for purposes of bidding on job openings and were treated as new employees. In effect, Satty had lost her job not because of the cutback but because she had taken maternity leave. Because she left for that reason rather than termination, the state denied her unemployment compensation, available only to workers who are involuntarily unemployed, when her temporary job ended.

Satty brought suit against her employer for sex discrimination under Title VII. The district court found for her, and that finding was affirmed on appeal. Both of these lower court decisions preceded the *Gilbert* opinion, however; so when the case reached the Supreme Court in 1977 Satty had good reason to fear that it would reverse the lower courts' favorable decisions. Yet this time the Court met working women halfway. Employers still were not obligated by Title VII to include pregnancy and childbirth in their sick leave, health, and disability programs, but they could not strip formerly pregnant employees of the seniority they earned before their leave when they returned to work. Sick leave and disability compensation were benefits, the Court reasoned, but canceling of accumulated seniority because of pregnancy was a burden placed solely and unfairly on women, a burden for which no "business necessity" could be found to defend Nashville Gas's position.

This distinction between benefit and burden allowed the Court to adhere to the reasoning of *Gilbert* (Satty's role as mother does not entitle her to pregnancy disability benefits) while simultaneously embracing the once rejected EEOC guideline (Satty's role as mother should not deprive her of rights attached to any other temporary disability, including preservation of seniority and right to reinstatement).

Brennan, dissenter in *Gilbert,* joined with Marshall in Powell's opinion, which concurred only in part. For Powell, the Court's dismissal of Satty's claim that her company's sick-leave policy was facially discriminatory did not satisfy. It was not enough to cite *Gilbert* and leave it at that, Powell argued, because there was always the possibility that more fact-finding—a wider examination of the employer's overall treatment of women, as Brennan had recommended with GE—would reveal a pattern of discrimination.

Stevens, though concurring in the judgment, thought that rather than distinguishing between a benefit and a burden the Court would do better to distinguish between the condition of pregnancy—which under *Geduldig* and *Gilbert* could legitimately be an excluded disability—and the pregnant woman herself. "This distinction," Stevens wrote, "may be pragmatically expressed in terms of whether the employer has a policy which adversely affects a woman beyond the term of her pregnancy leave," such as withdrawal of accumulated seniority for formerly pregnant employees.

The legal implications for working women in *Satty* were short lived, however, as the decision was essentially outstripped by an act of Congress. Lobbying by the Campaign to End Discrimination Against Pregnant Workers resulted in passage of the Pregnancy Discrimination Act of 1978, which, by revising the definition of terms in Title VII, made pregnancy a sex-based classification. Brennan's reasoning had found its way into law: *Gilbert* was overturned by Congress.

 ### The Pregnancy Discrimination Act of 1978

As the number of working women increased during the 1970s the ambivalent attitude of employers toward pregnancy and childbirth became more pronounced. On the one hand, employers argued that pregnancy and childbirth were temporarily disabling and inhibited women from working. On the other hand, they refused to insure women against lost wages or other job setbacks resulting from the "disability." In 1974 the Supreme Court ruled mandatory early maternity leave unconstitutional, and in 1976 it found that women on maternity leave were entitled to preserve their seniority but not to receive disability benefits during their absence from work. Still, it would take an act of Congress, guided by the spirit of Justice Brennan and the letter of the EEOC, to move the entire issue of pregnancy disability squarely into the arena of sex discrimination.

In his dissent in *General Electric Co. v. Gilbert* (1976), Brennan had argued that excluding pregnancy disability from otherwise comprehensive benefit packages meant that only women suffered an uncompensated disability and therefore were discriminated against on the basis of their sex under Title VII. The EEOC, in its 1972 guidelines on Title VII, suggested that pregnant women should be allowed to work for as long as medically

In 1978 Congress passed the Pregnancy Discrimination Act, amending Title VII to protect pregnant women from employment discrimination.

appropriate and to return to paid employment as soon as their doctors cleared them for employment after giving birth. Moreover, women should be compensated during the period of disability caused in pregnancy and childbirth on the same basis that employees were compensated for other disabilities. Congress adopted these two lines of reasoning in the Pregnancy Discrimination Act of 1978 (PDA), which amended Title VII to include pregnancy as a classification based on gender. Specifically, the PDA expanded Title VII's definition of sex discrimination.

The terms "because of sex" or "on the basis of sex" include, but are not limited to, because of or on the basis of pregnancy, childbirth, or related medical conditions; and women affected by pregnancy, childbirth, or related medical conditions shall be treated the same for all employment-related purposes, including receipt of benefits under fringe benefit programs, as other persons not so affected but similar in their ability or inability to work. . . .

The PDA seemed to fulfill for working women at least part of the elusive promise of "having it all"—full and equal participation in the workforce without being penalized for bearing children. Yet it also raised the question, albeit indirectly, of preferential treatment of women. It was not surprising, then, that the first two cases to reach the Supreme Court testing the PDA originated in complaints of sex discrimination made by male workers.

DISCRIMINATING AGAINST MEN: COVERAGE OF WORKERS' WIVES

Newport News Shipbuilding and Dry Dock Co. v. EEOC, 462 U.S. 669 (1983)

Prior to the Pregnancy Discrimination Act the Newport News Shipbuilding and Dry Dock Company of Eastern Virginia had provided comprehensive health insurance coverage to employees and their families—but extended only limited coverage for pregnancy to both female employees and to the wives of male employees. When the PDA became law in October 1978, the company dutifully amended its health insurance plan to include full coverage of pregnancy-related conditions for its female employees—but continued the limited coverage of pregnancy for employees' wives. The following September, a male employee filed a complaint with the EEOC charging that Newport News Shipbuilding had unlawfully failed to provide full coverage for his wife's hospitalization "caused by pregnancy." A month later, the United Steel Workers filed a similar complaint on behalf of another group of workers. Newport News Shipbuilding responded by filing suit in district court against the EEOC, the labor union, and the male employee who had originally brought the suit. The EEOC returned fire, accusing the company of sex discrimination against its male employees under Title VII as amended by the PDA. The district court dismissed the EEOC complaint and found for Newport News, concluding that the employer's plan was lawful because the PDA covered employees but not employee's dependents. On appeal, the Fourth Circuit Court of Appeals sitting en banc reversed, though not unanimously. Three judges stood with the district court in its interpretation that the PDA was designed to protect female employees who were temporarily unable to work, not the pregnant wives of male workers, whether the issue was disability compensation or medical insurance.

Stevens, writing for the majority, stated that the ultimate question was whether the company's plan violated Title VII. In other words, did it discriminate against male employees with respect to their compensation, terms, conditions, or privileges of employment because of their sex? He held that regardless of whether the PDA had been intended to include pregnant spouses, the fact that the employer provided insurance coverage for male employees' dependents that was less inclusive than for female workers' dependents was facially discriminatory against the male employees. The Court acknowledged that discussions in Congress over the PDA had focused on the circumstances of female employees, but argued that a law enacted to solve a particular problem does not limit its scope to that problem alone.

The EEOC guidelines, which the majority considered too weak for serious consideration in *Gilbert,* now constituted an important component of the Court's ruling. Stevens pointed to two interpretive guidelines issued by the EEOC after the PDA was passed but before Newport News Shipbuilding had amended its plan. The first reiterated an important aspect of antidiscrimination law, namely that the employer is free to provide *no* benefits or privileges to employees, but if it does choose to provide benefits must do so on a nondiscriminatory basis. Thus, an employer can choose to exclude all workers' spouses from health insurance coverage without violating Title VII but cannot exclude the spouses of one sex and include the other. The second guideline distinguished between level of coverage for employees and level of coverage for spouses or other dependents, stating that, again under Title VII, an employer can choose to cover employees more fully than their dependents but must cover pregnancy-related conditions of spouses at the same, albeit lower, level as all other conditions of spouses, male or female.

Dissenting justices Rehnquist and Powell thought the Court was reading too much into the PDA. The second clause of the act refers to "women affected by pregnancy" being treated the same as "other persons not so affected but similar in their ability or inability to work." This, Rehnquist construed, could only have been referring to female employees. Rehnquist argued that since the PDA did not reach beyond female employees, the overruled *Gilbert* decision should stand in this case. However, *Newport News* had one important distinction from *Gilbert.* The benefit at issue in the earlier case was disability compensation, which was awarded only to the person employed; in the *Newport News* case the benefit was medical insurance, which has traditionally covered workers *and* their dependents.

Newport News Shipbuilding had tried to comply with Title VII as amended by the PDA and was judged to have fallen short. Meanwhile, states were making laws in response to the PDA that some believed were inconsistent with its egalitarian intent, shifting the line from equal to preferential treatment for pregnant women. It was not long before a challenge was brought, under Title VII, to a state law that seemed to require employers to provide special treatment to pregnant workers.

SPECIAL VERSUS EQUAL TREATMENT FOR PREGNANT WORKERS

California Fed. Sav. & Loan Assn. v. Guerra, 479 U.S. 272 (1987)

In 1978, one step ahead of the PDA, the state of California had passed a statute requiring employers to grant employees up to four months of unpaid "pregnancy disability leave," a requirement the state enforcement agency interpreted to include a conditional right to post-leave reinstatement. When employee Lillian Garland took maternity leave in January 1982 from her job at California Federal Savings and Loan Association (Cal Fed) and attempted to return to work the following April, she was told that her receptionist job had been filled and that there were no other suitable vacancies. Garland filed a complaint with the state's Department of Fair Employment and Housing.

Cal Fed, along with a major trade association and the California Chamber of Commerce, issued its own challenge in district court, seeking to stop enforcement of the state law on the ground that it was preempted by Title VII as amended by the PDA. (Garland, meanwhile, was reinstated as a receptionist in November 1982.) Was a state law that required employers to provide pregnant workers with maternity leave when it imposed no such requirement for other temporarily disabled workers consistent with the PDA? The district court, citing *Newport News,* ruled in favor of Cal Fed, reasoning that the state law opened employers to charges of reverse discrimination under Title VII by requiring preferential treatment for one class of workers, pregnant women.

The Ninth Circuit Court of Appeals disagreed, declaring that the lower court's conclusion that the state law "discriminates against men on the basis of pregnancy defies common sense,

Los Angeles bank teller Lillian Garland (flanked here by her lawyer Patricia Shiu and feminist Betty Friedan) successfully sued her employer for giving away her job while she was on a four-month maternity leave.

misinterprets case law, and flouts Title VII and the PDA." The PDA was intended, the appeals court continued, "to construct a floor beneath which pregnancy disability benefits may not drop—not a ceiling above which they may not rise." In its opinion, the statute not only did not conflict with Title VII but furthered the goal of equal employment opportunity for women.

Such were the facts of the case when it reached the Supreme Court. Beneath this surface lurked a fierce tactical and philosophical controversy among advocates of women's rights that remains alive today: that of equal versus special treatment for pregnancy. In *Cal Fed,* this controversy produced two distinct feminist positions in response to the employer's argument that the state pregnancy disability law conflicted with the PDA's equal treatment philosophy and therefore should be declared invalid.

In essence, proponents of the equal treatment approach to pregnancy supported an interpretation of the PDA that took literally its directive that "women affected by pregnancy, childbirth, or related medical conditions shall be treated the same for all employment-related purposes . . . as other persons not so affected but similar in their ability or inability to work." The concern was not that pregnancy did not constitute a "real" difference between men and women, but they were worried that spotlighting those differences had historically resulted in worse, not better, treatment of female workers. Thus they agreed with the employer that the PDA required equal treatment, but they differed from the employer in arguing that extending pregnancy disability leaves to other disabled employees was the way to achieve that equality. By extending disability leaves to non-pregnant employees, the equal treatment advocates reasoned, Cal Fed would be complying with the California pregnancy statute without violating Title VII's guarantee of equal employment opportunity.

On the other side, the special treatment advocates argued that the special characteristics of pregnancy and the realities it created for women required some special accommodations for working women if their reproductive function was not to keep them at a disadvantage in the employment setting. If male employees did not suffer job setbacks to become parents, women employees should not face such setbacks either. They argued that the state pregnancy disability law was thus fully compatible with Title VII's goal of equal employment opportunity for women. By recognizing the special needs pregnancy creates for women, it placed working mothers on a more equal plane with working fathers.

The Supreme Court affirmed the decision of the Ninth Circuit, agreeing that the PDA established a floor, not a ceiling, on pregnancy benefits and that the PDA and the California Pregnancy Leave Statute shared the goal of promoting equal employment opportunity. Justice Marshall's majority opinion held that the special pregnancy disability leave provided by the California statute was "narrowly drawn" and therefore did not represent a return to archaic protective legislation that had been based on stereotypical notions about the abilities of pregnant workers. Thus did the "special treatment" feminists win the day.

Yet Marshall threw the "equal treatment" feminists a bone as well. "[E]ven if we agreed with the [employers' equal treatment] construction of the PDA," he wrote, "we would nonetheless reject their argument that the California statute requires employers to violate Title VII. . . . [The California statute] does not compel California employers to treat pregnant workers *better* than other disabled employees. . . . Employers are free to give comparable benefits to other disabled employees. . . ." Of course, being free to provide leave to other disabled employees did not mean that employers had an obligation to do so.

Justice Byron R. White's dissent in this case, joined by Justices Rehnquist and Powell, agreed with Cal Fed's argument. They pointed to the language of the second clause of the PDA to prove their point.

The PDA gave added meaning to discrimination on the basis of sex. . . . [Its] second clause . . . could not be clearer: it mandates that pregnant employees "shall be treated the same for all employment-related purposes" as nonpregnant employees similarly situated with respect to their ability or inability to work. This language leaves no room for preferential treatment of pregnant workers. . . . On its face, [the California statute] is in square conflict with the PDA and is therefore pre-empted.

Two other justices wrote opinions concurring with the majority, but on separate grounds. Justice Antonin Scalia thought it was unnecessary to come up with a definitive special treatment or equal treatment interpretation of the PDA. The California statute "cannot be preempted, since it does not remotely purport to require or permit any refusal to accord federally mandated equal treatment to others similarly situated," he wrote. "No more is needed to decide this case."

Justice Stevens, in contrast, agreed with Justice White that "Congress did not intend to 'put pregnancy in a class by itself within Title VII,' and the enactment of the PDA 'did not mark a departure from Title VII principles.'" But he concurred with the majority because Title VII allows the use of affirmative action policies to achieve its goal of equal employment opportunity and of removing barriers that have operated in the past (see p. 134). "It is clear to me," he concluded, "that the California Statute meets this test."

Did the *Cal Fed* decision mean progress for working women? In its equal treatment amicus brief, the National Organization for Women (NOW) pointed out that the California statute in question contained additional "special" provisions that harmed pregnant workers, such as giving employers the right to refuse to hire or train pregnant women. By creating a special four-month disability leave, NOW cautioned, the state might deter employers from hiring women of childbearing age. Proponents of equal treatment also feared that a four-month leave for mothers would only reinforce the disproportionate burden women carry for the responsibilities of childcare. In contrast, their opponents generally saw women's dominant role in childrearing as desirable and natural—or at least an entrenched reality that required recognition and accommodation. This notion of a woman's special responsibility to the child, which begins even before it is born, would occupy center stage in the third post-PDA case.

FERTILE WOMEN NEED NOT APPLY

Automobile Workers v. Johnson Controls, Inc.,
   499 U.S. 187 (1991)

While Title VII prohibits different treatment of men and women because of sex, it also creates an important (but very limited) exception to this prohibition. The "bona fide occupational qualification" (BFOQ) exception allows employers to discriminate on the basis of sex (and religion and national origin) if being of one sex is a "bona fide occupational qualification reasonably necessary to the normal operation of that particular business or enterprise" (see p. 121). The Supreme Court had applied the BFOQ exception on the basis of sex in *Dothard v. Rawlinson* (1977), ruling that women could be excluded from working as guards in certain male maximum security prisons because their "very womanhood"—that is, their vulnerability to sexual assault by males—meant they were unable to perform the central feature of a prison guard's job, to ensure prison security. The *Johnson Controls* case offered the Court an opportunity to further interpret Title VII's BFOQ exception, this time in the context of a pregnancy case.

Johnson Controls, a large manufacturer whose battery-making operations involved the use of lead, barred all women—except those who could medically document that they were infertile—from jobs involving lead exposure because such exposure, the company believed, could be harmful to developing fetuses. The company justified its policy on the basis of moral and ethical concern for the next generation—"fetal protection," as it came to be known. Plaintiffs claimed that this policy discriminated on the basis of sex. Studies had shown a reproductive risk from lead exposure to fathers as well as to mothers. Why, they asked, should a fifty-year-old female employee have to take a lower-paying job to avoid lead exposure while a healthy young male employee would be denied a leave of absence to lower his lead level in anticipation of becoming a father? The policy, they argued, harmed women by excluding them from jobs in the name of fetal protection and men by denying them any reproductive protection at all.

In fact, Johnson Controls had in earlier times allowed women to make batteries as long as they were duly warned of the dangers of lead exposure to their potential fetuses if they became pregnant. The policy changed when eight employees who had been exposed to levels of lead that exceeded the federal safety standard became pregnant and the company began to fear possible tort liability suits on behalf of children born with defects caused by lead. (In fact, the eight women's babies would show no birth defects.)

Instead, United Auto Workers and several Johnson Controls employees—a woman who had been sterilized to hold onto her job, a fifty-year-old divorced woman, and a male worker to whom the company had denied a leave of absence for the purpose of lowering the level of lead in his blood because he intended to become a father— brought a class action suit against Johnson Controls. The district court granted summary judgment to Johnson Controls. A divided appellate court affirmed, rejecting the idea that the company's sex-specific fetal protection policy constituted sex discrimination.

In the Supreme Court, the question was not whether the company's policy was discriminatory (all of the justices would agree that it was), but whether being of the male sex could be considered a BFOQ in this particular situation. The BFOQ defense, the Court noted, was available only where the employer's exclusion of one sex was based on a bona fide *occupational* qualification. "By modifying 'qualification' with 'occupational,'" said the Court, "Congress narrowed the

term to qualifications that affect an employee's ability to do the job."

Writing for the majority, Justice Harry A. Blackmun ruled that a fetal protection policy obviously discriminated on the basis of sex, both because it treated fertile men and fertile women differently and because it discriminated on the basis of pregnancy—which, after passage of the PDA, was now also defined as sex discrimination. And since no one, including Johnson Controls, had tried to argue that potentially or actually pregnant women were less capable of making batteries than nonpregnant employees, the BFOQ defense could not save the employer's argument. As for the company's concerns about the welfare of future generations, Blackmun reminded all concerned that Title VII "mandates that decisions about the welfare of future children be left to the parents who conceive, bear, support, and raise them, rather than to the employers who hire those parents or the courts."

Although all nine justices voted to reverse the Court of Appeals, Justices White and Scalia disagreed with some of the reasoning Blackmun employed on behalf of the Court's majority. White felt that a fetal protection policy could be justified if needed to avoid substantial tort liability and the accompanying, potentially ruinous, cost to the business. Scalia agreed with White, adding that there could be circumstances in which accommodating pregnant women in a job—on long sea voyages, for example—would be so expensive that a pregnancy-based exclusionary policy could be a BFOQ.

Nevertheless, White criticized the breadth of Johnson Control's fetal protection policy because it assumed that all women, regardless of age, were fertile unless they could document their sterility. But, he continued, the policy was also too narrow because it excluded fertile men. Scalia's concurrence pointed out that there was no need to bring men's fertility into the equation because the

A career officer in the air force, Capt. Susan Struck was considered an exemplary nurse and manager. Nonetheless, the air force discharged her. Struck's crime: becoming pregnant while stationed in Vietnam during the war.

Capt. Struck, who was not married, used only her accumulated leave time for childbirth and placed the baby up for adoption at birth. (For religious reasons she did not consider abortion an option, even though air force regulations at the time did permit its hospitals to perform abortions "when medically indicated.") Despite the minimal inconvenience she caused the air force, Struck was faced with an unwanted discharge because she had violated two entrenched regulations. The first: "A woman officer will be discharged from the service with the least practicable delay when a determination is made by a medical officer that she is pregnant" had been instituted to encourage birth control. In case that rule went unheeded it was backed up by a second: "The commission of any woman officer will be terminated with the least practicable delay when it is established that she . . . [h]as given birth to a living child while in a commissioned officer status."

Struck argued that those regulations violated her equal protection rights under the Fifth Amendment's Due Process Clause. She maintained that the air force's dismissal of women who became mothers but not men who became fathers was invidious discrimination. (The baby's father, also an air force officer, was not penalized.) Struck also charged that allowing women who had abortions to remain in service, but not women who delivered infants, was discriminatory. Struck did not prevail in lower courts, but the Supreme Court granted her petition for certiorari in October 1972.

At that point the air force backed down and granted Struck a waiver allowing her to continue service. The government then successfully main-

Although she made it clear that she did not plan to keep her baby, Capt. Susan Struck was discharged from the air force in 1970 for violating regulations prohibiting servicewomen from becoming pregnant or having babies. Struck, an unwed mother, admired her two-day-old daughter before giving her up for adoption.

tained that the case had become moot. Ruth Bader Ginsburg, who wrote the brief for Capt. Struck, has since commented that the removal of *Struck v. Secretary of Defense* from the Court's docket was unfortunate because the case so neatly linked disadvantageous treatment of a woman because of her pregnancy to sex discrimination. The rules clearly assumed that the birth of a child disabled a mother but not a father, which in Struck's case was especially untrue given that she never sought maternity leave and had surrendered her child for adoption, as she had informed the air force she would.

Perhaps the Court would have heeded Struck's plea to apply the strictest scrutiny to the air force's mothers-only discharge regulation. Ginsburg has also speculated that the reasoning in abortion decisions might have been altered if the Court had heard *Struck*. The Court might have perceived a sex equality dimension to the question of reproductive choice, instead of relying dominantly, as it did in *Roe v. Wade*, on the main themes of privacy or autonomy.

policy was already discriminatory under the PDA by reason that women were treated differently solely on the basis of their ability to become pregnant. Scalia also argued that the fact that pregnant women could make batteries safely was irrelevant because, even if the job was hazardous to their fetuses, they retained the right under Title VII to "make occupational decisions affecting their families."

 FAMILY LEAVE

Title VII, as amended by the PDA, now entitles women who become pregnant to the same benefits and privileges the employer extends to other workers who experience work disabilities and permits employers to craft policies (or states to pass laws) providing "narrowly tailored" benefits just for pregnant women. But what is the fate of women who work for employers who offer no or minimal benefits to all employees, including pregnant workers? Under such circumstances all Title VII can guarantee is that pregnant workers will be treated in the same way as their coworkers.

And what about fathers who want to bottle feed and bond with their babies? While some employers had traditionally allowed men to take a few days off when their wives gave birth as "paternity leave," they had never been legally required to

do so. Under Title VII, if an employer gives women infant care leave—as distinguished from childbirth and recovery leave—fathers, too, are entitled to such leaves (at least in theory, as such suits are rare).

The basic needs of temporarily disabled workers and working parents were finally given explicit consideration when President Bill Clinton signed into law the Family and Medical Leave Act (FMLA) in 1993. This act of Congress guaranteed *both* male and female employees (of companies with more than fifty workers) up to twelve weeks of unpaid leave of absence, with continuation of health benefits and a right to return to the same or similar job, in the event of their own serious health condition (including the birth of a child) and leave to care for a newly born or adopted child, or newly placed foster child. It also allowed for time off for employees of both sexes to care for a seriously ill parent, child, or spouse.

The FMLA signaled a new respect for the family obligations and responsibilities of working men and women and marked a decided shift away from old-fashioned "maternity leave" toward gender-neutral family leave by recognizing the parental needs and obligations of both mothers and fathers. The act was a victory for the equal treatment side of women's rights advocacy and for the notion that employers should not see child care, even for infants, as solely a mother's responsibility.

REPRODUCTIVE RIGHTS

CONTRACEPTION

The Right to Privacy

A person's right to privacy is nowhere explicitly guaranteed in the Constitution. Although it is now widely accepted as a fundamental right, there is no clause that overtly spells out an individual's right to privacy, and certainly the Framers offered little guidance about the parameters and limitations of such a right. The struggle to pinpoint a constitutional source for the right to privacy began over a century ago.

In 1888 legal scholar Thomas Cooley first coined the phrase the "right to be let alone." And in an influential 1890 *Harvard Law Review* article Boston lawyers Louis D. Brandeis and Samuel Warren made a compelling case for that right, arguing that "the sacred precincts of private and domestic life" ought to be protected. After his appointment to the Supreme Court Justice Brandeis reiterated his belief in the right to privacy in a 1928 dissent from a decision that upheld the government's right to wiretap telephones without warrants. But it would be nearly a half century before the right to privacy was recognized as the core issue in the battle over the legalization of birth control and reproductive rights.

The Court first considered reproductive rights in *Buck v. Bell* (1927), in which it upheld the constitutionality of a forced sterilization of a woman in a mental hospital because a popular "scientific" theory predicted that her feeblemindedness would be inherited by her child. Writing for the majority, Justice Oliver Wendell Holmes Jr. found that none of the woman's rights had been violated and that her sterilization was "better for all the world." The decision effectively permitted states to continue passing laws authorizing the sterilization of the mentally impaired or of habitual criminals.

But fifteen years later, in *Skinner v. Oklahoma* (1942), the Court found unconstitutional on equal protection grounds the forced vasectomy of a petty thief. Questioning whether criminality was an inherited trait, the Court pronounced the thief's crimes too minor to merit depriving him of "one of the basic civil rights of man"—the right to have children.

The Battle for Birth Control

Griswold v. Connecticut, 381 U.S. 479 (1965)

Eisenstadt v. Baird, 405 U.S. 438 (1972)

The first cases the Supreme Court heard linking reproduction to the "right to privacy" turned on the legalization of birth control. Congress's amendment of the Comstock Act in 1873 had made it a crime to send contraceptives, or information about them, through the U.S. mail or to sell them through interstate commerce. Many states then passed their own laws restricting the sale or use of birth control, but those statutes were narrowly interpreted by the courts. By the mid-1930s birth control devices were thus in fairly common use in the United States. Private physicians regularly prescribed them for their married patients, and some kinds of contraceptives were even available in drug stores. In Connecticut, however, a criminal statute dating from 1879 expressly forbade the use or prescription of any form of contraception—even for married people. Drafted by the outspoken temperance advocate P. T. Barnum (of circus fame), the statute was intended to protect public morals by discouraging illicit sexual conduct and extramarital affairs, presumably through the threat of pregnancy.

Although contraceptive bans existed in other states, the Connecticut statute was unique because it outlawed the *use* of birth control devices, allowing for prosecution not only of doctors, but also of their patients. And even though it was largely ignored by doctors in private practice, it served as a real deterrent to those practicing in public clinics—the places that provided service to low-income patients who were arguably most in need of access to birth control.

In 1935, despite the risk of prosecution, the Connecticut Birth Control League opened a women's health clinic in Hartford and began prescribing contraceptives to married women in need. Keeping a low profile, they provided services in the first year to over 400 women, mostly from low-income, immigrant communities. On the heels of the Hartford success, clinics were opened in several other cities across the state and all operated smoothly until 1938, when the League opened its Waterbury Maternal Health Center. Waterbury's large conservative Catholic population stood staunchly, and very vocally, against contraception. Although public officials were disinclined to take action against the clinic, members of the Catholic community demanded an investigation. As a result, the clinic was shut down, the director and two doctors arrested.

Seizing the opportunity to attack the statute in court, League members challenged the constitutionality of the convictions all the way to the Connecticut Supreme Court. It was an unlikely proposition, especially in the wake of a 1938 defeat in which that court had thrown out a similar appeal, saying that as long as the law remained on the books, it must be enforced—regardless of its wisdom. But public opinion favored birth control reform. Hopes that the court would adjust to catch up with public opinion were dashed, however, when *State of Connecticut v. Roger B. Nelson et al.* (1940) was announced. The court found that the 1879 statute allowed for no exception for doctors—regardless of whether contraceptives would preserve the health, or even the life, of their patients—and that doctors could indeed be prosecuted under the law. *Nelson* was a blow to birth control advocates across the country, but in Connecticut it was devastating. The decision effectively shut down every clinic in the state for two decades.

From 1941 to 1963 the Connecticut Birth Control League, now called the Planned Parenthood League of Connecticut (PPLC), proposed a new reform bill each legislative session. Ultimately every bill was rejected. At the same time, its leaders focused efforts on creating a legal case they hoped would press the boundaries of the law and force a reconsideration of *Nelson*. In 1961 they thought they had a winner—a case brought by clinic director Dr. C. Lee Buxton and several of his patients he deemed in medical need of contraception. Their case, *Poe v. Ullman*, went all the way to the Supreme Court.

In his eloquent petition, PPLC counsel Fowler Harper wrote:

When the long arm of the law reaches into the bedroom and regulates the most sacred relations between a man and his wife, it is going too far. There must be a limit to the extent to which the moral scruples of a minority, or for that matter a majority, can be enacted into laws that regulate the sex life of all married people.

He further maintained that Buxton's patients

complain that it is precisely their privacy in their homes and, indeed, in the most private part thereof that is invaded. They want to be let alone in the bedroom. They insist that marital intercourse may not be rationed, censored, or regulated by priest, legislator or bureaucrat. Certainly, they contend, the "liberty" guaranteed by the due process clause includes this, among the most sacred experiences of life.

Despite Harper's plea, the Supreme Court threw out the case, finding that no "substantial controversy" existed since the plaintiff had not been prosecuted.

In a lengthy dissent that would prove instrumental in the eventual overturn of the statute, Justice John Marshall Harlan relied on the Due Process Clause as protecting what a prior Court decision had called "the private realm of family life which the state cannot enter." He quoted from Justice Brandeis's 1928 dissent championing the "right to be let alone," and condemned the law for "allow[ing] the State to enquire into, prove and punish married people for the private use of their marital intimacy." Harlan concluded that a "statute making it a criminal offense for married couples to use contraceptives is an intolerable and unjustifiable invasion of privacy in the conduct of the most intimate concerns of an individual's private life."

In hopes of provoking a new legal action, the PPLC opened a New Haven clinic with a well-

Dr. C. Lee Buxton (left), medical director of the Planned Parenthood League of Connecticut, and Estelle Griswold, its executive director, were taken to police headquarters in 1961 for violation of an 1879 statute forbidding the use or prescription of contraceptives, even for married people. Buxton and Griswold had provoked their own arrest by publicizing the opening of their New Haven birth control clinic.

publicized kickoff. No officials took the bait; in fact no one seemed inclined to do anything about it until an outraged private citizen agitated for legal action. A rather reluctant investigation led to the arrests and convictions of PPLC medical director Buxton and executive director Estelle Griswold. The appeal of their convictions reached the Supreme Court in 1965.

Justice William O. Douglas wrote the opinion for the Court's 7–2 decision in *Griswold v. Connecticut* that finally struck down the Connecticut law. He invalidated the statute on the ground that it infringed on the constitutionally protected right to privacy of married persons. Although the right to privacy was not specifically enumerated in the Constitution, Douglas found that it was implicit in "penumbras" emanating from other rights guaranteed in the Bill of Rights.

[Previous] cases suggest that specific guarantees in the Bill of Rights have penumbras, formed by emanations from those guarantees that help give them life and substance. . . . Various guarantees create zones of privacy. . . . The present case, then, concerns a relationship [marriage] lying within the zone of privacy created by several fundamental constitutional guarantees.

Douglas held that the prohibition against using contraceptives, as opposed to making or selling them, sought to have "a maximum destructive impact" on marriage. "Would we allow," he asked, "the police to search the sacred precincts of marital bedrooms for telltale signs of the use of contraceptives? The very idea is repulsive to the notions of privacy surrounding the marriage relationship." He described marriage as "a coming together for better or for worse, hopefully enduring, and intimate to the degree of being sacred," and linked the right to use contraceptives to the protection of the marital bond, which had long received constitutional protection.

Although a seven-member majority agreed on the outcome in *Griswold,* there was disagreement about the constitutional basis for the decision. Justice Harlan rested his concurrence squarely on an expansive interpretation of the Due Process Clause, which he believed did not allow statutes (such as this contraceptive ban) that violate historic and cultural values "implicit in the concept of ordered liberty." Justice Byron R. White also cited due process as protecting "a realm of family life which the state cannot enter without substantial justification."

Justice Arthur J. Goldberg, in a concurrence joined by Justice William J. Brennan Jr. and Chief Justice Earl Warren, took a more expansive view to justifying the right to privacy. He looked to the Ninth Amendment, which Goldberg interpreted as incorporating rights not elsewhere enumerated in the Constitution so long as those rights were "so rooted in the traditions and conscience of our people as to be ranked fundamental." "Liberty protects those personal rights that are fundamen-

tal," he held, "and is not confined to the specific terms of the Bill of Rights."

The two dissenting votes came from Justice Hugo L. Black and Justice Potter Stewart, who joined each other's dissents. Stewart, who called the statute an "uncommonly silly law," thought married individuals should have the right to use birth control, but agreed with Justice Black that there was nothing in the text of the Constitution to protect such a right. Black cautioned that, without explicit guidance from the Constitution, the Court was exercising its judicial power in an arbitrary manner that threatened to diminish the power of the other two branches of government.

Griswold was a giant step toward the legalization of birth control, but it did not extend to contraceptive use by unmarried people. In 1971 the Court turned its attention to their rights in *Eisenstadt v. Baird.* At issue was the arrest of reproductive rights activist Bill Baird for handing out a package of contraceptive foam to an unmarried woman after a public lecture on overpopulation at Boston University. Distributing contraceptive devices without a doctor's or pharmacist's license was a felony offense under a Massachusetts law that also banned the distribution of contraceptives to unmarried persons.

The Court struck down the ban on equal protection grounds. Six justices found no rational basis in terms of protecting the public's health for a law that would, in effect, make an unwanted pregnancy the penalty for sexual promiscuity. They held that it was unacceptable under the Equal Protection Clause to single out unmarried people for such punishment. In his plurality opinion for the Court, Justice Brennan wrote:

Whatever the rights of the individual to access contraceptives may be, the rights must be the same for the unmarried and the married alike. If under *Griswold* the distribution of contraceptives to married persons cannot be prohibited, a ban on distribution to unmarried

When Estelle Trebert Griswold agreed to sign on as executive director of the Planned Parenthood League of Connecticut (PPLC), she was not sure exactly what a diaphragm was. The year was 1953, and although she had certainly heard about birth control, she was no crusader. She was a professional woman in her early fifties, married, but unable to have children. The funding for her current position as executive secretary of the New Haven Human Relations Council had recently run out, so she was in the market for a job, and the PPLC offices happened to be next door to her home. It just seemed like a logical proposition—a convenient job that might bring some exciting experiences, including the possibility for travel. When she accepted the job she never imagined the magnitude of the contribution she would make to the birth control legalization movement.

Born in 1900 to a middle-class Catholic family in Hartford, Estelle Trebert was not especially religious, nor was she one to follow the letter of the law. In school she was a self-described tomboy whose strong will got her in trouble from time to time. She was bright and energetic—skipping the fourth and seventh grades. It was a tremendous disappointment to her that her parents could not afford to send her to college. Instead, the independent-minded young woman decided to pursue a singing career, working at a bank to support herself while attending music school. Then, in 1922, despite objections from her parents, she moved to Paris. It was the first time she had ever left Connecticut.

Estelle's adventures abroad were cut short when her mother became seriously ill and she was forced to move back home. Not long after her return, she lost both her father and her mother. A series of short-term singing jobs brought her from New York to Chicago and back to Hartford again, where she was reacquainted with a former high school friend,

Richard Griswold. In 1927 the two were married and made a home in Mount Vernon, New York. Dick commuted into New York City for his job at a life insurance company and Estelle continued to travel for her singing career. But in 1935, when Dick was transferred to Washington, D.C., and Estelle's music tutor died, she decided to give up her music career. Instead, she began taking courses toward a medical technologist certificate at George Washington University. When Dick was called into active duty in naval intelligence and sent to Berlin in 1945, Estelle followed him to Europe, finding work with the United Nations Relief and Rehabilitation Agency, providing aid to East European refugees. Five years later, she and Dick were back in Hartford—Dick in advertising and Estelle working for the New Haven Human Relations Council.

PPLC board members could not help but be impressed with what they called Griswold's "phenomenally interesting experience." Her medical background, public relations savvy, and remarkable energy made her an ideal candidate for executive director of the PPLC. But Griswold took a couple of days to consider the offer. Recalling that an old high school friend had once been active in the league, she gave her a call to see what she could find out about the organization. Her friend reported rather skeptically, "It's practically dead. If you really want to work your head off to get it above ground and going again, there's no better place to work." That was all Griswold needed to hear. She was up for the challenge, and she accepted the PPLC's offer.

Griswold immediately pursued the league's primary objective: to overturn the 1879 statute outlawing the use and prescription of birth control. She also devoted herself to developing more outreach—to the greater public and especially to ethnic and low-income communities—insisting that the league "must reach and represent not only a small intellectual group but become a mass movement." And she soon proved herself a dynamo at achieving that goal. After just five short months on the job, PPLC president Molly Milmine told league members, "She admits to no experience with legislative or political activities, but at the rate she has caught up with us already, I see no reason why she cannot do almost anything."

Indeed Griswold did seem unstoppable. She refused to view a disastrous 1940 state supreme court decision that had forced the closing of every clinic across Connecticut as the last word on the subject. Instead, in 1955, with the help of new PPLC president Claudia McGinley, she devised and began implementing a referral program whereby Connecticut residents seeking counsel and prescriptions for birth control could be served at a clinic in Port Chester, just across the river in New York. She organized appointments and arranged transportation. In the PPLC's fifteen years of existence, this was the only real service it had been able to provide.

When the Supreme Court dismissed the PPLC's 1961 challenge to the Connecticut statute in *Poe v. Ullman* on the ground that there was no threat of prosecution under the statute, Griswold proudly told the press that the PPLC planned to open a new clinic as soon as possible, since the Court had declared the antiquated Connecticut anticontraception statute "a dead duck." And she stood by her promise. When the brand-new clinic was ultimately raided by the police, she could barely contain her delight. Thrilled at the prospect of challenging the constitutionality of the statute before the Supreme Court, she gladly provided evidence and information that

In 1965 plaintiff Estelle Griswold (left) triumphantly held a newspaper announcing that the Supreme Court had struck down an 1879 Connecticut law prohibiting the use of contraceptives.

would help the state put together the case against her and the clinic's medical director, Dr. C. Lee Buxton. But she made it clear that, although she welcomed the arrest, she would not be fingerprinted or accept bail, since she felt she had committed no crime, nor would she allow patients' files to be seized as evidence.

When the landmark *Griswold v. Connecticut* decision was handed down by the Supreme Court in 1965—finally voiding the 1879 statute against birth control and ending a forty-year battle—Griswold demurred from taking credit for the victory. But even though she felt the praise belonged to Buxton, the clinic's medical director, and Harper, the architect of the legal defense, many disagreed. "She was an inspiration of energy and determination and dedication to getting the job done," lauded McGinley. After Griswold's death in 1981 another former PPLC president, Lucia Parks, wrote, "Without her we might still have that birth control law. I am practically able to believe that, help or no help, and given time, Estelle Griswold could have gotten the Connecticut birth control law thrown out all by herself."

persons would be equally impermissible. It is true that in *Griswold* that right of privacy in question inhered in the marital relationship. Yet the marital couple is not an independent entity with a mind and heart of its own, but an association of two individuals each with a separate intellectual and emotional makeup. If the right of privacy means anything, it is the right of the *individual,* married or single, to be free from unwarranted government intrusion into matters so fundamentally affecting a person as the decision whether to bear or beget a child.

That final sentence was provocative, and its potential significance for the legalization of abortion—which was well on its way to fruition at the time—did not escape notice. When *Roe v. Wade* was handed down the following year, Brennan's defense of an individual's fundamental right to privacy in reproductive matters became precedent.

In 1977 the Court further extended its protection of the right to privacy—this time to minors—when a plurality struck down a ban on the distribution of contraceptives to anyone under the age of sixteen. *Carey v. Population Services International* overturned a New York state law that also banned the advertisement of contraceptives and prohibited anyone other than authorized pharmacists from distributing nonprescription contraceptives.

ABORTION

The Supreme Court wrote its most controversial women's rights decision on the emotional issue of abortion. In its landmark ruling, *Roe v. Wade* (1973), the Court declared that the Constitution safeguards a woman's right to terminate a pregnancy and limits the government's power to prohibit her from having an abortion or to regulate the medical procedure itself. The ruling touched off decades of intense criticism and political attack. Despite those attacks, a majority of the public gradually came to approve of the Court's decision. And in 1992 the Court reaffirmed *Roe v. Wade* while at the same time giving states somewhat more leeway to regulate abortion procedures.

Abortion Reform Laws

In the United States in the mid-twentieth century, women were not legally free to decide on their own whether to carry a fetus to term or to terminate a pregnancy. Laws on the books in most states severely restricted abortion, allowing the procedure—if at all—only under very limited circumstances such as rape or if the pregnancy posed a danger to the woman's life.

In practice, those laws were readily circumvented. A woman of means could travel to a state or foreign country where abortion was legal or find a reputable physician who would perform the operation despite the law. But women with fewer means often turned to less skilled doctors or illegal practitioners who operated, figuratively if not literally, in the back alleys of towns and cities across the country. Many women died from botched or unsanitary abortions.

By the 1960s a movement to repeal or rewrite restrictive abortion laws had gained strength nationally and in many individual states. The abortion reform movement drew from the work of family planning groups such as Planned Parenthood, antipoverty organizations, and the nascent women's liberation movement. But their efforts collided against the strong opposition of the Roman Catholic Church and significant public ambivalence about the morality of what were then termed "elective" abortions.

Despite those obstacles, the abortion reform movement claimed successes in a number of states by the end of the decade. Between 1967 and 1970, twelve states enacted liberalized abortion laws, usually permitting abortion in cases of rape, incest, or to protect the mother's health as well as her life. Then, in the first six months of 1970, three states, including New York, adopted so-called "repeal laws" that virtually eliminated any barriers to a woman's choice to terminate a pregnancy. Reformers also challenged abortion laws on constitutional grounds in the courts, but with less success. Still, the Supreme Court gave reformers some encouragement with its decision in 1965, *Griswold v. Connecticut*, striking down on privacy grounds a Connecticut law that banned the use of birth control by married couples. If the right to privacy extended to the marital bedroom, these reformers reasoned, it should also extend to a woman's control of her own body.

The First Decision: Roe v. Wade

Roe v. Wade, 410 U.S. 113 (1973)

Doe v. Bolton, 410 U.S. 179 (1973)

The abortion issue reached the Supreme Court in two separate cases brought by Norma McCorvey and Sandra Bensing under the assumed names Jane Roe and Mary Doe. They both said they had been pregnant in 1970 and unable to obtain an abortion under laws in their respective states. *Roe v. Wade* challenged a Texas law, enacted in 1857, that forbade all abortions except to save the pregnant woman's life. *Doe v. Bolton* challenged a "reform" law adopted in Georgia in 1968 that allowed abortions but only if they were performed in a hospital and approved by a hospital committee following an examination of the woman by two physicians other than her own doctor.

The Court—with two unfilled vacancies—heard argument in the two cases on December 13, 1971. Lawyers for the women challenging the laws felt encouraged by the questioning from the justices, but at the end of the term in June 1972 the Court unexpectedly scheduled a second round of arguments at the beginning of the new term in

October. The stated reason was to allow the justices who had joined the Court since the original argument—Lewis F. Powell Jr. and William H. Rehnquist—to participate in the decision. Years later, it was learned that Justice Harry A. Blackmun, who had been assigned to write an opinion striking down the laws, requested reargument after his initial draft failed to satisfy his colleagues.

Following the reargument, the Court issued its decision on January 22, 1973, striking down both the Texas and Georgia laws by 7–2 votes. Blackmun opened his lengthy opinion for the Court by acknowledging "the sensitive and emotional nature" of the issue and "the deep and seemingly absolute convictions" on both sides. The Court's responsibility, he continued, was to resolve the constitutional issue without "emotion" or "predilection." And after reviewing the Court's decisions in such areas as marriage, childrearing, and contraception, Blackmun concluded that as a constitutional matter the right to privacy was "broad enough to encompass a woman's decision whether or not to terminate her pregnancy."

As a matter of history, he recounted, abortion had been common and legal in ancient times and under common law. State laws restricting abortions dated from the mid-nineteenth century and appeared to have been aimed at protecting pregnant women from an unsafe medical procedure. The relative safety of the procedure weakened that consideration today, Blackmun said. Nor, he noted, did the states argue that the abortion laws were a means of discouraging illicit sexual conduct. Instead, the major justification for restricting a woman's right to an abortion was "the state's interest . . . in protecting prenatal life." But he rejected the state's argument that life began at the moment of conception and abortion could therefore be prohibited at any point of a pregnancy.

Instead, Blackmun continued, the balance between the state's interest and the woman's rights changed as the pregnancy progressed. In the first trimester, he said, the state could not regulate or prohibit abortions at all; the decision was for a woman and her doctor alone. In the second trimester—until the fetus was viable (capable of surviving outside the womb)—the state could regulate the abortion procedure "in ways that are reasonably related to maternal health." And in the final trimester, the state's interest in "promoting its interest in the potentiality of human life" could justify either regulating or banning abortion except if the procedure was necessary "for the preservation of the life or health of the mother."

Justices across the ideological spectrum joined Blackmun's opinion—from liberals William O. Douglas, William J. Brennan Jr., and Thurgood Marshall, to moderates Potter Stewart and Powell. Chief Justice Warren E. Burger joined the majority opinion too, but added in a concurring opinion that the decision did not permit "abortion on demand." In a dissenting opinion, however, Justice Byron R. White complained that the decision allowed for abortion to satisfy "the convenience, whim, or caprice of the putative mother." Justice Rehnquist joined White's dissent and added his own. The Court's "conscious weighing of competing factors," he said, was "far more appropriate to a legislative judgment than to a judicial one."

Roe: *The Aftermath*

The abortion decision received second play in most of the news media to the other big story of the day: the death of former president Lyndon B. Johnson. Still, the impact of the ruling on abortion laws in other states was immediately recognized. The *New York Times* carried a headline that read: "High Court Rules Abortion Legal the First 3 Months; State Bans Ruled Out Until Last 10 Weeks."

The ruling touched off a debate—partly legal, partly political—that continues to this day. Legally, supporters of restrictive abortion laws questioned the constitutional basis for the decision. They emphasized—as Rehnquist did in his dissent—that the Constitution includes no mention of the right to privacy that the Court cited as the basis for its ruling. They also noted that Blackmun himself had been ambiguous about the source of the privacy right when he said that it could be found either in the Ninth Amendment's protection for unenumerated rights or—"as we feel it is"—in the Fourteenth Amendment's Due Process Clause.

Abortion rights advocates generally celebrated the ruling, but a few came to have mixed feelings about the decision. Some legal experts sympathetic to the cause nonetheless echoed Rehnquist's view that Blackmun's opinion read more like legislation than a constitutional judgment. And over time some political and legal observers contended that abortion reform would have advanced more smoothly without the Court's sweeping decision and the polarized debate that it touched off.

Politically, the decision gave birth to a so-called "right-to-life" movement that supported antiabortion candidates at the local, state, and national levels. Most ambitiously, these antiabortion groups hoped to see *Roe* overturned—either by the Court itself or by a constitutional amendment. Neither of those goals was achieved. But right-to-life groups kept the issue on the agenda in Congress and in state and local legislative bodies around the country. The result was enactment of a host of restrictive abortion laws that challenged lower courts and ultimately the Supreme Court itself to continue defining the exact contours of the newfound right to abortion recognized in *Roe.*

The *Roe v. Wade* decision sparked an antiabortion movement that kept the issue on the agenda in Congress and in state and local legislative bodies around the country. The result was enactment of a host of restrictive abortion laws that ultimately forced the Supreme Court to define the exact contours of the newfound right to abortion recognized in *Roe.*

Abortion Funding

Maher v. Roe, 432 U.S. 464 (1977)

Harris v. McRae, 448 U.S. 297 (1980)

Rust v. Sullivan, 500 U.S. 173 (1991)

Abortion opponents won the Court's approval for one strategy for undercutting *Roe:* restricting women's ability to obtain funding for abortions under government health programs for the poor. In a pair of decisions within the first decade after *Roe,* the Court gave states and the federal government discretion to refuse to pay for abortions under Medicaid (except under limited circumstances) even if the programs did pay for the cost of childbirth. Then, in 1991, the Court extended those decisions by approving a federal regulation that prohibited any abortion counseling at family planning clinics receiving federal funds.

The Court followed similar reasoning in all three cases in rejecting arguments that the restrictions violated the equal protection rights of poor women. Since the government had no obligation to provide health services at all, it was not imposing an unconstitutional burden on poor women by refusing to pay for a particular medical procedure: abortions. The dissenting justices in each case complained bitterly that the Court was effectively denying poor pregnant women the choice that *Roe* theoretically had guaranteed to them.

In the first of the decisions, *Maher v. Roe* (1977), the Court upheld a Connecticut law that barred state Medicaid assistance for abortions in the first trimester of pregnancy unless a doctor

certified that the procedure was "medically necessary" for the woman's physical or mental health.
Writing for the 6–3 majority, Powell said that *Roe*
did not prevent the government from "favoring
childbirth over abortion." The law, he concluded,
"places no obstacles, absolute or otherwise, in the
pregnant woman's path to an abortion." For the
dissenters, Brennan said the decision reflected "a
distressing insensitivity to the plight of impoverished pregnant women." The Court's only new
member since *Roe*—John Paul Stevens—joined
the majority in upholding the law.

Three years later, in *Harris v. McRae*, the
Court upheld a more restrictive federal provision
known as the Hyde Amendment after its principal author: Henry Hyde, a Republican representative from Illinois. The Hyde Amendment prohibited the use of federal Medicaid funds in any
state to perform abortions "except where the life
of the mother would be endangered if the fetus
were carried to term; or except for such medical
procedures necessary for the victims of rape or incest." Thus, unlike the Connecticut law, the federal provision barred funding for abortions certified to be necessary for the mother's health unless
her life was at stake.

Despite the added restrictions, the Court's 5–4
majority treated the amendment as substantially
identical to the Connecticut law upheld earlier.
Stevens switched sides, however, from the previous ruling and voted to strike down the provision.
Under *Roe*, Stevens explained, "state interference
is unreasonable if it attaches a greater importance
to the interest in potential life than to the interest
in protecting the mother's health."

Through the 1980s Presidents Ronald Reagan
and George Bush aligned their administrations
with antiabortion groups in further efforts to
limit any governmental support for abortions.
One result was a regulation issued in 1988 by the
Department of Health and Human Services that
prohibited any abortion counseling by family

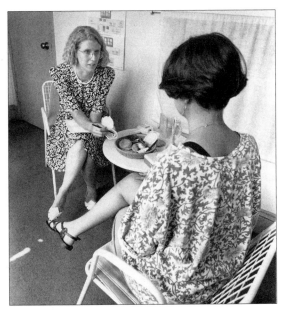

In 1991 the Court upheld a regulation issued three years earlier by the
Bush administration prohibiting abortion counseling in clinics that receive federal funds. The prohibition became known as the "gag rule" because it effectively silenced abortion counselors in federally funded clinics.

planning clinics that received federal funds under
Title X, a provision of the Public Health Service
Act. The provision, written three years before
Roe, stipulated that no federal funds could be
used in "programs where abortion is used as a
method of family planning." Doctors, clinics, and
the city and state of New York challenged the
provision, which became known as the "gag rule"
because it silenced abortion counselors. They argued that the regulation went beyond the language of the statute and in any event violated
women's abortion rights as well as the clinics' free
speech rights.

The Court, however, upheld the regulation in
Rust v. Sullivan in a 5–4 vote. For the majority,
Rehnquist, whom Reagan had elevated to chief
justice in 1986, echoed the previous funding decisions. "Congress' refusal to fund abortion counseling and advocacy leaves a pregnant woman
with the same choices as if the Government had

chosen not to fund family-planning services at all," Rehnquist wrote. Blackmun, in the main dissent, said the ruling left a woman's right to abortion "technically intact" but "rendered the right's substance nugatory [inoperative]."

Consent of Husband, Parents

Planned Parenthood Assn. of Central Mo. v. Danforth, 428 U.S. 52 (1976)

Bellotti v. Baird, 443 U.S. 622 (1979)

Planned Parenthood Assn. of Kansas City, Mo., Inc. v. Ashcroft, 462 U.S. 476 (1983)

Hodgson v. Minnesota, 497 U.S. 417 (1990)

Ohio v. Akron Center for Reproductive Health, 497 U.S. 502 (1990)

Antiabortion groups had less success in their efforts to undercut *Roe v. Wade* with laws requiring a woman to obtain her husband's consent or, in the case of a minor, one or both of her parents' consent before terminating a pregnancy. The Court firmly rejected any requirement to obtain a husband's consent. And it upheld parental consent or notification laws only if they allowed an unmarried minor to bypass the requirements by going to court to obtain the necessary approval for the abortion procedure from a judge.

Both issues reached the Court in a challenge to a Missouri law enacted within two years after *Roe*. The statute required written consent for an abortion from a husband or, in the case of a minor, a parent, unless a doctor certified that the procedure was necessary in order to preserve the life of the mother. Writing for the Court in *Planned Parenthood v. Danforth* (1976), Blackmun struck down the spousal consent provision by a 6–3 vote and invalidated the parental consent requirement by a 5–4 vote.

On the spousal consent issue, Blackmun acknowledged that the decision "ideally" should be made by both husband and wife. But, he continued, "Inasmuch as it is the woman who physically bears the child and who is the more directly and immediately affected by the pregnancy, as between the two, the balance weighs in her favor." Writing for the dissenters, White said it was "truly surprising" that the Court would require a state to "assign greater value to a mother's decision to cut off a potential human life than to a father's decision to let it mature into a live child."

The issues of parental consent or notification proved more difficult to resolve. Blackmun concluded that a "mature" minor's right to have an abortion must prevail over a parent's contrary decision. Three years later, in *Bellotti v. Baird*, the Court struck down a similar Massachusetts parental consent law, but with no majority consensus. In the plurality opinion, Powell suggested that every minor must have an opportunity to go to court to obtain approval for an abortion without first consulting or notifying her parents (a procedure known as a judicial bypass). A court must approve the procedure, Powell said, if the minor could show she was sufficiently mature and intelligent to make the decision on her own. If not, Powell continued, the minor should still have the opportunity to show the court that the abortion would be in her best interest.

In a 1983 decision, *Planned Parenthood v. Ashcroft*, the Court upheld, on a 5–4 vote, a Missouri law that contained a judicial bypass procedure that satisfied Powell's conditions. The Court's newest justice, Sandra Day O'Connor, wrote the pivotal opinion upholding the law. She said the statute was valid because it imposed "no undue burden" on the minor's right; Rehnquist and White joined her opinion. For the four dissenters, Blackmun said he would hold unconstitutional any provision that permitted a parent or a

The Supreme Court has held that a pregnant teenager who does not wish to obtain parental consent for an abortion may appear before a judge and ask the court's permission to terminate the pregnancy.

court to veto a minor's decision to obtain an abortion.

The close division on the consent issue persisted. In 1990 the Court revisited the issue in a pair of cases, *Hodgson v. Minnesota* and *Ohio v. Akron Center for Reproductive Health*. The Minnesota law required two-parent notification for an abortion on an underage woman but allowed her to seek a judicial bypass to get around this requirement. The Ohio statute imposed a twenty-four-hour waiting period for an abortion on a minor and required one parent to be notified; as an alternative, it allowed the minor to obtain court approval for an abortion upon showing "clear and convincing evidence" that the procedure was in her best interest.

The Court upheld the judicial bypass procedure in the Minnesota law by a narrow 5–4 vote, with O'Connor casting the swing vote. But the Court did so only after a different five-justice majority, led by Stevens, eliminated the two-parent notification on the ground that many young women did not live with both parents, either because the parents were divorced and one parent did not have custody, one parent was ill, or the absent parent had abused or deserted the child. Requiring a second parental notification, Stevens concluded, could be harmful to dysfunctional families. O'Connor provided the fifth vote because she was satisfied that the availability of a judicial bypass eliminated any "interference" with the minor's rights.

In the Ohio case, Justice Anthony Kennedy—writing his first abortion opinion since joining the Court in 1988—led the majority in dismissing concerns that the judicial bypass procedure unduly burdened a minor seeking an abortion. In dissent, Blackmun described the procedure as "a tortuous maze" designed to deter abortions.

In 1970 Dr. Jane E. Hodgson performed an abortion on a twenty-three-year-old mother of three who had been diagnosed with rubella. Hodgson had first consulted other prominent Minnesota obstetricians—all of whom agreed that the patient required an abortion because the chance of congenital mal-development with rubella contracted in the first month was very high. As she expected, Hodgson was arrested by the police and indicted for violating Minnesota's antiabortion law. She became the first licensed physician in the United States to be criminally charged for performing a medically approved abortion.

Dr. Hodgson, age fifty-five at the time of her arrest, was the only female obstetrician and gynecologist in St. Paul, Minnesota. Married, with two teenage daughters, she had long opposed Minnesota's antiabortion law. Hodgson had tried to use this case to challenge the law in court, on behalf of the mother, herself, and several like-minded physicians. But the court refused injunctive relief and did not issue a ruling before the mother reached the end of her first trimester, so Hodgson had proceeded with the abortion illegally.

Hodgson realized that she would have to be convicted to force a constitutional challenge to the state's abortion law. So she made every effort to be judged guilty—including waiving a jury trial. But if appeals from her conviction failed, Hodgson knew she would lose her license to practice medicine.

In pronouncing Hodgson guilty, the trial judge commended her courage and suspended her sentence to thirty days in jail. Her case was instantly appealed to the Minnesota Supreme Court. That court reversed her conviction shortly after the U.S. Supreme Court handed down its 1973 *Roe v. Wade* decision overturning as unconstitutional the restrictive abortion laws of Texas and Georgia.

The pioneering physician's crusade for abortion rights did not end there. She provided abortion

services to Minnesota women despite death threats and harassment by antiabortion demonstrators. Although Hodgson practiced at a hospital in St. Paul, she also traveled regularly to clinics in rural areas were her services were desperately needed. Most obstetricians in Minnesota, especially in rural areas, flatly refused to perform abortions either for fear of retaliation by antiabortion protesters or because they considered abortion to be immoral.

Turning again to the courts in 1986, Dr. Hodgson challenged a Minnesota statute requiring advance notice to both parents of any pregnant teenager's request for an abortion. The 1981 law applied even to cases where a parent had never lived with the teenager or did not have legal custody of her. In *Hodgson v. Minnesota* (1990) the Supreme Court struck down the statute because it did not include a provision to allow the pregnant teenager to obtain a judge's permission to bypass the parental notification requirement.

Abortion Procedure

City of Akron v. Akron Center for Reproductive Health, 462 U.S. 416 (1983)

Thornburgh v. American College of Obstetricians & Gynecologists, 476 U.S. 747 (1986)

Opponents of abortion won enactment of many other state and local laws regulating the procedures for a woman to obtain an abortion and for doctors to perform the procedure. Some laws required women to give written consent to an abortion; some went further and required that certain discouraging information be given to the woman, usually about the risks of an abortion. Some imposed a waiting period before a woman could obtain an abortion. Along other lines, some jurisdictions passed laws requiring an abortion to be performed in hospitals or with at least two doctors in attendance. And some laws barred specific types of abortion procedures or required doctors to determine the viability of the fetus before aborting it or to take steps to try to preserve the fetus's life if viable.

The Court charted an unsteady course in dealing with the varied restrictions. Some justices found virtually all of the restrictions unconstitutional as undermining *Roe,* while others voted to uphold almost all of them. Justices in the middle—notably Powell, Stevens, and, later, O'Connor—shifted positions from case to case. The appointment by Presidents Reagan and Bush of Antonin Scalia in 1986, Anthony Kennedy in 1988, and Clarence Thomas in 1991 strengthened the bloc for upholding abortion restrictions.

When it struck down the spousal consent provision in *Planned Parenthood v. Danforth* (1976), the Court accepted a separate provision that required the woman herself to sign a written consent to the abortion. In two subsequent cases, however, the Court overturned so-called "informed consent" provisions in an Akron, Ohio,

ordinance and a Pennsylvania state law. The Akron ordinance required a doctor to tell a woman about, among other things, "the physical and emotional complications" of an abortion and the availability of assistance for adoption and childbirth. Powell, writing for the 6–3 majority in *Akron v. Akron Center for Reproductive Health* (1983), struck down the law, saying much of the information "is designed not to inform the woman's consent but rather to persuade her to withhold it altogether." Three years later, in the Pennsylvania case, the Court voted 5–4 to strike down a similar state law in *Thornburgh v. American College of Obstetricians and Gynecologists* (1986).

The Court also voted to strike a part of the Akron ordinance that prohibited a doctor from performing an abortion until twenty-four hours after the pregnant woman signed a consent form. Powell noted that the provision added to the cost of the procedure by requiring a woman to make two trips to the facility where it was to be performed. The city, Powell said, had failed to show that the "arbitrary and inflexible waiting period" served any legitimate state interest.

The *Akron* case marked the first opinion by the Court's first woman justice, O'Connor, in an abortion case. O'Connor's appointment two years earlier had prompted much speculation from opposing groups about her likely views on abortion. Antiabortion groups drew encouragement from her opinion. Writing for the three dissenters, O'Connor criticized *Roe*'s trimester approach. The ruling, she said, did not give women an "unqualified 'right to an abortion,'" but only prohibited regulations that would result in "unduly burdensome interference" with a woman's freedom to terminate a pregnancy. Applying that standard, O'Connor voted to uphold all of the challenged provisions in the Akron law.

The majority in *Akron v. Akron Center for Reproductive Health* also voted to strike down a provision requiring any second-trimester abortion to be performed in a hospital, not a clinic. Powell said the procedure was safe in clinics and the hospitalization requirement unnecessarily added to the woman's cost. But in *Planned Parenthood v. Ashcroft,* decided the same day, Powell cast a pivotal vote in a 5–4 decision upholding a challenged provision of a Missouri law that required a second doctor to be present during any postviability abortion. Powell reasoned that the law included an implicit "emergency exception" if the woman's health or life would be endangered by waiting for the arrival of a second physician. But in *Thornburgh,* the Pennsylvania case decided three years later, Powell joined the majority in striking down a similar second-physician requirement because it did not allow an emergency exception.

The Pennsylvania law also stipulated that a physician performing a postviability abortion use the technique that "would provide the best opportunity for the unborn child to be aborted alive" unless the technique would pose a "significantly greater medical risk to the life or health of the pregnant woman." In *Thornburgh* the Court held 5–4 that the law was unconstitutional because it required "a 'trade-off' between the woman's health and fetal survival." In one of the dissenting opinions White said the decision "directly contradicts one of the essential holdings of *Roe*—that is, that the State may forbid *all* post-viability abortions except when *necessary* to protect the life or health of the pregnant woman."

Reconsidering Roe

Webster v. Reproductive Health Services, 492 U.S. 490 (1989)

With the justices so closely divided on the issue, abortion became a major focus of Supreme Court confirmation battles after Rehnquist's elevation to chief justice in 1986. Abortion rights groups, fearing a possible fifth vote on the Court for overturning *Roe,* helped defeat one Supreme Court nominee—Robert Bork in 1987—and lobbied hard in an unsuccessful fight to defeat another: Clarence Thomas in 1991. Meanwhile, the Justice Department under both Reagan and Bush was filing amicus curiae briefs in abortion cases explicitly urging the Court to overturn *Roe.*

The Court twice came within a hair's breadth of taking that course in cases challenging restrictive state abortion laws—first in 1989 and again in 1992. Abortion opponents could claim a measure of victory in both cases. The Court upheld all the challenged restrictions in the first case, from Missouri, and all but one of the provisions in the second case, from Pennsylvania. Both times, however, abortion opponents fell short of their ultimate goal. Instead, the Court ended in 1992 with a strongly worded opinion jointly authored by a pivotal group of three justices reaffirming abortion rights as an essential element of women's social and economic freedom.

The Missouri law challenged in the 1989 case, *Webster v. Reproductive Health Services,* opened with a preamble that directly contradicted *Roe* by declaring that "the life of every human being begins with conception." Substantively, the law went beyond previous abortion funding provisions by prohibiting state employees from performing abortions and banning the procedure altogether at public facilities. In addition, the law required doctors performing an abortion after the twentieth week of gestation to perform tests to determine the viability of the fetus.

The Court upheld each of the provisions on a 5–4 vote. In the plurality opinion, Rehnquist—joined by White and Kennedy—had little difficulty upholding the life-begins-at-conception preamble and the funding provisions. The preamble, Rehnquist said, "simply . . . express[ed] . . . [a] value judgment." The ban on abortions by public employees or in public hospitals, he continued, left pregnant women "with the same

Before becoming a judge Harry A. Blackmun served as resident general counsel to the world-renowned Mayo Clinic in Rochester, Minnesota, where he gained expertise in medical law. In preparing his opinion in *Roe v. Wade,* he returned to the clinic for several weeks to conduct medical and historical research about abortion. The father of three daughters, Blackmun paid a huge personal toll for *Roe:* he regularly received hate mail and death threats, and a shot was once fired into his apartment.

choices as if the State had chosen not to operate any public hospitals at all."

The testing requirement proved more problematic. Rehnquist acknowledged that the provision conflicted with *Roe*'s trimester approach by regulating the medical procedure to be used in determining viability. So, he called for abandoning what he termed *Roe*'s "rigid framework" and instead upheld the provision as a permissible requirement to further "the State's interest in protecting potential human life."

Justice Scalia, who provided a fourth vote for upholding the regulations, more explicitly called for overruling *Roe*. But O'Connor was not persuaded. She found each of the provisions valid under her undue-burden test. On that basis, she said, there was "no necessity" to reconsider *Roe*. In

an ominous dissent, Blackmun warned that *Roe* "survives" but was "not secure."

Casey: Reaffirming Roe

Planned Parenthood of Southeastern Pennsylvania v. Casey, 505 U.S. 833 (1992)

Two more justices had joined the Court by the time of the 1992 decision, *Planned Parenthood of Southeastern Pennsylvania v. Casey.* In their confirmation hearings, both David Souter in 1990 and Thomas in 1991 declined to give their views on abortion. But abortion groups feared that either or both would provide an additional vote for overturning *Roe*.

The Pennsylvania law in question included several provisions seemingly invalid under the Court's precedents. The law included a twenty-four-hour waiting period and an informed consent provision that appeared inconsistent with the ruling in *Akron v. Akron Center for Reproductive Health.* It required a woman to notify her husband before an abortion—a provision seemingly at odds with the Court's decisions barring a spousal consent requirement. Yet the law also included a parental consent provision that matched the Court's most recent decisions on the issue. And it imposed recordkeeping and reporting requirements for facilities where abortions were performed; those provisions also seemed in line with the Court's prior decisions.

The ruling, dramatically issued on the final day of the Court's 1991–1992 term, upheld all the provisions except one: the spousal notification requirement. But the result was less important than the stand taken by three centrist justices—O'Connor, Kennedy, and Souter—in getting there. In an unusual joint opinion, the three justices decisively rejected the arguments for overruling *Roe*. They relied in part on legal concerns: the "factual underpinnings" of *Roe*'s "central holding" had not been changed; the opinion had not proved to be unworkable, despite criticisms to the contrary; and overruling the decision in response to political criticism could undermine the Court's legitimacy.

The three justices began, though, by focusing directly on the importance of reproductive choice for women's lives and their liberties. In the process, they seemed to reconceive the right to terminate an unwanted pregnancy as one based more on the prohibition of gender discrimination than on the right to privacy. Women had relied for two decades, the justices said, on the availability of abortion. "The ability of women to participate equally in the economic and social life of the Nation has been facilitated by their ability to control their reproductive lives," they continued. The cost of overruling *Roe* for people who have relied on the decision, the justices concluded, cannot be dismissed.

Nonetheless, the three justices rejected *Roe*'s trimester framework, which they argued was not part of its "essential holding." That approach, they said, "undervalues the State's interest in potential life." Instead, they adopted O'Connor's long-held position that "[o]nly where state regulation imposes an undue burden on a woman's ability to make [the decision whether to procure an abortion] does the power of the State reach into the heart of the liberty protected by the Due Process Clause."

Using that standard, the three justices said the twenty-four-hour waiting period and informed consent provisions of the Pennsylvania law did not constitute an undue burden on women's rights—effectively overturning two parts of the *Akron* decision. The spousal notification provision, however, would "operate as a substantial obstacle," they said. They relied in part on detailed

Justices O'Connor, Kennedy, and Souter wrote a joint opinion in 1992 that reaffirmed the legality of abortion by rejecting state regulations that impose an "undue burden" on women seeking an abortion.

findings made by the lower court about the dangers of domestic violence against women by their husbands. With little discussion, the three justices ended by saying that the parental notification and recordkeeping provisions did not impose undue burdens and therefore were valid.

Abortion rights advocates were pleased with Souter's vote to uphold *Roe* and surprised by Kennedy's in the light of his vote in *Webster* to depart from the precedent. Blackmun and Stevens provided the necessary fourth and fifth votes for retaining *Roe*. They disagreed with the decision to uphold the various provisions of the Pennsylvania law, but Blackmun nonetheless praised O'Connor, Kennedy, and Souter by name for their "personal courage and constitutional principle" in recognizing the right to abortion.

In dissent, Rehnquist—joined as before by White and Scalia and now also by Thomas—called in vain for overturning *Roe*. The Court was wrong, Rehnquist said, in holding that a woman's decision to terminate her pregnancy was "a fundamental right." While outvoted on legal doctrine, though, the four justices provided the votes needed to uphold all but one of the challenged provisions and to signal to state and local governments some additional leeway in fashioning abortion regulations.

Stenberg v. Carhart —U.S.— (2000)

After *Casey* the composition of the Court changed. Justice White, who had maintained his opposition to *Roe* for two decades, retired in June 1993. President Bill Clinton named as his successor Ruth Bader Ginsburg, a pioneering women's rights advocate who nonetheless had criticized the Court's opinion in *Roe* for sweeping beyond the Texas case and effectively declaring unconstitutional all state abortion laws then existing. In her confirmation hearing, however, Ginsburg described abortion rights as "something central to a woman's life, her dignity."

A year later, Justice Blackmun retired. He had suffered a personal toll for writing the Court's opinion in *Roe*. The justice had received hate mail and death threats; once, a shot was fired into his apartment. On his retirement, however, Blackmun was unapologetic about the decision. "I think it was right in 1973, and I think it was right today," Blackmun said at his farewell news conference. "I think it's a step that had to be taken as we go down the road toward the full emancipation of women."

Clinton named as his successor Stephen G. Breyer, a federal appeals court judge and former Harvard Law School professor with a specialty in economic regulation issues. Breyer avoided specific questions about abortion in his confirmation hearings, but—along with Ginsburg—he proved to be a reliable vote for abortion rights once he reached the Court.

Justice Breyer wrote for the Court in *Stenberg v. Carhart,* a controversial abortion decision issued on the last day of the 1999 term. Speaking for a five-member majority, Breyer held unconstitutional the state of Nebraska's ban on a procedure opponents refer to as "partial-birth abortion." This rare procedure, which doctors call "dilation and extraction," is used only at the end of the second trimester when the fetus's head has grown too big to pass safely through the undilated cervix. The fetus is pulled out of the uterus and extracted feet first and the doctor collapses the skull to permit delivery of the head.

The Court struck down the law for failing to provide any exception to protect the *health*—not just the *life*—of the pregnant woman, as required by precedent. The law, Justice Breyer wrote, would "place some women at unnecessary risk of

Antiabortion demonstrators' efforts to discourage women and medical personnel from entering abortion clinics have forced the Supreme Court to weigh women's reproductive rights against the First Amendment's guarantee of free speech. Above, an Operation Rescue activist who tried to block a Planned Parenthood clinic is pulled away by pro-choice activists.

tragic health consequences." The Court also held that the law's vague wording made it so broad that it could be used to prosecute doctors for performing more common abortion procedures. Accordingly, the ban placed an "undue burden" upon a woman's right to choose an abortion, a violation of the standard established in *Casey*.

Seven other justices also wrote opinions, reflecting the divisiveness of the case. In a concurring opinion joined by Justice Ginsburg, Justice Stevens said that it was "impossible for me to understand how a state has any legitimate interest in requiring a doctor to follow any procedure other than the one that he or she reasonably believes will best protect the woman." Justice

O'Connor's concurring opinion was less deferential. She said that a statute that specifically prohibited the dilation and extraction procedure and included a health exception would be constitutional.

In an impassioned dissent, Justice Thomas called the decision "indefensible." The ruling, he said, "inexplicably holds that the States cannot constitutionally prohibit a method of abortion that millions find hard to distinguish from infanticide." Chief Justice Rehnquist and Justice Scalia joined Thomas's opinion. Separately, Justice Kennedy said the ruling "repudiates" *Casey*'s premise that the states "retain a critical and legitimate role in legislating on the subject of abortion."

When attorneys Linda Coffee and Sarah Weddington went looking in 1969 for a plaintiff who could help them challenge Texas's 100-year-old antiabortion law, they hoped for someone more solid than waiflike Norma Nelson McCorvey. Emotionally vulnerable and high strung, McCorvey lived an unsettled lifestyle. She had been married at sixteen, quickly divorced, and had already given up custody of two children by different fathers. And her account of being raped while traveling with the carnival that employed her as a ticket taker changed with each retelling. Still, she was a few months pregnant, wanted an abortion, and when approached was game to challenge the state for the right not to bear an unwanted child.

Besides, after months of tireless searching the only other potential test case they found was a married couple, David and Marsha King. The Kings were not expecting a child but objected on principle to the abortion statute on the ground that it infringed on their right to marital privacy. Coffee and Weddington had agreed to take up their case which, as *Doe v. Wade,* was also appealed up to the Supreme Court. But the suit was ultimately dismissed because, there not being a pregnancy, it did not present a real controversy.

When Coffee and Weddington met twenty-one-year-old McCorvey, she had already had a hard life. Growing up in a military family, Norma had moved every few years, finally ending up in Dallas. A poor student, she was rebellious and often in trouble. When Norma was thirteen her parents divorced, and she was forced to live with her mother, with whom she did not get along. Norma dropped out of school in the tenth grade and got a job as a car-hop at a drive-in. There she met Elwood "Woody" McCorvey, a sheet metal worker who, at age twenty-four, had already been twice divorced. They married, but separated when

Norma McCorvey kept her identity as "Jane Roe" quiet for more than a decade after *Roe v. Wade* was decided. In 1988 she began working at a Dallas abortion clinic, speaking at pro-choice rallies, and granting press interviews. McCorvey has since renounced the abortion rights movement.

Norma announced she was pregnant and Woody accused her of infidelity.

Again living with her mother, eighteen-year-old McCorvey tried to finish high school but felt "like a pool cue in a china cabinet." Instead she got a job as a waitress in a lesbian bar and moved in with a girlfriend. Her mother disapproved of her openly bisexual lifestyle, and pressured McCorvey into giving her custody of her baby, a daughter, a year after she was born.

Then McCorvey accidentally got pregnant a second time, this time giving up custody of the child to its father. When she found herself pregnant a third time while working for the traveling carnival, she was desperate to have an abortion.

McCorvey found her choices were limited. She could obtain a legal abortion in Colorado, California, or Georgia after fulfilling state residency requirements. Or she could do what most Texas women did: go to Mexico, where there were numerous clinics that openly performed illegal abortions. But both options required money, and she had none. (She had even moved in with her father to save on rent.) She thought her best hope was to find an illegal abortionist in Texas, but was informed that good ones cost at least $500 and with cheap ones she risked infection, injury, or death. Her last choice was to get through the pregnancy and give the child up for adoption. When she asked her doctor about this option, McCorvey was referred to a young lawyer named Henry McCluskey who arranged private adoptions. After hearing her story, McCluskey introduced her to Coffee and Weddington because he thought she might be the plaintiff for whom they had been looking.

Coffee and Weddington were young graduates of the University of Texas Law School who had decided to join forces to challenge the Texas law that prohibited abortion except to save the mother's life. Weddington had obtained an illegal abortion in Mexico during law school and knew what it was like to face an unwanted pregnancy (although she kept this fact secret until 1992). After graduating, Weddington found that there were few hiring opportunities for women at law firms so she took a job on an ethics project for the American Bar Association, coauthoring an important book on professional conduct for lawyers. Coffee gained a prestigious clerkship to a judge on the Fifth Circuit Court of Appeals after graduation, but then received only one job offer, from a small firm that hired her to practice bankruptcy law. Both women wanted to put their legal skills to work on a case that would fully challenge them. They initially took McCorvey's case for free and paid all the expenses out of their own pockets.

Coffee and Weddington decided they wanted to force the Texas court to reject the abortion law outright, not "reform" it to allow for abortions in cases

As young graduates of the University of Texas Law School, Linda Coffee (left) and Sarah Weddington (right) joined forces to challenge a century-old Texas law that prohibited abortion except to save the mother's life. Coffee worked on the procedural issues of the case that became *Roe v. Wade* while Weddington worked on its merits.

of rape or incest, or to preserve the mother's health, as other states had done. In preparing the case they decided not to mention McCorvey's allegations of being raped so that the court would not narrowly rule that abortion was legal only for rape victims. (In 1987 McCorvey would admit that she had not, in fact, been raped, and that she had originally made up that story in the hopes of getting a sympathetic doctor to perform an abortion.) Her lawyers chose to file the case under an assumed name—Jane Roe—to shield her from press scrutiny and to protect her privacy.

In 1970 Coffee filed suit in a Dallas federal courthouse against Henry Wade, the district attorney of Dallas County, seeking a court order to restrain him from enforcing the Texas abortion law. Wade's attorney countered that Jane Roe had no standing to sue because the law prohibited doctors from performing abortions, not pregnant women from seeking them. Coffee and Weddington quickly teamed up with a doctor named James Hallford, who had been arrested for illegally performing abortions, and added him as a plaintiff. They also enlarged the suit so that it would be brought on behalf of all women needing an abortion.

McCorvey did not have to testify at a hearing. Instead, she submitted a written statement explaining that she "wanted to terminate [her] pregnancy *(continued)*

(continued)

because of the economic hardship that [the] pregnancy entailed and because of the social stigma attached to the bearing of illegitimate children in our society." She did not show up for the trial, which was just as well since she was eight months pregnant and obviously past the stage where she could abort her baby. A three-judge court ruled in favor of McCorvey and Hallford on the ground that the Texas abortion law was an unconstitutional violation of a woman's right to "choose whether to have children."

By the time the decision was handed down McCorvey was recuperating from childbirth and the emotional strain of giving her baby up for adoption. When her lawyers told her they wanted to bypass the Fifth Circuit Court of Appeals and appeal her case directly to the Supreme Court, she exclaimed, "My God, all those people are so important. They don't have time to listen to some little old Texas girl who got in trouble." She was wrong. Of the many abortion cases presented to the Supreme Court on petition or appeal, the justices chose to hear *Roe v. Wade* and a Georgia reform law case called *Doe v. Bolton*.

As always, Coffee worked on the procedural issues of the case and Weddington on its merits. They unsuccessfully petitioned the Supreme Court to split the thirty-minute oral argument between them—an unusual but not unprecedented request. A nervous Weddington made the argument alone, with Coffee seated next to her at the counsel table. She gave an impressive performance by all ac-

counts, but had to repeat it the next term because the case was put down for reargument. Like most appellants, McCorvey did not make the trip to Washington, D.C., to hear her case argued. She had become increasingly difficult for her attorneys to locate during this time, because she stayed at friends' apartments and, she would later admit, abused drugs and alcohol.

The Court's decisive 7–2 decision came as a surprise even to Coffee and Weddington. When McCorvey read the news in her local newspaper she burst into tears. Connie Gonzalez, a store clerk who had become McCorvey's steady partner, was puzzled. Why was she so upset over the headline news of former president Lyndon B. Johnson's death? "I'm Roe," McCorvey revealed for the first time. When Weddington called to ask her how it felt to win her case on behalf of all women, McCorvey replied, "It makes me feel like I'm on top of Mount Everest."

A local Baptist paper was tipped off about Roe's real identity by Coffee's mother. McCorvey was interviewed and quoted as saying, "It's great to know that other women will not have to go through what I did." Although a few other papers picked up that story, McCorvey's identity mostly was kept quiet in the ensuing decade. She continued to keep a low profile working as an apartment manager.

Fifteen years after *Roe* McCorvey reemerged. She had decided she wanted to be in the spotlight and started granting press interviews—for a fee— and speaking at pro-choice rallies. She and Gon-

Abortion rights advocates hoped the ruling would invalidate similar laws in some other thirty states.

Antiabortion Demonstrations at Clinics

Frustrated by the inability to overturn *Roe v. Wade* in the courts or through a constitutional amendment, some militant elements of the antiabortion movement turned to direct action. A

group calling itself Operation Rescue took the lead in organizing demonstrations that sought to block women and medical personnel from entering clinics where abortions were performed.

The protest tactic pitted women's reproductive rights against the First Amendment's guarantee of freedom of speech. The Supreme Court tried to chart a middle course. It ruled that courts could impose some limits on antiabortion demonstrations as long as the restrictions did zalez began working at a Dallas abortion clinic and became immersed in the abortion rights movement. "[T]he issue is my life," she told an interviewer. "I think, I breathe, I eat, I drink nothing but 'choice' 24 hours a day, seven days a week."

But McCorvey soon found that she was taken for granted. She also felt snubbed by her better educated colleagues in the pro-choice movement. As she recalled in Cinemax's 1998 documentary, *Roe vs. Roe: Baptism by Fire:* "I've always been a rebel of sorts, and [the pro-choice organizers in Dallas] wouldn't basically call me whenever they had their rallies of fundraisers. . . . They really didn't want to have anything to do with me."

Still, it surprised nearly everyone when McCorvey crossed allegiances to join the antiabortion movement in 1995, making headlines across the country. The Reverend Flip Benham had befriended her when his Operation Rescue group rented space next door to the clinic where McCorvey worked and began protesting its activities. The evangelical preacher was warm and charismatic and paid attention to McCorvey in a way that leaders of the pro-choice movement never had. In her 1994 autobiography, *I Am Roe,* McCorvey aired her resentment toward Weddington and Coffee for not having helped her obtain an abortion, something she realized in retrospect that her lawyers could have done. "I was nothing to Sarah and Linda," she complained, "nothing more than a piece of paper." She was also miffed that her lawyers never visited her at the hospital when the baby she had origi-

nally hoped to abort was born.

Although the press made much of her defection, McCorvey's religious conversion had more to do with the acceptance and respect she earned from her fellow evangelical Protestants than with an ideological stance on the abortion issue. She joined Operation Rescue "to help women save their babies," although she continued to believe in a woman's right to first trimester abortions, particularly in cases of fetal deformities. Later she would criticize Operation Rescue's militant tactics of harassing abortion seekers entering clinics.

After three years, McCorvey broke with Operation Rescue. Benham's disapproval of her homosexuality and his constant pressuring her to move out of the house she shared with Gonzalez, by then her companion of more than twenty-five years, had made her angry. At age fifty-one McCorvey converted to Catholicism, her mother's religion (her father was a Jehovah's Witness), and declared herself against abortion in any situation, even in cases of rape or incest.

McCorvey's curious evolution from anonymous plaintiff to poster child for the pro-choice movement to antiabortion advocate has been a restless search for identity and acceptance. Perhaps being a symbol was too much responsibility for McCorvey's fragile nature. Yet in the 1998 Cinemax documentary she finally seemed to be making peace with herself. "I don't claim to be anything," she said. "I'm not a smart person. I'm not a beautiful woman. I'm O.K., and I'm O.K. with that."

not go too far in curbing free speech rights. Dissenting justices, however, complained that the rulings were inconsistent with free speech precedents and traditions.

The issue first reached the Court in an effort by a group of clinics to curb demonstrations by invoking a Reconstruction-era civil rights law that prohibits a conspiracy to deprive any person or class of persons of the equal protection of the laws. By a 6–3 vote, the Court in *Bray v. Alexandria Women's Health Center* (1993) rejected the argument. Writing for the majority, Justice Scalia said that the law did not apply because the demonstrations did not involve discrimination against women because of their sex.

In a pair of rulings one year later, however, the Court allowed women's clinics to use other legal tools to try to limit blockades and harassment of individual patients and staff members. In one decision, *Madsen v. Women's Health Center, Inc.,* the

Court in 1994 upheld parts of an injunction that a judge had issued against demonstrations at a women's clinic in Melbourne, Florida. Most importantly, the Court said a judge could order demonstrators to set up a "buffer zone" around clinics requiring protesters to keep a minimum distance—in this case, thirty-six feet—away from building entrances and driveways.

Significantly, the 6–3 decision was written by Chief Justice Rehnquist, who had consistently voted against abortion rights since the original *Roe v. Wade* decision. Nonetheless, Rehnquist said that an injunction limiting demonstrations could be justified by the government's "strong interest in protecting a woman's freedom to seek lawful medical or counseling services in connection with her pregnancy." Scalia, leading the dissenters, called the judge's order "misguided" and said the Court's ruling "ought to give all friends of liberty great concern."

In a second decision, *National Organization for Women, Inc. v. Scheidler,* issued earlier in 1994, the Court also ruled that women's clinics could sue demonstrators for damages under the federal antiracketeering law: the Racketeer Influenced and Corrupt Organizations Act, commonly known as RICO. That ruling exposed antiabortion protesters to the possibility of triple damages for any monetary harm suffered by the clinics as well as punitive damages.

Three years later, the Court applied the *Madsen* decision in a case arising from protests at clinics in Rochester and Buffalo, New York. A federal judge had ordered protesters to set up a fifteen-foot "fixed buffer zone" around clinic entrances and also to stay at least fifteen feet away from people entering or leaving the clinic—a so-called "floating bubble." Rehnquist wrote the Court's opinion in *Schenck v. Pro-Choice Network of Western New York* upholding the fixed buffer zone, but striking down the floating bubble because it improperly prevented protesters from "communicating a message from a normal conversational distance." Scalia dissented again, saying the ruling "makes a destructive inroad upon First Amendment law."

In June 2000 the Court decided *Hill v. Colorado,* in which it upheld a Colorado law that established a 100-foot zone around the entrance to any "health care facility." Within that buffer zone, people passing out literature, protesting, or counseling could not approach, without consent, within eight feet of passersby. The Court held that the law appropriately served the state interest in ensuring unimpeded access to health care facilities and was "content neutral" because it regulated the place where speech may occur without reference to the context of the expression. Justices Scalia, Kennedy, and Thomas dissented on the ground that the law unconstitutionally restricted free speech.

LEADING THE WAY

WOMEN BAR MEMBERS AND ADVOCATES

Belva A. Lockwood: First Woman Member of the Supreme Court Bar and First Woman to Argue Before the Supreme Court

"For the first time in the history of [the Supreme Court] a woman's name now stands on the roll of its practitioners," announced the *Evening Star*, Washington, D.C.'s widely read newspaper, in 1879. The brevity of this statement hid the dramatic story of Belva A. Lockwood, who had struggled for five years and virtually single-handedly to gain permission for women lawyers to practice before the Supreme Court of the United States. Although initially defeated both in Congress and the federal courts, Lockwood ultimately prevailed when she persuaded Congress to pass an act authorizing the admission of women to the bar of the Supreme Court. In 1880, twenty months after being admitted to practice, Lockwood became the first woman to argue a case before the Court.

Lockwood was an early and adamant woman suffragist who devoted her life to challenging the social axioms of nineteenth-century America. The head of her own law office in Washington,

D.C., she persistently claimed the right of women to pursue professional careers at a time when most Americans were certain that women whose husbands could support the family belonged at home. She not only desegregated the profession of law, but also changed the face of American politics when she ran for the United States presidency in 1884 and 1888.

Attorney Belva Lockwood adopted the tricycle as an efficient means of getting around Washington, D.C., to her court appointments.

FIRST LADIES OF
THE SUPREME COURT

In the early nineteenth century the justices traveled without their wives from their home states to Washington, D.C., and lived together in a boarding house while the Supreme Court was in session. This arrangement helped reinforce the unanimity of the Court's opinions under Chief Justice John Marshall and minimized domestic distractions. Sarah Wetmore Story, wife of Justice Joseph Story, broke up this cozy situation when she accompanied her husband to the nation's capital for the 1828 term. Later in the century, appointment to the Supreme Court regularly meant a move to the capital for the justice's family.

Being the wife of a justice historically entailed social obligations. On Mondays they were expected to receive visitors in their homes—sometimes as many as 300—and to provide music for dancing and a full tea spread. This practice died out during the Depression, and now Supreme Court spouses—there are two husbands—pursue their own interests and careers.

The spouses do get together three times a year, preparing lunch for each other in a room at the

The justices' wives posed for the traditional formal portrait in 1961. From left are (sitting) Mary R. Clark, Elizabeth S. Black, Nina P. Warren, Mercedes H. Douglas, and Winifred Whittaker; (standing) Ethel A. Harlan, Marjorie Brennan, and Mary Ann Stewart.

Supreme Court traditionally designated the Ladies Dining Room. In 1997 Justice Sandra Day O'Connor suggested the room be renamed to honor the memory of the chief justice's wife, Natalie Cornell Rehnquist, who died in 1991. A special section in the courtroom is reserved for the justices' spouses, so they may attend Court sessions whenever they wish.

Journey into Law and Politics

Belva A. Lockwood was born Belva Ann Bennett in Royalton, Niagara County, New York, in 1830. Her farm family background endowed her neither with advantage nor a tradition of rebellion. As a teenager she resembled numerous country girls who provided an extra pair of hands at home while teaching numbers and letters at the local schoolhouse. Widowed with a child at age twenty-two, she entered a local seminary and a year later its affiliated college (now Syracuse University), eventually becoming a teacher and school principal.

At thirty-six Belva Bennett McNall moved herself and her sixteen-year-old daughter, Lura, to Washington, D.C. In her 1888 self-portrait, "My Efforts to Become a Lawyer," written for *Lippincott's Monthly Magazine,* she said, "I sold out my school property in Owego, and came to Washington, for no other purpose than to see what was being done at this great political centre,—this seething pot,—to learn something of the practical workings of the machinery of government, and to see what the great men and women of the country felt and thought." She accepted a job at a school for girls. It paid poorly

The Evening Star.

Vᵒˡ. 53—Nᵒ. 8,086.   WASHINGTON, D. C., TUESDAY, MARCH 4, 1879.   TWO CENTS.

THE U. S. SUPREME COURT convened yesterday, after a recess of four weeks. All the justices were present except Associate Justice Hunt, who, it is feared, will never again take his seat on the bench. A number of opinions prepared during the recess were read. J. Hall Sypher, of New Orleans, and Mrs. Belva A. Lockwood, of Washington city, were admitted to practice. For the first time in the history of this court a woman's name now stands on the roll of its practitioners.

In 1879 the *Evening Star* reported that "For the first time in the history of this court a woman's name now stands on the roll of its practitioners." This brief mention downplayed Belva Lockwood's lobbying effort to gain women admittance to the Supreme Court bar.

but left her time to learn about the District government, to attend debates in Congress, and to listen to oral argument at the Supreme Court.

She was fascinated with law and lawmaking: "In my college course I had studied and had become deeply interested in the Constitution of the United States, the law of nations, political economy, and other things that had given me an insight into political life. I had early conceived a passion for reading the biographies of great men, and had discovered that in almost every instance law has been the stepping-stone to greatness. Born a woman, with all of a woman's feelings and intuitions, I had all of the ambitions of a man, forgetting the gulf between the rights and privileges of the sexes."

In 1869, newly married to dentist and Baptist minister Ezekiel Lockwood, who was nearly thirty years her senior, she decided to act on her ambition to become a lawyer. She had "wearied with the monotony of teaching" and believed that law "offered more diversity, more facilities for improvement, better pay, and a chance to rise in the world." She did not, she later recalled, "stop to consider that I was a woman." By this year Lockwood was also an established leader of the Washington, D.C., suffrage movement and a spokeswoman and lobbyist for the cause of women's equal employment. She may not have stopped to consider that she was a woman but she knew well that the bare handful of women attorneys in the United States in 1869 had credentialed themselves by reading law with a husband, relative, or family friend. The lack

of a legal mentor was a handicap but one she hoped to overcome by applying for admission to one of the several small law schools that were opening in those years (most for part-time, night study by government employees).

Lockwood first applied to become a student at the new Columbian Law School in the District of Columbia, but was refused admission because of her sex. Shortly thereafter, along with several other women, she matriculated at a second recently incorporated institution, the National University Law School (now George Washington University Law School), founded by men mistakenly believed to be sympathetic to women's interest in legal careers.

The recitations were sex segregated, "a compromise between prejudice and progress," and the women's degrees withheld because of a "growl by the young men, some of them declaring openly that they would not graduate with women." For Lockwood, who had earlier endured the death of the daughter born to her and Ezekiel, the action was "a heavy blow to my aspirations, as the diploma would have been the entering wedge into the court and saved me the weary contest which followed." Since she lacked the diploma, her name was not included in the list of male graduates whose membership in the D.C. bar was moved as a group before the District Supreme Court. Lockwood and Lydia Hall, a clerk at the Treasury Department, had no choice but to apply individually, which they did in the spring of 1872. The D.C. court deferred action by ordering that a special examination committee be constituted.

Lockwood endured days of questioning by this special bar committee but the examiners made no final decision on her application. Her colleague Hall abandoned the fight. Lockwood later singled out members of the bar as the culprits rather than local judges: "Judge Cartter . . . one year before . . . knowing that some women in the District were preparing for admission to the bar, had asked that the rule of court be so amended as to strike out the word 'male,' and it had been done . . . [but] the age of progress that had to some extent softened and liberalized the judges of the District Supreme Court had not touched the old-time conservatism of the bar." "Desperate enough for any adventure," Lockwood went south to work for the *Golden Age* and on behalf of the presidential campaign of Horace Greeley, a somewhat curious decision given Greeley's less than whole-hearted support of women's rights. Upon her return to Washington, she attempted to enroll at the Georgetown College Law School, failed, but was permitted to attend lectures at Howard University.

The "weary contest" continued into the winter and summer of 1873, although certain local justices of the peace, and Judge William Snell of the Police Court, had notified her that she would be recognized in their courts, as attorney, in the trial of any case. Finally, Lockwood took the step of writing two letters to President Ulysses S. Grant, the school's titular leader. The second one was short and brusque: *I have passed through the curriculum of study . . . and demand, my diploma."* Grant did not answer, but two weeks later the university chancellor presented Lockwood with her diploma. On September 24, 1873, she was admitted to the District of Columbia bar. She thus became, after African American attorney Charlotte E. Ray, the second woman attorney in the capital, and one of the very few in the nation, to be licensed to practice law.

Washington Activist and Career Woman

Lockwood had been a resident of Washington for seven years when she was admitted to the D.C. bar. She had used these years to prepare for a legal career and to launch herself as an activist in the cause of women's rights and, slightly later, international peace and arbitration. In establishing a law practice, she could rely on no one but herself. Success required that she find men and women willing to hire a woman attorney, and judges at least tolerant of courtroom appearances by a woman. Lockwood succeeded on both counts at a time when religious belief, social mores, and the law itself maintained that women were driven by emotion, not intellect; that female reproductive capacity was diminished by thinking (and vice versa); and that a married woman, by law, "merged" with her husband. In this context it is all the more impressive that, without the springboard of a socially prominent family, or prior longtime residence in Washington, Lockwood built a solo law practice that survived for forty years.

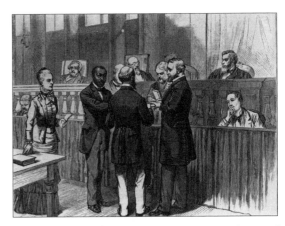

Once a member herself, Belva Lockwood (left) moved the admission of Samuel R. Lowery, the first Southern African American attorney admitted to the Supreme Court bar.

Portrait of a Legal Career

When Lockwood was admitted to the District bar in September of 1873, at least one member of the legal establishment, District of Columbia Judge Arthur MacArthur, remarked that he did not believe that women lawyers "will be a success." Lockwood proved him wrong. She built a practice that brought her regularly before the civil, criminal, and equity courts, as well as state courts where sex discrimination did not prevent her from obtaining permission to practice law. She developed a specialization in pension and land claims. The staff of her law office processed thousands of Civil War veterans' pension claims between the early 1870s and the 1890s, and Lockwood appeared repeatedly before the United States Court of Claims on behalf of these and other claims petitioners. She participated in litigation before United States district courts and eventually, at the Supreme Court of the United States.

Lockwood always maintained a law practice in her name and delegated courtroom appearances and arguments only when she was out of town. Several historians have argued that female attorneys of the nineteenth and early twentieth centuries disliked speaking in court, or thought it inappropriate, and elected to remain in back offices, supporting the work of a male partner or superior. In Lockwood's case, however, there is evidence that she "hung around" police court prior to her 1873 admission to the D.C. Supreme Court bar and, once admitted, was willing, even anxious, to be part of the spittoon and boots world of justice. Moreover, the docket books also demonstrate that despite sex discrimination, once in court Lockwood had her share of wins and perhaps no more than her share of defeats. While repeatedly the victim of discrimination, Lockwood used persistence, intelligence, and propriety—for she was ever the decorous, modestly attired woman of her time—to overcome and to succeed.

Lockwood won general respect for her legal accomplishments. Unlike the brutal social and political lampoons prompted by her work on behalf of women's rights, or her introduction of the tricycle as a mode of local transportation for working women, very few cartoons belittled her work as an attorney. Her professional life, moreover, inspired other women, several of whom lived in or came to Washington and were mentored by her. She earned a living from her law practice, but also relied upon her good sense as a businesswoman for additional income. She made investments in property, rented rooms in the twenty-room house that she purchased, lent money at interest and, beginning in 1884, cultivated another career as a lyceum speaker.

And yet, Judge MacArthur's prediction that women lawyers would not be successful was not entirely incorrect. Despite the full and public careers of pioneering attorneys such as Lockwood, only a small number of women entered the profession in the remaining decades of the nineteenth century. Historian Virginia G. Drachman has written that it was not until the 1930s—sixty years after Lockwood's career began—that "women [lawyers] had achieved modest professional success and recognized the limits of their progress, a pattern that barely changed until the mid-1970s." It is against this background that Lockwood's achievements must be understood as the singular accomplishments of an extraordinary woman who by intellect and force of will forged her way in circumstances so hostile that few other women could or would follow.

Once admitted to practice before the local courts of the District of Columbia, Lockwood settled into a practice that resembled the work of male colleagues with small practices. Her professional profile was one of a repeat player, appearing frequently enough to be well known to the

Having presented her first oral argument before the Supreme Court in 1880, Belva Lockwood argued her last, and most publicized, case, *U.S. v. Cherokee Nation*, in 1906, at the age of seventy-six. She won a share of the multi-million dollar award for the Eastern Cherokees, her clients in the complex, multi-party case challenging several treaties of removal, relocation, and compensation.

judges on the D.C. courts. Half of her cases in the courts' equity division were divorce actions. As a woman attorney she attracted female clients, and represented wives as complainants against defendant husbands far more frequently than men. When she represented men in divorce actions, the men were always complainants, never defendants. After divorce actions, her most frequent equity work involved injunction proceedings, lunacy proceedings, and actions requesting the partition of land.

The post–Civil War emphasis on gentility and the proper sphere of women (in the home) made the thought of women working in the criminal courts particularly egregious, even loathsome. If courts in general represented a male world, criminal court was the stage upon which played all of society's morally repugnant dramas from which women were to be shielded. Lockwood could have

refused criminal cases. Yet, despite her religious rectitude and middle-class aspirations, criminal court cases and criminal court argument were as acceptable to her as any other kind of legal work. In fact, once Lockwood began arguing criminal cases in 1875, this side of her courtroom practice was as active as that involving the law division. A number of her clients were women charged with some form of larceny, burglary, or assault—including one charge of infanticide.

In 1884 Lockwood took on an even more public persona that drew her away from Washington and courts of law. Late in the summer of that year she accepted the nomination of the small Equal Rights Party to be its presidential candidate. Lockwood became the first American woman to run a full presidential campaign and used the publicity of the campaign to launch herself onto the paid lecture circuit and, later still, to become a leading activist in the movement on behalf of international peace and arbitration (as a member and officer of the Universal Peace Union and the International Bureau of Peace).

Her local practice was never again as robust. After 1890, on several occasions, she wrote to close friends that business was slow. In these times she relied on rents, her pension as Ezekiel's widow, and lecture fees. During many of these years, Lockwood also supported her widowed mother and, later, the orphaned son who survived her daughter, Lura. Along with Lockwood's niece, Clara B. Harrison, Lura had read law and worked as a law clerk in her mother's practice.

The Supreme Court of the United States: A Male Bastion No More

In 1874 Lockwood was engaged by a client, Charlotte Van Cort, to file a case against the government for the use and infringement of a patent. Lockwood anticipated the need to argue the cause before the U.S. Court of Claims and, in

April 1874, asked Washington attorney A. A. Hosmer to move her admission to the Claims Court bar. Lockwood was not prepared for the Claims Court judges' flat refusal to admit her, as she was a member of the District of Columbia bar who was also well known in federal government departments doing business with the Court of Claims. Although she was weary of such struggle, Lockwood again refused to back down. In a lonely and often discouraging five-year contest, she not only won bar membership for herself at the Claims Court and at the U.S. Supreme Court, but also the right of all qualified women attorneys to be admitted to practice before federal courts.

The confrontation began when, in a written opinion rejecting her application, Court of Claims judge Charles Nott asserted that "admission to the bar constitutes an office. Its exercise is neither an ordinary avocation nor a natural right. It is an artificial employment, created not to give idle persons occupation, nor needy persons subsistence, but to aid in the administration of public justice." Nott went on to argue that the common law of marriage might make it impossible "to hold a woman to the full responsibility of an attorney," and concluded by maintaining, "The position which this court assumes is that under the Constitution and laws of the United States a court is without power to grant such an application, and that a woman is without legal capacity to take the office of attorney." Lockwood writes of this decision, "[I] was crestfallen but not crushed. [I] had already filed Mrs. Van Cort's case in the Clerk's Office—had been promised a large fee and did not mean to be defeated. [I] took her testimony in the case . . . prepared with great care an elaborate brief, and asked leave for [my] client to read it to the Court. This, they had no power to deny, as it is the privilege of every applicant to plead his own case, and sat by Mrs. Van Cort until the hearing was completed."

Lockwood should have been prepared for the Nott decision both because of the general opposition to women professionals in the United States at that time, and because of the U.S. Supreme Court decision only the year before in *Bradwell v. Illinois* (see p. 2). In that case, the justices maintained that the privilege of earning a livelihood as an attorney was not a right that a state need grant to women under the Privileges and Immunities Clause of the Fourteenth Amendment. While Lockwood correctly maintained that the *Bradwell* decision had no precedential value as it applied only to states, and she had applied for admission to the bar of a federal court, *Bradwell* had created a new symbolic, if not legal, hurdle for women attorneys.

Her application put the Claims Court judges in a difficult position. On the one hand the Supreme Court of the District of Columbia, a court constituted under federal law, now licensed women attorneys. On the other hand, the majority and concurring opinions in *Bradwell* offered no particular inducement to do so. Uncertain, chagrined perhaps about the effects of the Claims Court decision on a hometown colleague, Judge Nott waffled in his concluding statement: "It is to be understood that the decision of this court does not rest upon those grounds which would make its judgment final. We do not, in legal effect, pass upon the individual application before us, but refuse to act upon it for want of jurisdiction. Our decision is not necessarily final, and there is express authority for saying that if we err, the Supreme Court can review our error and give relief to the applicant by mandamus."

At the time of the Court of Claims action, Lockwood was forty-three years old and married to an increasingly frail man in his seventies. She supported an extended family and had practical as well as philosophical reasons to fight the Nott decision. She believed unequivocally that women should have the equal opportunity of earning a living and knew that denial of federal court licensing would significantly affect the growth of her practice. Thus, as soon as Nott delivered the court's decision in May 1874, Lockwood turned to Congress, lobbying for legislation "that no woman otherwise qualified, shall be debarred from practice before any United States Court on account of sex or coverture." Neither house took action beyond referring her petition to committee, where it languished for the remainder of 1874 and all of 1875.

Undeterred, she reshaped her strategy. Lockwood and her supporters knew that the rules of the U. S. Supreme Court permitted an attorney to apply for permission to practice at that court after practicing in a state, or the District of Columbia, Supreme Court for three years. By late September 1876 she had met that requirement. She reasoned that success with the justices of the Supreme Court would end resistance to her candidacy in all of the federal courts. Proceeding with her plan, she presented her credentials to them. Former representative from Ohio, woman suffrage supporter, and respected local attorney Albert G. Riddle moved her admission.

Lockwood again met with defeat. Speaking for his colleagues on November 6, 1876, Chief Justice Morrison R. Waite announced:

By the uniform practice of the Court from its organization to the present time, and by the fair construction of its rules, none but men are permitted to practice before it as attorneys and counselors. This is in accordance with immemorial usage in England, and the law and practice in all the States, until within a recent period, and that the Court does not feel called upon to make a change until such a change is required by statute or a more extended practice in the highest courts of the States.

Lockwood returned to Congress and over the course of the next two years continued stubbornly to plead the case of women attorneys' right to equal treatment. She succeeded in February 1879 when the more reluctant Senate, following the earlier lead of the House of Representatives, approved the historic "Act to relieve certain legal disabilities of women." With one sentence, Congress delivered the legislative fiat invited by Chief Justice Waite: "That any woman who shall have been a member of the bar of the highest court of any State or Territory or of the Supreme Court of the District of Columbia, for the space of three years, and who shall have maintained a good standing before such court, and who shall be a person of good moral character, shall, on motion, and the production of such record, be admitted to practice before the Supreme Court of the United States."

Lockwood later wrote with candor about the days before the final Senate vote.

I grew anxious, almost desperate, called out everybody who was opposed to the bill, and begged that it might be permitted to come up on its merits, and that a fair vote might be had on it in the Senate. I have been interested in many bills in Congress, and have often appeared before committees of Senate and House; but this was by far the strongest lobbying that I ever performed. Nothing was too daring for me to attempt. I addressed Senators as though they were old familiar friends. . . .

The victory was significant: Despite the Nott and Waite rulings Lockwood, virtually alone, using tenacity and political savvy, had pushed a reluctant Congress to enact a concrete measure supporting women's equal rights.

The justices of the Supreme Court had no choice but to admit her. On March 3, 1879, Riddle again moved her admission to the bar. It was approved and Lockwood became the first woman licensed to practice law before the Supreme Court of the United States. Several days later, the judges of the Court of Claims followed suit and she was admitted to the bar of that court. Twenty months later, the case of *Kaiser v. Stickney* presented Lockwood with the opportunity to become the first woman member of the Supreme Court bar to participate in oral argument.

Kaiser involved the validity of a trust-deed used to secure a bank note and came on appeal from the District of Columbia Supreme Court (general term). Lockwood had been participating in the case as cocounsel with local attorney Mike L. Woods. When the case reached the U.S. Supreme Court, Woods began argument on November 30, 1880. According to Court documents, Woods continued to argue the case on December 1, joined by "Mrs. Belva A. Lockwood." Her words were not recorded but papers filed with the Court show that Lockwood, despite her opposition to the restrictive married women's property laws of her day, attempted to persuade the Court to set aside the deed in question on the ground that a married woman alone had signed it. The Court ruled against Lockwood's clients, saying that they both had signed the deed, and that it was valid.

In the years after *Kaiser*, Lockwood appeared at the Court to move the admission of applicants for membership in the Court's bar. She also participated as cocounsel in a few federal court cases that were appealed to the Court, but she did not argue another case at the Supreme Court until 1906. Lockwood undoubtedly hoped for more Supreme Court cases, both for the prestige and the fees that they would bring to her. The nature of her local and pension claims practice made such representation unlikely. In fact, only a few Washington attorneys made frequent appearances before the Court. Yet even while working local cases Lockwood seemed to find high-profile suits. In 1893, for example, she filed a legal brief in New York on behalf of the heirs of Myra Clark Gaines. Well known around the country and at the Supreme Court for her tenacious struggle to win inheritance of her father's property in New Orleans, Gaines had probably been Lockwood's friend.

Lockwood had sought bar membership not only for the good that it might bring to her law practice but also to establish equal opportunity for all women attorneys. Yet, even after winning the right to practice in the federal courts, Lockwood did not have the last word. In 1894 she brought an original action at the U.S. Supreme Court, *In Re Lockwood*, in which she argued that the state of Virginia violated her constitutional rights by refusing to grant her a license to practice in its courts. Her decision to act was very much in character and she was, undoubtedly, encouraged by her previous successes in overcoming adverse law. *Bradwell* had not been overruled, but a number of states now licensed women attorneys.

As in the 1870s, Lockwood was motivated primarily by the desire to conduct business and, presumably, gave little or no thought to the possibility of a legal decision that would diminish women's legal position. She had prevailed before. Strategically, however, she erred badly. Chief Justice Melville W. Fuller ruled that the state of Virginia did not violate the U.S. Constitution when it refused to license Lockwood as an attorney. His opinion left states free to exclude women from those defined as "persons" under the law.

Career's End

Lockwood maintained a legal practice well into old age. At seventy-six she argued two days before the U.S. Supreme Court as counsel for the Eastern Cherokee. *United States v. Cherokee Nation* was a complex, multiparty case involving claims of money due under several treaties of removal, relocation, and compensation. Lockwood entered the Court with more than thirty years of experience as a claims attorney. She was thoroughly familiar with the long and torturous history of Cherokee claims, having first litigated on behalf of certain Cherokee as early as 1875. She reveled in the prospect of Supreme Court argument, relished the prospect of public notice, and needed the sizable contingency fee as a financial cushion for her old age. Lockwood presented her oral argument before the members of Chief Justice Fuller's Court on January 17 and 18, 1906. Her presentation won respectful notices from the local press and victory for her clients, who went on to share in the multi-million dollar award. The *Sun* reported that "Mrs. Lockwood . . . spoke with great rapidity, but with clearness, and her arguments were followed closely by the Justices on the bench, several of them interrupting her to ask questions upon different points she made."

Lockwood continued local and Court of Claims legal work, spurning retirement because of her restless energy and her need for an income. She died on May 19, 1917, at the age of eighty-six. The extraordinary late-twentieth-century growth in the number of women attorneys in the United States and the consequent increase in women state and federal judges was made possible by determined women such as Lockwood, who opened up law schools and federal courts to women.

The First Women Members of the Supreme Court Bar, 1879–1900

In the twenty years after Lockwood forced the Supreme Court to allow women to join its bar in 1879, twenty-one other women joined her as members of that elite bar. Their names, dates of admission, and other relevant information are set forth in the table on p. 217.

These twenty-one women lawyers ranged in age from thirty-six to sixty-one at the time of their admission. They practiced in seven different states as well as the District of Columbia. Nearly all of the first women admittees practiced in big cities. They came from both coasts and the midwest, but not from the south. The five women who lived in the nation's capital conveniently did not have to travel far to be sworn in or to conduct business in the Supreme Court. Their high proportion may also be explained by the existence in

The corporation counsel for the District of Columbia and a law professor at Howard University, Albert Gallatin Riddle moved the admission of Belva A. Lockwood, Laura D. Gordon, and Carrie B. Kilgore, three of the first four women to join the Supreme Court bar. A champion of women's suffrage, Riddle had formerly been elected to Congress from the state of Ohio.

Washington, D.C., of two law schools that admitted women, the Washington College of Law and Howard University Law School.

Respected local attorney Albert G. Riddle moved the admission of Lockwood as well as two other women, Laura D. Gordon and Carrie B. Kilgore, neither of whom were local. Riddle was a former representative from Ohio and a champion of women's suffrage. He also mentored Marilla M. Ricker, who read law in his office in preparation for the District of Columbia bar exam, which she passed with the highest grade of that year. Many of the other women evidently asked their representatives in Congress to move their admission, a practice that was also common for men.

Once they became members these women began to move each other's admission to the Supreme Court bar. For example, in 1890 Ada M. Bittenbender, the third woman member of the Supreme Court bar, moved the admission of Emma Gillett, the seventh woman member. The

Women Admitted to the Supreme Court Bar

Name	Date of admission to Supreme Court bar	State and year of original admission	State and year of birth	Residence at time of admission to Supreme Court bar	Name and affiliation of movant
1. Belva A. Lockwood	March 3, 1879	D.C., 1873	NY, 1830	Washington, D.C.	Albert Riddle, Howard Law
2. Laura D. Gordon	February 2, 1885	CA, 1879	PA, 1838	San Francisco, CA	Albert Riddle, Howard Law
3. Ada M. Bittenbender	October 15, 1888	NE, 1883	PA, 1848	Lincoln, NE	Henry Blair, U.S. Senate
4. Carrie B. Kilgore	January 8, 1890	PA, 1886	VT, 1838	Philadelphia, PA	Albert Riddle, Howard Law
5. Clara Shortridge Foltz	March 4, 1890	CA, 1878	IN, 1849	San Diego, CA	Thomas J. Clurie, U.S. House
6. Lelia Robinson Sawtelle	April 8, 1890	MA, 1882	MA, 1850	Boston, MA	George Hoar, U.S. Senate
7. Emma M. Gillett	April 8, 1890	D.C., 1883	WI, 1852	Washington, D.C.	Ada Bittenbender
8. Kate Kane	May 19, 1890	WI, 1878	NH, 1840	Chicago, IL	Robert Ingersoll
9. Marilla M. Ricker	May 11, 1891	D.C., 1882		Washington, D.C.	Emma Gillett
10. Myra Bradwell	March 28, 1892	IL, 1890	VT, 1831	Chicago, IL	Atty. Gen. Miller
11. Fannie O'Linn	October 17, 1893	NE		Chadron, NE	J. Bryan, U.S. House
12. Kate H. Pier	January 31, 1894	WI		Milwaukee, WI	W. F. Vilas, U.S. Senate
13. Ellen Spencer Mussey	May 25, 1896	D.C., 1893	OH, 1850	Washington, D.C.	Watson Newton
14. Alice A. Minick	January 18, 1897		NE	Lincoln, NE	Belva Lockwood
16. Caroline H. Pier	January 18, 1897		WI	Milwaukee, WI	Kate H. Pier
16. J. Ellen Foster	December 20, 1897	IA, 1872	MA, 1840	Washington, D.C.	Ellen Mussey
17. Catharine McCulloch	February 21, 1898	IL, 1886	NY, 1882	Chicago, IL	Charles Beale
18. Clara L. Power	April 3, 1899	MA		Boston, MA	Atty. Gen. Griggs
19. Kate Pier	February 1, 1900	WI		Milwaukee, WI	Kate H. Pier
20. Harriet H. Pier	February 1, 1900	WI		Milwaukee, WI	Kate H. Pier
21. Victoria Conkling-Whitney	April 9, 1904	MO		St. Louis, MO	Chas. F. Joy

Note: Some information on admittees is unavailable.

Ellen Spencer Mussey (left) moved the admission of more than twenty women to the Supreme Court bar between 1897 and 1920, many of them affiliated with the Washington College of Law, the first law school established by and for women, which she cofounded with Emma Gillett (right) in 1898. Mussey also wrote briefs for at least three cases before the Supreme Court and argued a fourth, *Shelton v. King*, in 1912.

following year, Gillett, in turn, moved the admission of fellow Washingtonian Marilla Ricker, the ninth woman member. Kate H. Pier moved the admission of her sister, Caroline H. Pier, in 1897, as well as her mother, Kate Pier, and her other sister, Harriet H. Pier, both in 1900. Ellen Spencer Mussey alone moved the admission of more than twenty women to the Supreme Court bar between 1897 and 1920, many of them affiliated with the Washington College of Law, the first law school established by and for women, which she founded together with Emma Gillett in 1898.

As members of the Supreme Court bar, these women were in a small minority. Of the 250 to 350 attorneys who joined each term, just a few were women. For example, in the 1883 term there were 279 new admittees and no women. In the 1889 term there were 322 new admittees, five of whom were women. It took the Court until 1920, or forty-one years from the time it opened its bar to women, to admit its first 100 women.

Prior to joining the Supreme Court's bar, these women had achieved many other "firsts" for women in the legal profession. They were either the first woman to attend, or graduate from, their law school; the first woman to join their state's bar; or the first woman to hold a particular position within the legal profession, such as law school dean. In breaking down barriers to women's entry into the legal profession and achieving a high degree of professional success while doing so, these women were recognized as the leading women lawyers of their day.

The backgrounds of these pioneers parallel one another in many respects. Like many early women lawyers, most of them practiced with their lawyer husbands, either as apprentices or upon graduation from law school. This arrangement was common because early women lawyers were excluded from other legal apprenticeship opportunities and because it was convenient: working for a father or husband helped resolve potential conflicts between domestic and professional duties. Absence of children at home also contributed to women's ability to pursue legal careers with concentrated energy and drive. Nearly all of these women were either childless or had grown children at the time of their admission to the Supreme Court.

These women had entered the legal profession for three main reasons. First, they were rebelling against being isolated in their domestic duties at home, or in "feminine" professions, such as teaching, that paid them low wages and relegated them to low status. Second, they discovered that they enjoyed the practice of law and the income it provided. Third, they were passionate about women's rights issues and saw law as a means to further their feminist goals.

These women were well known to each other. They worked in conjunction with one another in the woman suffrage movement, were active in the same professional and voluntary associations, and corresponded with one another about personal and professional issues. Their practice of supporting each other's applications for admission suggests the efforts of an "old girls' network" of "sisters in law" who promoted women's opportunities in the legal profession.

Although few of them had litigation experience, many of these women presumably hoped to practice before the Supreme Court. Pervasive sex discrimination prevented most of them from doing so, however, as few clients or male colleagues were willing to hire women to file briefs or present oral argument in the Supreme Court. Yet securing appellate work was difficult for male advocates as well, the vast majority of whom never had the opportunity to practice before the Court. Still, joining was important for both men and women lawyers because they became licensed to perform appellate work in the Supreme Court should a client ever need such services. Admission to practice before the Court also enabled them to boast of being members of an elite bar, which was a mark of professional status. When Kate Kane joined in 1890 she said she felt prouder than "a czar of the Russias or a President of the United States."

It is not surprising then that only four of the first twenty-one women members of the Supreme Court bar actually practiced there. Bittenbender and Foltz each filed one brief, while Lockwood and Mussey each presented oral argument in at least one case and filed briefs in multiple cases.

Ada M. Bittenbender represented her husband's and her own temperance interests when she filed a brief, cosigned by her attorney husband, in *State of Nebraska Ex Rel. Henry C. Bittenbender and Ada M. Bittenbender v. Excise Board of the City of Lincoln, Nebraska* during the Supreme Court's 1916 term. The case involved the question of whether an 1858 act of the Nebraska territorial legislature had repealed an act passed three years earlier prohibiting the sale of intoxicating liquor. On May 21, 1917, the Supreme Court dismissed their appeal for want of jurisdiction.

Clara Shortridge Foltz also cosigned a brief, with A. C. Searle, which was filed on behalf of Alfred Clarke during the Court's 1896 term. The appeal involved a California superior court's adjudication of Clarke's insolvency. It is unclear at what stage of the litigation Foltz became involved. On January 25, 1897, the Supreme Court dismissed *Clarke v. McDade* for want of a final judgment and the absence of a federal question.

Ellen Spencer Mussey briefed at least three cases and argued one before the Supreme Court. Each time the justices ruled in her favor. In *Glavey v. United States,* heard during the Court's 1900 term, Mussey was joined in the brief filed on behalf of Glavey by Robert D. Benedict, who presented oral argument. This case, originally filed in the Court of Claims, involved Glavey's claim for recovery of unpaid salary due him as a steam vessel inspector commissioned by the U.S. Secretary of the Treasury. The Court of Claims dismissed Glavey's claim, ruling for the defendant United States on the ground that Glavey's commission had never become effective. On May 27, 1901, the Court reversed the Court of Claims judgment, holding that Glavey was entitled to compensation for services performed for the government as an appointed special investigator of foreign steam vessels.

Next, during the 1905 term, Mussey filed a brief as sole legal representative of José Casuela Geigel in *La Compania de Los Ferrocarriles de Puerto Rico v. Jose Casuela Geigel.* This case involved a contract claim filed by Geigel in the U.S. District Court for the District of Puerto Rico. Mussey's Supreme Court brief argued that the appeal should be dismissed for want of jurisdiction because the claim involved less than the required minimum amount in controversy. The Supreme Court dismissed the appeal, with costs granted to Geigel on December 6, 1905.

Finally, Mussey briefed and argued *Shelton v. King* in the Court's 1912 term. This was her first and only oral argument; she was, after Lockwood, the second woman to plead before the high court.

Or, as one of the many newspapers that recorded the event put it, "Mrs. Ellen Spencer Mussey . . . won the distinction of being the second fair Portia to argue a case before the United States Supreme Court." On May 26, 1913, the Court upheld the validity of a trust in favor of Mussey's client. Her appearance before the Court represented a significant advance in the law practice she had taken over when her husband died in 1892. Before his death, Mussey had spent her time counseling clients and drafting documents within the confines of the law office, not performing such supposedly "masculine" duties as litigating in court.

Lockwood was more active in the Supreme Court bar than the other three advocates. Twenty months after being admitted she presented oral argument in *Kaiser v. Stickney* (1880), giving her the distinction of being the first woman to argue before the Court. (See p. 215 for details of her litigation before the Supreme Court.)

After 1900 women continued to join the Supreme Court bar at a slow but steady pace. But, as was true for men as well, opportunities for filing briefs or arguing cases remained infrequent. As of 1920 only thirteen out of ninety-seven women bar members had actually argued a case before the Court. It was not until the late 1970s that the proportion of women joining the Supreme Court bar, and the number of women filing briefs and arguing cases, began to increase significantly.

Women Advocates Before the Court

Legend has it that when Dolley Madison and a group of the first lady's friends arrived one day at the Supreme Court in the middle of an oral argument, the great advocate Daniel Webster stopped his oration, bowed to the ladies, and started again from the beginning. Although such excessive gallantry was not standard practice in the early nineteenth century, it was customary for wives of Washington dignitaries to dress up in the latest fashions and come to the Supreme Court to observe oral arguments.

The passive, decorative role women then played in the life of the Court contrasts sharply with the professional one they do today. This gradual transformation did not begin until 1880, ninety-one years after the Court's inception, when a woman was finally permitted to leave the spectator ranks and join the show.

That was the year that Lockwood became the first female attorney to argue a case before the Supreme Court. The previous year she had forced the Court, through congressional intervention, to license her to practice before it. In doing so Lockwood opened the doors for successive women attorneys to file petitions and briefs at the Supreme Court, to join its bar and to move the admission of other attorneys, and to argue cases before the bench.

Before examining the contributions of the women advocates who followed in Lockwood's footsteps, however, it is appropriate to consider claims that two earlier women, Lucy Terry Prince and Myra Clark Gaines—neither of whom were lawyers—personally pleaded their own land dispute cases before the Supreme Court. (The practice of presenting one's own case without the intermediary of an attorney is called arguing "pro se.") No official court documents have been discovered to support these claims.

Lucy Terry Prince (c. 1725–1821)

Lucy Terry Prince, an African American, is usually hailed in reference books as the first woman to address the Supreme Court of the United States. The popularizer of this legend is Massachusetts historian George Sheldon, who described the event in his 1893 article "Negro Slavery in Old Deerfield," which was published in the *New England Magazine* and widely circulated. He wrote that Prince was permitted to argue her

Vermont land claim suit in 1796 before the "Supreme Court of the United States ... presided over by [Justice] Samuel Chase of Maryland." Apparently, Chase was so impressed by Prince's eloquence that he complimented her on making "a better argument than he had heard from any lawyer at the Vermont bar."

Her performance would have been all the more extraordinary considering her background. She was taken from Africa as a child in 1730 and eventually sold to a Deerfield, Massachusetts, innkeeper named Ebenezer Wells. She purchased her freedom in 1756 after her marriage to Abijah Prince, a free black. In 1762 a wealthy Deerfield landowner deeded Prince's husband 100 acres of land in the newly opened territory of Guilford, Vermont. The Princes and their six children took up residence there in the 1780s. Hungry for land, they had also obtained a grant of 300 acres of wilderness tract in nearby Sunderland.

The predatory behavior of a wealthy Sunderland neighbor, Col. Eli Bronson, is the basis for the legendary suit. He set up a claim to the Princes' property and, according to Sunderland historian Giles B. Bacon, "by repeated law suits obtained about one-half of the home lot, and had not the town interposed [the Princes] would have lost the whole." A prominent citizen, Bronson allegedly hired Royall Tyler, a future chief justice of the Vermont Supreme Court, and Stephen R. Bradley, a future Vermont senator, as his counsel. The Princes were said to have engaged Isaac Tichenor, a future governor of the state, to defend their claim.

In his article, Sheldon wrote that Prince argued before "the Supreme Court of the United States," although there is no evidence to suggest that she made the trip to Philadelphia (where the Court was then lodged) to do so. Sheldon based his assumption on a letter written by a Guilford historian named Rodney Field—who was neither an eyewitness to the event nor a contemporary of

No official records have been found documenting the alleged oral arguments of Lucy Terry Prince, a freed slave, before Associate Justice Samuel Chase in 1796. This oil portrait of Prince, one of the first published African American poets, is purely imaginary; no likeness of her exists.

the Princes—that simply stated that she appeared before a "United States Court."

A more likely scenario, given Chase's favorable comparison of Prince to other Vermont lawyers, would be that she argued before Justice Chase when he was riding circuit in Vermont. (In those days circuit courts were presided over by one Supreme Court justice and one district court judge.) Justice Chase did sit at one session of court in Vermont while on circuit at Bennington in May 1796, which coincides with the time that the litigation would have taken place. But the court records show no cases in which Prince or Bronson were associated. Perhaps Lucy Terry Prince was a principal or a witness in a federal district court or the state superior or supreme court.

There is no doubt that Prince, an eloquent storyteller renowned for her keen memory, must have been an effective oral advocate before whatever court she did appear. In fact, she merits a place in history whether or not she argued before Justice Chase. Her lyrical thirty-line doggerel, "The Bars

Fight," which accurately recounts the dramatic events surrounding an Indian raid on Deerfield that she witnessed in 1746, was printed in 1855. This accomplishment distinguishes her as one of the first published African American poets.

Myra Clark Gaines (1803–1885)

The other woman mistakenly reported to have pleaded her case before the Supreme Court is perpetual litigant Myra Clark Gaines. The gallant orator Daniel Webster is alleged to have been the opposing advocate.

This myth probably arose because Gaines brought her land claim case before the Supreme Court an astonishing twenty-one times (her heirs pursued it thrice posthumously) between 1836 and 1891, and before some thirty different justices. Passionate and dogged in her pursuit of her inheritance claim to valuable New Orleans properties, Gaines was wealthy and shrewd enough to employ the most seasoned oral advocates to argue on her behalf. Over a period of five decades she employed more than thirty lawyers, seventeen of whom died in her service. There is no evidence, however, that she ever pleaded her own case against Webster or any other advocate. (In fact, Webster was one of the advocates she retained in her service.) But she did present her own argument in a state court trial, having stepped in after her counsel, infuriated by the judge's bias, stormed out. Gaines was also active in helping her lawyers prepare briefs.

At issue was the mysterious disappearance of a will drafted by her Irish immigrant father, Daniel Clark, when he died in 1813. In the will Clark named Myra his legitimate daughter and heir to the large fortune he had accumulated. Her Creole mother, Zulime Carriere, held no record of her marriage to Clark, which they had kept secret because she had not obtained an annulment from her first husband, a French wine merchant and

The land dispute case of Myra Clark Gaines, involving her claim to valuable New Orleans property, came before the Supreme Court an astonishing twenty-one times in the nineteenth century and was heard by some thirty different justices.

bigamist. Upon Clark's death the will disappeared, and his sisters and business partners claimed that Myra was illegitimate and therefore ineligible to inherit from her father under Louisiana's unique civil code. Because hundreds of New Orleans residents stood to lose their land if she won her claim, she was forced to resort constantly to federal courts to obtain the fair trial that hostile local courts did not always provide. The Supreme Court held that Myra Clark Gaines was her father's legitimate heir shortly before she died in 1885, deeply in debt from a lifetime of legal expenses. It took a few more lawsuits for her grandchildren to force the city of New Orleans to pay them their due.

Pioneers of the Bar

Lockwood thus remains unchallenged as the first woman either to file a brief or present oral argument at the Supreme Court. Subsequent female advocates also qualified as pioneers in various ways.

Opposing the proposed sale by Congress of her tribe's sacred burial ground in Kansas City, Lyda Burton Conley (1874–1946), of Wyandotte and English ancestry, became in 1910 the first Native American woman to argue before the Supreme Court. (The first Native American was probably Elias C. Boudinot, a Cherokee, in 1870.) Along with her sisters Helena and Ida, Conley protested Congress's proposal in 1906 to transfer the bodies and sell off the Huron cemetery, which would have violated the government's treaty with her tribe. The Conley sisters padlocked themselves in the cemetery, built a fortified shack to dwell in, and, for seven years, fended off government officials and realtors (but not other Wyandottes) with their father's shotgun.

Conley had long realized the value of the coveted piece of real estate where her parents and a sister were buried, and had equipped herself with a law degree from Kansas City School of Law in 1902 to defend it by peaceful means. She unsuccessfully filed suit for a permanent injunction in district court against the Secretary of the Interior. After losing an appeal, she left her sisters to hold the fort in 1909 while she traveled to Washington to argue the case before the Supreme Court. Conley argued pro se; she did not become a member of the Supreme Court bar until 1915. A draft of the argument she delivered at the Court, written in her own hand, reveals that she used biblical imagery to enhance her plea. "Like Jacob of old I too, when I shall be gathered unto my people, desire that they bury me with my fathers in Huron Cemetery, the most sacred and hallowed spot on earth to me," she wrote. "I cannot believe," she added, "that this is superstitious reverence any more than I can believe that the reverence every true American has for the grave of Washington at Mount Vernon is a superstitious reverence."

In *Conley v. Ballinger, Secretary of the Interior* (1910), the Court held that in making the treaty the United States had "bound itself only by

honor, not by law" and that the Wyandotte tribe had no legal right to the cemetery. However, the Conley sisters' tenacious defense of their ancestors' graves so swayed public opinion that Congress repealed the sale, which had since been transacted. The three sisters were buried in the Huron Cemetery, which is now a green oasis in downtown Kansas City.

The first female African American lawyer to join the Supreme Court bar—Chicago Law School–trained Violette N. Anderson—did so eleven years after Conley. She was admitted in 1926 on motion of James A. Cobb, a local African American judge in the District of Columbia. The first African American woman to petition the Court pro se was Jama A. White, who contested

Lyda Burton Conley argued a case before the Supreme Court in 1910 demanding that the U.S. government honor a treaty with her tribe safeguarding its sacred burial ground, the Huron cemetery in Kansas City.

her expulsion from Portia Law School. She was expelled for neglecting to tell a coal and groceries dealer that she was separated from her husband and for refusing to pay for the merchandise herself once her marital status was discovered. (She had billed her husband's account despite their separation because a court had ordered her husband to pay her expenses.) The Massachusetts Supreme Court rejected White's claim against the law school, and, acting as her own attorney, she petitioned the U.S. Supreme Court unsuccessfully in 1933.

It is not known which black woman lawyer filed the first brief or argued the first case in the Supreme Court. (The first African American man to argue was probably J. Alexander Chiles in 1910.) One possibility is Constance Baker Motley, who, as associate counsel for the NAACP Legal Defense and Education Fund from 1945 to 1966, argued ten desegregation cases, winning nine. She helped prepare the briefs in the landmark case of *Brown v. Board of Education,* which found segre-

As associate counsel for the NAACP Legal Defense and Education Fund, Inc., from 1945 to 1966, Constance Baker Motley argued ten segregation cases before the Supreme Court. She was probably the first black woman attorney to argue a Supreme Court case.

gated schools unconstitutional. She also argued James Meredith's suit for admission to the University of Mississippi, and Charlayne Hunter-Gault's case that forced the University of Georgia to open its doors to black students. Impressed with her oral arguments before the Supreme Court, Attorney General Ramsey Clark persuaded President Lyndon B. Johnson to appoint Motley to be the first black woman federal judge in 1966.

The first women to argue against each other in the Supreme Court were Elizabeth R. Rindskopf and Dorothy Toth Beasley, the attorneys in *Paul J. Bell, Jr. v. R.H. Burson, Director, Georgia Department of Public Safety* (1971). Beasley, an assistant attorney general of Georgia, again opposed a woman advocate two years later in *Doe v. Bolton.* Her opponent, Margie Hames, representing abortion-seeker Mary Doe, prevailed and the Court struck down a Georgia law that allowed only residents of the state to obtain abortions. "She didn't get it simply because she was female," Attorney General Arthur Bolton later told historian David J. Garrow as to why Beasley, the only female out of a staff of some twenty-six deputies, was given the task of defending Georgia's 1968 abortion law. Beasley, who had briefly worked with Hames in private practice, was simply considered the best advocate for the job.

Doe was argued the same day as *Roe v. Wade,* its companion case. Jay Floyd, who defended the Texas antiabortion statute in *Roe,* argued against Sarah Weddington and her cocounsel, Linda N. Coffee. "It's an old joke," chided Floyd when he began his *Roe* presentation, "but when a man argues against two beautiful ladies like this, they are going to have the last word." His misplaced humor did not go over well. Hames told Garrow that she remembered finding Floyd's comment "very chauvinistic." She "thought [Chief Justice] Burger was going to come right off the bench at him. He glared him down. He got the point right away that this was not appropriate in court."

When the assistant solicitor general assigned to an immigration case was unexpectedly called out of the country in 1949, government lawyer Patricia H. Collins (now Patricia Dwinnell Butler, right) took over and successfully argued the government's case before the Supreme Court. Her husband, Assistant Attorney General Sal Andretta (second from left), had persuaded Solicitor General Phil Pearlman (left) to reassign her the case. Attorney General Tom C. Clark is standing between the Andrettas.

There was no place for gallantry in the 1977 case of *Danielle Gandy et al. v. Organization of Foster Families for Equality and Reform et al.*, which marked the first time four women collectively argued one case. The counsel tables had never before been so "female" as when Louise Gruner Gans, Helen L. Buttenwieser, and Maria L. Marcus successfully represented individual foster families and an organization of foster parents in their suit for an injunction against New York City's procedures for removing foster children. Attorney Marcia Robinson Lowry argued the city's case.

Women of the Office of the Solicitor General

The best source of women advocates has been the Office of the Solicitor General (OSG), the elite corps that represents the United States in the Supreme Court. The OSG has supplied a steady trickle of women to argue the government's position since 1972, when Harriet Sturtevant Shapiro was hired as the first regular woman attorney. There was at least one earlier instance, however, of a woman on the Solicitor General's staff appearing before the Supreme Court, although that episode seems to be an exception. In 1949 Patricia H. Collins successfully argued *Johnson v. Shaughnessy*, an immigration case, when she was a lawyer in the Office of the Assistant Solicitor General, which was subsequently renamed the Office of Legal Counsel.

The reason she got the assignment is revealing. When Robert Ginnane, an associate in the OSG who had been assigned the case, was called suddenly to France, Collins's husband, Assistant Attorney General Sal Andretta, prevailed on Solicitor General Phil Pearlman to select his wife to step in and argue the government's case. Collins (now Patricia Dwinnell Butler) recalls that the bailiff of the Supreme Court complimented her on her performance: "with that [stentorian] voice of yours, you can come back any time." But Justice Felix Frankfurter's needling did not encourage her to request assignment for further oral arguments.

Twenty-three years after that episode, Shapiro joined the staff as an assistant solicitor general and paved the way for other women attorneys at OSG. In 1999, five out of twenty lawyers on the staff were women. Now more than seventy years old, Shapiro is a seasoned advocate who holds the record—seventeen—among women staffers for most arguments. In terms of gender law cases, Shapiro argued the government's position in *Schlesinger v. Ballard* (1975) and *Newport News Shipbuilding & Drydock Co. v. Equal Employment Opportunity Commission* (1988). Her record puts her just ahead of Amy L. Wax, now a law professor, who argued fifteen cases for the government during her tenure at the OSG from 1987 to 1994. They may both soon be overtaken by assistant solicitor general Beth S. Brinkmann, who as of 1999 had argued thirteen cases since joining OSG in 1993.

Several former OSG staffers continue to specialize in appellate advocacy and appear before the Supreme Court. Kathryn A. Oberly, who argued ten cases in her four-year stint at OSG from 1982 to 1986, specializes in representing accounting firms. In 1989 she argued for Price Water-

In 1972 Harriet Sturtevant Shapiro (back row, second from left) became the first woman attorney to work at the Office of the Solicitor General (OSG), the elite corps that represents the United States before the Supreme Court. Pictured in this 1972 OSG staff photo: (back row) Bradford Reynolds, Shapiro, Andrew Frey, Harry Sachse, Edward Korman, Mark Evans, Keith Jones, Allen Tuttle, and Ray Randolph; (front row) Sam Huntington, Philip Lacovara, Daniel Friedman, Solicitor General Erwin Griswold, Lawrence Wallace, and Richard Stone. Shapiro has since argued seventeen cases before the Supreme Court, more than any other woman from the OSG.

house in the high-profile Supreme Court case brought by Ann Hopkins, who successfully claimed she had been denied partnership because of her gender (see p. 130). Maureen E. Mahoney argued eight times when she served as a deputy solicitor general; she has returned to argue two more cases before the Supreme Court since leaving OSG in 1993 to join a law firm. Mahoney had also argued one case before joining OSG, having been invited by the Supreme Court through a special appointment to present argument. She was probably the first woman invited by the Court to appear as an advocate.

There has yet to be a female solicitor general, but the first female attorney general, Janet Reno, has argued once before the Supreme Court. In 1996 she chose to present the government's position, as amicus curiae, in *Maryland v. Jerry Lee Wilson,* three years after being appointed to the top job at the Justice Department.

Most Appearances Before the Court

But these contemporary women advocates do not compare, in terms of numbers of cases argued, with a handful of pioneers who worked as appellate lawyers for various branches of the federal government. The earliest of these professional advocates was Mabel Walker Willebrandt (1889–1963), who served as assistant attorney general in the 1920s, and prosecuted scores of violators of the National Prohibition Act. Because the Act was difficult to enforce, she spearheaded the use of tax laws to prosecute illegal distributors of liquor. "Prohibition Portia," as she was nicknamed, argued twenty-one times before the Supreme Court, all Prohibition- or tax-related cases, before retiring from the Justice Department in 1929.

Willebrandt's service at the Justice Department overlapped for one year with that of Helen R. Carloss (1890–1948), another female public servant

As an assistant attorney general during Prohibition, Mabel Walker Willebrandt spearheaded the use of tax laws to prosecute illegal distributors of liquor.

who several times represented the United States before the Supreme Court. She had left her native Mississippi to attend law school at George Washington University and then was hired to handle tax litigation for the federal government. So engaged from 1928 to 1947, Carloss argued sixteen times before the Supreme Court and filed numerous briefs—including five in tax cases that were jointly prepared with Willebrandt (among others) in 1929. A brief they filed on May 13, 1929 (along with Attorney General William D. Mitchell and special assistant attorney general Alfred A. Wheat) for the Commissioner of Internal Revenue was likely the first instance of two women's names appearing on the same Supreme Court brief.

In his memoir, *The Court Years, 1939–1975,* Justice William O. Douglas described Carloss as "a gray-haired lady from Mississippi." If seen by a stranger, he mused, "she would doubtless be identified as a housewife. But she was an advocate *par excellence*—brief, lucid, relevant and powerful. Typical of the complex and important questions which she presented is *Kirby Petroleum Co. v. Commissioner* . . . concerning the right of the lessor of oil and gas land to the depletion allowance where the lease is for a cash bonus, a royalty and a share of the net profits."

Another outstanding appellate lawyer and dedicated public servant, Bessie Margolin (1909–1996) is best remembered for her talent for oral argument. She joined the Department of Labor shortly after passage of the 1938 Fair Labor Standards Act, and specialized in interpreting that New Deal law, which spelled out federal wage and hour policy. Margolin rose to become assistant solicitor in charge of Supreme Court litigation, and then, in 1963, was promoted to associate solicitor for the Division of Fair Labor Standards. As such, she was responsible for all litigation under the Fair Labor Standards Act, the Equal Pay Act, and the Age Discrimination in Employment Act. Margolin argued twenty-seven cases before the Supreme Court.

The daughter of Russian-Jewish immigrants, Margolin had been born in New York City but was sent to a Jewish Children's Home in New Orleans after her mother died. She attended Tulane University and graduated from its law school. She then pursued a doctorate in law at Yale University. Margolin started her career working on the legal staff at the Tennessee Valley Authority, the New Deal project intended to bring electricity to rural communities.

Justice William O. Douglas remembered Margolin as

crisp in her speech and penetrating in her analyses, reducing complex factual situations to simple, orderly problems. Typical perhaps of the worrisome but important issues which she argued was *Phillips Co. v. Walling* (324 U.S. 490), holding that an exemption from the Fair Labor Standards Act of employees "engaged in any retail . . . establishment" does not include warehouse and central office employees of an interstate retail-chain-store system. As [Chief Justice] Earl Warren said at a dinner honoring her retirement, she helped put flesh on the bare bones of the Fair Labor Standards Act and made it a viable statutory scheme.

The women's all-time record for arguments before the Supreme Court belongs to Beatrice

A brilliant attorney in the criminal division of the Justice Department and an expert on the government's right to search and seizure, Beatrice Rosenberg argued some thirty cases before the Supreme Court, a record for women advocates.

Rosenberg (1908–1989), a low-profile but brilliant government attorney who, as an authority on search and seizure, argued more than thirty cases before the high court. (The men's twentieth-century record belongs to John W. Davis who, as solicitor general from 1913–1918 and as a private lawyer, argued 140 cases.) In his autobiography, Justice Douglas remembers Rosenberg as being superior to many better-known appellate lawyers with grand reputations. "[L]esser lights and lawyers not well known brought greater distinction to advocacy at the appellate level," he wrote, "Oscar Davis . . . , Daniel Friedman and Beatrice Rosenberg (all of the Department of Justice) made more enduring contributions to the art of advocacy before us than most of the 'big-name' lawyers."

Born in Newark, New Jersey, Rosenberg was a high school classmate of William J. Brennan Jr., who became a Supreme Court justice. (She herself was reportedly considered for a Supreme Court nomination by Richard M. Nixon in 1971.) Rosenberg then graduated from Wellesley College and New York University Law School. She began her government career as a lawyer in the

Justice Department's criminal division in 1943. When she left in 1972, Rosenberg had worked her way up to becoming chief of the criminal division's appellate section. As an appellate lawyer Rosenberg quietly earned accolades from her peers. In 1970 she became the first woman to win the Tom C. Clark Award, which is given by the Bar Association of the District of Columbia for outstanding government service by a federal or local lawyer.

Rosenberg spent the last seven years of her career before she retired in 1979 hearing job discrimination cases—including those involving sexual harassment—on the appeals board of the Equal Employment Opportunity Commission (EEOC). She also litigated appeals and helped persuade the Justice Department that sexual harassment was a form of gender discrimination. Practical and quick witted, she served at the EEOC as a masterful mentor to a pride of appellate lawyers tackling employment discrimination cases. When she died in 1989 the D.C. bar inaugurated the Beatrice Rosenberg Award "for outstanding government service by a bar member whose career contributions to the government exemplifies the highest order of public service."

Although she does not come close to Rosenberg in terms of quantity of cases, Ruth Bader Ginsburg deserves singling out as an advocate for the quality of the arguments she used to persuade the Supreme Court to strike down laws that treat men and women differently. As a cofounder of, and then general counsel to, the Women's Rights Project at the American Civil Liberties Union (ACLU), Ginsburg was the architect of a comprehensive litigating strategy designed to end overt sex discrimination in the law. She argued six times before the Court, losing only one case, *Kahn v. Shevin* (1974). Initiated by an ACLU affiliate in Florida, that case had not been selected to go before the Court by Ginsburg who, presciently, felt the timing was wrong.

The cases Ginsburg argued or briefed read like a list of landmarks in a gender law textbook: *Reed v. Reed* (1971), *Frontiero v. Richardson* (1973), *Weinberger v. Wiesenfeld* (1975), *Edwards v. Healy* (1975), *Turner v. Department of Employment Security* (1975), *Califano v. Goldfarb* (1977), and *Duren v. Missouri* (1979). She also filed influential amicus curiae briefs in many other equal protection cases, including in the landmark *Craig v. Boren* (1976). Ginsburg went on to be appointed to the United States Court of Appeals for the District of Columbia Circuit in 1980 and then, in 1993, to the Supreme Court.

Getting the Assignment

Working as an appellate lawyer for the federal government has been the most direct route to gaining the opportunity to argue a case before the Supreme Court. Many of the cases heard in recent terms were between the federal government and an individual or other private party. Attorneys seeking to represent private parties sometimes participate in so-called "beauty contests" to peddle their services. Affluent clients often make the rounds of a handful of top lawyers who specialize in appellate work—where the number of women is traditionally low—and ask questions about how each candidate would handle the case and how experienced that attorney is at arguing before the justices. The prestige of arguing a case before the Supreme Court, and the reduction over the past decade in the number of cases the Court has agreed to hear each term, make the competition for assignments correspondingly stiff.

However, many women (and men) simply wind up arguing before the Supreme Court not because they were selected to jump in at the appeals level and lend their expertise, but because they have ridden the case from the local level. In other words, clients often stick with the attorney who filed their original suit regardless of whether he or she is an experienced appellate lawyer. These advocates generally do not return a second time unless they are lucky enough to be hired by another client whose case is reviewed by the Supreme Court.

How many women argue before the Supreme Court each term? Only 17 percent of the lawyers who argued before the Supreme Court in the 1999 term, and 10 percent in the 1986 term, were women. This is a big improvement from the 1966 term, when that figure was barely 1 percent, and from the 1976 term, when it was a mere 5 percent. But these figures do not keep pace with the increasing numbers of women entering the legal profession or joining the Supreme Court bar.

To become a member of the Court's bar one must be proposed by two nonrelated members of that bar who swear that the applicant has been a member in good standing of the bar of the highest court in their state for at least three years. Once admitted, members are qualified to file briefs and other papers and to argue before the bench, although most join simply for the prestige of being a member of an elite bar. In 1996 nearly a quarter of the attorneys admitted to the Supreme Court bar were women. That figure was up from 18 percent in 1986 and 5 percent in 1976. Perhaps a good indicator of the swelling female ranks of the Supreme Court bar occurred on March 2, 1998. On that day Susan Orr Henderson, Karen Orr McClure, and Joanne Orr, attorneys from Indiana, became the first three sisters to be sworn in simultaneously.

Do women advocates have a harder time getting clients? Legal experts, and the advocates themselves, generally say the answer is no. Former deputy solicitor general Mahoney, who is now carving out her own practice specializing in appellate advocacy, told the *Washington Post* in 1997, "I've always been convinced that when I lost a client, I lost for a . . . legitimate reason," not because of gender. "There are credentials you need,"

she emphasized, "and right now a lot more men have those credentials." Like Mahoney, who clerked for Chief Justice William H. Rehnquist, those credentials often include a clerkship for a justice and a stint at the OSG arguing for the United States.

One way to get appellate work in the Supreme Court is to specialize in a particular area of law. Betty Jo Christian, a partner at the Washington firm of Steptoe & Johnson, is a good example. Having served as commissioner of the Interstate Commerce Commission in the 1970s, she is considered a top expert on transportation and railroad law. Combining this expertise with appellate skills has made her an attractive choice for railroad companies in suits interpreting the government's transportation and interstate commerce laws, many of which Christian helped formulate. She has argued four times before the Supreme Court and has prepared briefs either for a party or as amicus curiae in countless other cases.

Academic jobs at prestigious law schools are also aids to engagement in a Supreme Court case. Kathleen M. Sullivan, now dean of Stanford Law School, is perhaps the most high-profile woman in this category. Professor Sullivan helped prepare the brief challenging Georgia's antisodomy statute in *Bowers v. Hardwick* (1986), and was on the briefs representing abortion clinics in *Rust v. Sullivan* (1991).

A good indication that women advocates are making progress and becoming true contenders was the selection in 1999 of Mahoney, over stiff competition from leading male advocates, to represent the House of Representatives in a suit against the Commerce Department challenging the Census Bureau's proposal to use a new method for conducting the population count. This action was one of the most highly prized assignments for the Supreme Court bar that term.

In 1999 the House of Representatives hired Maureen Mahoney (right, addressing Justice John Paul Stevens at left) to argue a high-profile case against the Commerce Department challenging the Census Bureau's proposal to use a new method for conducting the population count.

Dressing for Success

While male advocates have followed a formal dress code, women advocates, absent any rules, have had to improvise. In her day, Belva Lockwood wore prim black dresses befitting her profession, but her arrival at the Supreme Court drew considerable attention because she came on a tricycle, which she found more economical than a horse and carriage. When Mabel Walker Willebrandt was named assistant attorney general in 1923, she had a skirt made out of pinstripe material and a black coat to "[call] the attention of her gentlemen colleagues of the bar to her ability to conform to the regulations of what a well-dressed lawyer should wear before the Supreme Court."

At that time, the dress code for men was cutaways and striped trousers, also called a morning suit.

Although male advocates representing parties other than the United States have long stopped sporting that uniform, lawyers in the Office of the Solicitor General continue to honor the tradition. The office keeps half a dozen outfits on hand and most staffers borrow one that fits when they have a Supreme Court appearance. But when Deputy Solicitor General Jewel Lafontant (now Lafontant-Mankarious), a very stylish dresser, became the first woman from the OSG to argue a case in 1973, she took a cue from Willebrandt and had a skirt and suit specially made for her with a one-button cutaway, pinstriped skirt, and jabot ruffled

In 1973 Jewel Lafontant became the first woman from the Office of the Solicitor General to argue a case before the Supreme Court. For the occasion she had a tailor make her a skirt and jacket that resembled the pinstriped cutaway coat and pants worn by her male colleagues.

Five years later the justices heard the first argument delivered by a woman in another type of uniform—a military one. Lieut. Colonel Kim L. Sheffield presented the respondent's case in *U.S. v. Scheffer* (1997) wearing her regulation U.S. Air Force attire.

Other women advocates have chosen clothes that gave them confidence. Raya Dreben, the lawyer who argued Gwendolyn Hoyt's 1961 case against all-male juries, bought a new hat for her first appearance before the Court. She was asked to remove it, however, because Court policy did not permit women lawyers to wear hats in the courtroom. Ginsburg summoned the image of her mother, Celia, when arguing before the Court: "I wear her earrings and her pin and I think how pleased she would be if she were there."

The first woman to argue a case wearing pants was Marguerite M. Buckley in October 1973. She had previously distinguished herself in 1964 as the first woman to wear a miniskirt while being admitted to the Supreme Court bar. Having been thrown out of a courtroom by a municipal court judge for wearing pants, Buckley chose a black pantsuit for her argument in the Supreme Court as much to make a political statement as to be comfortable. "He wasn't overwhelmed," commented the clerk of the Court, Michael Rodak Jr., when the *Washington Post* asked Chief Justice Warren E. Burger's reaction. But Buckley had called ahead to ask permission, and was told by Rodak that the justices did not mind what she wore as long as it was "neat and clean."

Husbands and Wives

The process of preparing for a Supreme Court argument takes months and is usually nerve wracking. An advocate only has thirty minutes to make the argument, but she does not know how long she will be able to speak before a justice jumps in with a question. Advocates prepare answers to

blouse. Apparently she had dismissed as "too large" then-acting attorney general Richard Kleindienst's offer of his morning suit for her first Court appearance. Harriet S. Shapiro also declined to "get dressed up in those crazy costumes that don't fit very well" for her first argument, which took place later in the 1973 term, and instead wore her own suit. Other women from the OSG have generally followed her lead by wearing dark (but not brown) suits or dresses.

Women who work at the Supreme Court as courtroom deputies (there has yet to be a female clerk or marshal of the Court) also wear the traditional cutaways with pants. This tradition started in 1992 when Sandy Nelsen, assistant to the clerk of the Court, appeared in her usual spot at the clerk's desk in the courtroom during oral argument wearing a morning suit. Clerk William Suter had decided it was appropriate that they *both* be dressed according to tradition.

possible questions and outline themes and points they intend to deliver, whether in response to a question or through a narrative. It is difficult to predict which tangent a justice's line of questioning might take, and an advocate must be prepared for anything. First-timers are often coached by veterans, who help them stage mock arguments by playing the role of the justices. Even veterans continue to do mock arguments no matter how many times they have appeared before the Court. Horror stories abound of advocates who are humiliated because they get off track or fail to think fast enough to answer a justice's question.

Some male advocates have had the good fortune of collaborating with their wives on their presentation. The first couple to argue a case together before the Court was probably Alice L. Robie and Melvin L. Resnick in a death penalty case called *Crampton v. Ohio* (1971). Resnick presented the argument for Ohio, while Robie, who had cowritten the brief, sat next to him at counsel table. (The oral advocate is routinely accompanied at counsel table by a second attorney, who helped prepare the briefs.) They were both assistant prosecuting attorneys at the time and are now serving as judges on the Sixth District Court of Appeals and the Supreme Court of Ohio, respectively.

At least one woman advocate making her first Supreme Court appearance has been coached at home by a husband who was a veteran. Benna Ruth Solomon, a lawyer for the city of Chicago, and David Strauss, a professor at the University of Chicago Law School, delivered arguments a week apart in 1997. Strauss, who had already appeared fifteen times before the Court, admitted that he had a tougher time sitting with his two young daughters watching his wife, who had clerked for Justice Byron R. White, deliver an argument than he had performing himself. "It's harder because you can't do anything with your energy, your nervousness. You just have to sit there," he told the

Chicago Tribune. For others sitting in the courtroom, Solomon's argument was a treat to observe. "It was one of the very best arguments of the term," a regular observer commented.

Another woman advocate, Cornelia T. L. Pillard, an assistant solicitor general, argued six days before her husband, David Cole, a professor at Georgetown University Law Center in 1994. But they were not much help to each other because neither had ever argued before the Supreme Court and they were preparing unrelated cases. The stress level in their household was enormous. "It's like the Iron Man Triathalon of the law," Pillard told the *Chicago Tribune.* "There's so much training and preparation, it's . . . the ultimate challenge."

And Ruth Bader Ginsburg reports that not only did her husband, Martin D. Ginsburg, now Georgetown University Law Center professor, read drafts of her briefs and listen to rehearsals of her arguments, but her son and daughter also routinely chimed in with their questions and suggestions during dinner-table conversations.

Rolling with the Punches

The gallantry shown women in Daniel Webster's day has long since been replaced by professional courtesy. And female advocates are not cut any slack during the ordeal of oral argument because they are women. Does their gender give them an advantage in arguing sex discrimination cases? Justice Douglas implicitly answered that question in *The Court Years,* in his description of how four hapless women so irritated him during their arguments that he jokingly considered rolling back all the progress the Supreme Court had granted women in equal protection cases.

In the sixties and seventies, more and more women appeared as advocates. Their average ability and skill were the same as the male advocates and their presence was no cure for the mediocrity of most arguments

by Frank B. Gilbert

My mother, Susan Brandeis Gilbert (1893–1975), was the first and so far only daughter of a Supreme Court justice to argue a case before the Court. Of course her father, Louis D. Brandeis, who served from 1916 to 1939, absented himself in this case. In 1925 she and her partner Benjamin Kirsh represented Joseph Margolin, a lawyer who was convicted and fined $250 for charging his client a $1,500 fee for handling an insurance claim with the Veterans' Bureau. The federal statute limited to $3 any fee for services to a beneficiary.

Mother came into the case after the conviction was upheld in the Court of Appeals for the Second Circuit. She was practicing law in New York City and had been a special assistant to the U.S. Attorney in a major antitrust litigation in the 1920s, the Trenton Potteries *case. After graduating from Bryn Mawr, she had spent a year campaigning for women's suffrage and then went to the University of Chicago Law School because no major eastern law school would admit women.*

In discussing the case many years later, Mother said that she felt that the odds were against her gaining a reversal because the treatment of veterans was at issue. The opposing lawyer was William Donovan, who had been a hero in World War I and who would during World War II be the head of the OSS, the predecessor of the CIA.

"The United States of America may appear by its learned, skilled and able officers, whereas the claimant must plead his own cause," Mother reasoned in her argument before the Court. "To prohibit the employment of counsel is seriously and substantially to impair, if not to destroy, the enforcement" of a claim against the government.

Speaking for the Court (absent Justice Brandeis), Justice James C. McReynolds affirmed the decision of the lower courts. "We find no reason which would justify disregard of the plain language of the section under consider-

> **Brandeis's Daughter in Supreme Court Today To Argue New York War Insurance Fee Case**

When Susan Brandeis argued a veteran's insurance claim case before the Supreme Court in 1925, her father, Justice Louis D. Brandeis, absented himself from the bench. Susan's appearance before the Court, the first and only argument by the daughter of a justice, made the front page of the *New York Times.*

ation," he wrote in Margolin v. United States *(1925).*

Right after her Court appearance and before the decision, Grandfather wrote Mother, who was then thirty-two, "You are certainly getting fine publicity and fruits will come later if you will raise your professional performance as high as your abilities and hard work would make possible. Lovingly, Father."

During the Roosevelt and Truman administrations Mother was considered for appointment as a federal district judge. She became the second woman to serve on the New York State Board of Regents, the body that sets standards for secondary education in the state and deals with many educational issues including state aid to the schools. Like her father, she was an early Zionist. In the last twenty-five years of her life she was active in the development of Brandeis University, founded in 1948 and named in honor of her father.

before us. I remember four women in one case who droned on and on in whining voices that said, "Pay special attention to our arguments, for this is the day of women's liberation." Several of us did express the view that any law which drew a line between men and women was inherently suspect. That view had not prevailed over the majority saying a discrimination classification would be sustained if "reasonable." During this argument by the four wondrous Amazons, I sent a note along the bench saying I was about to change my mind on sex classifications and sustain them if they were "reasonable."

While presenting a case to the justices is perhaps the most difficult task a lawyer can perform, it also confers enormous prestige and can be an exhilarating experience. Despite her abilities, even Ginsburg felt the same fears that strike most advocates, men or women, her first time arguing before the Supreme Court. Yet she also recalls on the Court's film for visitors how powerful the experience made her feel.

The first time I argued a case here I didn't have lunch . . . because I didn't know whether I could keep it down. I was initially terribly nervous, and after about

Ruth Bader Ginsburg's son James and nephew David attended her 1979 oral argument in *Duren v. Missouri,* one of six cases she argued before the Supreme Court.

two minutes into the argument I looked up at these guys and I said, "I have a captive audience. They have no place to go for the next half hour. They must listen to me." And it was a feeling of power. And then there was the challenge of rolling with the waves, sometimes the punches.

THE FIRST FEMALE LAW CLERKS

Lucile Lomen: First Woman Law Clerk

Lucile Lomen was a twenty-three-year-old law student at the University of Washington when Justice Douglas chose her as his law clerk in 1944.

Born in Nome, Alaska, on August 21, 1920, she decided to become a lawyer while she was still in grade school. She attributed her interest in law to her grandfather, Gudbran J. Lomen, a Republican lawyer who had been appointed to the Alaska Territorial Court by Calvin Coolidge in 1925 and reappointed by Herbert Hoover in 1930. Her father, who owned the local newspaper, the *Nome Gold Digger,* had not gone to college.

Graduating from Queen Anne High School in Seattle in 1937, she accepted a one-year tuition scholarship from Whitman College, a small liberal arts college in Walla Walla, Washington, from which Justice Douglas had graduated seventeen years earlier. Like Douglas, she was an outstanding student at Whitman. Elected to Phi Beta Kappa, she graduated with honors in 1941.

Pursuing her ambition to become a lawyer, Lomen went to the University of Washington Law School. She did not consider Harvard, for in 1941 the Harvard Law School did not admit women. The University of Washington Law School had admitted women from the time it opened its doors in 1899. In 1941, there were three women enrolled in the law school, including Lomen.

by Ruth Bader Ginsburg

The first woman to clerk at the Supreme Court was Lucile Lomen, who was engaged by Justice William O. Douglas for the 1944 term. It happened this way: The nation was at war, and the west coast deans who recommended clerks to Douglas found no student worthy of his consideration. Douglas wrote to the Dean at the University of Washington Law School.

When you say you have "no available graduates" whom you could recommend for appointment as my clerk, do you include women? It is possible I may decide to take one, if I can find one who is absolutely first-rate.

The Dean recommended, and Douglas hired, Lomen. Douglas later reported that she was "very able and very conscientious." Lomen eventually became General Electric's counsel for corporate affairs.

When Douglas again thought about hiring a woman six years later he had in mind a "two for." As he described his thinking:

It may be that [my] second law clerk should be someone who is an accomplished typist, someone who can a half or three-quarters of the time help Mrs. Allen [Douglas's secretary]. In this connection it might be desirable to consider getting a woman [law school graduate], a woman who can qualify as a lawyer and who can assist the regular law clerk for part of the time and help Mrs. Allen part of the time. If that procedure is worked out the woman selected might stay for more than one year, say two years, perhaps even three.

(Now before you put down Douglas for hopelessly chauvinist thinking, consider this. If push comes to shove, a justice generally can do for herself what a law clerk does. But our secretaries are the people who keep us going. At the Supreme Court, they manage the office and contend with the ceaseless paper flow and mail floods, sparing us from countless distractions so we can concentrate on the job of judging.)

Justice Douglas never found his double duty person, and it was not until the 1966 term, two decades after Lomen's service, that another woman came to the Court as a clerk. (I have it on reliable authority, however, that the idea was kept alive. In 1960, one of my law teachers, who selected clerks for Justice Felix Frankfurter, suggested that I might do. The justice was told of my family situation: I was married and had a five-year-old daughter. For whatever reason, he said "No." In recent years, I might add, the justices have seen from the best evidence—law clerks they have engaged—that motherhood need not impede diligent service.)

For the 1966 term Justice Hugo L. Black engaged Margaret Corcoran, daughter of a prominent Democrat,

She was an outstanding law student—first in her class, law review editor, vice president of the law review board, and recipient of a prize for the best student essay on constitutional law, which the law review published. While achieving those honors, she worked as a part-time secretary in the dean's office at the law school.

During Lomen's first semester, the United States entered World War II. She remembered clearly the consternation of her fellow law students on December 8, 1941, and their eagerness to enlist. Many finished the school year, but only a small number of them returned the following autumn. In 1941 there were eighty-four law students at the University of Washington; in 1943 there were thirty-five, eight of whom were women.

The war also affected recruitment of Supreme Court law clerks. Concerned about finding a

Thomas Corcoran, known around town as "Tommy the Cork." Black was not entirely pleased with Margaret's performance. He thought she didn't work hard enough. One time, for example, she told him she couldn't review thirty-five petitions for certiorari (asking the Supreme Court to review a case) over the weekend, because of plans to attend VIP dinners with her father. She was, in these extracurricular activities, a dutiful daughter. Corcoran was a widower and sometimes needed a substitute for a spouse at special events.

In 1968, Martha Field, now professor of law at Harvard, clerked for Justice Abe Fortas. In 1971 Barbara Underwood, who became a law professor and a prosecutor and is now principal deputy solicitor general, clerked for Justice Thurgood Marshall. Justice Douglas took the lead again in the 1972 term, when his selection committee engaged two women. He wrote when told the news:

The law-clerk-selection committee has informed me that my two clerks for next year are women.
That's Women's Lib with a vengeance!

That same term—1972—Justice Byron R. White engaged a woman as a law clerk and the following year Justice William H. Rehnquist did the same. The 1972 term, Scott Armstrong and Bob Woodward relate in The Brethren, was not a vintage year in Justice Douglas's chambers. Midway through the term, one of the clerks asked the justice about a note she had received from him. "Excuse me, Mr. Justice," she said, "I've been looking at this note[.] I'm afraid I don't understand it." "I'm not run-

ning a damn law school," the justice responded, "read my opinions on the subject." The clerk sent her boss a note:

I'm very sorry I made a mistake on this case. I'm sure there will be other times this year when I will make other mistakes. However, I've found that civility in professional relationships is most conducive to improved relationships. You can afford to be basically polite to me.

Things went downhill from there. Eventually, the justice hired a third law clerk, a young man, with whom he had better rapport. The other woman engaged by Douglas for the 1972 term got along well enough with her boss, but had a problem of a different sort. She liked a young man who worked on the Court's staff, a man whose father served as messenger for Chief Justice Warren E. Burger. The young man had been active in urging improvement in working conditions in the marshal's office. Douglas's clerk and the young man first dated, then began living together. He was black and she was white. He continued to press for better working arrangements for staff people. He was fired; she kept her job. The two eventually married.

After the 1973 term women law clerks no longer appeared as one-at-a-time curiosities. From 1973 through 1980 the Justices engaged 34 women and 225 men as law clerks. From 1981, Justice Sandra Day O'Connor's first term on the Court, through 1997, 162 women and 446 men were hired. In the 1998–1999 term, the law clerk contingent for active Justices included 13 women and 23 men; the numbers remained about the same—12 women and 22 men—in the 1999–2000 term.

first-rate law clerk for the 1944 term, Douglas began canvassing law school deans before Christmas in 1943. He first wrote to Dean Judson F. Falknor of the University of Washington because Falknor had supplied him with four of his last five clerks. He told the dean that he was aware that the choices would be limited because of the war, but nonetheless he wanted to stay with his "practice of taking men from Ninth Circuit law

schools." Although Douglas used the word "men" in his letter, that did not mean he would not consider a woman. Nine months earlier, he had told Falknor he might take a woman if she "is absolutely first-rate."

Dean Falknor could confidently recommend Lomen, but still he thought he had a problem: no woman had ever been chosen for a clerkship at the Supreme Court. Two years earlier he had fi-

Justice William O. Douglas chose Lucile Lomen to become his law clerk in 1944 partly because so many male law students had dropped out to enlist in World War II.

nessed the problem by recommending a very able male student a couple of ranks below the top student, who was a woman. The male student was Vern Countryman, who turned out to be one of Douglas's most successful law clerks. Now this option was not available to Dean Falknor, for Lomen was the only student in her class who qualified for a clerkship. So his choice was either to recommend her or to recommend no one.

Dean Falknor called Lomen into his office and discussed the matter with her. He told her that he wanted to recommend her. "The only fly in the ointment," he said, "is your sex." In her case, however, he thought that might not be a bar because of her Whitman connection. "The fact that you went to Whitman," he said, "makes it easier because the justice can check with Whitman people he knows."

Dean Falknor wrote Douglas on December 20, saying that he and his colleagues recommended Lomen without hesitation. "In our opinion," he wrote, "she is absolutely first-rate in every respect." He described her outstanding academic record at Whitman College and pointed out that in addition to her excellent record she had been very active in student activities. He then gave the names

of three persons at Whitman who could give "an accurate appraisal of her intellectual activities"— Professor Chester C. Maxey, Dean William R. Davis, and S. B. L. Penrose, Whitman's retired president. Praising her sterling academic accomplishments in the law school, Falknor mentioned that she had worked in his office as a part-time secretary. "I have never had anyone working for me," he continued, "who has been more courteous, cooperative, and conscientious. She comes from a very fine family [and] is a young woman of the highest character and refinement. She has a pleasing appearance and an extraordinarily pleasant personality. I know that you would like her, and my colleagues and I believe that she has the capacity to do an excellent job for you."

Dean Falknor's recommendation of Lomen impressed Douglas, who did exactly what Falknor thought he would do. He checked with one of the Whitman scholars named in his letter. Douglas knew all three men quite well. Penrose was president of Whitman when Douglas was there, and Douglas had taken a philosophy course with him. Davis, an English professor with whom Douglas had taken seven courses, had been his advisor and father confessor. Maxey, a highly respected, tough-minded political scientist, was a close friend and fraternity brother. Douglas chose Maxey to appraise Lomen for the clerkship. "This job of being a law clerk is a pretty mean one," Douglas wrote to Maxey on December 27. "It entails tremendously long hours and is very exacting. As you can imagine, fumbles are costly."

Professor Maxey strongly supported Lomen for the clerkship. On January 10 Douglas sent an excerpt from Maxey's letter to Vern Countryman, his clerk for the 1942 term, asking for his observations. "Beyond that," Douglas wrote, stating the nub of his concern, "I wonder if you would give me your reaction as to how you think a girl would fare as a law clerk in these surroundings which you know so well."

Women in Key Positions at the Supreme Court

Statutory Officers

Librarian	Shelley L. Dowling	1989–present
	Helen Newman	1948–1965

Auxiliary Officers

Counsel	Jane Petkofsky	1999–present
	Mary Ann Willis	1995–1999
	Susan Golz	1977–1978
Curator	Gail Galloway	1978–present
	Catherine Skefos	1974–1976
Director of Data Systems	Donna J. Clement	1994–present
Personnel Officer	Elizabeth Saxon	1985–1987
Public Information Officer	Kathleen Arberg	1999–present
	Toni House	1982–1998

Other Senior Managers

Associate Librarian	Betty Clowers	1972–1976
	Helen Lally	1965–1967
Deputy Librarian	Rosalie Sherwin	1996–present
Deputy Marshal	Sharron Dubose	1997–present
	Dina Zucconi	1980–1983
Deputy Reporter	Christine Fallon	1989–present
Police Lieutenant	Eileen Cincotta	1995–present
Special Assistant to the Administrative Assistant	Vanessa Yarnall	1988–present

Countryman, who was in training at an army air force base in North Carolina, responded immediately. He told Douglas that he had known Lomen quite well at the University of Washington. "She is a very intelligent woman," he wrote, "and she is an indefatigable worker. She appears to be a very healthy young woman, with stamina enough to keep on working long and busy hours." Responding specifically to Douglas's main concern, Countryman continued: "As to how a girl would fare on the job, I can't see that sex would make any difference except on the point of maintaining contact with other offices. On that score, she would not be able to keep as well informed as to what your brethren were doing as a man could, unless, of course, your brethren also employed female clerks. But I doubt if that point is of any importance—certainly not enough to warrant choosing a man instead, unless you are satisfied that the man is absolutely first-rate because I am sure that Lomen is just that."

Justice Douglas received Countryman's reply on January 14. On January 29, he wrote Dean Falknor saying he would take Lomen as his clerk for the following term. Lomen, said Douglas, should "plan to report for work by the third week of September so as to get broken in before sessions of the Court actually start." Dean Falknor

Eileen Cincotta, a veteran on the police force since 1978, was elevated to the position of lieutenant in 1991—the first woman to achieve that rank. In 1985 she had also been the first woman promoted to the position of sergeant.

responded that Lomen was very pleased to receive the clerkship.

On August 24, Lomen wrote Douglas saying that she would report for duty on September 11. "I deeply appreciate the opportunity of serving as your law clerk," she wrote, "and I am highly honored to became a member of your staff." At the time, Douglas was at his cabin near Lostine, Oregon, and had not planned to return to Washington until the first week of October.

Lomen arrived in Washington, D.C., the Friday before Labor Day, 1944. For a young woman who had never been east of Spokane, war-time Washington seemed overwhelming. She said the city was as David Brinkley described it in *Washington Goes to War*. She checked into the YWCA on 17th and K Streets, where she planned to stay only until she found suitable quarters near the Court, but such quarters were so difficult to find that she received special permission to stay at the YWCA for the period of her clerkship.

Bright and early the day after Labor Day, she took a streetcar to the Court. When she arrived at Douglas's chambers, no one was there. Learning

that Douglas's secretary, Edith Waters, and law clerk, Eugene A. Beyer Jr., would not be in until 11 o'clock, she began to look around the Court. Encountering a small group of women being given a tour of the building, she quietly joined them without introducing herself. Near the end of the tour, the Court guide showed the women two impressive circular staircases that ended in a dome. Pointing to the dome, he said, "This will remind Miss Lomen of an igloo." She was astonished. "He not only knew who I was," she later recalled, "but he knew I was from Alaska and the whole business." This was her first lesson about the Court—it was a small, self-contained world in which there were few secrets.

During Lomen's first three weeks at the Court, Douglas was still in Oregon. In that period, she learned her duties as a law clerk and began writing certiorari memos. She also became acclimated to life at the Court. Edith Waters introduced the other secretaries, and Lomen became a part of their social group. She would be a bridge between them and the law clerks. She recalled that the clerks accepted her "pretty well." So did the chief justice and justices. Yet she sensed differences with the clerks. She thought it had to do mostly with age, legal education, and geography. Soon after she arrived at the Court, a fellow clerk asked where she was from. She answered Seattle, and he said, "Oh, you'll like it here. We have another westerner. [Byron] Kabot's from Wisconsin." In relating the story, she said: "I nearly died. But, indeed, Kabot and I, of the whole ten, thought differently . . . than the way the other eight thought. They were all east-coast fellas [and] Kabot . . . was hired from [Chicago]. So everybody but me had been educated . . . at [Chicago,] Harvard, Yale, and Columbia. I was [also] younger. . . . I never knew if my problem was because I was a woman or because I was younger, or what."

Lomen met Douglas one morning during the first week of October. She was working on certiorari petitions when he came into Chambers. He said how do you do, apologized for not putting her on the payroll earlier, said he had to get to work, walked into his office, and closed the door— all in less than a minute. She soon learned that this was typical Douglas office behavior. He did not say good morning when he arrived or goodnight when he left. She remembered him as being rather "distant" and "cool" in Chambers. He was "all business"; there were no pleasantries, no small talk, just work. At first, she did not know what to make of him and finally concluded that he was shy. Since she was shy herself, she understood.

Determined to succeed, she tried to work as quickly as he did, which was impossible, for, as she later said, she had never known anyone who could do legal research as fast as Douglas could. She did her best to keep up. She said that she had never worked so hard in her life. She worked six- teen hours a day, and often she remained at the Court all night to complete assignments. She would catch a few hours sleep on a leather couch in the office and awaken when the cleaning crew came in at 5:00 a.m. The only real sleep she got was on weekends; she would go to bed at 9:00 p.m. on Saturdays and sleep until noon on Sun- days. She took responsibility for the correctness of every statement of law and fact in Douglas's opinions. She went over the content of his opin- ions with him, and sometimes disagreed with him. Carol Agger Fortas, the wife of Justice Abe Fortas, urged her to stand up to Douglas at such times. Lomen said she did, but she could not re- member winning any arguments. That did not bother her, for she said that he was there to de- cide cases and she was there to help him.

What did bother her was Douglas's failure to tell her how she was doing. Although he never criticized her work, he never praised it either. Concerned, she wrote to her professor at Whit- man, Chester Maxey, stating the problem and ask- ing for his views. Maxey wrote back saying that if

Douglas had been dissatisfied he would have told her in no uncertain terms. Since that had not oc- curred, he said, "You are doing all right."

Later, Justice Douglas let Lomen know indi- rectly that he valued her work by inviting her to his home several times for dinner or a party. There she saw another side of him. He was, she recalled, "a delightful fellow"—relaxed, warm, and jovial. But back at the office he reverted to his work mode—all business.

The 1944 term went by quickly. In spring, Jus- tice Douglas offered to help Lomen find a job. She thanked him and said that she already had two job offers—one from the Justice Department and another in Seattle. She turned down the for- mer and returned to Washington State, where she took a job at the state attorney general's office. This pleased Justice Douglas, for his standard ad- vice to law clerks was, "Go back to your roots."

In 1945 Justice Douglas sent Lomen an in- scribed photo. She responded with a chatty, handwritten letter, which she concluded by say- ing, "I recognize the incomparable value of last year's experience and I am grateful to you for the opportunity which you gave me. I certainly hope to be a better lawyer because of it."

After three years at the Washington State at- torney general's office, Lomen sought a position in the legal department of the General Electric Company. Justice Douglas recommended her "without any qualification whatsoever." She wanted Justice Douglas's help because one of the executives had serious doubts about hiring a woman for the position. "She has a fine mind and a firm foundation in the law," Douglas wrote. "She has great capacity for work, is thorough, re- liable and dependable in every respect." Lomen got the position.

She worked at General Electric from 1948 to 1983, holding important positions in the company in the northwest and finishing her career at cor- porate headquarters in the east. After she retired,

Margaret Corcoran, who clerked for Justice Hugo L. Black during the 1966 term, had graduated from Harvard Law School the previous year. She was the daughter of Thomas Corcoran, the powerful New Deal Democrat who was a former clerk to Justice Felix Frankfurter and Justice Hugo Black's close friend. According to the diary of his wife, Elizabeth, Justice Black "gave Margaret a straight-from-the-shoulder-talk about how much work there was to being a clerk; he told her that she wouldn't have time for dating and having fun." Once hired, Corcoran ignored this warning, both disappointing and inconveniencing the justice. She often accompanied her widowed father to social events at night, balked at taking work home on weekends, and was absent from work for days in a row. Tragically, Corcoran took her own life not long after her clerkship.

❦

Martha Aschuler Field, who clerked for Justice Abe Fortas during the 1968 term, graduated first in her class with the highest record yet achieved at the University of Chicago Law School. "That is why Justice Fortas 'took a chance on me,'" she acknowledges, "which is what it was considered to hire a woman." Since 1978 she has taught

Federal Courts and Constitutional Law as Langdell Professor of Law at Harvard University. Field has argued appeals in the Courts of Appeals and the Supreme Court of the United States and has tried cases in courts in Philadelphia, where she served for a short period as an assistant district attorney. She is the author of *Surrogate Motherhood* and coauthor with Valerie Sanchez of *Equal Treatment for People with Mental Retardation*.

❦

Barbara Underwood, who clerked for Justice Thurgood Marshall in the 1971 term, had graduated first in her class at Georgetown University Law Center and had then served as a clerk to Judge David L. Bazelon at the U.S. Court of Appeals for the D.C. Circuit. After her Supreme Court clerkship she became a professor of law at Yale Law School and at Brooklyn Law School.  While on leave from Yale she tried cases as an assistant district attorney in New York County; she later became chief of appeals and counsel to the district attorney in Kings County, and senior executive assistant district attorney for legal affairs in Queens County, all in the state of New York. In 1993 she became chief assistant U.S. attorney for the eastern district of New York, leaving after five years to become the principal deputy solicitor general in Washington, D.C. Underwood has argued two sexual harassment cases before the U.S. Supreme Court: *Burlington Industries v. Ellerth* (1998) and *Davis v. Monroe County Board of Education* (1999).

Lomen returned to Seattle, where she died on June 21, 1996, at the age of seventy-five.

Shortly before her death, Lomen reflected on the significance of her Supreme Court clerkship. She said that newspaper articles in 1944 about her as the first woman to clerk at the Court were embarrassing. "You know," she tried to explain, "there was nothing unusual about it. I mean it was unusual that I was a woman [law clerk], but I was just a lawyer, and that is all I wanted to be." Her year at the Court, she acknowledged, was not easy, but she said that it was "very rewarding." She then added, "I would not have given up the experience for anything."

NEAR MISSES: WOMEN CONSIDERED FOR APPOINTMENT TO THE SUPREME COURT

The first woman to be seriously considered for appointment to the Supreme Court was Florence Ellinwood Allen, a judge from Ohio. In 1934 President Franklin D. Roosevelt appointed her to the U.S. Court of Appeals for the Sixth Circuit, where she became the first woman to receive a lifetime judgeship on a court of general jurisdiction. Almost immediately, a host of supporters—from little-known women lawyers in small towns to well-connected New Deal officials—promoted her for a series of vacancies on the Supreme Court. The most eminent female legal professional in the country, Allen was endorsed by professional women's organizations and by prominent female judges. She also earned the backing of several male judges and of maverick progressive senators William Borah and George Norris.

Although Eleanor Roosevelt had openly advocated Allen's appointment to the federal appeals court in 1934, the first lady never used her influence to lobby for Allen's subsequent elevation to the Supreme Court. Roosevelt did, however, later predict that one day a woman would sit on the Supreme Court, and that the first female justice "might make a little bow to Florence Allen, who by her own distinguished career helped to make it possible."

Allen's "candidacy" spanned twelve Supreme Court appointments and two Democratic administrations. Although she vigorously sought to fill each Court vacancy, Allen never publicly declared herself a candidate because it was considered inappropriate for would-be nominees to promote themselves. Yet her ambition was hardly disguised: it was Allen's own secretary who orchestrated the campaign to secure her nomination. Although she met the political, professional, and geographic representational standards for Supreme Court selection, Allen did not have a large enough constituency to demand the recognition of a Supreme Court seat. Women's influence in politics had dwindled in the 1920s and was not revived until the 1970s.

The last vacancy for which Allen was considered arose in 1949, when she was sixty-five. India Edwards, director of the Women's Division of the Democratic Party, urged President Harry S Truman to select Allen for the seat vacated that year by Justice Wiley B. Rutledge. According to Edwards's oral history, Truman replied, "Well, I'm willing. I'd be glad to. I think we ought to have a woman. But I'll have to talk to the Chief Justice about it and see what he thinks." "No," was the president's verdict, "the Justices don't want a woman. They say they couldn't sit around with their robes off and their feet up and discuss the problems." To which Edwards replied, "They could if they wanted to."

Despite her efforts, Allen was realistic about her prospects.

Do not block in the future too optimistically because there are some things that will never happen in our

When President Franklin D. Roosevelt appointed Florence Ellinwood Allen to the U.S. Court of Appeals for the Sixth Circuit in 1934, she became the first woman to hold a lifetime judgeship on a court of general jurisdiction. The most eminent woman legal professional in the country, Allen was considered for appointment to the Supreme Court many times.

lifetime. In other words, when my friends delightfully tell me they hope to see me on the Supreme Bench of the U.S., I know two things: First, that will never happen to a woman while I am living, and second, that perhaps it is just as well not to mention that possibility at the present time because there is a certain type of lawyer that immediately becomes fighting mad when that possibility is mentioned.

Allen retired from the Sixth Circuit in 1959. The previous year President Dwight D. Eisenhower, a Republican, had selected Potter Stewart as his fifth and last appointee to the Court. It had been a close call: Stewart sat next to Allen on the U.S. Court of Appeals for the Sixth Circuit bench.

During the 1960s women's groups became more insistent on pressing for a woman to join the Supreme Court. In 1965, for the first time, they endorsed three women candidates: federal district judge Sara Hughes, North Carolina Supreme Court judge Susie M. Sharp, and Shirley M. Hufstedler of the Superior Court of Los Angeles. President Lyndon B. Johnson

nonetheless appointed his friend, Abe Fortas, an accomplished lawyer, for the vacancy left by Justice Arthur J. Goldberg. Undeterred, women's groups became increasingly savvy about the nomination process and the National Women's Political Caucus routinely supplied the White House with a list of qualified women, including federal and state judges, law professors, and members of Congress from which to choose. Professional groups of mixed sexes also began to join the clamor for a woman on the Court.

President Richard M. Nixon considered elevating Judge Mildred Lillie from a California appeals court to the U.S. Supreme Court in 1971, but the American Bar Association (ABA) rated her as "unqualified," effectively killing her chances. According to Nixon's chief of staff, John Erlichman, the president also considered appointing Jewel LaFontant, an African American woman, to the Supreme Court, but instead named her the first female deputy solicitor general in 1973. With a president serious about appointing a woman for the first time, retired chief justice Earl Warren and retired justices Goldberg and Tom C. Clark took the opportunity to endorse the idea of a woman on the Court.

When President Gerald R. Ford had a vacancy to fill on the Supreme Court in 1975, he told his attorney general, "Don't exclude women from the list" of potential appointees. He revived the practice of submitting names to the ABA's Committee on the Federal Judiciary for evaluation. (Nixon had discontinued the practice in 1971 after two nominees were spurned.) Ford's initial list contained eleven names—none female—but a second, greatly expanded list held many women's names. Included were two prominent women judges: U.S. district judge Cornelia G. Kennedy of Michigan, and Shirley M. Hufstedler, who had been appointed to the U.S. Court of Appeals for the Ninth Circuit. Carla A. Hills, secretary of Housing and Urban Development, also on the list, was the preference of First Lady Betty Ford, who was publicly pressuring her husband to choose a woman. Future nominees Sandra Day O'Connor and Ruth Bader Ginsburg, as well as trial or appellate judges Dorothy Nelson, Julia Mack Cooper, Susie M. Sharp, and Constance Baker Motley were also named on the lengthy list.

Cornelia G. Kennedy, a conservative Republican who had been appointed district judge for the eastern district of Michigan by Nixon five years earlier, was the only woman to make the shortlist. The ABA rated her "qualified," which put her behind several "highly qualified" men on the list. Chief Justice Warren E. Burger weighed in during the selection process with an assessment that there were no women with impressive qualifications "in sight." Still, Kennedy's ranking signified that the ABA was now persuaded as to the viability of women candidates. Kennedy went on to be appointed to the U.S. Court of Appeals for the Sixth Circuit in 1979.

With the women's movement now in full swing, the public declared its readiness for a

Cornelia G. Kennedy became the first woman to receive a rating of "qualified" from the American Bar Association's Committee on the Federal Judiciary when it evaluated potential nominees for a Supreme Court vacancy in 1975. Five years later, Kennedy was appointed to the U.S. Court of Appeals for the Sixth Circuit.

female justice. In 1972 the Harris Poll reported that 57 percent of the women and 50 percent of the men surveyed would like to see a woman on the Supreme Court "now." When President Ford ultimately settled on John Paul Stevens instead of Kennedy, women's groups were outraged and demanded representation on the Court. Members of the Supreme Court spoke up as well. Justices William J. Brennan Jr. and Thurgood Marshall publicly expressed their eagerness to be joined by a woman on the bench. Justice Potter Stewart recalled his admiration for Florence Allen, with whom he had served on the Sixth Circuit.

During his 1976 presidential campaign Jimmy Carter promised to appoint a woman to the Supreme Court if a vacancy occurred during his tenure in office. Privately, he favored Hufstedler, the appeals court judge previously considered by Ford. President Johnson had named her to the Ninth Circuit in 1968, when she became, more than thirty years after Allen, only the second woman appointed to a U.S. Court of Appeals. Carter brought Judge Hufstedler to Washington, D.C., to launch the newly created Department of Education as its first secretary in 1979 and to be in position if a vacancy occurred. But no justice retired during the Carter administration, and the president never had the opportunity to make a nomination.

When Ronald Reagan campaigned against Carter in 1980 he also pledged to appoint a woman. "One of the first Supreme Court vacancies in my administration will be filled with the most qualified woman I can find, one who meets the high standards I will demand for all my appointments." In November 1980, in anticipation that a woman would soon join their ranks, the justices quietly decided in their weekly conference to use the designation "Justice" instead of the traditional "Mr. Justice." They were nine months ahead of the game.

On August 19, 1981, Reagan made good his campaign pledge by nominating Sandra Day O'Connor, a judge on the Arizona Court of Appeals, to the Supreme Court. While Allen had clearly been the only qualified, well-positioned female candidate of her time, O'Connor's selection was somewhat of a surprise. The previous April, Reagan had been secretly informed that Justice Stewart would announce his resignation in July. As a result, Attorney General William French Smith and other advisors had time to quietly check out potential candidates. Almost half of the names on their initial list of twenty-five were women—a higher proportion than ever before. By the time the list was winnowed to five, only two women, O'Connor and Kennedy, remained. O'Connor was the only candidate interviewed directly by the president and his top aides.

In addition to her strong political backing and impressive academic credentials, O'Connor received a "qualified" backing from the ABA's Committee on the Federal Judiciary (which, incidentally, was now chaired by a woman). Although

Had a vacancy occurred during his administration, President Jimmy Carter would have elevated appeals court judge Shirley M. Hufstedler to the Supreme Court. Carter even brought her to Washington, D.C., in 1979 to head the new Department of Education so that she would be in position to take a seat on the Court.

O'Connor met "the highest standards of judicial temperament and integrity," the committee also expressed concern over her limited practice as an attorney and her short experience on the bench. Yet, when she took her seat in October, she was the only justice with experience in all three branches of government. Reagan expressed satisfaction with his choice of O'Connor: "I am proud that for the first time in our history, a woman . . . now sits on the Supreme Court of the United States. But I'm proudest of this appointment not because Justice O'Connor is a woman, but because she is so well qualified."

When Justice Brennan suddenly announced his retirement in 1990, President George Bush, who had been in office for two years, was ready with a shortlist of eighteen candidates. Carla A. Hills, now the U.S. trade representative, appeared on it, as did Pamela A. Rymer of the U.S. Court of Appeals for the Ninth Circuit. But only Edith H. Jones of the U.S. Court of Appeals for the Fifth Circuit, which was in Bush's home state of Texas, made it to the shortlist of four. Jones ended up a finalist against the eventual victor— the little-known David Souter of New Hampshire. After spiriting the two candidates to Washington for interviews, Bush opted for Souter, although his advisors were evenly split between the candidates. Souter had published little in the way of controversial opinions and was considered a safer choice to make it through the grueling confirmation process.

When for the first time in twenty-six years a Democratic president got the chance to make an appointment to the Supreme Court, he choose the second woman to become a justice. But gender was not the primary criterion in Bill Clinton's selection process. Nor was Ruth Bader Ginsburg Clinton's immediate choice; he picked her after considering several men. Indeed, it took Clinton eighty-seven days, far longer than his two Republican predecessors, to decide on a nominee.

Initially, the president favored politicians over sitting judges. But first choice Mario Cuomo preferred to keep his job as governor of New York. Secretary of the Interior Bruce Babbitt was willing, but environmentalists protested the prospect of their ally leaving the cabinet. Clinton then seriously considered several judges, including female U.S. Court of Appeals judges Amayla Kearse (who would have been the first African American woman on the Court), Stephanie K. Seymour, and Patricia Wald. Chief Judge Judith Kaye of New York's highest tribunal was also on the shortlist but publicly asked to be removed from consideration. Clinton decided to interview Stephen G. Breyer, the chief judge of the U.S. Court of Appeals for the First Circuit, who became his eventual choice for a second vacancy.

Finally, Clinton settled on Ginsburg, a Carter appointee on the U.S. Court of Appeals for the District of Columbia Circuit, who, as a litigator and law professor, had pioneered equal rights for women. She addressed the issue of being the second woman named to the Court in her acceptance speech at the White House.

The announcement the President just made is significant, I believe, because it contributes to the end of the days when women, at least half the talent pool in our society, appear in high places only as one at a time performers.

Justice Ginsburg likes to tell the story of how in 1853 Sarah Grimké, an antislavery lecturer and women's rights proponent from South Carolina, visited the Supreme Court and was invited to sit in the chief justice's chair. In a letter home, Grimké recalled that the justices laughed when she "involuntarily exclaimed," "Who knows, but this chair may one day be occupied by a woman." Gender equality in the nomination process has come a long way since an outstanding candidate like Florence Allen was shut out because she was a woman. But Grimké's prophecy, while no longer laughable, has yet to come true.

WOMEN ON THE SUPREME COURT

Sandra Day O'Connor: First Woman Justice

Sandra Day O'Connor, the first woman appointed to the Supreme Court, was born March 26, 1930, to Harry A. Day and Ada Mae Wilkey Day in El Paso, Texas. She grew up on the Lazy B Ranch, 198,000 acres of land with more than 2,000 cattle, twenty-five miles from the town of Duncan in southeastern Arizona. Her grandfather, Henry Clay Day, had founded the ranch in 1880, some thirty years before Arizona gained statehood. The ranch house, a simple, four-room adobe building, had neither running water nor electricity until Sandra Day was seven. In the drought years of the Great Depression, her family confronted real hardship, but the ranch eventually prospered.

Day's sister and brother, Ann and Alan, were born in 1938 and 1939; she therefore spent her first eight years as an only child, and most of these years on a remote ranch. Her early childhood friends were her parents, ranch hands, a bobcat, and a few javelina hogs. She learned to entertain herself and to find diversion in books. Her mother spent hours reading to her from various books and the *Los Angeles Times*, the *New Yorker*, and the *Saturday Evening Post*. By the age of eight she was also mending fences, riding with the cowboys, firing her own .22 rifle, and driving a truck. At age five Sandra Day began to spend the school months with her maternal grandmother, Mamie Wilkey, in El Paso in order to attend Radford School, a private school for girls. She spent each summer at the ranch. Day lived with her grandmother from kindergarten through

Sandra Day O'Connor had the support of her husband, John, and sons Scott, Brian, and Jay when she was appointed to the Arizona State Senate in 1969. She won re-election to the state senate in two successive terms and was elected majority leader in 1972, the first woman to hold such office anywhere in the United States.

high school, with a one-year interruption at age thirteen, when homesickness impelled her to return to Arizona. During her years in El Paso she was deeply influenced by her grandmother's strong will and high expectations.

Day graduated from high school at sixteen and entered Stanford University. She earned a degree in economics with great distinction in 1950. In her senior year she began to study law and then continued at Stanford Law School. There she served on the *Stanford Law Review* and won membership in the Order of the Coif, a legal honor society. She graduated in 1952, third in her law school class of 102 students. That same year Sandra Day married John Jay O'Connor III, whom she had met while working on the law review.

O'Connor set out to find a job as a lawyer but was repeatedly turned down by firms that would not hire women. The one job offer she received was for a position as a legal secretary. Ironically, almost thirty years later, Attorney General William

French Smith, who had been a senior member of the firm that made the offer, would be instrumental in O'Connor's appointment to the Supreme Court. Instead of becoming a secretary, O'Connor accepted a position as a deputy county attorney in San Mateo, California. She recalls how that job "influenced the balance of my life because it demonstrated how much I enjoyed public service."

John O'Connor graduated a year after his wife and joined the U.S. Army Judge Advocate General Corps, in which he served for three years in Frankfurt, Germany. While overseas, Sandra Day O'Connor worked as a civilian lawyer for the Quartermaster Corps. The couple returned to the United States in 1957 and moved to Maricopa County, Arizona. In the next six years they had three sons, Scott, Brian, and Jay.

In 1958, after the birth of her first child, O'Connor opened her own firm with a partner, Tom Tobin. She stopped working, however, after Brian's birth. From 1960 to 1965, besides being a full-time mother, O'Connor did a variety of volunteer work. She wrote questions for the Arizona bar exam, helped start the state bar's lawyer referral service, sat on the local zoning commission, and served as a member of the Maricopa County Board of Adjustments and Appeals. In 1965 she served as a member of the Governor's Committee on Marriage and Family, worked as an administrative assistant at the Arizona State Hospital, acted as an adviser to the Salvation Army, and volunteered in a school for blacks and Hispanics. During these years O'Connor also became actively involved in Republican politics. She worked as a county precinct officer for the party from 1960 to 1965, and as district chairman from 1962 to 1965. "Two things were clear to me from the onset," O'Connor has remarked about that period in her life. "One is, I wanted a family and the second was that I wanted to work—and I love to work."

O'Connor returned to regular employment in 1965, as an assistant state attorney general, while also continuing her volunteer work. In 1969, when Isabel A. Burgess resigned from her seat in the Arizona Senate to accept an appointment in Washington, D.C., O'Connor was appointed as her replacement. O'Connor won reelection to the state senate in two successive terms. She was elected majority leader in 1972, the first woman to hold such office anywhere in the United States. Among her Republican colleagues, her voting record was moderate to conservative, although she differed with some of them on issues such as discrimination and in her support of the Equal Rights Amendment. In addition, she served as cochair of the state committee to elect Richard Nixon to the presidency.

In 1974 O'Connor won a hard-fought election to a state judgeship on the Maricopa County Superior Court, on which she served for the next five years. Republican leaders encouraged her to run for governor in 1978, but she declined. In 1979 the Democratic governor selected O'Connor as his first appointee to the Arizona Court of Appeals. There, she decided appeals on subjects spanning workmen's compensation, divorce, criminal convictions, torts, and real property. Twenty-one months later, on August 19, 1981, President Reagan fulfilled

The family of Sandra Day O'Connor attended her confirmation hearings before the Senate Judiciary Committee in 1981. She was confirmed unanimously, becoming the first woman to sit on the Supreme Court bench.

a campaign promise to appoint a woman to the Supreme Court and nominated O'Connor to the seat vacated by Justice Potter Stewart.

In her Senate confirmation hearings, O'Connor expressed cautiously conservative views on capital punishment, the rule excluding illegally obtained evidence from trials, and busing for desegregation, while declining to be pinned down on the question of abortion. When asked how she wanted to be remembered, O'Connor replied, "Ah, the tombstone question. I hope it says, 'Here lies a good judge.'" On September 15, 1981, seventeen of the eighteen members of the Judiciary Committee recommended her approval. One voted "present" because O'Connor had declined to condemn the Supreme Court's 1973 abortion decision, *Roe v. Wade*. The Senate confirmed her appointment 99–0, and O'Connor took the oath of office September 26, 1981. When she began her first term in October, O'Connor brought to the Court experience from service in all three branches of government and was the only sitting justice who had been elected to public office.

In her first five terms O'Connor usually voted with the conservative faction of the Court. In her best-known opinion of her first term, however, O'Connor was joined by the liberal wing of the Court in a 5–4 ruling that a state-supported university in Mississippi could not constitutionally exclude men from its school of nursing. By the end of the 1984 term, O'Connor had come to be identified as a restrained jurist, a strong supporter of federalism, and a cautious interpreter of the Constitution.

In subsequent terms O'Connor often voted with the centrist Lewis F. Powell Jr., and the two were in the majority on 5–4 rulings more often than any other justices. While O'Connor generally sided with her conservative colleagues, she frequently wrote her own, narrower concurrence. "It has become almost commonplace for 5–4 rulings by the Court's conservative bloc to be em-

Sandra Day O'Connor's appointment to the Supreme Court generated many cartoons poking fun at the demise of the all-boys clubhouse. Six months before her nomination, the justices quietly had voted to replace the honorific "Mr. Justice" with "Justice" in anticipation of a woman joining their ranks.

broidered—and often limited—by an O'Connor concurrence," one observer commented in 1989. "Even though none of the other justices agree completely with her views, they in effect become the law because of her position near the center of the Court's ideological spectrum." O'Connor came under increasing scrutiny as the swing vote on a Court often sharply divided over issues such as affirmative action, the death penalty, and abortion. "As O'Connor goes, so goes the Court," another observer would declare in 1990. When David Souter joined the Court that fall, he voted the same way as O'Connor in every 5–4 decision during his first term.

Among O'Connor's noted opinions are those dealing with issues of religious freedom. A concurring opinion she wrote in *Lynch v. Donnelly* (1984) on the constitutionality of a government-sponsored nativity scene has subsequently established the legal standard for determining when such displays violate the Constitution's prohibition on government establishment of religion. A year later, another O'Connor concurrence was important in outlining the constitutional bounds on a state-prescribed "voluntary moment of silence" for school children. According to O'Connor, the challenged law was unconstitutional in that its purpose was to encourage prayer, but it might have passed muster had it not favored "the child who chooses to pray . . . over the child who chooses to meditate or reflect."

Two recent opinions written by O'Connor give further insight into her views on religious matters. In *Agostini v. Felton* (1997) O'Connor wrote a decision overruling a 1985 decision in which the Court had held that a federally funded program that paid for public school teachers to teach remedial education classes on the premises of religious (or parochial) schools was unconstitutional. The Court had reasoned that spending government money in this way resulted in an "excessive entanglement" between church and state. The 1985 decision meant that public school teachers could not conduct remedial lessons on the premises of parochial schools, but had to teach elsewhere. Sometimes classes would even be held in trailers parked right next to a religious school. Writing for a majority of five, O'Connor concluded that the Court's understanding of the Constitution had so changed in the intervening twelve years that the 1985 decision was no longer good law.

Also in 1997, O'Connor dissented vigorously from the Court's decision in *City of Boerne v. Flores.* O'Connor objected to the Court's current understanding of the Constitution's guarantee of the right to religious "free exercise." O'Connor strongly disagreed with the view that, so long as a law applies to the public generally and does not directly discriminate against religion, it is constitutional. In her dissent she wrote that, if complying with a law would require a person to violate his or her religious beliefs in a significant way, that person should be exempted from complying with the law, unless the government has a "compelling interest" in enforcing the law. For example, suppose a generally applicable law requires people to go bareheaded in public places, and a certain religion requires its members to cover their heads in public. Under the Court's interpretation of the Constitution, it is possible that members of the religion would have to comply with the law, since it does not specifically target the religious practice for unfavorable treatment. In contrast, O'Connor's dissent in *City of Boerne* argued that, unless the government can show there is a very important reason for its law, the Constitution gives members of the religion the right to follow their religious practice and to be exempted from the law.

In other opinions, O'Connor has endorsed affirmative action for minorities if "narrowly tailored" to correct a demonstrated wrong, but not

otherwise. In a landmark 1989 opinion, *City of Richmond v. J. A. Croson Co.,* O'Connor's opinion for the Court concluded that government programs setting aside a fixed percentage of public contracts for minority businesses violate equal protection. In a second major decision on the issue, *Adarand Constructors, Inc. v. Pena* (1995), O'Connor wrote for the majority in concluding that all racial classifications, imposed by federal or state governments, must be analyzed under a "strict scrutiny" analysis. This means that an affirmative action program that gives benefits based on race is constitutional only if the government can show that the program serves a very important government interest and is narrowly designed to serve that interest. The decision has called into question a number of governmental affirmative action programs.

O'Connor has also written two significant opinions interpreting federal sexual harassment laws. In *Harris v. Forklift Systems, Inc.* (1993), lower courts had rejected the claim of a woman employee whose supervisor repeatedly made her the target of unwanted sexual innuendoes. Even though the lower courts found that a reasonable woman would have found the supervisor's conduct offensive, they nevertheless held that the conduct did not create an "abusive work environment" because the woman had not suffered a serious psychological injury. A unanimous Supreme Court reversed this decision in an opinion written by O'Connor. Explaining that harassing conduct is actionable before it "leads to a nervous breakdown," the Court held that federal law does not require a harassed employee to establish psychological injury. Instead, he or she need only show that a reasonable person would think a work environment was hostile or abusive.

In *Davis v. Monroe County Board of Education* (1999), the Court considered whether a school board could be sued for "student-on-student" sexual harassment. The case involved a fifth grader who said another student had sexually harassed her by making many off-color remarks and touching her inappropriately. The fifth-grader's mother said that she had repeatedly complained about the problem to the school principal, but nothing was done. Writing for a five-member majority, O'Connor held that under federal law a school board could be held liable for the student's conduct if the board had deliberately refused to do anything about the student's misconduct. O'Connor rejected the argument that this decision would teach "little Johnny" the wrong lesson about federalism. Instead, she argued, it would ensure that "little Mary may attend class."

On the highly charged issue of abortion, O'Connor searched for a middle ground in a series of decisions in the 1980s and ultimately found one in 1992. In *Planned Parenthood of Southeastern Pennsylvania v. Casey*, O'Connor, Justice Anthony Kennedy, and Justice Souter wrote a joint plurality opinion that limited but declined to overturn the Court's original 1973 recognition of the right to abortion.

Consistent with her own tenures as a state legislator and state judge, O'Connor has favored limiting intrusions by federal courts on state powers, especially in criminal matters. She has taken a similarly restrained view of federal judicial power with respect to the legislative and executive branches. Legal scholars have had difficulty categorizing O'Connor's jurisprudence. Her opinions are conservative and attentive to detail, but also open minded; they reflect no profound ideology and rarely contain any sweeping rhetoric. Critics say that her opinions have no passion, no lofty vision, and lack a personal tone. O'Connor has been compared to Justices Powell and John Marshall Harlan, "whose careers were distinguished by a devotion to pragmatic resolution of the issues before them." She is portrayed as a justice "who looks to resolve each case and no more, one with no overarching philosophy that might preor-

dain a result." O'Connor has described her careful approach to joining an opinion as "a little like walking through a patch of recently poured concrete." "You look back and see those steps forever. You see them! They aren't easily covered up or removed. It makes me want to tread softly."

O'Connor is a tall, striking woman, with glittering eyes and an unflinching gaze. She speaks with quiet, confident authority. Her former law clerks describe her as very much in control, committed, intense, a perfectionist—but also warm, down-to-earth, and irrepressibly upbeat. Shortly after taking her seat, O'Connor established a morning exercise class in the Court gym for the women employees. She plays tennis and golfs regularly, often with one of her more athletically inclined law clerks. Her chambers are noted for long hours and sometimes seven-day work weeks, punctuated with popcorn, Mexican brunches, or mandatory outings to the Smithsonian or to go fishing or white-water rafting. On the Saturdays when she meets with her law clerks to discuss upcoming cases, she brings in a homemade lunch for the group. In fall 1988 O'Connor was diagnosed with breast cancer; the day before her surgery she fulfilled a speaking engagement at Washington and Lee University, and she was back on the bench ten days later, without missing an oral argument.

Ruth Bader Ginsburg: From Litigator to Justice

Ruth Bader Ginsburg was born in Brooklyn, New York, on March 15, 1933. Although her birth certificate listed her as "Joan Ruth," the first and middle names were reversed by her mother when she entered kindergarten. Her father, Nathan Bader, was a Russian-Jewish immigrant who worked first as a manufacturer of fur coats and later as a haberdasher. Celia Amster Bader, Ginsburg's mother, was born in this country four months after her family emigrated from Austria. Ruth was the second of Celia and Nathan Bader's two children, but her older sister, Marilyn, died of meningitis at the age of eight.

Both of her parents showered attention on Ruth, now their only child. Nathan Bader was a warm and doting father who would have spoiled his daughter, Ginsburg has said, if her mother had allowed it. But it was Celia Bader who was the primary influence on Ginsburg's early intellectual development. An avid reader who had graduated from high school at the age of fifteen, Celia immediately went to work as a secretary in New York's garment district. She was proud of her eldest brother, a student at Cornell University, and a portion of her earnings helped to sustain his education. Celia accepted for herself the contemporary assumptions about women's proper roles as wife and mother. But she envisioned a different life for her daughter.

Celia accompanied Ruth on weekly trips to the local public library to select books on which Ruth would thrive. And she saved every bit she could manage to put away for Ruth's college education. Although Celia did not work outside the home after her marriage, she passed on to Ruth a deep sense of the importance of independence and achievement. "She was not a career woman," Ginsburg later said, ". . . but she had tremendous intellect."

Celia was never to see the fruition of her hopes for her daughter: she developed cervical cancer during Ruth's high school years and died in June 1950, one day before Ruth's graduation. Although devastated by the loss, Ruth nevertheless left home that fall to enter Cornell, with the aid of scholarships granted on the basis of her outstanding high school record. There she once again excelled academically, becoming a member of Phi Beta Kappa and graduating first among the women in her class. A constitutional law course piqued Ginsburg's interest, but—as she wrote to a cousin during her junior year of college—she had "deep doubts" about whether she had sufficient aptitude for a career in the law.

One person who believed she had the requisite aptitude was Martin Ginsburg, a fellow Cornell student who was one year ahead of Ruth. Martin had his own legal ambitions—encouraged by Ruth, as he encouraged hers—and entered Harvard Law School during Ruth's senior year at Cornell. Following her graduation from college in 1954, the two were married. Although opposites in many ways—he gregarious and warm, she reserved and measured in her speech—the couple respected each other's talents and supported each other's dreams.

Their plans were interrupted by the Korean War, then winding down, which forced them to relocate to Fort Sill, Oklahoma, shortly after their wedding. There Martin took up his duties as an artillery officer, while Ruth secured a job with a nearby Social Security office. When she started work, she told the office supervisor that she was pregnant. As a result, he decided she was unfit to travel to Baltimore for a training session, and she was assigned to a lower-paying job. Although Ginsburg did not yet consider herself a feminist, this early brush with gender discrimination left its mark.

In 1956, after nearly two years in Oklahoma, the Ginsburgs—now including daughter Jane, born the previous year—arrived in Cambridge, Massachusetts, where Martin resumed his studies at Harvard Law School and Ruth began hers. One of only nine women in a class of over five hundred, a wife, and mother of a fourteen-month-old as well, Ruth might justifiably have found law school overwhelming. But thanks to her own drive and intellect—and to her husband's willingness to share equally in childcare and domestic responsibilities—she not only stayed afloat but rose to the top. After her first year she was invited to join the law review.

Ruth Bader Ginsburg was photographed with her daughter Jane (age ten) shortly before the birth of her son James in 1965. An assistant professor at Rutgers Law School, Ginsburg felt compelled to hide her pregnancy from her employer for fear of losing her job.

Further challenges still awaited her. During Ruth's second year of law school her husband was diagnosed with a cancerous condition that was usually fatal. While he underwent surgery and radiation, Ruth kept up with her classes and law review work, and collected notes from able students in her husband's courses. She edited and typed the notes, along with Martin's third-year paper. Amazingly, he not only recovered but graduated with his class, getting the highest grades he had ever achieved. In the spring of his last year at Harvard, he accepted an offer from a law firm in New York City, and Ruth transferred to Columbia Law School, where she graduated tied for first in her class.

Despite her stellar academic credentials, Ginsburg had a difficult time finding a job. Not a single New York law firm was willing to hire her, apparently—as Ginsburg has speculated—because of her status as "a Jew, a woman, and a mother to boot." With the aid of her teacher, Gerald Gun-

ther, Ginsburg eventually secured a clerkship with Judge Edmund L. Palmieri of the federal district court in Manhattan and threw herself into her work, determined to prove that a wife and mother could handle the job. Twenty years later, Judge Palmieri rated her among the best law clerks he had ever had. During her clerkship, one of Ginsburg's Harvard Law School professors recommended her for a Supreme Court clerkship with Justice Felix Frankfurter, but then told her the justice was unwilling to take a chance on a woman who had a five-year-old child and a husband not far removed from a bout of cancer.

After the two-year clerkship ended Ginsburg became a research associate on a comparative law project sponsored by Columbia Law School. Ginsburg was assigned the task of studying Sweden's system of civil procedure, which required her to learn Swedish and spend time there observing the operation of Swedish courts. While abroad, she was struck by the progress Swedish women had made in the workforce as compared to their American counterparts. It was this experience, she later said, that "first stirred feminist feelings" in her. Ginsburg ultimately became associate director of the comparative law project, and coauthored a book on Sweden's judicial system. She also translated into English, together with her coauthor, Anders Bruzelius, Sweden's Code of Judicial Procedure.

In 1963 Ginsburg joined the faculty of Rutgers Law School in Newark, New Jersey, a job she would keep for the next nine years. The second woman on the faculty, she felt sufficiently insecure about her position that when she became pregnant with her second child—James, born in 1965—she hid her condition from her dean and colleagues. James was a lively child and Ginsburg told his school that when the teachers needed to contact a parent about a problem, they should alternate calls between mother and father rather than routinely calling only the mother.

Ginsburg's personal experience with gender issues came to coalesce with a professional interest in the subject. After reading Simone de Beauvoir's *The Second Sex* in the early sixties, Ginsburg began to see sex discrimination as a societal problem: women were routinely being denied choices and opportunities that were open to men. In response to requests from her students, Ginsburg began reading cases and law journals to prepare a course on sex discrimination. She was surprised to find that there was little to research. Equality issues were rarely litigated, and legal scholars had given them little attention.

All that was soon to change, however. After passage of the 1964 Civil Rights Act there was federal legislation on the books prohibiting employment discrimination on the basis of gender as well as race. The problem was enforcing it. The New Jersey chapter of the American Civil Liberties Union (ACLU), like ACLU chapters across the country, was beginning to hear from women who felt they had been victims of discrimination. And many of these cases—including one on behalf of a school teacher involuntarily placed on unpaid maternity leave when her pregnancy began to show—were referred to Ginsburg for litigation.

Ginsburg soon joined forces with the national office of the ACLU to launch a campaign to secure greater legal recognition of women's rights and equal citizenship stature. At the time, the Supreme Court had long held that discrimination on the basis of race was constitutionally "suspect"—that is, the Court would view such legislation with what amounted to a presumption that it was unconstitutional. But legislation that treated women differently from men—whether disadvantaging women or giving them special benefits—was accorded no such "heightened scrutiny." The Supreme Court had upheld legislation exempting women from jury duty, restricting working hours for women but not for men, and forbidding women to work as bartenders. Ginsburg saw that

part of her task was to convince the courts that such "protective" legislation was doing women no favors. Rather, it was perpetuating a stereotype of women as the weaker, dependent sex, and thereby limiting their opportunities and choices.

In 1971 Ginsburg and the ACLU helped to win a landmark victory in a Supreme Court case called *Reed v. Reed,* which involved an Idaho statute that disfavored women as administrators of estates of the deceased. For the first time ever, the Court struck down legislation on the ground that it unconstitutionally discriminated against women. Although Boise, Idaho, attorney Allen Derr argued the case, Ginsburg, together with ACLU legal director Melvin Wulf, wrote the brief, aided by law students from New York University, Rutgers, and Yale. On the strength of the victory in *Reed,* the ACLU established a Women's Rights Project (WRP) in 1972. Ginsburg agreed to serve as codirector during the project's first year. She was to research and argue cases for the WRP, while the other codirector, Brenda Feigen Fasteau, managed the project's day-to-day operations.

At the same time, Ginsburg left Rutgers to become the first tenured woman professor at Columbia Law School, where she taught civil procedure, conflict of laws, constitutional law, and sex discrimination law. Part of her arrangement with the school was that she would devote half her hours in the 1972–1973 academic year to the WRP. Thereafter, she served as counsel to the project. Through it all, she successfully continued to juggle family and professional responsibilities. Diane Zimmerman, one of her former Columbia students and now a law professor herself, has recalled that the few other women teaching law at the time had often chosen not to have families. "These women were awe-inspiring," she said, "but not people we would have felt comfortable emulating. . . . [By contrast,] we had Ruth Ginsburg, who had kids she liked to talk about, a husband that she loved and admired, who was accessible to us as a model for the possibility of being a woman and not having to engage in those strategies if they weren't comfortable for us."

At the WRP, Ginsburg was carefully orchestrating a legal campaign. Her goal was to convince the Supreme Court that gender discrimination, similar to race discrimination, was generally prohibited by the Equal Protection Clause of the Constitution. She drew inspiration from Thurgood Marshall, who had successfully led the NAACP Legal Defense Fund's fight against racial segregation. Like Marshall, Ginsburg adopted a gradual approach: bringing the easier cases first, trying to choose clear winners, and building incrementally on each victory. One of her ACLU colleagues recalls Ginsburg's insisting that the WRP develop the law "one step at a time. . . . Don't ask them to go too far too fast, or you'll lose what you might have won. She often said, 'It's not time for that case.'"

To underscore her point that even legislation ostensibly benefiting women was in fact perpetuating stereotypes that harmed both sexes, Ginsburg often provided representation in cases involving male plaintiffs. One case particularly close to her heart was *Weinberger v. Wiesenfeld,* which involved a young widower, Stephen Wiesenfeld, whose wife had died in childbirth. Wiesenfeld wanted to work only part time so he could care personally for his infant son. Because he was a man, however, he was ineligible to receive the Social Security benefits that would enable him to do so. Ginsburg won the case, which she later said "epitomized for me all that we were doing in the 70's."

Between 1972 and 1979 Ginsburg argued six cases before the Supreme Court and filed petitions for review and amicus curiae briefs in many more. Her calm, deliberative speaking style served her well in oral argument. Those who were present during her arguments observed that the

justices would "[sit] up straight when she spoke," and she lost only one of the cases she argued. Guiding Ginsburg through the thickets of these arguments—when several justices at once may pepper an advocate with tough questions—was the memory of her mother. Ginsburg has said that her mother continually admonished her to "be a lady," by which she meant "hold fast to your convictions and self-respect. . . , but don't snap back in anger."

A high point in Ginsburg's efforts was *Craig v. Boren,* a 1976 decision holding that sex discrimination warranted review under an "intermediate" standard of scrutiny. In effect, the Court ruled that gender-based legislation would not be as difficult to defend as legislation based on race, but it would be far harder to defend than legislation based on some "non-suspect" criterion such as intelligence or age. Ginsburg did not argue *Craig,* but she filed an influential amicus brief, and sat beside counsel for the prevailing parties at the argument.

By 1980 Ginsburg had developed a national reputation based on both her academic work and the cases she had litigated for the WRP. That year, President Jimmy Carter nominated her to fill a vacancy on the United States Court of Appeals for the District of Columbia Circuit, one of the highest-profile federal courts in the country. The Ginsburgs relocated to Washington, D.C., where Martin, who had been teaching and practicing tax law in New York, is now a professor at Georgetown University Law Center and also maintains an "of counsel" relationship to a law firm with a D.C. office.

While the shift from partisan advocate to impartial member of the judiciary might have been difficult for some, for Ginsburg—with her cautious, deliberative temperament—the transition appears to have been smooth. During her thirteen-year tenure on the Court of Appeals, she displayed, in the words of legal commentator Jeffrey Rosen, "an affinity for resolving cases on narrow procedural grounds rather than appealing to broad principles of social justice; a preference for small steps over sweeping gestures; and an aversion to bold assertions of judicial power." Defying critics who predicted that her decisions would reflect her liberal, activist past, Ginsburg sometimes sided with the conservative members of the Court of Appeals. "One of the most sacred duties of a judge," she said, "is not to read her convictions into the Constitution."

Among Ginsburg's notable majority opinions for the Court of Appeals are *Abourezk v. Reagan* (1986) and *Walker v. Jones* (1984). In *Abourezk* Ginsburg parsed the complexities of the Immigration and Nationality Act to determine that the act did not authorize the denial of visas to aliens invited to address United States audiences, on college campuses or elsewhere, based solely on the State Department's view that the mere presence of the alien in this country would be detrimental to national security. *Walker* held members of Congress accountable for denying equal pay to a woman hired to supervise the House of Representatives' restaurant facilities. Ginsburg's pursuit of doctrinal clarity within the constraints of prior court decisions, evident in her *Abourezk* and *Walker* opinions, is equally evident in many other opinions, among them her delineation of copyright law as applied to commissioned works in *Community for Creative Non-Violence v. Reid* (1988), and her explanation of the concept of standing to sue in *Dellums v. U. S. Nuclear Regulatory Comm'n* (1988) (dissenting opinion).

Ginsburg's vision of the judge's role is grounded in her awareness of cases' contexts. Ginsburg, one former law clerk has said, "looks at the world as a collection of particulars. . . . She likes to look at larger questions through the lens of smaller stories of people's lives." In an effort to give her law clerks a sense of the real-world effects of judicial decisions, she periodically led them on tours of the local detention facilities where some of the criminal defendants who figured in D. C. Circuit cases were incarcerated. Her practical orientation also shows in her concern that law and legal process be transparent both to participants in particular cases and to the public. For example, in a concurring opinion in *Tavoulareas v. Washington Post* (1987), Ginsburg laid out detailed guidance for trial court judges on how to arm juries to understand and accurately apply libel law.

By virtue of her careful drafting of opinions and her sensitivity to doctrinal nuance, Ginsburg gained the respect of her colleagues on the Court of Appeals. She also developed a reputation as a judge who could forge a consensus in difficult or divisive cases. A former clerk has described Ginsburg as someone who "knows how to disagree without being disagreeable and has mastered the art so well she pulls people her way."

In 1993 Justice Byron R. White retired from the Supreme Court, creating the first opportunity in twenty-six years for a Democratic president to fill a Supreme Court vacancy. At the beginning of his search for a replacement, President Bill Clinton announced that he was looking for someone with "a fine mind, good judgment, wide experience in the law and the problems of real people, and someone with a big heart." Because several of his nominations to other top government posts had already foundered as a result of embarrassing revelations about the nominees, Clinton also wanted to choose someone beyond reproach—a sure-fire winner, or, as he put it, someone who would make people "stand up and say, 'Wow.'"

After a three-month search Clinton finally settled on Ginsburg, calling her "the Thurgood Marshall of gender equality law." He also noted that she had been "a force for consensus-building" on the Court of Appeals and predicted that she would serve the same crucial function on the Supreme Court.

After winning easy confirmation in the Senate, Ruth Bader Ginsburg was applauded by Chief Justice William H. Rehnquist and President Bill Clinton at her swearing-in ceremony in 1993.

As might have been expected, criticism of Ginsburg's nomination came from conservatives who were still—despite her record on the Court of Appeals—suspicious of her past as a feminist crusader. But opposition also came from a less expected quarter: the feminist movement itself. In part this was a result of the emergence of a "second wave" of feminists, who perhaps misunderstood Ginsburg's philosophy that the law should treat men and women as persons of equal stature and dignity. But another reason some feminists opposed Ginsburg's elevation to the Supreme Court was that she had publicly expressed doubts about the Court's reasoning in *Roe v. Wade,* the 1973 case in which the Court had given constitutional protection to a woman's right to choose to have an abortion.

Ginsburg had criticized the Court's opinion in *Roe* in a 1993 lecture in part on the ground that it had gotten ahead of public opinion on the abortion issue. State legislatures in the 1970s were beginning to liberalize their abortion laws, she pointed out. Had the Supreme Court merely struck down the

statute at issue in *Roe,* instead of going on to construct an elaborate trimester-based scheme, the process of legislative liberalization might have continued gradually, without the political divisions engendered by the Court's decision.

In accepting the nomination during a White House Rose Garden ceremony on June 14, 1993, Ginsburg articulated her philosophy of judging, borrowing a phrase from Chief Justice William H. Rehnquist: "A judge is bound to decide each case fairly, in accord with the relevant facts and the applicable law, even when the decision is, as he put it, not the one the home crowd wants." She also expressed her gratitude to the social forces and the individuals that had made it possible for her to attain the position in which she found herself. She was indebted, she said, to "a revived women's movement in the 1970s that opened doors for people like me, [and] to the civil rights movement of the 1960s from which the women's movement drew inspiration." She also thanked her husband, who had been her "best friend and biggest booster"; her mother-in-law, Evelyn Ginsburg, "the most supportive parent a person could have"; and her grown children, who had had "the taste to appreciate that Daddy cooks ever so much better than Mommy, and so phased me out of the kitchen at a relatively early age." She saved a final expression of appreciation for her mother, Celia Bader, "the bravest, strongest person I have known, who was taken from me much too soon." She continued, "I pray that I may be all that she would have been, had she lived in an age when women could aspire and achieve, and daughters are cherished as much as sons."

Easily winning confirmation in the Senate on a vote of 96 to 3, Ginsburg took the oath of office on August 10, 1993. Ginsburg's record on the Supreme Court thus far has been characterized as one of "judicial minimalism": restrained, cautious, and non-ideological. Ginsburg has garnered this reputation because many of the majority opinions she has authored centered on procedural questions. In such cases, she could draw on knowledge gained in teaching civil procedure for seventeen years, and on her keen eye for the detail that leads to the just resolution of a complex case. To characterize Ginsburg's jurisprudence solely from these majority opinions is misleading, however, because she does not choose the cases she writes for the Court, but is assigned by a senior colleague to write them to carry out the consensus reached at the Court's conference. More revealing are Ginsburg's separate writings, in which she employs her trademark clarity and analytical sophistication in the service of core principles of fairness and equality.

Among Ginsburg's significant dissents are those dealing with reliability and notice in the criminal process. In her first term, Ginsburg dissented from the Court's decision in *Romano v. Oklahoma.* The majority held that disclosing to a jury in the capital sentencing phase of a defendant's trial the information that a prior jury had already sentenced the defendant to death did not infect the jury's life-or-death deliberations. Revealing this information to the jury, Ginsburg thought, created a constitutionally unacceptable risk that the jurors would believe the defendant's fate was not fully their responsibility. Her concern for the fairness of the criminal process is similarly reflected in a variety of cases, including two more recent dissents, *Muscarello v. United States* and *Portuondo v. Agard,* in which Ginsburg objected to the Court's failure to resolve textual ambiguities in favor of criminal defendants.

The most notable of Ginsburg's separate writings show that she has never retreated from the vision of an equal opportunity society characteristic of her legal career. In opinions addressing issues ranging from school desegregation (*Missouri v. Jenkins*) to affirmative action (*Adarand v. Pena*) to legislative redistricting (*Miller v. Johnson*), Gins-

burg has shown her awareness of the long history and persistence of racial discrimination and the importance of allowing legislatures, state and federal, to adopt remedial measures to counteract the lingering effects of discrimination.

Ginsburg's best-known opinion for the Court, *United States v. Virginia,* is of a piece with her separate writings and with her legal advocacy for the WRP. This important gender discrimination case raised the very same equal protection issue Ginsburg had several times presented to the Supreme Court as an advocate. Now sitting on the Court, she wrote for a solid majority that the 150-year-old male-only admissions policy at Virginia Military Institute (VMI) violated the equal protection principle. The fact that most women (and men) were unable or unwilling to endure VMI's rigorous program was irrelevant, Ginsburg reasoned; rather, the focus must be on the exceptional woman who was both able and willing. The Court emphasized that governmental sex discrimination will be held unconstitutional unless it is supported by "an exceedingly persuasive justification." As Professor Kenneth Karst has written, the VMI decision brought to fruition Ginsburg's constant endeavor at the WRP: to establish that official sex discrimination should be subjected to exacting judicial scrutiny of its asserted justifications, and that asserted justifications based on generalized assumptions about "the way men or women are" will not pass that scrutiny.

In general, Ginsburg's performance as a justice has been consistent with her record as a judge: meticulous attention to detail, analytical rigor, and clarity of expression. She has also been an active participant during oral argument. In some ways, Justice Ginsburg has departed from Supreme Court tradition. She furnished her chambers, a large suite of rooms on the second floor, with modern art, beige curtains, and chrome-and-glass furniture from her D. C. Circuit office. More significantly, Ginsburg agreed to a flexible

Passionate about opera, Justice Ruth Bader Ginsburg (left) appeared in period costume in a 1986 production by the Washington Opera Company. Justice Antonin Scalia (right) also moonlighted as an extra.

schedule for one of her first-term law clerks—a man who needed time off during the day to care for his two grade school age children, because his wife had a demanding job as an economist. "I thought, 'This is my dream of the way the world should be,'" Ginsburg said, explaining her decision. "When fathers take equal responsibility for the care of their children, that's when women will truly be liberated."

Justice Ginsburg was diagnosed with colorectal cancer in September 1999, but was able to take her place on the bench for the Court's opening session a mere three weeks after her surgery. While Ginsburg's conscientious work habits are legendary (she has been known to work in taxis on the way to the theater and to read her mail by flashlight during previews at the movies), she does find time for relaxation. She enjoys reading novels, biographies, and mysteries; water-skiing and horseback-riding; and excursions with her children and grandchildren. And she has a passion for opera. Not only is she a loyal fan of the Washington Opera, she has even appeared on stage, in full period costume, as an extra.

GLOSSARY

ABOLITIONIST.   An opponent of slavery.

ABRIDGED.   Diminished or reduced.

ACT.   A written law that has been passed by Congress.

ACTIONABLE.   Subject to, or affording ground for, a law suit.

ADJUDICATION.   An act of judgment by a court.

ADVOCATE.   An attorney who speaks for the cause of another in court.

AFFIRM.   To uphold a decision of a lower court.

AFFIRMATIVE ACTION.   Steps taken by an organization to remedy past discrimination in hiring, promotion, or education; for example, by recruiting minorities and women.

ALIENAGE.   The status of being born in a foreign country.

ALIMONY.   An allowance made to one spouse by the other for support pending or after legal separation or divorce.

ALLEGATION.   An accusation that has not been proven.

ALLEGE.   Assert without proof or before proving.

AMENDMENT.   An addition or change to the U.S. Constitution.

AMICUS CURIAE.   Latin for "friend of the court." A person or group, not a party to a case, who submits views (usually in the form of written briefs called amicus briefs) on how the case should be decided.

ANTITRUST.   A kind of law that protects trade and commerce from unlawful restraints and monopolies or unfair business practices.

APPEAL.   The procedure by which a case is taken to a superior court for a review of the lower court's decision.

APPEALS COURT.   (*See* Courts of appeals.)

APPELLANT.   The party who appeals a lower court's decision to a higher court and who is usually seeking reversal of that decision.

APPELLATE COURT.   A court with jurisdiction to review decisions of lower courts.

APPELLEE.   The party responding to an appeal and generally seeking to affirm the lower court's decision.

ARBITRARY.   Unreasonable, capricious; not done in accordance with established legal principles.

ARGUMENT, or ORAL ARGUMENT.   The oral presentation of a case to supplement the arguments presented in the written briefs. Advocates are usually allotted one half-hour to argue their case before the Supreme Court.

ATTORNEY GENERAL. The chief law enforcement officer of the United States.

BAR, or BAR ASSOCIATION. An organization of lawyers qualified or licensed to practice in a certain jurisdiction.

BENEFICIARY. The person designated to receive the income of a trust estate.

BILL. A draft of a proposed law being considered by a legislature.

BILL OF RIGHTS. The first ten amendments to the Constitution guaranteeing citizens basic constitutional rights and liberties.

BONA FIDE OCCUPATIONAL QUALIFICATION (BFOQ). An employment requirement that is reasonably necessary to the normal operation of a particular business or enterprise.

BRIEF. A document prepared by an attorney as the basis for an argument in court, setting out the facts of, and the legal arguments in support of, the case.

BURDEN OF PROOF. The duty of proving a disputed assertion or charge in a lawsuit by showing that the weight of the evidence is on one party's side.

CASE. A legal dispute or controversy brought to a court for resolution.

CERTIORARI, WRIT OF. An order from an appellate court to an inferior court to send up the records of a case that the appellate court has elected to review. This is the primary method by which the Supreme Court exercises its discretionary jurisdiction to accept appeals for a full hearing. The Supreme Court grants certiorari (or "cert" in the vernacular) in less than 1 percent of cases that are appealed from federal and state appeals courts. "Certiorari" is Latin for "to be more fully informed."

CIRCUIT COURT. (See Courts of appeals.)

CIVIL LAW. All law that does not involve criminal matters. Civil law usually deals with private rights of individuals, groups, or businesses.

CIVIL SUIT, or CIVIL ACTION. A lawsuit brought by one or more individuals against another person, a business, or the government.

CLASS ACTION. A lawsuit brought by one or more persons who represent themselves and all others similarly situated.

CLAUSE. A paragraph, sentence, or phrase in a legal document or in the Constitution.

COMMON LAW. The body of law that develops over time from custom and from judgments of courts, as opposed to statutory law, which is written by legislatures. Sometimes called case law.

COMPARABLE WORTH. A legal theory that women in traditional female jobs should be paid the same as men in traditional male jobs when the two kinds of work involve comparable skill, effort, or responsibility.

COMPENSATORY DAMAGES. A monetary award, equivalent to the loss sustained, to be paid to the injured party by the party at fault.

COMPLAINT. The first legal document filed in a civil lawsuit. It includes a statement of the wrong or harm done to the plaintiff by the defendant and a request for a specific remedy from the court.

CONCURRING OPINION, or CONCURRENCE. An opinion that agrees with the result reached by the majority (the judgment), but that demonstrates a different analysis or gives the law or facts a different emphasis in reaching that result.

CONFERENCE. The justices' weekly meetings in a private conference room during which they secretly deliberate cases as well as other business before the Court. Conferences are held on Wednesday and Friday afternoons during weeks that arguments are heard.

CONTEMPT OF COURT. Any act to embarrass, hinder, or obstruct the court in the administration of justice.

CONTRACT. To contract is to make a legal agreement. A contract is a legally enforceable agreement between two or more people to take a certain action in exchange for payment in some form.

CONVICTION. Final judgment or sentence that the defendant is guilty as charged.

COUNSEL. A lawyer engaged in the trial or management of a case in court.

COUNSEL OF RECORD. The lawyer who appears for a party in a lawsuit and who is entitled to receive, on the party's behalf, all pleadings and other formal documents from the court.

COURTS OF APPEALS. The intermediate level appellate courts in the federal system having jurisdiction over particular regions known as circuits. Also called circuit courts. Decisions and verdicts of the United States District Courts are appealed to the United States Circuit Courts of Appeals, where cases are decided by judges, not juries.

COVERTURE. The condition of women during marriage prior to the late nineteenth century whereby they were legally "covered," or protected, by their husbands. As such, women's legal rights were suspended.

DAMAGES. Compensation in money imposed by law for loss or injury.

DECISION. The formal outcome of a case as decided by the court.

DEED. A signed and usually sealed document containing some legal transfer, bargain, or contract.

DEFENDANT. In a civil action, the party denying or defending itself against charges brought by the plaintiff. In a criminal action, the person indicted for the commission of a crime.

DICTA, OR OBITER DICTA. Statements by a judge or justice expressing an opinion and included with, but not essential to, an opinion resolving a case before the court. Dicta are not necessarily binding in future cases.

DISENFRANCHISEMENT. The act of depriving someone of the right to vote.

DISPARATE IMPACT. The adverse effect of a facially neutral employment practice that nonetheless discriminates against applicants for hire or promotion.

DISPARATE TREATMENT. A type of employment practice that intentionally discriminates on the basis of race, sex, age, national origin, or disability.

DISSENTING OPINION, or DISSENT. A formal written expression by a justice who has a different point of view on major or minor issues in a case and that rejects the result reached by the majority.

DISTRICT COURTS. The trial courts of general jurisdiction in the federal system. United States district courts make findings of fact and law in civil cases and render verdicts in criminal cases.

DOCKET. A calendar listing cases set to be tried.

DUE PROCESS. Government procedures based on fair and regular principles. The Fifth and Fourteenth Amendments guarantee persons that they will not be deprived of life, liberty, or property by the government until fair and usual procedures have been followed.

DUE PROCESS CLAUSE. Clause of the Fifth and Fourteenth Amendments declaring that no person may be deprived of life, liberty, or property without due process of law.

EN BANC. With all judges present and participating.

ENFRANCHISE. To be granted the right to vote.

EQUAL PROTECTION CLAUSE. Clause of the Fourteenth Amendment declaring that no person can be denied the equal protection of the laws. This clause has been interpreted to mean that no individual or class of individuals can be denied rights enjoyed by others who exist in similar circumstances except under narrow conditions.

EQUITY.   Law based on principles of fairness rather than on strictly applied statutes.

EXECUTIVE BRANCH.   The administrative branch of government that includes a chief executive (e.g., the president), executive offices, and agencies that carry out the laws.

FACIAL DISCRIMINATION.   Discrimination that is explicit or intentional.

FACIALLY.   Explicitly.

FEDERAL.   Relating to the federal government as opposed to state government.

FEDERALISM.   The system of divided and allocated powers between the states and the federal government.

FIAT.   A decree or authoritative order.

GENDER.   Sex.

GENDER-BASED CLASSIFICATIONS.   Laws that classify or treat men and women differently.

GOVERN.   To serve as a precedent or deciding principle.

GRAND JURY.   Group of twelve to twenty-three persons impaneled to hear, in private, evidence presented by the state against an individual or persons accused of a criminal act to determine if the accused should be formally charged with a crime.

HEARING ON THE MERITS.   Presentation of the central issues in a case.

HEIGHTENED SCRUTINY,   also called the INTER-MEDIATE STANDARD OF SCRUTINY,   or the MIDDLE-TIER STANDARD OF SCRUTINY.   The standard of review used by the federal courts for gender-based classifications under which the party seeking to uphold a statute that classifies individuals on the basis of their gender must carry the burden of showing an "exceedingly persuasive justification" for the classification. This burden is met only by demonstrating that the classification serves "important governmental objectives" and that the discriminatory means employed are "sub-

stantially related to the achievement of those objectives."

HOLDING.   The legal principal underlying a court decision; it is the part of the decision that is legally binding as precedent on subsequent similar cases.

HOSTILE WORK ENVIRONMENT.   A type of sexual harassment where the victim is not threatened with retaliation by the harasser but is nonetheless subjected to harassment that is sufficiently severe and pervasive as to create a hostile work environment.

INDICTED.   A person is indicted when he or she is charged with specified offenses.

INDICTMENT.   A formal written statement, based on evidence presented by the prosecutor, from a jury. Decided by a majority vote, an indictment charges one or more persons of specific crimes.

INFERIOR COURT.   (*See* Lower court.)

INFRINGE.   To encroach upon in a way that violates the law.

INJUNCTION.   An order from a court commanding or preventing a specific action.

INTERMEDIATE STANDARD.   (*See* Heightened scrutiny.)

INVIDIOUS DISCRIMINATION.   A type of discrimination that is offensive or objectionable because it involves prejudice or stereotyping.

JUDICIAL BRANCH.   The portion of government that interprets laws and judges legal questions.

JUDICIAL BYPASS.   A procedure by which a pregnant minor who does not wish to obtain parental consent for an abortion may appear before a judge and ask the court's permission to terminate the pregnancy.

JUDGMENT OF THE COURT.   The final ruling of a court, independent of the legal reasoning supporting it.

JURISDICTION. The power of a court to hear a case in question, which exists when the proper parties are present and when the point to be decided is within the issues authorized to be handled by the particular court.

JURISDICTIONAL STATEMENT. An appellant may appeal a case to the Supreme Court directly from a federal district court by filing a jurisdictional statement explaining why the case merits Supreme Court review.

JUROR. A member of a jury.

JURY. A body of men and women selected to examine certain facts and determine the truth in a legal proceeding.

JURY DUTY. A citizen's obligation to serve on a jury.

JURY POOL. The group of citizens summoned for jury duty from which the attorneys will select a jury panel.

JURY SELECTION. The process of deciding which of the citizens summoned to compose the jury pool will be selected to actually serve as jurors on the panel.

JURY SERVICE. The act of serving as a juror.

LEGISLATION. Laws or statutes enacted by a legislature.

LEGISLATIVE BRANCH. The portion of government that passes the laws.

LEGISLATURE. A body of persons having the power to make laws.

LEGITIMATE. To legitimize a child born out of wedlock.

LIABILITY. Legal responsibility.

LITIGANT. A person or group engaged in a lawsuit.

LITIGATE. To carry on a legal contest by judicial process.

LITIGATION. The judicial process by which a legal contest or lawsuit is carried out.

LOWER COURT. A court that ranks below another in the appellate system and from which cases are appealed to a superior court. All courts below the U.S. Supreme Court are lower courts.

LYCEUM. An association providing public lectures.

MAJORITY OPINION, or OPINION OF THE COURT. An opinion joined by a majority of the nine justices explaining the legal basis for the Court's decision and regarded as binding precedent in future decisions.

MANDAMUS. Latin for "we command." An order issued from a superior court directing a lower court or other authority to perform a particular act.

MANSLAUGHTER. The killing of a person without malice or premeditation, but during the commission of an illegal act.

MERITS. The central issues of a case.

MIDDLE-TIER STANDARD. (*See* Heightened scrutiny.)

MINOR. A person who has not yet reached the age of majority.

MONOPOLY. A person or group having exclusive ownership over a specific commodity.

MOOT. Unsettled or undecided. A question presented in a lawsuit that cannot be answered by a court either because the issue has resolved itself or conditions have changed so that the court is unable to grant the requested relief.

MOTION. A request made to a court for a certain ruling or action.

MOTION FOR ADMISSION. To recommend an applicant for admission to the bar. Prior to 1970 admission to the Supreme Court bar was granted only after an appearance by the applicant in person or on oral motion in open court. Today most applicants obtain admission on written motion, without either the applicant or the movants (two are required) appearing personally in Court.

OPINION. The formal opinion by a judge or court of the legal reasons and principles upon which a decision is based.

ORAL ARGUMENT. (*See* Argument.)

ORDINANCE. Local law enacted by a city, suburb, town, municipality, or other local entity.

ORIGINAL ACTION. A case brought directly to the Supreme Court without first having been heard in lower court.

PAROLE. A conditional release of a prisoner serving an unexpired sentence.

PARTY. A person or group of persons involved in a lawsuit.

PER CURIAM. An unsigned or collectively written opinion issued by a court.

PEREMPTORY CHALLENGE, or PEREMPTORY STRIKE. The act of excusing a prospective juror during the pretrial jury selection in which each side is given the right to dismiss a certain number of potential jurors without giving a reason.

PETIT JURY. A body of citizens who sit to review evidence and testimony in order to try to reach a unanimous verdict on questions of the fact in criminal and civil proceedings. Traditionally, juries were composed of twelve citizens; since 1970 the Supreme Court has upheld the legality of state juries with fewer than twelve persons. Also known as a trial court jury.

PETITION. A formal written request.

PLAINTIFF. The injured party in a civil case who brings an action against the alleged wrongdoer. The party who brings the original suit in a state or federal court.

PLURALITY. An opinion announcing the judgment of a court with supporting reasoning that is not endorsed by a majority of the judges participating.

PRECEDENT. A previously decided case that may be used as the basis for ruling on a current similar case.

PRIVILEGES AND IMMUNITIES CLAUSE. Clause of the Fourteenth Amendment stating that "No State shall make or enforce any law which shall abridge the privileges and immunities of citizens of the United States."

PROBATE. The process of proving to a court that a will is genuine and distributing the property according to the terms of the will.

PRO SE. A Latin term meaning "for oneself" or "on one's own behalf," which is typically used to describe a person who represents him- or herself in court (without an attorney).

PROVISION. A clause in a statute.

PUNITIVE DAMAGES. A monetary award (separate from compensatory damages) imposed by a court for punishment purposes to be paid by the party at fault to the injured party.

QUID QUO PRO. A Latin term meaning something given or received for something else. A type of sexual harassment where the victim is threatened with retaliation in terms of a change in employment or academic status if he or she does not submit to the harasser.

RATIONAL BASIS TEST, RATIONALITY TEST, or the REASONABLENESS STANDARD. The most lenient standard of judicial review, requiring only that the law in question have a basis in reason and serve a "legitimate" governmental objective beyond mere administrative convenience. A classification that is reviewed under this standard is presumed to be constitutional, which means it is up to the party challenging the law to prove that it is irrational or arbitrary.

REAL PROPERTY. Land and all items attached to it such as houses and crops.

RECUSE. The action of a judge not to participate in a case because of conflict of interest or other disqualifying condition.

REGULATION. Rule made by a government agency.

RELIEF. The monetary benefit or other restitution that a court in a civil suit grants to a party that has suffered loss or injury.

RESPONDENT. The party answering to a petition for review in court. Appellee.

REVERSE. An action by an appellate court setting aside or changing a decision of a lower court.

RULING. The outcome of a court's decision either on some point of law or on the case as a whole.

SCRUTINY. The level of review under the Equal Protection Clause that federal courts apply to classifications that distinguish on the basis of race, gender, age, national origin, or other characteristics.

Rational Basis Scrutiny (least suspect)	Intermediate or Heightened Scrutiny	Strict Scrutiny (most suspect)
Income Age Physical handicap Sexual orientation Many other classifications	Gender	Race Religion National origin

SENTENCE. The formal pronouncement by a court or judge in a criminal proceeding that specifies the punishment to be inflicted on the convict.

SEPARATION OF POWERS. The constitutional doctrine establishing that each of the three branches of the government—the legislative, executive, and judicial—is independent and exercises unique powers.

SEXUAL HARASSMENT. Unwanted sexual conduct, sometimes including promises or threats, that either 1) creates a hostile learning or workplace environment, or 2) involves express or implied conditions in which rejection of or submission to such conduct will affect the victim's employment or academic status.

SIMILARLY SITUATED. Two groups of people are similarly situated if they exist in similar circumstances with respect to the objectives of the legislation in question.

SOLICITOR GENERAL. The attorney who serves under the attorney general and who represents the United States in cases coming before the Supreme Court.

STANDING. The right of parties to bring legal action because they are directly affected by the legal issues raised.

STATUTE. A law passed by a federal or state legislature.

STATUTORY. Relating to a statute.

STATUTORY RAPE. The act of unlawful sexual intercourse with a person who is under the age of consent, even if he or she is a willing and voluntary participant in the sexual act.

STAY. A court order issued to stop or suspend a judicial proceeding while some related matter is resolved.

STRICT SCRUTINY. The highest standard of review, or level of scrutiny, applied to classifications based on a characteristic that is common to a group of people. This standard presumes that the classification is unconstitutionally discriminatory unless the law's supporters are able to show that it is necessary to achieve a "compelling" governmental objective and that it achieves that objective in the least intrusive way.

SUFFRAGE. The right to vote.

SUIT. An action or process in a court for the recovery of a right or claim.

SUPREME COURT. The Supreme Court of the United States, which is composed of one chief justice and eight associate justices, is the highest court in the United States. The Supreme Court is charged with ruling on appeals from the United States Circuit Courts of Appeal and from state supreme courts. The Court also functions as a trial court in specified disputes, including those that occur between states.

SUSPECT CLASSIFICATION. When a given law denies equal protection to individuals based on their race, national origin, or religion, it creates a suspect classification, or suspect category. *Strict scrutiny* is applied to suspect classifications.

TEMPERANCE. Moderation or abstinence in the use of alcoholic beverages.

TERM. The Supreme Court term begins on the first Monday in October and the justices hear oral arguments through late April. The Court continues to announce opinions and hand down orders, as it has been doing throughout the term, in May, June, and sometimes into July. Following the announcement of its last opinion in cases that have been argued during the term, the Court rises for its summer recess.

THREE-JUDGE COURT. A special federal court made up of appellate and trial court judges created to expedite the processing of certain issues made eligible for such priority treatment by congressional statute.

TORT. An injury or wrong to the person or property of another.

TRUST. A property interest held by one person for the benefit of another.

WARRANT. A judicial order authorizing an arrest or search and seizure.

WRIT. A judicial order of a court commanding the recipient to perform or not to perform certain specified acts.

TIMELINES

TIMELINE OF MAJOR CASES

Slaughter-House Cases (1873)
Bradwell v. Illinois (1873)
Minor v. Happersett (1875)
Strauder v. West Virginia (1880)
Lochner v. New York (1905)
Muller v. Oregon (1908)
Adkins v. Children's Hospital of D.C. (1923)
Buck v. Bell (1927)
West Coast Hotel Co. v. Parrish (1937)
Ballard v. United States (1946)
Goesaert v. Cleary (1948)
Poe v. Ullman (1961)
Hoyt v. Florida (1961)
Griswold v. Connecticut (1965)
Phillips v. Martin Marietta Corp. (1971)
Reed v. Reed (1971)
Stanley v. Illinois (1972)
Eisenstadt v. Baird (1972)
Roe v. Wade (1973)
Doe v. Bolton (1973)
Frontiero v. Richardson (1973)
Corning Glass Works v. Brennan (1974)
Cleveland Board of Education v. LaFleur (1974)
Kahn v. Shevin (1974)
Geduldig v. Aiello (1974)

Schlesinger v. Ballard (1975)
Taylor v. Louisiana (1975)
Weinberger v. Wiesenfeld (1975)
Stanton v. Stanton (1975)
Planned Parenthood of Central Mo. v. Danforth (1976)
General Elec. Co. v. Gilbert (1976)
Craig v. Boren (1976)
Califano v. Webster (1977)
Califano v. Goldfarb (1977)
Maher v. Roe (1977)
Dothard v. Rawlinson (1977)
Nashville Gas Co. v. Satty (1977)
Los Angeles Department of Water and Power v. Manhart (1978)
Duren v. Missouri (1979)
Orr v. Orr (1979)
Caban v. Mohammed (1979)
Parham v. Hughes (1979)
Personnel Administrator of Mass. v. Feeney (1979)
Califano v. Westcott (1979)
Bellotti v. Baird (1979)
Wengler v. Druggists Mut. Ins. Co. (1980)
Harris v. McRae (1980)
Kirchberg v. Feenstra (1981)
Michael M. v. Superior Court of Sonoma Cty. (1981)

County of Washington v. Gunther (1981)

Rostker v. Goldberg (1981)

Mississippi Univ. for Women v. Hogan (1982)

Planned Parenthood Assn. of Kansas City, Mo., Inc. v. Ashcroft (1983)

Akron v. Akron Center for Reproductive Health (1983)

Newport News Shipbuilding & Dry Dock Co. v. EEOC (1983)

Lehr v. Robertson (1983)

Arizona Governing Committee v. Norris (1983)

Hishon v. King & Spalding (1984)

Thornburgh v. American College of Obstetricians and Gynecologists (1986)

Meritor Savings Bank v. Vinson (1986)

California Fed. Sav. & Loan Assn. v. Guerra (1987)

Johnson v. Transportation Agency, Santa Clara Cty. (1987)

Price Waterhouse v. Hopkins (1989)

Webster v. Reproductive Health Services (1989)

Hodgson v. Minnesota (1990)

Ohio v. Akron Center for Reproductive Health, Inc. (1990)

Automobile Workers v. Johnson Controls, Inc. (1991)

Rust v. Sullivan (1991)

Franklin v. Gwinnett County Public Schools (1992)

Planned Parenthood of Southeastern Pennsylvania v. Casey (1992)

Bray v. Alexandria Women's Health Center (1993)

Harris v. Forklift Systems, Inc. (1993)

National Organization for Women, Inc. v. Scheidler (1994)

J.E.B. v. Alabama ex rel. T.B. (1994)

Madsen v. Women's Health Center, Inc. (1994)

United States v. Virginia (1996)

Schenck v. Pro-Choice Network of Western New York (1997)

Oncale v. Sundowner Offshore Services, Inc. (1998)

Lorelyn Penero Miller v. Madeleine K. Albright (1998)

Gebser v. Lago Vista Independent School Dist. (1998)

Burlington Industries, Inc. v. Ellerth (1998)

Faragher v. City of Boca Raton (1998)

Davis v. Monroe County School Bd. of Ed. (1999)

Stenberg. v. Carhart (2000)

TIMELINE OF EVENTS

1828 Sarah Wetmore Story becomes the first wife of a justice to accompany her husband to Washington, D.C., for the Supreme Court term.

1839 Mississippi becomes the first state to recognize the right of women to hold property in their own names, though permission from their husbands is required.

1848 Declaration of Rights and Sentiments is adopted at the first Women's Rights Convention in Seneca Falls, N.Y.—a landmark document in the history of women's rights.

➤ New York passes Married Women's Property Act, granting married women a measure of control over their property and earnings. The act becomes a model for other states; by 1900 every state has passed similar legislation.

1852 Maximum hours of employment for women are set by law in Ohio, the first state to do so.

1868 *Chicago Legal News* is founded by Myra Bradwell.

➤ The Fourteenth Amendment is ratified by the states, federally guaranteeing newly freed slaves the right to vote, but limiting the vote to males.

1869 Elizabeth Cady Stanton and Susan B. Anthony found the National Woman Suffrage Association (NWSA), the radical, militant, women-only group of the women's suffrage movement. A more moderate group, the

American Woman Suffrage Association, is founded shortly thereafter, signaling a historic split in the American women's movement.

➤ First state (Iowa) licenses a woman, Arabella B. Mansfield, to practice law.

➤ Myra Bradwell is denied admission to the Illinois bar because she is a married woman.

1870 First woman receives law degree from an accredited institution, Union College of Law in Chicago.

➤ Wyoming becomes first state to have sexually integrated grand juries.

1873 An amendment to the 1872 Comstock Law adds birth-control information to the list of obscene materials that cannot legally be circulated by mail.

1873 Susan B. Anthony and other suffragists are tried in court for illegally voting in an election.

1878 National Woman Suffrage Association drafts a constitutional amendment prohibiting disenfranchisement because of sex and introduces it in Congress. The proposal becomes known as the Anthony Amendment, after Susan B. Anthony, the leader of the fight for suffrage.

1879 Belva Ann Lockwood becomes the first woman admitted to the Supreme Court bar.

➤ Connecticut passes a law forbidding the use or prescription by doctors of any form of contraception.

1880 Belva Ann Lockwood becomes first woman to argue a case before the Supreme Court.

1884 As the candidate of the National Equal Rights Party, Belva Ann Lockwood becomes the first woman to mount a national campaign for the presidency.

1890 National American Woman Suffrage Association (NAWSA) is founded, merging the larger, more militant, NWSA with the more conservative AWSA.

➤ Wyoming grants women the right to vote in all elections, becoming the first state to do so.

1898 Washington College of Law (now the law school at The American University), the first law school established by and for women, is founded in Washington, D.C.

1899 National Consumers' League is founded, seeking protective legislation for workers, the end of child labor, better working conditions for women, and safer consumer products.

1908 Florence Kelley and the National Consumers' League lead a campaign for state minimum wage laws for women.

1910 Lyda B. Conley becomes the first Native American woman to argue before the Supreme Court.

1912 A minimum wage law for women is adopted in Massachusetts; other states follow.

1916 Jeannette Rankin of Montana is elected to Congress, becoming its first female member.

1917 National Woman's Party leader Alice Paul and other suffragists are arrested and jailed for demonstrating outside the White House.

1920 The Nineteenth Amendment to the Constitution guaranteeing women the right to vote is ratified.

1921 Margaret Sanger founds the American Birth Control League to increase the distribution of birth control information and to provide lists of clinics and doctors willing to dispense contraceptives.

1923 Alice Paul proposes the first version of the Equal Rights Amendment in Congress. Most major women's rights organizations oppose it because it threatens labor legislation protective of women.

1925 Susan Brandeis becomes the first daughter of a justice to argue before the Supreme Court.

1926 Violette N. Anderson becomes the first African American woman admitted to the Supreme Court bar.

1933 Frances Perkins becomes the first female cabinet member when President Franklin D. Roosevelt appoints her Secretary of Labor.

➤ Prohibition is repealed; several states pass laws prohibiting women from working in bars.

1934 Florence Ellinwood Allen becomes the first female federal judge to serve on a court of general jurisdiction when President Roosevelt appoints her to the U.S. Court of Appeals for the Sixth Circuit.

1938 The Fair Labor Standards Act establishes a national minimum wage for workers of both sexes and brings substantial gains in workplace equality for women.

1940 A federal immigration law is enacted allowing American mothers, but not American fathers, the right to transmit their U.S. citizenship to children born out of wedlock in a foreign country.

1942 The National War Labor Board issues General Order No. 16 encouraging employers to pay women as much as men.

1944 Lucile Lomen becomes the first woman law clerk at the Supreme Court.

1953 *The Second Sex,* by French writer Simone De Beauvoir, is published in the United States and becomes a central document in the women's liberation movement.

1960 The first birth control pill is introduced on the market.

1963 Betty Friedan's book *The Feminine Mystique,* calling for women to become independent wage earners, becomes a bestseller.

➤ The Equal Pay Act is passed in Congress.

1964 The Civil Rights Act of 1964, including the Title VII subchapter prohibiting employment discrimination because of sex, race, color, religion, or national origin, is passed in Congress. The Equal Employment Opportunity Commission (EEOC) is set up as the act's enforcement mechanism.

1966 The National Organization for Women (NOW) is founded.

1967 President Lyndon B. Johnson amends his executive order requiring that businesses that have contracts with the federal government implement affirmative action policies to include women as a category eligible for preferential treatment.

➤ Congress lifts the 2 percent ceiling on women's enrollment in the armed forces and allows women to serve on draft boards and in positions of command.

➤ States begin enacting liberalized abortion laws, permitting abortion under certain circumstances.

1968 The EEOC determines that sex is not a bona fide occupational qualification requirement for being a flight attendant.

1971 The Equal Rights Amendment (ERA) passes in the House of Representatives by a vote of 350–15.

➤ The National Women's Political Caucus is organized to field more women candidates.

➤ Two women advocates (Elizabeth R. Rindskopf and Dorothy Toth Beasley) argue against each other in the Supreme Court—a first.

➤ The first husband and wife team (Alice L. Robie and Melvin L. Resnick) argue a case before the Supreme Court.

1972 The ERA passes in the Senate by a vote of 84–8.

➤ Title IX of the Education Act Amendments of 1972 is passed, banning discrimination in most federally assisted educational programs and related activities, including sports.

➤ An amendment to Title VII extends its coverage from private employers to state and local governments and educational institutions. The EEOC is given authority to sue private employers directly.

➤ American Telephone & Telegraph Company (AT&T) ends sex segregation in employment.

1975 District judge Cornelia G. Kennedy is rated "qualified" by the American Bar Association's Committee on the Federal Judiciary, the first woman to receive such a rating for a Supreme Court nomination.

1976 The U.S. Military Academy at West Point, New York; the U.S. Naval Academy at Annapolis, Maryland; and the U.S. Air Force Academy at Colorado Springs, Colorado admit their first women students under a 1975 law directing them to do so. (The U.S. Coast Guard Academy at New London, Connecticut, admitted women in 1975.)

➤ The Hyde Amendment prohibiting the use of federal Medicaid funds in any state to perform abortions except to save the mother's life, or in cases of rape and incest, is passed in Congress.

1977 Indiana becomes the thirty-fifth state to ratify the ERA; only three more states are needed for the three-quarters majority necessary for ratification.

1978 The Pregnancy Discrimination Act is passed in Congress as an amendment to Title VII of the 1964 Civil Rights Act.

➤ The ERA deadline for ratification is extended by three years; several states have rescinded earlier ratification.

➤ The Women's Armed Forces Integration Act is passed, integrating separate women's corps that were formed during World War II into the armed forces.

1980 President Jimmy Carter reactivates registration for the draft and calls for compulsory registration of both men and women. Congress authorizes male-only registration.

➤ The justices drop the traditional designation "Mr. Justice" in favor of "Justice."

1981 Sandra Day O'Connor becomes the first female Supreme Court justice.

1982 The deadline for ratification of the Equal Rights Amendment expires.

1988 The Department of Health and Human Services issues a regulation prohibiting abortion counseling by family planning clinics that receive federal funds under the Public Health Services Act, enacted in 1970.

1991 The Anita Hill–Clarence Thomas hearings provoke a national debate about sexual harassment. Congress passes the Civil Rights Act expanding Title VII to include compensatory and punitive damages for gender discrimination in the workplace.

1993 The Pentagon opens select combat positions to women.

➤ The Family and Medical Leave Act is passed in Congress.

➤ Ruth Bader Ginsburg is appointed to the Supreme Court.

1995 The Congressional Accountability Act makes Congress subject to Title VII.

1997 First female cadets enroll at Virginia Military Institute.

BIBLIOGRAPHY

PRINCIPAL SOURCE

The main source used in preparing this book is a legal textbook that discusses all aspects of sex discrimination:

Babcock, Barbara Allen, Ann E. Freedman, Susan Deller Ross, Wendy Webster Williams, Rhonda Copelon, Deborah L. Rhode, and Nadine Taub. *Sex Discrimination and the Law: History, Practice, and Theory.* 2d ed. Little, Brown, and Company, 1996.

GENERAL BOOKS ABOUT THE SUPREME COURT

Biskupic, Joan, and Elder Witt. *The Supreme Court and Individual Rights.* 3d ed. Congressional Quarterly, 1997.

_____. *The Supreme Court at Work.* 2d ed. Congressional Quarterly, 1997.

Cushman, Clare, ed. *The Supreme Court Justices: Illustrated Biographies, 1789–1995.* 2d ed. Congressional Quarterly, 1995.

Hall, Kermit L., ed. *The Oxford Companion to the Supreme Court of the United States.* Oxford University Press, 1992.

O'Brien, David M. *Storm Center: The Supreme Court in American Politics.* 3d ed. W. W. Norton, 1993.

Raskin, Jamin B. *We the Students: Supreme Court Cases for and about High School Students.* CQ Press, 2000.

Schwartz, Bernard. *A History of the Supreme Court.* Oxford University Press, 1993.

The Supreme Court Yearbook. Congressional Quarterly, 1989– .

GENERAL BOOKS ABOUT WOMEN'S RIGHTS

Banner, Lois. *Women in Modern America: A Brief History.* 3d ed. Harcourt Brace College Publishers, 1995.

Chafe, William Henry. *The American Woman: Her Changing Social, Economic, and Political Roles, 1920–1970.* Oxford University Press, 1972.

Coontz, Stephanie. *The Way We Never Were: American Families and the Nostalgia Trap.* Basic Books, 1992.

Davis, Flora. *Moving the Mountain: The Women's Movement in America Since 1960.* Simon & Schuster, 1991.

Faludi, Susan. *Backlash: The Undeclared War Against American Women.* Crown Publishers, 1991.

Flexner, Eleanor. *Century of Struggle: The Women's Rights Movement in the United States.* Rev. ed. Harvard University Press, 1975.

Goldstein, Leslie Friedman. *The Constitutional Rights of Women: Cases in Law and Social Change.* Rev. ed. University of Wisconsin Press, 1989.

Hoff, Joan. *Law, Gender, and Injustice: A Legal History of U.S. Women.* New York University Press, 1991.

Lynn, Naomi B., ed. *Women, Politics, and the Constitution.* Haworth Press, 1990.

Otten, Laura A. *Women's Rights and the Law.* Praeger, 1993.

Rosenberg, Rosalind. *Divided Lives: American Women in the Twentieth Century.* Hill and Wang, Noonday Press, 1992.

CHAPTER I
ROMANTIC PATERNALISM

Barry, Kathleen. *Susan B. Anthony: A Biography of a Singular Feminist.* New York University Press, 1988.

Bordin, Ruth Birgitta Anderson. *Women and Temperance: The Quest For Power and Liberty, 1873–1900.* Temple University Press, 1981.

DuBois, Ellen Carol. *Feminism and Suffrage: The Emergence of an Independent Women's Movement in America, 1848–1869.* Cornell University Press, 1978.

Foner, Philip S. *Women and the American Labor Movement: From Colonial Times to the Eve of World War One.* Free Press, 1979.

Friedman, Jane M. *America's First Woman Lawyer: The Biography of Myra Bradwell.* Prometheus Books, 1993.

Kessler-Harris, Alice. *Out to Work: A History of Wage-Earning Women in the United States.* Oxford University Press, 1982.

_____. *A Woman's Wage: Historical Meanings and Social Consequences.* University Press of Kentucky, 1990.

Salmon, Marylynn. *Women and the Law of Property in Early America.* University of North Carolina Press, 1986.

Sklar, Kathryn Kish. *Florence Kelley and the Nation's Work: The Rise of Women's Political Culture, 1830–1900.* Yale University Press, 1995.

Stanton, Elizabeth Cady, Susan B. Anthony, and Mathilda Joslyn Gage. *History of Woman's Suffrage. Vol. 1: 1848–1861.* 2d ed. Charles Mann, 1887.

CHAPTER 2
JURY DUTY

Kerber, Linda K. *No Constitutional Right to Be Ladies: Women and the Obligations of Citizenship.* Hill and Wang, 1998.

CHAPTER 3
SEX DISCRIMINATION: THE
SEARCH FOR A STANDARD

Blair, Anita K. "The Equal Protection Clause and Single-Sex Public Education: *United States v. Virginia* and Virginia Military Institute." *Seton Hall Constitutional Law Journal* 6 (1996): 99–1012.

Brake, Deborah L. "Sex as a Suspect Class: An Argument for Applying Strict Scrutiny to Gender Discrimination." *Seton Hall Constitutional Law Journal* 6 (1996): 953–66.

Darcy, R., and Jenny Sanbrano. "Oklahoma in the Development of Equal Rights: The Era, 3.2% Beer, Juvenile Justice, and *Craig v. Boren.*"

Oklahoma City University Law Review 22 (fall 1997): 1009–49.

Fox-Genovese, Elizabeth. "Strict Scrutiny, VMI, and Women's Lives." *Seton Hall Constitutional Law Journal* 6 (1996): 987–90.

Ginsburg, Ruth Bader. "Sex Equality and the Constitution: The State of the Art." *Women's Rights Law Reporter* 14 (spring/fall 1992): 361–66.

_____. "Speaking in a Judicial Voice." *New York University Law Review* 67 (December 1992): 1185–1209.

Ginsburg, Ruth Bader, and Barbara Flagg. "Some Reflections on the Feminist Legal Thought of the 1970s." *University of Chicago Legal Forum* (1989): 9–21.

Markowitz, Deborah L. "In Pursuit of Equality: One Woman's Work to Change the Law." *Women's Rights Law Reporter* 14 (spring/fall 1992): 335–359. The essay on Ruth Bader Ginsburg as a litigator is greatly indebted to this source.

Rhode, Deborah L. *Justice and Gender: Sex Discrimination and the Law.* Harvard University Press, 1989.

Rosen, Jeffrey. "Like Race, Like Gender?" *The New Republic,* February 19, 1996, 21–27.

Seymour, Stephanie K. "Women As Constitutional Equals: The Burger Court's Overdue Evolution." In *The Burger Court: Counter-Revolution or Confirmation,* edited by Bernard Schwartz, 66–82. Oxford University Press, 1998.

CHAPTER 4
WOMEN IN THE FAMILY:
FROM SUBORDINATES
TO EQUAL PARTNERS

Berry, Mary Frances. *Why ERA Failed: Politics, Women's Rights, and the Amending Process of the Constitution.* Indiana University Press, 1986.

Coontz, Stephanie. *The Way We Never Were: American Families and the Nostalgia Trap.* Basic Books, 1992.

Ginsburg, Ruth Bader. "Some Thoughts on Benign Classifications in the Context of Sex." *Connecticut Law Review* 10 (summer 1978): 813–827.

Kurz, Demie. *For Richer, For Poorer: Mothers Confront Divorce.* Routledge, 1995.

Mansbridge, Jane J. *Why We Lost the ERA.* University of Chicago Press, 1986.

Phillips, Roderick. *Untying the Knot: A Short History of Divorce.* Cambridge University Press, 1991.

Williams, Joan. "Is Coverture Dead? Beyond A New Theory of Alimony." *Georgetown Law Journal* 82 (September 1994): 2227–2290.

CHAPTER 5
SINGLE SEX SCHOOLS

Bellman, Amy B. "The Young Women's Leadership School: Single-Sex Public Education After V.M.I." *Wisconsin Law Review* 1997 (July–August 1997): 827–64.

Colom, Wilbur O. "The Trials of a Mississippi Lawyer." *New York Times Magazine,* May 15, 1983, 62–64.

Corcoran, Carrie. "Single-Sex Education After VMI: Equal Protection and East Harlem's Young Women's Leadership School." *University of Pennsylvania Law Review* 145 (April 1997): 987–1033.

Gilligan, Carol. *In A Different Voice: Psychological Theory and Women's Development.* Harvard University Press, 1982.

Nemko, Amy H. "Single-Sex Public Education After VMI: The Case for Women's Schools." *Harvard Women's Law Journal* 20 (spring 1998): 19–77.

Sadker, Myra, and David Sadker. *Failing At Fairness: How America's Schools Cheat Girls.* C. Scribner's Sons, 1994.

Staton, Carolyn Ellis. "Sex Discrimination in Public Education." *Mississippi Law Journal* 58 (fall 1988): 323–48.

Von Lohmann, Fred. "Single Sex Courses, Title IX, and Equal Protection: The Case for Self-Defense for Women." *Stanford Law Review* 48 (November 1995): 177–216.

CHAPTER 6
DIFFERENT TREATMENT OF WOMEN

Brownmiller, Susan. *Against Our Will: Men, Women, and Rape.* Simon & Schuster, 1975.

Cole, David. "Strategies of Difference: Litigating for Women's Rights in a Man's World." *Law and Inequality* 2 (February 1984): 33–96.

Czapanskiy, Karen B. "Volunteers and Draftees: The Struggle for Parental Equality." *UCLA Law Review* 38 (August 1991): 1415–1481.

Elshtain, Jean Bethke. *Women and War.* University of Chicago Press, 1995.

Erickson, Nancy B. "The Feminist Dilemma Over Unwed Parents' Custody Rights: The Mother's Rights Must Take Priority." *Law and Inequality* 2 (August 1984): 447–472.

Faludi, Susan. *Stiffed: The Betrayal of the American Man.* W. Morrow & Company, 1999.

Holm, Jeanne. *Women in the Military.* Rev. ed. Presidio, 1993.

Jones, Pamela R. "Women in the Crossfire: Should the Court Allow It? [Note]." *Cornell Law Review* 78 (January 1993): 252–301.

Kerber, Linda K. *No Constitutional Right to Be Ladies: Women and the Obligations of Citizenship.* Hill and Wang, 1998.

Oberman, Michelle. "Turning Girls Into Women: Re-evaluating Modern Statutory Rape Law."

Journal of Criminal Law and Criminology 85 (summer 1994): 15–79.

Olsen, Frances. "Statutory Rape: A Feminist Critique of Rights Analysis." *Texas Law Review* 63 (November 1984): 387–432.

Thompson, Sharon. *Going All the Way: Teenage Girls' Tales of Sex, Romance, and Pregnancy.* Hill and Wang, 1995.

CHAPTER 7
DISCRIMINATION IN THE WORKPLACE

Bass, Stuart L., and Nathan S. Slavin. "Avoiding Sexual Discrimination Litigation in Accounting Firms and Other Professional Organizations: The Impact of the Supreme Court Decision in *Price v. Waterhouse v. Ann B. Hopkins.*" *Women's Rights Law Reporter* 13 (spring 1991): 21–34.

Blau, Francine D., Marianne A. Ferber, and Anne E. Winkler. *The Economics of Women, Men, and Work.* 3d ed. Prentice-Hall, 1998.

Faludi, Susan. "Diane Joyce." *Ms. Magazine,* January 1988, 62–65, 90–92.

Fogel, Walter. *The Equal Pay Act: Implications for Comparable Worth.* Praeger, 1984.

Goldin, Claudia. *Understanding the Gender Gap: An Economic History of American Women.* Oxford University Press, 1992.

Hopkins, Ann Branigar. *So Ordered: Making Partner the Hard Way.* University of Massachusetts Press, 1996.

Matthaei, Julie A. *An Economic History of Women in America: Women's Work, the Sexual Division of Labor, and the Development of Capitalism.* Schocken Books, 1982.

Reskin, Barbara F., and Heidi I. Hartmann, eds. *Women's Work, Men's Work: Sex Segregation on the Job.* National Academy Press, 1986.

Urofsky, Melvin I. *A Conflict of Rights: The Supreme Court and Affirmative Action.* Scribner's Sons, 1991.

U.S. Congress. House. Representative Griffiths of Michigan speaking on the lack of enforcement of the sex provisions of Title VII of the Civil Rights Act of 1964. 89th Congress, 2d session. *Congressional Record* (June 20, 1996), vol. 112, pt. 10: 13689–13694.

U.S. Federal Glass Ceiling Commission. *Good for Business: Making Full Use of the Nation's Human Capital: the Environmental Scan: A Fact-finding Report of the Federal Glass Ceiling Commission.* U.S Department of Labor, 1995.

CHAPTER 8
SEXUAL HARASSMENT

Gorney, Cynthia. "Teaching Johnny the Appropriate Way to Flirt." *New York Times Magazine,* June 13, 1999.

MacKinnon, Catherine A. *Sexual Harassment of Working Women: A Case of Sex Discrimination.* Yale University Press, 1979.

Patai, Daphne. *Heterophobia: Sexual Harassment and the Future of Feminism.* Rowman & Littlefield, 1998.

Rosen, Jeffrey. "In Defense of Gender-Blindness: A Practical and Philosophical Proposal for Sexual Harassment Law." *The New Republic* (June 29, 1988): 25–28, 30–35.

Ross, Susan Deller. "Sexual Harassment Law in the Aftermath of the Hill-Thomas Hearings." In *Race, Gender, and Power in America: The Legacy of the Hill-Thomas Hearings,* edited by Anita Faye Hill and Emma Coleman Jordan, 228–241. Oxford University Press, 1995.

Segrave, Kerry. *The Sexual Harassment of Women in the Workplace, 1600–1993.* McFarland, 1994.

CHAPTER 9
PREGNANCY AND CHILDBIRTH

Kay, Herma Hill. "Equality and Difference: The Case of Pregnancy." *Berkeley Women's Law Journal* 1 (fall 1985): 1–38.

Law, Sylvia A. "Rethinking Sex and the Constitution." *University of Pennsylvania Law Review* 132 (June 1984): 955–1040.

Ross, Susan Deller. "Legal Aspects of Parental Leave: At the Crossroads." In *Parental Leave and Child Care: Setting A Research and Policy Agenda,* edited by Janet Shibley Hyde and Marilyn J. Essex, 93–124. Temple University Press, 1990.

Williams, Wendy W. "Equality's Riddle: Pregnancy and the Equal Treatment/Special Treatment Debate." *New York University Review of Law & Social Change* 13 (spring 1985): 325–80.

CHAPTER 10
REPRODUCTIVE RIGHTS

Alderman, Ellen, and Caroline Kennedy. *The Right To Privacy.* Knopf, 1995.

Allen, Anita L. *Uneasy Access: Privacy for Women in a Free Society.* Rowman & Littlefield, 1988.

Chesler, Ellen. *Woman of Valor: Margaret Sanger and the Birth Control Movement in America.* Simon & Schuster, 1992.

Cleghorn, Amy S. "Justice Harry A. Blackmun: A Retrospective Consideration of the Justice's Role in the Emancipation of Women." *Seton Hall Law Review* 25 (winter 1995): 1176–1218.

Faux, Marian. Roe v. Wade: *The Untold Story of the Landmark Supreme Court Decision That Made Abortion Legal.* MacMillan, 1988.

Garrow, David J. *Liberty and Sexuality: The Right to Privacy and the Making of* Roe v. Wade. University of California Press, 1998.

Gordon, Linda. *Woman's Body, Woman's Right: Birth Control in America.* Rev ed. Penguin Books, 1990.

McCorvey, Norma. *I Am Roe: My Life,* Roe v. Wade, *and Freedom of Choice.* HarperCollins, 1994.

O'Hara, Megan, and Ilene Findler. Roe vs. Roe: *Baptism by Fire.* A "Cinemax Reel Life" documentary. Cinemax, 1998. [Television documentary programmed January 28, 1998.]

Rubin, Eva. *Abortion, Politics and the Courts:* Roe v. Wade *and Its Aftermath.* Greenwood, 1987.

Tribe, Laurence H. *Abortion: The Clash of Absolutes.* W. W. Norton & Company, 1992.

CHAPTER II
LEADING THE WAY

First Ladies of the Supreme Court

Ginsburg, Ruth Bader, and Laura W. Brill. "Remembering Great Ladies: Supreme Court Wives' Stories." *Journal of Supreme Court History* 24, no. 3 (1999): 255–268.

Belva Lockwood

This essay is adapted from:

Norgren, Jill. "Before It Was Merely Difficult: Belva Lockwood's Life in Law and Politics." *Journal of Supreme Court History* 23, no. 1 (1999): 16–40. For citations, see that work. (Jill Norgren is working on a full-length biography of Lockwood.)

Further Reading

Drachman, Virginia G. *Sisters in Law: Women Lawyers in Modern American History.* Harvard University Press, 1998.

_____, comp. *Women Lawyers and the Origins of Professional Identity in America: The Letters of the Equity Club, 1887 to 1890.* University of Michigan Press, 1993.

Lockwood, Belva A. "My Efforts to Become A Lawyer." *Lippincott's Monthly Magazine,* February 1888, 215–229.

Stern, Madeleine B. "The First Woman Admitted to Practice Before the United States Supreme Court: Belva Ann Lockwood." In *We the Women: Career Firsts of Nineteenth-Century America,* edited by Madeleine B. Stern, 205–234. New York, Schulte, 1963.

Winner, Julia Hull. "Belva Lockwood: That Extraordinary Woman." *New York History* 39 (October 1958): 321–340.

The First Women Members of the Supreme Court Bar, 1879–1900

This essay is adapted from:

Clark, Mary L. "The First Women Members of the Supreme Court Bar, 1879–1900." *San Diego Law Review* (winter 1999): 36–87.

Further Reading

Babcock, Barbara Allen. "Feminist Lawyers." *Stanford Law Review* 50 (May 1998): 1689–1708.

Drachman, Virginia G. *Sisters in Law: Women Lawyers in Modern American History.* Harvard University Press, 1998.

_____, comp. *Women Lawyers and the Origins of Professional Identity in America: The Letters of the Equity Club, 1887 to 1890.* University of Michigan Press, 1993.

James, Edward T., Janet Wilson James, and Paul S. Boyer. *Notable American Women: A Biographical Dictionary.* 4 vols. Belknap Press of Harvard University Press, 1971–1980.

Morello, Karen Berger. *The Invisible Bar: The Woman Lawyer in America, 1638 to the Present.* Random House, 1986.

Women's Legal History Biography Project at the Robert Crown Law Library at Stanford Law School. [Web site–URL address: *http://www. stanford.edu/group/WLHP/*]

A few early women bar members have been the subjects of more extensive research:

Babcock, Barbara Allen. "Clara Shortridge Foltz: 'First Woman.'" *Valparaiso University Law Review* 28 (summer 1994): 1231, 1268–1269.

Bittenbender, Ada M. "Women in Law." *Chicago Law Times* 2 (July 1988): 301–309.

Clark, Mary L. "The Founding of the Washington College of Law: The First Law School Established by Women for Women." *American University Law Review* 47 (February 1988): 613–676. [Mussey and Gillett are discussed.]

Hathaway, Grace. *Fate Rides A Tortoise: A Biography of Ellen Spencer Mussey.* John C. Winston Company, 1937.

Women Advocates Before the Supreme Court

Biskupic, Joan. "Women Are Still Not Well-Represented Among Lawyers Facing Supreme Test: Despite Gains for Female Advocates, High Court Is Largely a Man's Venue." *Washington Post,* May 27, 1997, p. A03.

Clarke, Nell Ray. "Women in the Supreme Court." *Equal Rights* 14 (April 9, 1927): 70–72.

Douglas, William O. *The Court Years, 1939–1975: The Autobiography of William O. Douglas.* Random House, 1980.

Epstein, Cynthia Fuchs. *Women in Law.* 2d ed. University of Illinois Press, 1993.

Greenburg, Jan Crawford. "This Couple Argues Before Highest Court." *Chicago Tribune,* October 15, 1997, p. 6.

Harmon, Nolan B. *The Famous Case of Myra Clark Gaines.* Louisiana State University Press, 1946.

Kansas City Public Library. The Conley Sisters [web site] at *http://www.kckpl.lib.ks.us/kscoll/ people/lconley.htm.* Considerable information about Lyda B. Conley is provided at this web site.

McGuire, Kevin T. *The Supreme Court Bar: Legal Elites in the Washington Community.* University Press of Virginia, 1993.

O'Donnell, Alice L. "A Long Way, Baby: Women and Other Strangers Before the Bar." *Supreme Court Historical Society Yearbook* (1977): 59–62, 114.

Smith, J. Clay, Jr., ed. *Rebels in Law: Voices in History of Black Women Lawyers.* University of Michigan Press, 1998.

Stern, Robert L., Eugene Gressman, Stephen M. Shapiro, and Kenneth S. Geller. *Supreme Court Practice.* 7th ed. Bureau of National Affairs, 1993.

Wertheimer, Barbara Mayer. *We Were There: The Story of Working Women in America.* Pantheon Books, 1977.

Lucy Terry Prince

Most sources perpetuate the story of the legendary argument by Lucy Terry Prince, who is sometimes called Luce. David R. Proper finds no documentation for "the Supreme Court argument" in his biography:

Proper, David R. *Lucy Terry Prince: Singer of History.* Pocumtuck Valley Memorial Association & Historic Deerfield, Inc., 1997.

For a well-considered argument in support of the likelihood that Prince did appear before Justice Chase, see:

Smith, J. Clay, Jr. *Emancipation: The Making of the Black Lawyer, 1844–1944.* University of Pennsylvania Press, 1993.

For historical accounts of Prince's argument, see:

Holland, Josiah Gilbert. *History of Western Massachusetts the Counties of Hampden, Hampshire, Franklin, and Berkshire: Embracing an Outline, or General History, of the Section, an Account of Its Scientific Aspects and Leading Interests, and Separate Histories of Its One Hundred Towns.* S. Bowles and Co., 1855.

Merriam, Robert L. *Lucy Terry Prince.* Conway, MA, [R.L. Merriam], 1983.

Sheldon, George. "Negro Slavery in Old Deerfield." *New England Magazine* 8, March 1893, 54–57.

Prince's poetry is discussed in most works on African American poetry and in:

Kaplan, Sidney. "Lucy Terry Prince: Vermont Advocate and Poet." In *The Black Presence in the Era of the American Revolution, 1770–1800,* 209–211. New York Graphic Society, 1973.

Susan Brandeis

Goldman, Sheldon. *Picking Federal Judges: Lower Court Selection from Roosevelt through Reagan.* Yale University Press, 1997.

Paper, Lewis J. *Brandeis.* Prentice-Hall, 1983.

Urofsky, Melvin I., and David W. Levy, eds. *Letters of Louis D. Brandeis. Vol. 5: 1921–1941. Elder Statesman.* State University of New York Press, 1978.

The First Female Law Clerks

Black, Hugo L., and Elizabeth Black. *Mr. Justice and Mrs. Black: The Memoirs of Hugo L. Black and Elizabeth Black.* Random House, 1986.

McGurn, Barrett. "Law Clerks: A Professional Elite." *Supreme Court Historical Society Yearbook* (1980): 98–101.

Reuben, Richard C. "Not Year of the Woman For Supreme Court Clerks." *Chicago Daily Law Bulletin* (October 6, 1992): 2.

Urosky, Melvin I., ed. *The Douglas Letters: Selections from the Private Papers of Justice William O. Douglas.* Adler & Adler, 1987.

Woodward, Bob, and Armstrong, Scott. *The Brethren: Inside the Supreme Court.* Simon & Schuster, 1979.

Lucile Lomen: First Woman Law Clerk

This essay is reprinted from:

Danelski, David J. "Lucile Lomen, First Woman to Clerk at the Supreme Court." *Journal of Supreme Court History* vol. 24, no. 1 (1999): 43–49. For citations see that work.

Near Misses: Women Who Have Been Considered for Appointment

Abraham, Henry J. *Justices and President: A Political History of Appointments to the Supreme Court.* 3d ed. Oxford University Press, 1992.

Cook, Beverly B. "The First Woman Candidate for the Supreme Court: Florence E. Allen." *Supreme Court Historical Society Yearbook* (1981): 19–35.

_____. "Women as Supreme Court Candidates: From Florence Allen To Sandra O'Connor." *Judicature* 65 (December 1981/January 1982): 314–326.

Ginsburg, Ruth Bader, and Laura W. Brill. "Women In the Federal Judiciary: Three Way Pavers and the Exhilarating Change President Carter Wrought." *Fordham Law Review* 64 (November 1995): 281–290.

Goldman, Sheldon. *Picking Federal Judges: Lower Court Selection from Roosevelt Through Reagan.* Yale University Press, 1997.

Tuve, Jeanette E. *First Lady of the Law: Florence Ellinwood Allen.* University Press of America, 1984.

Sandra Day O'Connor: First Woman Justice

This essay is an updated version of:

Huber, Peter William. "Sandra Day O'Connor." In *The Supreme Court Justices: Illustrated Biographies, 1789–1995,* edited by Clare Cushman, 506–510. 2d ed. Congressional Quarterly, 1995.

Further Reading

Greenhouse, Linda. "From the High Court: A Voice Quite Distinctly a Woman's." *New York Times,* May 26, 1999, sec. A, p. 1.

"The Jurisprudence of Justice Sandra Day O'Connor." *Women's Rights Law Reporter* 13 (summer/fall 1991): 149–170.

Maveety, Nancy. *Justice Sandra Day O'Connor: Strategist on the Supreme Court.* Rowan & Littlefield Publishers, 1996.

Spaeth, Harold J. "Justice Sandra Day O'Connor: An Assessment." In *An Essential Safeguard: Essays on the United States Supreme Court and Its Justices,* edited by D. Grier Stephenson Jr., 81–98. Greenwood Press, 1991.

Ruth Bader Ginsburg: From Litigator to Justice

Roberts, Edith Lampson. "Ruth Bader Ginsburg." In *The Supreme Court Justices: Illustrated Biographies, 1789–1995,* edited by Clare Cushman, 531–535. 2d ed. Congressional Quarterly, 1995.

Rosen, Jeffrey. "The New Look of Liberalism on the Court." *New York Times Magazine,* October 5, 1997, 60–65, 90–97.

The *Washington Post,* July 18–20, 1993, ran these three articles under the series title "*Ruth Bader Ginsburg: Her Life and the Law*":

Biskupic, Joan. "Ruth Bader Ginsburg: Her Life and the Law. Pt. 3. Looking at Human Problems, with Judicial Restraint." *Washington Post,* July 20, 1993, p. A1.

Van Drehle, David. "Ruth Bader Ginsburg: Her Life and the Law. Pt. 1. Conventional Roles Hid a Revolutionary Intellect; Discrimination Helped Spawn a Crusade." *Washington Post,* July 18, 1993, p. A1.

_____. "Ruth Bader Ginsburg: Her Life and the Law. Pt. 2. Redefining Fair with a Simple, Careful Assault: Step-By-Step Strategy Produced Strides for Equal Protection." *Washington Post,* July 19, 1993, p. A1.

Juvenile Literature

Ayer, Eleanor H. *Ruth Bader Ginsburg: Fire and Steel on the Supreme Court.* Dillon Press, 1994.

Brown, Drollene P. *Belva Lockwood Wins Her Case.* Albert Whitman, 1987.

Dunnahoo, Terry. *Before the Supreme Court: The Story of Belva Ann Lockwood.* Houghton Mifflin, 1974.

Emert, Phyllis Raybin. "Belva Lockwood Opening Doors." In *Top Lawyers and Their Famous Cases,* 65–79. The Oliver Press, 1996.

Fox, Mary Virginia. *Lady for the Defense: A Biography of Belva Lockwood.* Harcourt Brace Jovanovich, 1975.

Huber, Peter William. *Sandra Day O'Connor.* Chelsea House, 1990.

Katz, Bernard, and Jonathan Katz. *Black Woman: A Fictionalized Biography of Lucy Terry Prince.* Pantheon Books, 1973.

(The books and chapters on Belva Lockwood present basic facts about her life and career. They draw, however, on dated research. Jill Norgren will be writing an updated biography for young readers.)

INDEX

Note: Page numbers in italics refer to photographs or illustrations.

Beasley, Dorothy Toth, 224
Beauvior, Simone de, 255
Bellotti, Francis X., 107
Bellotti v. Baird (1979), 193
Bender, Paul, 59
Benedict, Robert D., 219
Benham, Flip, 205
Bennett, Wallace, 146
Bensing, Sandra, 189
Beyer, Eugene A., Jr., 240
Beyer, Tom, 130
BFOQ (bona fide occupational qualification), 121, 122, 127, 178–179, 181
Bible, Teresia, 35
Birth control, 182–188
Bittenbender, Ada M., 216, 217, 219
Black, Elizabeth S., *208*, 242
Black, Hugo L., 29, 185, 236–237, 242
Blackmun, Harry A., *198*, 200
    on *Automobile Workers v. Johnson Controls, Inc.* (1991), 179
    on *Batson v. Kentucky* (1986), 35–36
    on *Califano v. Webster* (1977), 78
    on *Craig v. Boren* (1976), 51
    on *Dothard v. Rawlinson* (1977), 123
    on *Frontiero v. Richardson* (1973), 44
    on *Meritor Savings Bank, FSB v. Vinson* (1986), 154
    on *Michael M. v. Superior Court, Sonoma Cty.* (1981), 115
    Mississippi Univ. for Women v. Hogan (1982) dissent, 89
    Ohio v. Akron Center for Reproductive Health, Inc. (1990) dissent, 194
    Parham v. Hughes (1979) dissent, 110
    on *Planned Parenthood of Southeastern Pa. v. Casey* (1992), 200
    Planned Parenthood v. Ashcroft (1983) dissent, 193–194
    on *Planned Parenthood of Central Mo. v. Danforth* (1976), 193
    on *Price Waterhouse v. Hopkins* (1989), 133
    on *Roe v. Wade* (1973), 189–190
    Rust v. Sullivan (1991) dissent, 193
    on *Stanton v. Stanton* (1975), 49, 79

Webster v. Reproductive Health Services (1989) dissent, 198
Blackstone, William, 1
Blair, Henry, 217
Bolton, Arthur, 224
Bona fide occupational qualification (BFOQ), 121, 122, 127, 178–179, 181
Borah, William, 243
Boren, David, 54
Bork, Robert, 197
Bosley v. McLaughlin (1915), 19
Boston Globe, 107
Boudinot, Elias C., 223
Bowers v. Hardwick (1986), 230
Bowman, James, 35
Bradley, Joseph P., *5*, 6, 7
Bradley, Stephen R., 221
Bradwell, Bessie, 8, 10
Bradwell, James B., 3, 9, 10
Bradwell, Myra Colby, 3–4, 8–10, 217
Bradwell, Thomas, 10
Bradwell v. Illinois (1873), 2–4, 6–7, 9, 213, 215
Brandeis, Louis D., 17, 22, 182, *234*
Bray v. Alexandria Women's Health Center (1993), 205
Breedlove v. Suttles (1937), 16
Brennan, Marjorie, *208*
Brennan, Peter J., 144, 190
Brennan, William J., Jr., *169*, 246
    on *Arizona Governing Committee v. Norris* (1983), 151
    on *Califano v. Goldfarb* (1976), 71–72, 74
    on *County of Washington v. Gunther* (1981), 147
    on *Craig v. Boren* (1976), 49–50, 55
    Dothard v. Rawlinson (1977) dissent, 127
    draft registration regulations and, 102
    on *Eisenstadt v. Baird* (1971), 185
    on *Frontiero v. Richardson* (1973), 44, 69
    Geduldig v. Aiello (1974) dissent, 169–170
    General Elec. Co. v. Gilbert (1976) dissent, 171–172, 173

Ginsburg's strict scrutiny argument and, 63
    on *Griswold v. Connecticut* (1965), 185
    on *Johnson v. Transportation Agency, Santa Clara* (1987), 137
    on *Kahn v. Shevin* (1974), 76
    Lehr v. Robertson (1983) dissent, 111
    on *Meritor Savings Bank, FSB v. Vinson* (1986), 154
    Michael M. v. Superior Court, Sonoma Cty. (1981) dissent, 116
    on *Nashville Gas Co. v. Satty* (1977), 173
    on *Orr v. Orr* (1979), 79, 80
    Parham v. Hughes (1979) dissent, 110
    Personnel Administrator of Massachusetts v. Feeney (1979) dissent, 105
    on *Price Waterhouse v. Hopkins* (1989), 133
    Rosenberg and, 228
    Rostker v. Goldberg (1981) dissent, 103
    on *Schlesinger v. Ballard* (1975), 100
    on statutory rape, 113–114
    on *Weinberger v. Wiesenfeld* (1975), 71
    on women for Supreme Court, 245
The Brethren (Armstrong and Woodward), 237
Brewer, David J., 17
Breyer, Stephen G., 112, 113, 161, 200–201, 247
Brinkley, David, 240
Brinkmann, Beth S., 226
British common-law, 68
Bronson, Eli, 221
Brown, John R., 122
Brown v. Board of Education (1954), 224
Bruzelius, Anders, 254
Bryan, J., 217
Buckley, Marguerite M., 232
Buck v. Bell (1927), 182
Bunting, Josiah, III, 67
Burger, Warren E., 38, 92, 224, 232, 245
    Caban v. Mohammed (1979) dissent, 109
    on *Califano v. Webster* (1977), 78

on U.S. Court of Appeal for D.C.
Circuit, 256–257
on U.S. Supreme Court, 258–260
on U.S. Supreme Court female law
clerks, 236–237
Weinberger v. Wiesenfeld (1975),
70–71, 72–73, 229, 256
Gittes, Betty, 106
Glavey v. United States (1900), 219
Goesaert, Margaret, 22
Goesaert, Valentine, 22
Goesaert v. Cleary (1948), 21–26
Goldberg, Arthur J., 185, 244
Goldberg, Robert, 102
Goldfarb, Hannah, 71
Goldfarb, Leon, 71
Goldmark, Josephine, 17, 22
Golz, Susan, 239
Gonzalez, Connie, 204–205
Goodell, Charles Ellsworth, 145
Gordon, Laura D., 216, 217
Gotcher, Emma, 17
Governmental objective test
Califano v. Goldfarb (1976), 73–74
Califano v. Westcott (1979), 81–82
Craig v. Boren (1976), 49–50
Kahn v. Shevin (1974), 76
Rostker v. Goldberg (1981), 101,
102–103
Schlesinger v. Ballard (1975),
99–100
VMI gender discrimination and,
57–58, 95
Graebner, James, 136
Graham, Michael, 52
Grant, Ulysses S., 12, 210
Greeley, Horace, 210
Grimke, Sarah, 247
Griswold, Erwin, *226*
Griswold, Estelle Trebert, 184, 186,
187
Griswold, Richard, 186
Griswold v. Connecticut (1965),
182–185, 187, 189
Grove City College v. Bell (1984),
96
Gunther, Alberta, 146, *147*

Hall, David, 54
Hall, Lydia, 209–210

Hallford, James, 204
Hames, Margie, 224
Happerset, Reese, 7
Hardy, Charles, 155
Harlan, Ethel A., *208*
Harlan, John Marshall, 28–29, 31, 184,
185, 252
Harper, Fowler, 184, 187
Harris, Teresa, 155
Harrison, Clara B., 212
Harris Poll, 245
Harris v. Forklift Systems, Inc. (1993),
155–156, 251
Harris v. McRae (1980), 192
Harvard College, 86
Harvard Law School, 242, 253–254
Hawley v. Walker (1914), 19
Hayden Rider, Equal Rights Amend-
ment, 83–84
Head of the household, 1, 68, 79–81
Kirchberg v. Feenstra (1981) on,
82–83
Health and Human Services, U.S. De-
partment of, 192
Health concerns, protective laws on,
17–18
Healy v. Edwards (1973), 29, 31
Hellegers, André E., 166
Helmer, Bessie Bradwell, 10. *See also*
Bradwell, Bessie
Henderson, Susan Orr, 230
Hester, Ezra G., 144
Hill, Anita, 156
Hills, Carla A., 244–245, 246
Hill v. Colorado (2000), 206
Hiring practices, 121–128
height/weight requirements, 123,
127–128
mothers with pre–school age chil-
dren, 121–122
Hishon, Elizabeth Anderson, 128–129,
131
Hishon v. King & Spalding (1984),
128–129
H.L. v. Matheson (1981), 115
Hodgson, Jane E., *195*
Hodgson v. Minnesota (1990), 194
Hogan, Joe, 87, 88, *90,* 90–92
Holmes, Oliver Wendell, Jr., 182
Holtzman, Elizabeth, 85

Hopkins, Ann Branigar, 129, *130,*
130–132, 227
Hopkins, Tela, 132
Horowitz, Pamela, 124
Hosmer, A. A., 213
Hospitalization requirement for abor-
tion, 196–197
Howard University Law School, 210,
216
Hoyt, Clarence, 28, 30
Hoyt, Gwendolyn Rogers, 28, 30–31,
232
Hoyt v. Florida (1961), 28–29, 30–31,
32
Hufstedler, Shirley M., 244, 245, *246*
Hughes, Charles Evans, 21
Hughes, Sara, 244
Hulett, Alta, 9
Hunt, Ward, 12
Hunter-Gault, Charlayne, 224
Huntington, Sam, *226*
Hyde, Henry, 192

I Am Roe (McCorvey), 205
Idaho v. Freeman (1982), 85
Illegitimacy, Equal Protection Clause
and, 39
Illinois Bar Association, 10
Immigration and Nationality Act,
257
"Informed consent" for abortion, 196
Ingersoll, Robert, 217
Intermediate scrutiny test, 39, 58
Califano v. Webster (1977) and,
77–78
Craig v. Boren (1976) and, 49–50,
55, 256
*Mississippi Univ. for Women v.
Hogan* (1982) and, 58
Weinberger v. Wiesenfeld (1975), 74
International Bartenders Association,
22

J. E. B. v. Alabama ex rel T. B. (1994),
35–36, 58
Jaramillo, Jacqueline, 168
Jefferson, Thomas, 113
Johnson, Betty, 139
Johnson, Elizabeth, 168
Johnson, Frank, 43

ILLUSTRATION CREDITS